Janice Hall

973-729-2247

ROADMAP
TO YOUR FUTURE

ROADMAP
TO YOUR FUTURE
A Quick Guide to Progressions & Transits

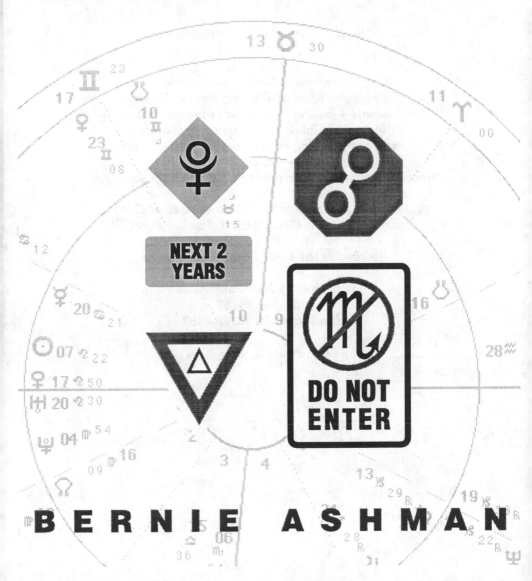

NEXT 2
YEARS

DO NOT
ENTER

BERNIE ASHMAN

International Standard Book Number 0-935127-30-5
Library of Congress Catalog Card Number 94-072197

Printed in the United States of America

Published by ACS Publications
P.O. Box 34487
San Diego, CA 92163-4487

First Printing, July 1994

In order to more fully include women in our language, this book will randomly vary the use of masculine (he, his, him) and feminine (she, her, hers) pronouns. All discussions apply to both sexes.

Table of Contents

PART I
ROOTS

CHAPTER ONE

PREDICTION AND LIFE PROCESSES

This book discusses two important areas of predictive astrology: **secondary progressions and transits**. A key focus of the book is a complete discussion of **planetary aspects**.

Chapter One is a general overview of predictive astrology. Chapters Two and Three are a brief review of astrology's primary symbols, *i.e.*, planets, signs, houses, and planetary aspects. Chapter Four covers transits. Chapter Five describes the progressed horoscope. Chapter Six defines the progressed Sun; Chapter Seven discusses the importance of other progressed planets. Chapter Eight explains the progressed Ascendant and Midheaven.

Chapters Nine through Twelve are an interpretation of aspects formed by progressed and transiting planets to natal planets, Ascendant, Midheaven and Moon's Nodes. It is the interaction of our birthchart planets with progressed and transiting planets that offers useful symbolism to comprehend current trends.

I would like to immediately emphasize that **to understand predictive astrology one must understand the birthchart**. Progressions and transits indicate our use of birthchart potentials in the present.

THE NEW PREDICTIVE ASTROLOGY

What's New?

What separates the new predictive astrology from the old traditional fortune telling is the emphasis on self-understanding. Comprehending **life processes** becomes the focus rather than seeing our actions as isolated "means" leading to various "ends." I am not belittling the importance of accomplishing life goals. The new astrology encourages us to acknowledge entire processes as we accomplish our desired goals.

The old-fashioned fortune-teller was (and still is) more concerned with external events. I really do question the accuracy of the fortune-teller's ability to predict physical events. For instance, consider the fortune-teller's perspective. He observes that an individual has a major aspect formed by Venus and Uranus in the birthchart. The forecast is that the person is "destined" to experience separation (Uranus) in his relationships (Venus).

A modern astrologer would concentrate more on the planetary **themes**. The individual creates the options. This same Venus-Uranus aspect could be indicative of experimentation (Uranus) in relationships (Venus). Perhaps the individual is attracted to people (Venus) who have quite different backgrounds (Uranus). The relationships may be very harmonious. Each respects the other's need for space, individuality and freedom (Uranus).

The new predictive astrology concentrates on the understanding and inward challenges presented by the various life experiences we encounter whether it is relationships, aging, etc. When we truly understand the processes of life, we can then apply this understanding to other situations.

IS LIFE PREDICTABLE?

I have found some events in my life predictable through astrology. The psychological, emotional and spiritual intensity of my life can be measured with even more accuracy through predictive astrology. One sees major aspects when one has major events, but one can have major aspects without major — or any — outer events! The key to successfully experiencing one's own progressed chart is to embrace one's birthchart. The progressed chart symbolizes human beings in the present or a future time period relying on the wisdom of the birthchart as life challenges them.

We need to comprehend our strengths and weaknesses. As will be seen, the different forms of predictive astrology essentially involve the movement through time of one's birthchart symbols (*i.e.*, planets, signs, and houses).

There is no way to forecast with absolute certainty how a person will manifest birthchart themes. Even individuals with very similar charts can be motivated in completely different directions. There may be similarities that overlap. For instance, perhaps a person with the Sun in Pisces becomes an artist while another individual chooses social work. Of course, the same individual can be quite capable of multiple expressions related to the Piscean theme. Other contrasting chart themes further complicate the matter of prediction. It is the mixing of key birthchart themes that indicates how a person might express a strong progressed or transiting movement in his chart.

ASTROLOGY AS A CELESTIAL COMPASS

Since the dawn of civilization, humans have observed the movement of the heavens. In a sense, the earliest celestial interpreters grew and gathered food in accordance with the moon's phases. Early navigators of the sea relied upon the skies to give them support in maintaining a sense of direction.

For modern folks such as you and me, astrology can be applied to the rhythm of our lives. The birthchart represents a **blueprint of consciousness**. Possible harmonies and disharmonies are indicated. Some astrological themes are definitely more troublesome, indicating that a person may need to be quite determined and flexible to get good results.

Many of the lessons and challenges for an individual are symbolized in the birthchart. However, our particular **choices** are what make life so meaningful, unpredictable, and exciting!

The birthchart is a **compass** that can help us to perceive and accept our long and shortcomings. It is not an all-knowing and seeing crystal ball. The birthchart reminds us to keep true to our initial goals. Astrology points to staying flexible enough to alter our goals if needed. This is probably one of the most important messages in predictive astrology: giving ourselves the freedom to grow and walk away from outworn identities is essential!

Astrology reminds us that life is a continuous process. I believe this current life is an extension of numerous previous lives. It does not matter whether you as the reader can accept this theory or not. The current life is most relevant. Past lives or the past of this lifetime does not have to limit us. As a matter of fact, it is the "past" that may give us the strength to persevere through hard times and to fulfill our goals.

AUTHOR'S TIP: CLARITY IS WITHIN

You can be your greatest source of clarity. I view astrology as an ally to remind me of my direction. Astrology can be a great tool to gain a broader perspective concerning a major life decision. The clarity that I seek is often beckoning to me to simply change directions or rise above fixed opinions.

As we proceed into the chapters that discuss progressions and transits, I feel it is important to remember that the clarity resides within us. The beauty of modern predictive astrology is that it can remind us that we are beings striving to find continuing meaning within life's ups and downs.

CHAPTER TWO

THE BIRTHCHART: ROOTS OF PREDICTION — PROMISES, PROMISES!

Sometimes I fantasize life in the womb. It is shortly before the time of birth. A person is having a last-minute conversation with herself, awaiting the final countdown into life. Perhaps she is making her final resolutions for the life about to begin. An individual may make a promise to be less judgmental, more giving; to accept more responsibility; to avoid drugs and alcohol; to be a faithful spouse, etc. Some of us may relive certain memories at this delicate time of insulated protection. We have the greatest of intentions.

Some folks may be quite eager to get here. The idea of starting new goals and beginning a new lifetime is exciting. The slate is clean again.

Others may feel rather skeptical of the new life. Perhaps it will be another promising opportunity becoming a repeated failure. The same old frustrating pitfalls reside in our consciousness, awaiting their opportunity to entrap us.

IS BIRTH AN ACCIDENT?

I believe we attract the birthchart we need to fulfill our creative potentials. Our time, date, and place of birth are no more accidental than is the sunrise or sunset. It is the time of one's birth as well as the date and geographical location that create one's astrological rhythms as found in the birthchart or horoscope.

The birthchart represents the beginning of a person's astrological cycle. It is filled with many symbolic messages. They can be decoded into a meaningful language by an adept astrologer.

ROOTS

The birthchart is truly the root of all predictive astrology. However, the most powerful roots of all predictive astrology reside with the "will" of the individual. It cannot be stressed enough that the birthchart symbolizes many different potentials for each individual. It is the **freedom of choice** and perhaps the unpredictability of the spiritual forces in the universe that make predictive astrology a unique form of astrology.

ASTROLOGY'S PRIMARY SYMBOLS, THREE KEYS: PLANETS, SIGNS, AND HOUSES

To unlock the coded messages of the birthchart or horoscope one must have a basic grasp of the **planets**, **signs**, and **houses**. This is especially important if one hopes to understand the progressed horoscope.

In my first book, *Astrological Games People Play*, I describe the basic **themes** of the planets, signs, and houses. It may help the reader to refer to the tables that are included in the book. I am including in this chapter a brief discussion of the planets, signs, and houses.

BUILDING BLOCKS

I decided to include a brief review chapter because I wanted to emphasize the importance of the birthchart symbolism. The birthchart offers the building blocks for the current life cycles, such as progressions and transits. The beginnings of our life are symbolically shaped by our birthchart. It is our movement through time as we live our lives that is in synchronicity with the symbolic movement of our birthchart.

CHANGING GEARS

As complex as interpreting the birthchart can be, it is simpler to interpret than progressions and transits. I feel it is like going from ordinary driving to race car driving. Suddenly the skills of the driver must meet the demands of an entirely different contour. There is little room for error. Perhaps this comparison is a bit extreme, but the birthchart is at least a stationary entity. The symbolism is in no way limited, but at least we are looking at a particular blend of themes that are given to us as standard equipment. The birthchart is like a still photograph that is constantly changing in the midst of our growth and development symbolized by the challenges of progressions and transits.

What follows is intended to be only a brief review of astrology's thirty-four primary symbols. In the chapters that follow, I will give a brief definition or theme for progressed symbols. Transits will be discussed in a similar manner.

PLANETS IN PREDICTIVE ASTROLOGY

The planets do act as symbolic motivators in predictive astrology. The main focus of this book in the predictive discussions will be upon the planets.

It is the planetary movements through the signs (and birthchart houses) that point to the challenges of current life themes. This will be seen in the most commonly used predictive techniques: progressions and transits. It is the movement of the action-oriented planets in relation to the birthchart planets, signs, and houses that gives us a lot of useful information about the past, present, and future.

FIRST KEY: TEN PLANETS

The planets are the most dynamic astrological symbols. They symbolize our brains stimulated into **action**. Our consciousness makes itself known to us through the planets. Whether the action is more obvious as with the fiery Sun or more subtle as with watery Neptune, the action is real whether visible or hidden.

The **fire planets (Mars, Sun, and Jupiter)** symbolize forceful energy and the broadcasting of self. The **earth planets (Venus, Mercury, and Saturn)** indicate stabilizing energy and the maintaining of self. The **air planets (Mercury, Venus, and Uranus)** typify mental energy and serve to communicate self. The **water planets (Moon, Pluto, and Neptune)** represent instinctual energy and the feeling side of self.

SECOND KEY: TWELVE SIGNS

The signs are more subtle than the planets. Someone once described the planets as answering the question "What happened"? While the signs ask "Why"? or "How"? The signs **describe** planetary actions by giving a **shading** or **coloration**.

An easy example is comparing someone with the Sun (planet) in Sagittarius (sign) to a person with the Sun (planet) in Capricorn (sign). The same planet, the fiery Sun indicative of creative vitality, is channeled through two quite different signs. Generally the fiery Sagittarius is more spontaneous than earthy Capricorn. The Capricorn is possibly more organized than the Sagittarius. Even though this is comparing only one astrological trait of the horoscope there will be some truth to the previous statements. The Sun represents our fiery vitality which vivaciously broadcasts our identity through a sign.

The **fire signs (Aries, Leo, and Sagittarius)** color with enthusiasm and dynamic bursts of energy. The **earth signs (Taurus, Virgo, and Capricorn)** color with caution and practicality. The **air signs (Gemini, Libra, and Aquarius)** color with thought and communication. The **water signs (Cancer, Scorpio, and Pisces)** color with sensitivity and intuition.

THIRD KEY: TWELVE HOUSES

The final key to unlocking the birthchart is the houses. For beginners, this is perhaps the most difficult key to find when you need it! It has kept many a student of astrology locked out of the chart.

The houses **focus** the action-oriented planets and the weaving nature of the signs into meaningful reality. This reality may be quite subjective as found in the dreamy **water houses (4th, 8th, and 12th)** to concrete as in the efficient **earth houses (2nd, 6th, and 10th)** to the need for immediate self-expression as found in the enthusiastic **fire houses (1st, 5th, and 9th)** to the mental realm as found in the communicative **air houses (3rd, 7th, and 11th)**.

INTERPRETING THE COSMIC MIX

The art of interpreting birth or progressed charts **begins with a firm grasp of astrology's primary symbols**. A planet placed in a particular sign residing in a specific house represents a living energy in an individual's consciousness.

There are myriad ways to express these cosmic mixes of astrology's symbols. Though the basic themes remain the same, each individual may differ in the intensity of the expression. Some individuals may choose to repress the energy more than others with the same theme. Also, one's upbringing and/or culture can greatly alter behaviors. However, it has been my experience that major astrological themes will still surface with a basic similarity in the lives of individuals even if the objective behavior is different. The key issues have common roots.

Each of us is a complex mixture of the astrological symbols as the thirty-four primary symbols will be found in everybody's chart. However, the cosmic mixes are capable of many different combinations — reflecting the major life challenges each of us needs to encounter in one form or another.

SOME EXCELLENT BOOKS

There are many fine books written on the subject of chart interpretation. Find one you like and see if it fits into your style of thinking.

The Only Way to...Learn Astrology series by Marion March and Joan McEvers is a classic! It is currently a six-volume series that covers an amazing range of subjects. It is written in a style that is easy to read. Beginners to advanced astrologers can delight in these treasures. These are two astrologers with a passion for astrology that comes across dramatically in their work!

Joan Negus has written several wonderful books. *Basic Astrology* and its companion workbook with the same title are excellent for the beginner. Negus is exceptionally talented in presenting astrological concepts in a clear and insightful manner.

The Inner Sky by Steven Forrest is a gem worth reading. This is a great book for someone new to astrology. The planets, signs, and houses are described very clearly. Mr. Forrest has an ability to proceed with order, humor, and wisdom making the book a pleasure to read. I highly recommend this book!

Another excellent book is Maritha Pottenger's *Complete Horoscope Interpretation*. Ms. Pottenger has an unusual ability to find **themes** that have a **repeating** nature in the chart. Her methods of chart interpretation are very progressive and can be of great benefit to any students or practitioners of astrology.

In my first book, *Astrological Games People Play*, I discuss astrological **"chords"**, *i.e.*, the corresponding planet, sign, and house. For instance, Pluto (planet), Scorpio (sign), and the eighth house each belong to the eighth chord. I explain how understanding each of the twelve astrological chords aids one in understanding chart interpretation.

IS THERE A "BAD" CHART?

My answer to this question is an emphatic No! I am not saying that there are not individuals with more intense energies that do require a lot of soul searching and careful self-examination. These individuals do need to keep clear about their motives for actions in order to avoid potentially destructive or self-defeating behavior. In every chart there will exist more flowing themes and others that require much effort to get the best results. Certain chart themes do seem to indicate how the individual has come into this lifetime to make good on a lot of previously unfulfilled promises.

NOTHING MORE, NOTHING LESS

My basic premise concerning our time of birth is that we attract the chart we need — nothing more and nothing less. This is basically why I feel there is no truly "bad" or "good" chart. We are born at the moment the cosmos reflects our potentials.

Our choices greatly determine our destiny. I do not believe there is a fate that controls us.

"AUTHOR'S TIP"

Become completely familiar with the basic **themes** of the planets, signs, and houses. Make this your ally and it will come through for you when interpreting progressions and transits.

CHAPTER THREE

THE DANCE OF THE PLANETS: ASPECTS

Next in importance after the thirty-four primary symbols are the **planetary aspects**. Sometimes when the three main keys will not open the door, planetary aspects will "pick" the lock.

Essentially a planetary aspect is the angular distance separating planets. Take a glance at Gloria Steinem's chart on Page 12. Notice the aspect grid under the chart. Aspect symbols are placed in the boxes such as conjunction (♂), opposition (☍), etc.

The aspects represent different levels of intensity that require a **blending of both planetary themes**. The aspect itself, and the nature of the planets themselves, greatly determine how powerfully the symbolism will manifest in our personal expression.

The intensity level of the aspects ranges from the powerful conjunction to the ease of the trine. The table that follows lists the astrological symbol for each aspect and the angular distance separating the planets.

Aspect	Angular Distance	Symbol	Suggested Orb
Conjunction	0°	♂	8
Sextile	60°	⚹	5
Square	90°	□	8
Trine	120°	△	5
Quincunx	150°	⚻	3
Opposition	180°	☍	8

Notice the column marked **"Suggested Orb."** The orb of an aspect is the distance by degree from being exact. Very few aspects are exact. The **closer to exact** the orb is, the more significant that aspect is.

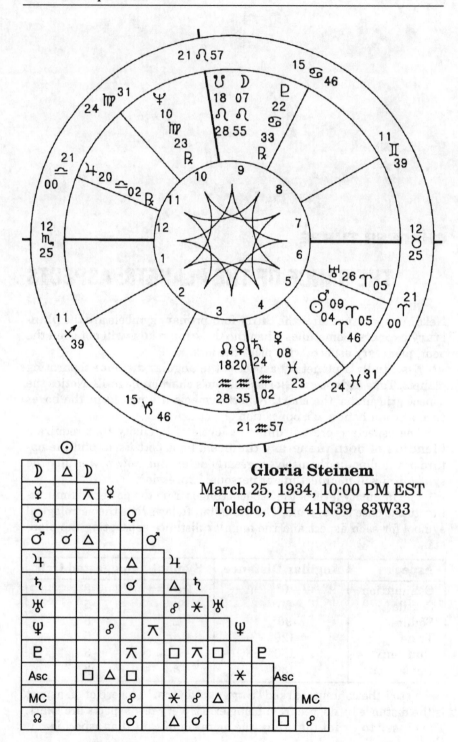

Gloria Steinem
March 25, 1934, 10:00 PM EST
Toledo, OH 41N39 83W33

The orb, or distance from exact, in birthchart or natal astrology is a lot wider than in predictive astrology. With progressions and transits, the orb I use is narrow. For most progressions, I use no more than one degree. Depending on the transit I will go as wide as five degrees (sometimes even wider). In other words, progressions symbolize an individual's recognition of planetary themes as the progressed planet gets to about one degree of the natal (or a progressed planet reaches within one degree of another progressed planet). The aspect will often last until the progression moves one degree past the natal planet.

Transits are more unpredictable in my opinion. Perhaps it is because they really do symbolize inner and outer changes. Even though the symbolism may grow stronger as the aspect gets more exact, wide orbs can still work, especially transits to natal Sun! Transiting aspects to highly charged natal planets can also denote important time periods even with a wider orb.

The aspect discussions have been separated into two groups: **intense** and **soft**. The **intense aspects**, conjunction (♂), square (□), quincunx (⚻), and opposition (☍), symbolize drives to action and solving life conflicts. These aspects are generally more indicative of inner energies that one may feel a need to resolve. I am not saying that intense aspects indicate bad energies. On the contrary, the planets involved in these aspects can combine into powerful creative symbolism.

The **soft aspects**, sextile (⚹) and trine (△), point to a flow in one's nature. Individuals can feel ease. Charts with a lot of soft aspects may require a push to action. One may need to watch extremes regarding soft or intense aspects. In soft aspects, one can lose awareness of limits. In the intense aspects, a person can be driven to compulsive actions.

INTENSE ASPECTS: THE CONJUNCTION (♂) 0°

The conjunction is when two planets are located so close together in the chart they could be holding hands. This aspect has a **self-orientation**. Two planets are welded or "fused" together. For instance, the Sun conjunct Saturn could be expressed as learning how to mix pleasure (Sun) and business (Saturn). Creativity (Sun) may need discipline (Saturn). This can be a person with a drive to be a leader. The power of the fiery Sun is given focus by serious Saturn. Both planets are mutually dependent upon the other. In a sense, the two become one.

Many astrologers consider the conjunction to be the most intense aspect, symbolizing energy that can easily grab our attention in everyday life. The conjunction at its best can denote a rugged determination to fulfill the symbolism of **both** planets. At its worst, this aspect can indicate extreme me-focus. One can be too consumed by a compulsive drive.

SQUARE (□): 90°

The **square** aspect is when two planets are separated by ninety degrees. This aspect is second in intensity to the conjunction. In some ways, the square denotes more conflict.

Planets in a square occupy signs that denote friction. Their themes naturally rub each other the wrong way. This is an **elemental** clash. A planet in Aries square a planet in Capricorn presents a dilemma. Fiery Aries wants to act now and think later. Earthy Capricorn is worried about the consequences and is more prone to caution. Aries is impatient while Capricorn steadily and patiently grasps situations. For Aries, the strategy is "go;" Capricorn is "wait" and make sure the coast is clear.

Squares can work for or against us. Understanding the issues and needs of **both** camps is important. Resolving a square is a test of **endurance** and ability to **channel** personality drives.

A rule of thumb to remember: mutable signs (Gemini, Virgo, Sagittarius, and Pisces) can square or oppose each other. The same is true of cardinal (Aries, Cancer, Libra, Capricorn) or fixed (Taurus, Leo, Scorpio, Aquarius) signs.

QUINCUNX (⚻): 150°

The **quincunx** involves two planets separated by an angular distance of 150°. As in the square, the planets occupy signs that have clashing **elements**. Planets in fire signs must adjust to accommodate the needs of earth and water. Planets in air signs must stretch to integrate the full potential of planets in earth or water signs.

The quincunx calls for gaining **clarity about inner motivations for actions**. It can be a very psychological aspect. It is an aspect indicating a type of **yoga** or union is needed. This can be a very empowering energy, if one can resolve **both** planets involved. Not being pulled into extremes is an excellent start.

A hunger for fulfillment may be at the root of this aspect. Growth can be tremendous.

OPPOSITION (☍): 180°

The **opposition** is when two planets face each other across the chart. This 180° angle represents two opposing forces that want to be brought together. We often act out our oppositions in our **relationships.**

The tension inherent in the opposing signs and planets can be **synthesized into balanced self-expression.** A planet placed in Aries opposing a planet in Libra has a challenge of balancing identity (Aries) with expectations of others (Libra). The identity focus and self-interests of Aries get tested within relationship-oriented Libra. Arian abruptness can be tempered by Libran diplomacy. The Arian call to action can motivate indecisive Libra.

Planets involved in opposition aspects indicate two separate dimensions of ourselves on a seesaw. If we try to deny one part of the opposition, the other side swings to an extreme. A person with Venus opposing Uranus could deny his individuality (Uranus) or his desire to please others (Venus). A desire to live individuality out through others can occur. Too much concern about how others feel about us (Venus) could use a more impersonal (Uranus) nature at times. A balanced (Venus) approach to relationships can slow down extreme or eccentric tastes (Uranus). Simplicity and a calm approach to life (Venus) can balance inconsistent behavior (Uranus).

SOFT ASPECTS: SEXTILE (✶): 60°

In the **sextile,** two planets occupy signs that are separated by 60°. **A rule of thumb to remember: fire signs (Aries, Leo, Sagittarius)** can sextile (or oppose) **air (Gemini, Libra, Aquarius); earth signs (Taurus, Virgo, Capricorn)** can sextile (oppose) **water (Cancer, Scorpio, Pisces).**

The sextile is indicative of **stimulation.** It can be a mental aspect. Integrating the energies shown by both planets in a sextile can arouse excitement. Action-oriented Mars may be moved by the faith of Neptune in the sextile. The Mars themes associated with courage could stimulate dreamy Neptune to act on ideals.

One may scatter energy in the sextile. Restlessness and too many changes of directions can lead to frustration.

TRINE (△): 120°

In the trine, two planets occupy signs that are separated by 120°. **A rule of thumb to remember: planets within the same element can trine each other.** The element (fire, earth, air, or water) that is showcasing a particular trine is a good clue as to the nature of the aspect. The trine is an **expansive** aspect. People may go to extremes: too much confidence or personal focus with lots of fire trines; too much practicality or materialism with earth; excessive rationalizing with air; or oversensitivity with water trines. A flowing harmony can be characteristic of this aspect. One may take the nature of the planets involved in a trine for granted. "I know this is a strength I possess, but so what?" Trines can symbolize escapism, running to paths of least resistance. The trine at its best points to positive attitudes and confidence. This can be a proud part of our personality.

DISASSOCIATE ASPECTS

I wanted to leave this section out for all of the beginners. When I was studying Spanish in college, I was horrified to learn of idioms or the usage of a language contrary to the usual pattern of that language. Misery! Something else to learn.

Disassociate aspects are formed by planets not placed in the signs you would expect to find them. This occurs when a planet is placed in the beginning or near the end of a sign. For instance, a natal Sun located at 1° Sagittarius would be exactly square a natal Mars located at 1° Pisces. However, the natal Sun is still square natal Mars located at 29° Aquarius. The orb is only 2° wide. These **"out of sign" or disassociate** aspects may not indicate the same intensity as the more natural aspects. They must be recognized! This would still be an important square in the chart.

AUTHOR'S TIP

Keep it simple! With so many predictive systems available I would advise the reader to first learn secondary progressions and transits. (I must confess my fondness for solar arc directions.) Both progressions and transits will keep you busy enough! Both complement the other.

Remember, all of this astrology is about a real person. She has feelings and concerns like you and me. Learn to tune into the key themes first. It will begin to make sense as you put it together. Take your time and do not force anything to happen. Look at both progressions and transits. See if major aspect hits or other major cycles coincide with events in that person's life.

The chapters that follow will describe the "parts" of the predictive cycles that speak of the major chapters in our lives. I believe each of us seeks to have a clearer and deeper understanding of ourselves. Our life's processes are echoed in the symbolism of progression and transits.

HELPFUL HINTS OUTLINE

I would like to list a few predictive guidelines. Getting a "feel" for astrology is a key issue for many folks. With predictive astrology it is even more challenging. The following guides will make your entrance into this area of astrology a bit easier.

1. **Rule one is that it all begins with the birthchart!** The blueprint of our consciousness indicates certain themes that are strong in each individual's chart. The organic nature of our birthchart is challenged by the secondary progressions and transits (Chapter Two).

2. Tune into the **repeating themes** in the birthchart. Why? It will help you determine the strength of a current cycle occurring in a chart for action on the mental or physical planes. An example of a repeating theme is a person having the Sun in Scorpio and many planets placed in the 8th house. There is a repeating theme of the 8th principle ("chord"). This repeating theme gains even more strength with a powerfully placed Pluto by house position and/or aspecting other planets in the chart. Transiting Pluto could be more

intensely experienced on the emotional level or in creative self-expression for this person than an individual lacking a natal emphasis on this particular theme. (This is not always the case. Individuals moving in Plutonian directions such as obtaining more personal power, searching for deeper emotional content or a heartfelt life passion may be just as intense in expressing a transiting Pluto [Chapters Two and Seven]).

3. **Progress your own chart!** What major transits or progressions occurred during key transitions? Look back at the major events in your life. Notice the transits and progressions surrounding these happenings. Also, look at major transits and progressions and see what did not happen. I have seen some astrologers get very disappointed (including myself), when a hoped-for reality did not occur. The transits and progressions may have symbolically pointed to a desired outcome of a situation. Life might not always give us an event according to our own imagined plan. It should be said that some of these current patterns manifest just as much within a person as in an outer, observable event. I have seen numerous situations where a transit of Neptune or Jupiter was experienced more on the subconscious or spiritual level.

4. The **progressed Sun changing signs or houses** is extremely important as this is a rare event. In a lifetime of 80 years, a person will not experience more than two or three changes by sign or house. **Even if the Sun is not changing sign or house, I feel it is still important to note the current position of the progressed Sun by sign and house.** I have had my progressed Sun in the practical and result-oriented Capricorn for about the last fifteen years. This adds quite a focus to the idealism of my natal Sagittarian Sun. I did a consultation for a woman yesterday born with the Sun in Libra. She had some knowledge of her birthchart and could not understand her love of travel. I discussed her progressed Sun that has been in Sagittarius for the past twenty years! (Chapter Six)

5. The **transits of the outer planets** (Saturn, Uranus, Neptune, and Pluto) are symbolic of **dynamic life processes**. The faster transiting planets act more like symbolic "triggers." Dane Rudhyar referred to these outer planets as "ambassadors of the galaxy." Is a person in the midst of a key transit cycle involving one of these planets? **A Saturn return or any other intense aspect formed by transiting Saturn to natal Saturn is important**. It describes the structure of the present and our real challenges. The **house position of Saturn** (and the house ruled by Saturn in the birthchart) is just as important. Any of the outer transiting planets changing houses is worthy of notice. People's consciousnesses adjust to new frames

of reference. Any outer planet forming intense aspects to either natal planets or the Nodes of the Moon are other key areas (Chapters Four, Nine, and Twelve).

6. **Outer transiting planets crossing any one of the four angles of the chart.** The 1st house is associated with identity and our personal style; the 4th house is security and residency needs; the 7th house denotes social interactions and partnerships; the 10th house is pointing to ambition and career desires (Chapters Four, Ten, and Eleven).

7. **Transits of Jupiter** can be times when some needed inspiration and relief will be welcomed. These transits are not easily felt by a person in the midst of very difficult life challenges. Saturn and Pluto transits will often dominate the present as well as progressed planets (and angles) contacting sensitive birthchart points. A Jupiter transit conjunct the natal Sun or another key birthchart motif, might still show a person enjoying some new learning or travel to help process a time period (Chapter Four).

8. **A progressed planet crossing an angle** of the chart or aspects formed by the progressed Ascendant and Midheaven to natal planets. Progressed planets conjunct the Ascendant are usually symbolic of powerful new orientations towards the world. A progressed Mars crossing the Ascendant might indicate new assertive power; the progressed Sun conjunct the Ascendant might be a show of new confidence. The shadow side can be just as prevalent and need balance. Mars in this instance can be expressed as self-hate or an overly aggressive nature; the Sun could be an overly inflated ego (Chapters Five, Six, Ten, and Eleven).

9. **The progressed Moon by sign and house.** One's comfort needs, residency situations, and instinctual drives are symbolized. This symbolic "trigger" can activate other aspects formed by transits or progressions already in progress (Chapter Seven).

10. **The progressed Ascendant or Midheaven changing signs or houses.** New life chapters are probably beginning (Chapter Eight).

11. **The faster progressed planets changing signs or houses.** This can be especially important if one of these planets enters a sign (or house) heavily accentuated in the birthchart. For example, an individual could have the Sun and other planets placed in Aquarius and now the progressed Venus is moving into this sign. Aspects formed by the fast progressions to natal planets are symbolic of potential new experiences associated with these planets (Chapter Seven).

12. **Note if any secondary progressed planets are changing direction.** A new direction in regard to expressing the planet's symbolism is indicated. Going from direct to retrograde does not always mean a more repressed expression. Changing from retrograde to direct does not guarantee a more outward show of this planetary theme (Chapter Five).

13. Learn the **planetary cycles** such as transiting Saturn and the progressed Moon remain about two to two-and-one-half years in a sign; certain aspects will occur at certain ages for a person such as the Saturn return at approximately ages 29-30, 58-59, and 87-88. Knowing which cycles occur at certain time periods along the life cycle helps reveal the climate of the present and future. Learning the different speeds of transiting and progressed planets increases your understanding (Chapters Four, Six, Seven, and Nine).

14. **The hard or intense aspects** (conjunction, square, quincunx, and opposition) formed by current patterns to the natal chart **are more likely to translate into events.** The softer aspects (sextile and trine) more often than not point to talents, opportunities, and mental attitudes. They are not nearly as dramatic in indicating major life transitions (Chapter Three).

15. **Each pattern can be expressed and understood in a multitude of ways.** Experiences might be on the mental, physical, emotional, or spiritual level. Interpreting a range of possibilities for ourselves or clients makes for a broader selection of choices! Opportunities will be more perceivable (Chapter One).

PART II
TRANSITS

CHAPTER FOUR

TRANSITS

Transits refer to the current positions of the planets. They do not emanate directly from our birthchart. They denote environmental situations. Transits also represent internal growth in an individual's life as much as visible changes.

For example, transiting Saturn conjunct an individual's natal Mercury, could denote "get real" and "get down to business" with mind or tongue. There might be an internal shift of more serious, cautious or even negative thinking. A tangible external result as in accomplishing a difficult task is possible. The mind (Mercury) is applied to the real world (Saturn).

COSMIC BREATH

Sometimes when I do public lectures, I explain transits in terms of breathing. For instance, Saturn represents a deep "in-breath" of life energy followed by a slow and cautious "out-breath." Transiting Saturn can symbolize a tremendous focusing time in one's life. This is quite true when transiting Saturn is aspecting a key planet in one's chart such as the Sun or Moon. Likewise, transiting Saturn moving across one's Ascendant or 7th house can be indicative of focusing upon identity (1st house) or relating to others (7th house). Transiting Saturn represents taking control, restructuring, and defining life themes.

We recognize a tornado by its funnel-shaped cloud. I feel that transits have a symbolic energy form. Saturn is linear in nature. It denotes our upbringing in a culture and knowing what truths to "swallow" to fit into society. Saturn is indicative of our ability to make choices within "the system" that promote growth.

Transiting Saturn (♄)

Process:	Maturation
Life Challenges:	Clear reality testing
	Self-expression through career
	Accepting responsibility
Key Allies:	Focusing power
	Concentration
	Self-growth
	Feeling of accomplishment
	Discipline
Illusions:	Power hunger (need to control)
	Fear of commitment or responsibility
	Surrender to cultural stereotypes
	Lack of versatility and imagination
	Pressured excessively by time
Orbital Period:	29 years 167 days
Sign Cycle:	Approximately 2 1/2 Years

GOD OF TIME

In mythology, Saturn was associated with Cronus, the god of time. Cronus was a Titan who overthrew his father, Uranus, to become ruler of the universe. Cronus was later overthrown by one of his sons, Zeus.

Transiting Saturn represents a bookmark in our lives. Many of us feel the pressures of time as Saturn moves through our charts. This planet indicates periods of time when we do a lot of **reality testing**.

COSMIC CHIROPRACTOR

The ancients called Saturn the Lord of Karma. I view Saturn as a planet of growth. Granted it may symbolize a period of more responsibility and hard work. Increased inner strength and wisdom are often the outcome of a key Saturn transit in one's life. Saturn represents a cosmic chiropractor, symbolizing where life adjustments may be needed as we grow older.

Saturn symbolically tests our patience and determination. I have found in many charts (including my own) that the full fruition of a particular Saturn transit may come years after the actual transit occurs. For example, Saturn's transit of an individual's Sun may be denoting a need to better face reality and make more concrete goals. It may take years of small steps and much practice for the individual to grow confident with the process. Saturn transits reflect an evolving process more often than immediate gratification. We are investing heavily in the present to pave the way for a successful future.

TRANSIT CYCLES
It takes Saturn approximately two to two and one half years to move through a sign. Saturn transited through Sagittarius as I began writing this book.

Saturn may take a longer or shorter time to transit through a birthchart house. It depends on the size of the house. The entrance into a new house usually is indicative of life changes. Saturn crossing the natal 10th house often is indicative of career concerns. One may have a change of focus regarding ambitions. Saturn tends to indicate a more serious tone in the life circumstances associated with its current house.

TRANSITING SATURN ASPECTING PLANETS
Transiting Saturn aspecting a particular natal planet points to developing issues denoted by that planet. Also, this is a process that may go on for a year or two due to the slow movement of transiting Saturn. Processes connoted by transiting Saturn when aspecting a natal planet include: discipline, focusing, leadership, confidence, and career aspirations. (See Chapters Nine through Twelve for a complete discussion of aspects.)

TRANSITING URANUS (♅)

Process:	Individualization
Life Challenges:	Clear Sense of Individuality
	Developing Future Goals
	Respecting Freedom of Others
	Understanding Cultural & Global Trends
Key Allies:	Free Thinking
	Sharing of Ideas
	Subcultures
	Friendship
	Innovative Mentality
Illusions:	Legend in Our "Own" Minds
	Rights of Others Not Important
	Reactionary Consciousness
	Impatience & Selfishness
	Fear of Freedom
	Rebelliousness
Orbital Period:	84 years, 5 days
Sign Cycle:	Approximately 7 years

URANUS: COSMIC BREATH
Uranus denotes hyperventilation! Our vision or desire for the future can make us impatient with the present. Whereas, Saturn connotes focus and stability, Uranus symbolizes unpredictable bursts of energy and instability. Uranus can represent one's tendency to race against

time. This planet is a key theme in rock musician Bruce Springsteen's chart. The Saturn/Uranus conjunction was square his natal Sun during the publicity of his separation from actress-model Julianne Phillips.

Uranus was a key planet in the chart of actor James Dean. The rebel planet ruled Dean's Aquarian Sun and was placed in his natal 7th house. Uranus in the 7th house can denote strong individualistic themes in relating to others. Transiting Uranus was conjunct Dean's natal Mars on the day he was killed in an automobile accident, 9/30/55.

COSMIC LIGHTNING
Saturn reminds me of a methodical movement with a step-by-step vision. Uranus symbolism is like bolts of lightning. This planet can symbolize a fast and ingenious mental nature, one who can see the future quite clearly. One can quickly perceive entire processes. Our internal sense of time is turned ahead.

Saturn symbolizes a slowing down of life rhythms; Uranus denotes a tremendous speeding-up. When transiting Uranus contacts a sensitive birthchart symbol, a person can experience sudden life changes. Doors may open that were previously not seen. Some individuals who have been knocking very hard find an opening. Tennis star Steffie Graf had transiting Uranus opposing her natal Gemini Sun during her rise to world recognition as the number one woman's tennis player.

During a Uranus transit a person must watch out for too much "me" focus. This can occur with Uranus transiting the Moon, Venus, Sun, Midheaven, or Ascendant.

Some people need to be focusing on self. I have seen clients who ignored their own needs for years. Self-sacrifice is all they had lived. During a Uranus transit they have angered those they were serving by pursuing their own interests. A Uranus transit does point to developing one's individuality. It can be a vitally refreshing period of time.

TRANSITING URANUS ASPECTING PLANETS
When transiting Uranus aspects a natal planet, physical or consciousness changes are often denoted. Once again, the planet being aspected must be considered. The sign and house of this planet would also need to be noted.

Transiting Uranus conjuncting an individual's 5th house Sagittarius Sun could denote experimental (Uranus) creative pursuits (Sun and 5th house). This could symbolize new (Uranus) love relationships (5th house).

Transiting Uranus often symbolizes the spark needed to ignite energy floating in our subconscious. When Uranus transits across one's 1st, 4th, 7th, or 10th houses it acts as a symbolic alarm clock. This movement denotes a wake-up in consciousness. Maybe we have thought about trying a new career, hobby, or relationship but put it on the back burner for years. It is amazing how many sudden changes are really long cherished goals! (See Chapters Nine through Twelve for a complete discussion of aspects).

SATURN AND URANUS: A DYNAMIC POLARITY

Saturn and Uranus form an interesting polarity. History (Saturn) needs those questioning individuals (Uranus) who are not afraid to change its course; cultures and laws (Saturn) are needed to protect against anarchy (Uranus); society and government (Saturn) thrives off free individuals and subcultures (Uranus); people must be careful not to sacrifice their entire individuality (Uranus) to cultural expectation and myths (Saturn). Each of these transiting planets symbolizes important challenges as we mature into young or older adults.

TRANSITING NEPTUNE (Ψ)

Process:	Expressing personal and universal love
Life Challenges:	Creating ideals
	Self acceptance
	Finding union
	Finding internal peace
	Transcending anxiety of life pressures
	Avoiding divine discontent
Key Allies:	Faith in a higher power (Grace)
	Spiritual values
	Creativity
	Surrendering rigid concepts
	Compassion
	Charisma
	Vision
	"Watching"
Illusions	Sleepy consciousness
	Denial of reality
	Escape from responsibility
	Denial of intangible
	Stagnated Growth
	Self-Indulgence and Addictive Habits
Orbital Period:	164 Years 290 Days
Sign Cycle:	Approximately 14 Years

NEPTUNE: COSMIC COBWEBS

Neptune's presence in astrology offers symbolism that explains one's deepest intuition. This planet denotes venturing beyond logic and reality into the area of the mind that is moved by ideals and fantasy.

There is a divine discontent in Neptune symbolism and each 12th chord motif (*i.e.*, Pisces and 12th house) that is unlike any other astrological symbol. The placement of Neptune in one's birthchart connotes in what manner we deal with divine discontent, perfection and idealism. (Planets placed in the sign Pisces and 12th house should also be noted.)

The transits of Neptune can denote periods when we feel disoriented. Our inner timing may be out of synch with physical events. Neptune's symbolism can manifest in a spectrum as wide as charisma, glamour, aesthetic talent, falling in love, spiritual awareness to substance abuse and loss of values. This planet is indicative of our ability to feel compassion and empathy for others.

There are times when Neptune symbolism can feel like we have walked into a spider web. We keep pulling away the web from our face. Our compulsive drives for perfection can give the impression the web is still clinging to our skin. The more we persist in removing the web the more frustrating it feels. Sometimes Neptune transits can represent learning to quiet our minds. Our drives to perfection may need to be adjusted so we can feel contentment and peace.

COSMIC BREATH

Neptune is a peculiar motif. It reminds me of trying to eat chicken broth with a fork. We probably need Twilight Zone music when transiting Neptune is aspecting our Ascendant and key birthchart planets (or Moon's Nodes!) to really capture the mood.

When Neptune transited over my natal 9th house Venus in Sagittarius, I began listening to a lot of music. I already liked music. It helped me stay in touch with my thoughts. I chose different types of music almost daily to match my moods during that transit.

Neptune is like not breathing at all. It is like complete relaxation where breathing does not exist. It can denote escaping from time through various addictions. It is the timeless symbolism found in a very creative work. The writer, artist, or musician captures the muse consciousness.

During Neptune transits an individual will sometimes overcome addictions to people, substances, and other escapist behavior. Neptune transits in one's chart can represent a spiritual hunger. Many folks get into meditation and relaxation therapies such as biofeedback during a Neptune transit. "Right brain" therapies may become quite attractive. People may discover astrology or psychic forms of counseling. The higher intuitive symbolism associated with Neptune denotes a person seeking to feed the right brain. Experiences with yoga and meditation can truly be satisfying. This could also denote a person's interest in music, dance or art. Bruce Springsteen dramatically burst into learning guitar at age 13 while transiting Neptune conjuncted his natal Venus in Scorpio. Both planets have an association with aesthetic pursuits.

Neptune indicates that faith in our intuition will integrate our energies. We need to come full circle and see the relationship of our thoughts and the life we are creating.

Transiting Pluto (♇)

Process:	Tuning into personal power
Life Challenges:	Maintaining a clear sense of personal power
	Finding emotional happiness
	Establishing balanced relationships
	Learning to forgive
	Understanding the grieving process
	Understanding subconscious patterns
Key Allies:	Focusing power
	Concentration
	Intimate relationships
	Seeing the "Big Picture"
	Understanding of death and rebirth
	Release of pain and negative thoughts
Illusions:	Compulsive addictions
	(sex, substance, relationship)
	Power hunger
	Emotional starvation
	Exaggerated self-importance
	Lack of self-respect
Orbital Period:	248 years 157 days
Sign Cycle:	Approximately 14 to 30 years

PLUTO: COSMIC COMPOST

I recently met with a client having just gone through some intense growth symbolized by transiting Pluto in her chart. I was explaining the symbolism of Pluto to the young lady in terms of finishing a cycle and starting another. Suddenly the client's eyes opened widely. She stated that Pluto reminded her of composting a garden. You take food waste and recycle it into the soil to help something new grow. Pluto is the cosmic composter.

Pluto transits denote rebirth. Attitudes and behaviors can get transformed greatly. A person experiencing a Pluto transit could achieve transformative growth through starting a business as much as studying psychology. Pluto self-mastery themes can take unlimited forms. Financial success for some people during the present Pluto in Scorpio era may give them the confidence and insights for psychological transformation. (I said these transits can get unpredictable!)

COSMIC BREATH

Pluto symbolizes a deep in-breath of energy like Saturn. Unlike Saturn symbolism, this in-breath may take a lot longer than Saturn to exhale into the world. It can be years after a Pluto transit aspects our Ascendant, Sun, Moon, or another planet that we comprehend the past. It may take years for consciousness to catch up with the actual events that occur during these transits.

Pluto denotes a lot of internal processing. Some people are more attracted to this than others. Pluto transits connote our deepest subconscious urges wanting to become conscious. We may not always like what we see. The in-breath of Pluto can reside in our consciousness for years. Lucky is the person who takes the time to understand this energy. It can unlock many of our deepest psychological processes.

PLUTO AND INNER STRENGTH

An individual can accomplish amazing growth and overcome destructive habits during Pluto transits. A person may survive the death of a child, parent, or spouse during a Pluto transit. These transits could denote a psychological death or the end of a cycle. Recently I did a consultation for a person with transiting Pluto in Scorpio conjuncting natal Saturn in Scorpio. She was grieving the death (Pluto and Scorpio) of her father (Saturn). The client was learning a lot about her own psychological strength. She was trying to forgive her father and release her anger.

Another client with transiting Pluto in Scorpio conjunct natal Saturn in Scorpio was grieving a different type of loss. She had left a place of business to start her own business after fifteen years on the job. Her close friends at work were so jealous (Pluto and Scorpio) they did not give her a going-away gift. She was rejected by employer and employees. She went through a very emotional period and felt like something in her life had truly died.

The circle deepens during Pluto transits. Some people truly suffer. They have difficulty with material that surfaces from the unconscious. This material from the unconscious can empower us or weaken us. The choice is always our own. We can learn how to master this very forceful energy. It need not be compulsive energy.

Transiting Jupiter (♃)

Process:	"In Search of the Promised Land"
Life Challenges:	Maintaining a Positive Life Perspective
	Trusting Oneself
	Benevolence
	Sensible Risk Taking
Key Allies:	Knowledge
	Travel
	Philosophy
	"Luck"
	Faith
Illusions:	Dogmatism
	Lack of Growth beyond Cultural Myths
	Judgmental
	Not Knowing One's Limits
	Lack of Faith
Orbital Period:	11 Years 351 Days
Sign Cycle:	One Year

JUPITER: COSMIC BREATH

I have known more than one astrologer disappointed by transiting Jupiter. There was much anticipation for something "good" or "big" to happen.

Jupiter transits are similar to those of Uranus in that both motifs symbolize futuristic thoughts. A key difference between Jupiter and Uranus symbolism is that Uranus is more result-oriented. Uranus transits often do denote an individual wanting to break into new situations. Our first civilian astronaut, Christina McAuliffe, had transiting Uranus in Sagittarius conjunct natal Jupiter in Sagittarius when the tragic explosion of the Challenger occurred in 1986. It is interesting that Ms. McAuliffe was a teacher (Jupiter in Sagittarius) breaking into new territory (Uranus). She was going to teach two classes beamed back on live television from the seven-day space odyssey.

Jupiter is "softer" in symbolism. Like Uranus, Jupiter can connote relationship or lifestyle changes. Jupiter is expansion. It is a build up of energies but not as intensely as Saturn or Pluto. Uranus symbolism moves so fast through consciousness that a build up is not needed. Jupiter is the Buddha belly symbolism. It represents a huge in-breath followed by a short, strong out-breath.

JUPITER AS A CATALYST

Jupiter transits often symbolize faith and inspiration issues more than external change. Outward success may follow the faith and inspiration a person is experiencing.

I have observed that individuals do have a drive for outward success if a Jupiter transit follows a key Saturn or Pluto transit rather closely in time. Sometimes this can be true if transiting Jupiter follows a Uranus transit. It is as though a person's consciousness and willpower have been stretched to such a point that she welcomes the encouraging touch denoted by transiting Jupiter.

Jupiter transits can symbolize that relaxation and rest are needed. I have seen where a person is ready to have fun! Traveling or another leisurely activity is very attractive. If Jupiter occurs simultaneously with a key Saturn or Pluto transit in one's chart, a person may not experience much lightness in thought or action.

JUPITER AND DENIAL

Transiting Jupiter can denote a period when a person denies the reality of a situation. We want so badly to have harmony with Jupiter. People sometimes stay in relationships or careers that they have outgrown. The eternal optimist of Jupiter believes it will get better no matter how difficult the problem. We can be like a person excited about finding fool's gold.

WE CREATE OUR LUCK

Good things may happen to us during a transit of Jupiter in our chart. **Usually a person has been working hard to create what appears to be a lucky break**.

I have seen disillusionment with Jupiter. People can wonder if their hard work will ever be rewarded. Sometimes Jupiter's rewards are related to our drives for self-growth. It can be our exploration of new studies or areas of interest that leads us into a profitable life on a material or consciousness level.

JUPITER AND IMPATIENCE

People do sometimes leave relationships, careers, etc., during key Jupiter transits (*i.e.*, aspects to Sun or Venus and transits of 7th house). The "Grass is Greener" game mentioned in my first book, *Astrological Games People Play,* can be a dominating theme. It is important to become aware of underlying motivations for change during Jupiter (and Uranus) transits. Discipline and organization can be aggravating words when going through a Jupiter transit. Limits are not desired.

TRANSIT CYCLES

Jupiter takes about a year to move through a sign. Jupiter is the fastest moving of the planets beyond the orbit of Mars. It takes about twelve years to return to the sign it occupied at your birth. This is called a **Jupiter Return**. Aspects made by transiting Jupiter last from two to three weeks. These aspects are briefer than those made by the outermost transiting planets. Jupiter transits connote the seeking of knowledge. People may seek a broader life perspective. Jupiter denotes seeking opportunity. This planet symbolizes travel on mental and physical planes.

TRANSITS OF THE PERSONAL PLANETS (SUN, MOON, MERCURY, VENUS, AND MARS)

The planets closest to the earth are the personal planets. They move through our charts quickly. These planets require much less time to move through a sign than the outermost planets (*i.e.*, Jupiter, Saturn, Uranus, Neptune, and Pluto).

The fast-moving transits do not symbolize the depth and potential for transformative growth as the outer planets. Personal planets do act as symbolic "triggers." Each of these planets, especially Mercury, Venus, and Mars can denote the activation of a slower-moving transit (or a progression).

An individual with transiting Uranus opposing the Sun could be deciding to leave a troublesome relationship. Perhaps the confidence (Sun) to resolve this situation to preserve independence (Uranus) is lacking. This aspect may already be operating for several months but the person has taken no action. Then comes the faster transiting Mars to conjunct the Sun. The person may find the assertion (Mars) strength to move ahead. The goal and insight (Uranus) just needed an energy burst (Mars) to satisfy the ego (Sun) needs of the present.

The swift Moon (☽) requires only 2 1/2 days maximum to transit through a sign; the Sun (☉) only about 30 days. Mercury (☿) only about two to three weeks; Venus (♀) no more than approximately six weeks; Mars (♂) about two months. Aspects made by these transits to our natal planets denote activity for only a matter of days. This is in great contrast to the slower-moving outer planets. Their aspects can last for years!

The transiting Moon can symbolize mood and domestic changes; the Sun a short period of dramatic display or creative energy; Mercury can denote important communication or information; Venus can symbolize relating to others as well as aesthetic interests; Mars can connote assertion and physical energy.

Aspects formed by the transiting Sun, Moon, Mercury, and Venus are not included in this book. They are not being given individual attention because they are too ephemeral in nature.

Some people even compare transits to progressions. In my opinion this is not as reliable as comparing transits to the natal chart. There is a complete delineation of the aspects formed by transiting Jupiter, Uranus, Neptune and Pluto to each natal (and progressed) planet, Ascendant, Midheaven, and Nodes of the Moon in Chapters Nine through Twelve.

PART III
SECONDARY PROGRESSIONS

CHAPTER FIVE

SYMBOLIC TIME PIECES: PROGRESSIONS

You consult a road map to see how far it is from your present location to the city of your destination. The scale on the map explains that one quarter of an inch is equal to twenty-five miles. You determine that you will be traveling one inch of the map or a distance of one-hundred miles. If you take this concept of distance, but now think in terms of a smaller length of time equaling or symbolizing a greater length of time, you are already on the way to understanding progressions.

A DAY EQUALS A YEAR
It may sound strange to find out that in the system known as secondary progressions, each day following the day of birth is equivalent to a year of time. However, it really is no more peculiar than one quarter of an inch equaling twenty-five miles. In secondary progressions, if a person is born June 1, 1947, his progressed twenty-second birthday planetary positions will be listed under June 23, 1947.

SYMBOLIC AND ACTUAL SKY
Progressions indicate the movement of the planets only days after the birth. A person's planetary positions for age ninety are found only ninety days following birth. This is a symbolic sky as the planets are not really occupying these portions of the sky on the individual's ninetieth birthday.

In the predictive system known as transits, the planets are in a real portion of the sky. Today is October 19, 1992. The planetary ephemeris shows that the transiting Moon is moving through Leo. As stated in Chapter Four, transits are the positions of the planets as they are currently moving through the sky. This may sound a bit peculiar but the planets on June 22, 1947 mentioned earlier as progressed planets were actually transits when they occupied real portions of the sky on that day. We are infants during the first years of our transits and adults when we look back at these same planetary movements in terms of progressions.

Both of these systems are valid. Progressions are small units of time equaling or "symbolizing" greater units of time. Remember the map example. Transits are similar to the actual distance we need to travel while progressions resemble the scale on the map where one quarter of an inch equals twenty-five miles.

Both progressions and transits are important. The symbolic one-hundred miles and the actual one-hundred miles are both valid and meaningful. Progressions (especially secondary) and transits are predictive systems that can be used to better comprehend past, present and future time periods.

There are other types of progressions in addition to secondary. Each involves the symbolic equivalent of one unit of time with another. For example, minor progressions equate one lunar month after birth with one year of a person's life. Tertiary progressions equate a day after birth with a lunar month in the life. Converse progressions apply the above principles, but move everything **backward rather than forward.**

All progressed positions did occur in the sky at a particular time. There is another system known as **directions** involving positions which did not ever occur in the sky. In directions, the whole chart is rotated a certain amount, depending on the type of directions being used. My favorite form of directions is **solar arc directions**! Everything in the natal chart is moved the same distance as was traveled by the Sun in secondary progressions. Since the Sun moves about one degree per year in secondary progressions, to find the positions of planets in solar arc directions for a person's twenty-fifth birthday, approximately, twenty-five degrees are added to each natal planet in the chart. For example, if the natal Moon is 10 Aries, the solar arc directed Moon (for age twenty-five) would be 5 Taurus. You can figure the solar arc directed Ascendant in this manner. Aspects are considered between solar arc planets and natal planets. The orb is still one degree. You do not consider the aspects formed by solar arc planets to each other because their angular distances from one another are the same as they were in the natal chart.

In Ascendant arc directions, the whole chart is moved the distance the secondary progressed Ascendant has moved. Some people even use symbolic arc directions. This system moves everything an arbitrary number of degrees per year, *i.e.*, three, five, seven and one-half degrees per year, etc.

Return charts involve constructing a chart for the exact moment in time a planet returns to its exact natal position by degree, sign,

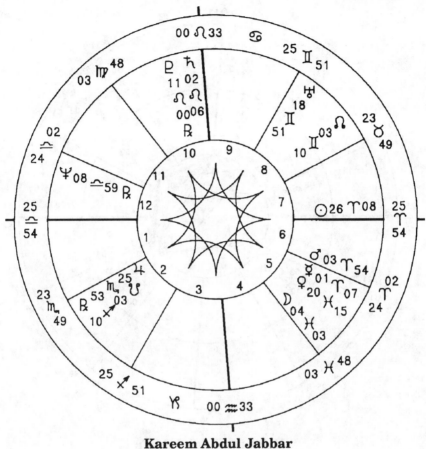

Kareem Abdul Jabbar
April 16, 1947, 6:30 PM EST
New York, NY 40N42 74W0

minute, and second in the zodiac. A **Solar Return** is erected for the
exact time the transiting Sun reaches the precise position of your natal
Sun. The longitude and latitude of birth or the longitude and latitude of
the place of residence can be used to construct the chart. This chart
gives a general overview of a year.

   Lunar Returns are popular. They occur about once a month. It is
possible to do return charts for the other planets. Current life spans
would not include a Neptune or Pluto Return.

THE PROGRESSED HOROSCOPE
Look at the birthchart (above) for famous basketball star Kareem Abdul Jabbar (formerly known as Lew Alcindor). This chart represents
the positions of the planets at Kareem's birth on April 16, 1947.

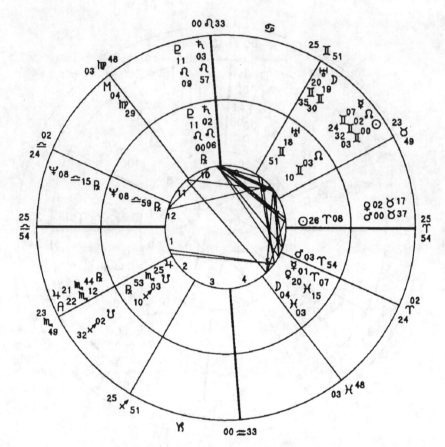

Kareem Abdul Jabbar
Progressed to April 16, 1982
New York, NY   40N42   74W0

Now look at the same chart above, but this time notice the planets placed outside of the birthchart wheel. These are the secondary progressed positions for age thirty-five. **Remember this assumes that one day equals one year.** Therefore, we count thirty-five days following the birth in the planetary ephemeris which is May 21, 1947. This progressed birthday is equivalent to April 16, 1982 (thirty-fifth birthday).

SLOW AND FAST PROGRESSIONS

Notice that the slower progressed planets have barely moved since birth. They still occupy the same signs and houses. The fastest of the slow planets is Jupiter which has changed houses (moving retrograde from second into first house) moving approximately four degrees. The next in speed is Saturn which has traveled less than two degrees; Uranus less than two degrees; Neptune and Pluto less than one degree.

The faster moving planets have made some definite changes in Kareem's chart. The progressed Sun has already changed signs twice. It moved into Taurus at age four and entered Gemini at age thirty-five (written as 0♊3' in the chart). It takes the progressed Sun approximately thirty years to move through an entire sign. The progressed Sun moves about one degree per year. The house position of the progressed Sun is also important. Kareem's Sun has progressed into the eighth house.

The fastest-moving of the progressed planets is the Moon. It stays in one sign from two to two-and-one-half years. Kareem's progressed Moon on April 16, 1982 is located at nineteen degrees of Gemini in the 8th house. The progressed Moon is a very important indicator as to what is capturing our attention during its movement through the signs and houses.

Kareem's autobiography *Giant Steps* was released in December, 1983. He had both the Sun and Moon by secondary progression in Gemini which is a sign greatly associated with communication and writing! The progressed Mercury in Kareem's chart is located at seven degrees Gemini, twenty-four minutes. It has moved a little more than two signs since birth. The progressed Venus is placed in Taurus, two degrees and seventeen minutes. It has changed signs twice since birth. Progressed Mars has changed signs in Kareem's chart since birth going from three degrees and fifty four minutes of Aries to zero degrees and thirty seven minutes of Taurus.

WHAT ABOUT THE HOUSES?

The houses can each be progressed. However, I would advise only paying special attention to the progressed first house or the progressed Ascendant and the progressed tenth house or progressed Midheaven. These two "angles" are quite significant. If they contact a natal planet an individual will probably express these themes.

Look again at Kareem's charts on Page 36 and 37. Notice the birthchart Ascendant (25♎54') has progressed into Scorpio (written as 22♏12'). Actually Kareem's Ascendant entered Scorpio by progression at age six. In *Astrological Games People Play*, I described the Ascendant as related to one's self-image. The Ascendant can act as a persona. Kareem has characteristically been described as a private and moody person. This can be typified by the sign Scorpio.

Kareem's Midheaven or 10th house has moved from the birthchart position (0♌33') to four degrees Virgo and thirty-two minutes (4♍29'). Kareem's progressed Midheaven has entered the freedom-oriented eleventh house of his birthchart. He has been adopting more of a carefree

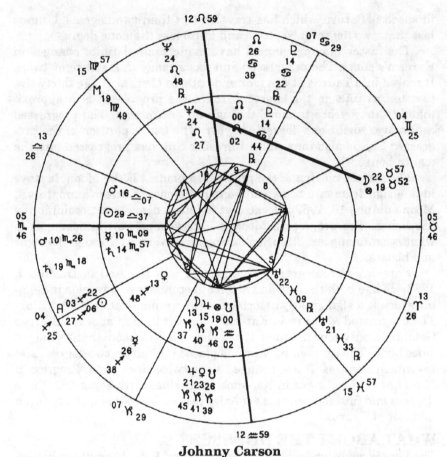

Johnny Carson
Inner Chart - October 23, 1925, 7:17 AM CST 40N59 94W44
Outer Chart - Progressed to October 23, 1962 40N59 94W44

attitude the past few years. His public image (10th house) is of a freer individual. There will be more on the progressed angles (Ascendant and Midheaven) later.

PROGRESSED ASPECTS

The fast-moving planets in progressions are catalysts that symbolize changes in our consciousness. It is often the relationship of these faster-moving progressions to natal planets (aspects) that indicates changes of life direction, important choices, consciousness changes, meeting obstacles and challenges related to the particular planets involved.

For instance, the chart of Johnny Carson is above. Notice the line drawn from his progressed Moon in Taurus to the natal Neptune in his tenth house.

Carson's progressed Moon was moving into a ninety degree aspect or a square in 1962. This was the year "Here's Johnny!" became a popular phrase. Mr. Carson became the TV host of the *Tonight Show*. The progressed Moon can very much represent a symbolic "trigger" and shows our consciousness extremely focused in terms of its sign and house position. Aspects made by the progressed Moon refine this focus even more. Neptune has symbolism related to the arts. Media is quite pronounced in Carson's birthchart. The planet Neptune (associated with film and imagination) is placed in his career-oriented tenth house.

Carson's progressed Moon is placed in an earth sign Taurus that can be indicative of financial change. Carson was to become the highest paid TV host. It is important to remember that this is only one isolated predictive factor. One would need to consider the other progressed planets with fast motion (Sun, Mercury, Venus, and Mars) as well as the progressed Ascendant and Midheaven. Also, the transits for this time period would need to be included.

PAGES VERSUS CHAPTERS

The speed of the planets is just as important with progressions as with transits. Since progressions are basically slow-moving entities, the faster-moving planets offer useful symbolism for a particular time period being considered. An exception to this is when a planet changes direction, (*i.e.*, going from direct to retrograde or vice versa).

The slowest-moving transits (*i.e.*, the outer planets) offer valuable symbolism as we move along our life cycle. The slowest-moving planet, Pluto, transits or moves through a sign in thirteen to approximately thirty years. Each sign contains thirty degrees. Progressed Pluto will not even move three degrees in a ninety-four year lifetime.

However, **long-term aspects** held for years and years (using the one-degree orb) by progressed outer planets to one another or inner planets that are retrograde **are keys to major enduring character issues**. For instance, a person could have progressed Uranus sextile progressed Jupiter for twenty years! This is an enduring theme pointing to a love of independence and being exhilarated through travel. Learning and teaching are a strong tendency.

Due to my own progressed Mars turning retrograde, I have progressed Mars square my natal Jupiter from age 34 through 56! This is a good example of a planet turning retrograde and still being used both internally and externally. I learned how to harness some of my fire energy and direct it productively into creative pursuits. Directing energy (Mars) into writing (Jupiter) this and other books is one form. It is good to be aware of these long-term aspects formed by progressed planets as they are endless chapters!

The fast-moving "triggering" action of the progressed Moon is similar to the faster moving transits (Sun, Moon, Mercury, Venus, and Mars). Each of these fast-moving planets can make numerous aspects in a given year as they form different angular relationships with our natal planets.

The progressed Moon and fast-moving personal planets by transit are analogous to the pages in a book. The remaining progressions and the slower-moving transits are more like chapters. The progressed Moon and fast transits symbolize more immediate daily needs. The progressed Sun, Ascendant, Midheaven and other key progressed planets along with the slower-moving transits are indicative of major cycles that contain many days in our lives.

For instance, an aspect made by the fast transiting Mercury to a natal planet will last for only a few days. An aspect made by the slow transiting Pluto could continue for three years! An aspect made by progressed Mercury lasts for about two years.

It should be mentioned that though the progressed Moon moves like a fast transit (approximately one degree per month), its movement through the signs and houses is more like another chapter in our lives. The progressed Moon changing signs or houses is important. The progressed Moon remains in a sign or house approximately two to two-and-one-half years. Aspects made by other progressed planets can also be important. This is especially true if the aspect corresponds to another important cycle or cycles occurring simultaneously. Progressed aspects formed by the Sun, Ascendant, Midheaven, Venus, Mercury, and Mars can be indicative of important chapters in our lives.

RETROGRADE MOTION IN SECONDARY PROGRESSIONS

A planet having retrograde motion simply means that, observed from the Earth, that planet "appears" to have a backward motion. Except for the Sun and Moon, each planet can have retrograde motion. In reality, the planet is moving forward. Since astrology is a language of symbols, retrograde motion is said to denote a different expression than if the planet had direct (forward) motion. Most of the astrology books speak of retrograde in terms of inwardly-directed behavior.

I have seen people quite forcefully project the themes of retrograde planets. A progressed planet changing direction, either from direct to retrograde or retrograde to direct, is symbolic of a new life chapter. A dramatic energy shift can occur. I have a friend who at about age ten had natal Mercury turn retrograde. At age thirty-five it turned direct. The friend told me that shortly after age ten she became a much quieter child. It was interesting to learn that when Mercury turned direct at age thirty-five, my friend was faced with numerous decisions. The Mercury turning direct, combined with some key transits at that time, seemed to denote more confidence in her perceptions and communication abilities.

When a progressed planet has been retrograde for several years and then turns direct, or vice/versa, it may take a few years to grow accustomed to the switch. Progressed Mercury remains retrograde about 25 days or years in secondary progression; progressed Venus about 42 years; progressed Mars about 63 years. The progressed planets beyond Mars stay retrograde for many years. Progressed Jupiter will remain retrograde almost 120 years! Saturn, Uranus, Neptune, and Pluto stay even longer.

It depends when during a retrograde cycle a person is born as to whether a progressed planet might later change direction. It is quite possible an outer planet will not change direction in one's life. Saturn stays retrograde for about 150 days or 150 years in secondary progression. I was born November 24, 1947 with Saturn moving direct. Ten days later on December 4, 1947, Saturn turned retrograde. This means that since age ten (one day equaling one year) my progressed Saturn has been retrograde and will be my entire life. Uranus was retrograde for me at birth. It will remain retrograde my entire lifetime.

A change of direction by a progressed Saturn whether from direct to retrograde or retrograde to direct can be quite significant if occurring later in life. Most of us have been fully indoctrinated by our culture's agenda and values well before our first transiting Saturn Return at about age twenty-eight to thirty. If progressed Saturn changes direction after age thirty this can denote a radical change of direction in a person's life. Saturn turning retrograde could connote a more reflective life period starting and even pulling away from what one was taught to be true by society. It can symbolize a person's deep processing and attempt to find his own values. Saturn turning direct could symbolize a person's challenge to live his ideals or inner reality. This could be someone wanting to more fully change the community or culture. It could even denote a person surrendering ideals and giving into societal pressures.

Many astrologers teach students to basically ignore the outermost planets in secondary progression. I am saying to take a good look at their direction. A progressed Jupiter, Saturn, Uranus, Neptune, or Pluto changing direction can be quite significant, as are the long-term aspects formed by outer progressed planets to each other.

CHAPTER SIX

THE PROGRESSED SUN (☉)

Organic Process:	Expressing and experiencing the true self
Life Challenges:	Maintaining a creative vitality
	Expanding one's self-expression
	Expressing love for self and others
Key Allies:	Self-confidence
	Inspired life attitude
	Humor
	Spontaneous expression of love
	Strong willpower
Illusions:	"Stuck in the mud"
	Forgetting to be happy
	Blocked expression of love
	Egomania
	A dictator
Sign Cycle:	Approximately 30 Years

LONG CHAPTERS OF SELF-UNFOLDING

There is no single factor in secondary progressions as important as the progressed Sun. It is a predictive factor that outweighs any other isolated predictive symbol in my opinion.

The progressed Sun represents chapters within a chapter. It stays in one sign for approximately thirty years — more than one third of an average lifetime. This alone should indicate that the progressed Sun plays a major role in our self-development. Its position by sign and house as well as any aspects formed must be taken into consideration. There are certain years in a person's life when the Sun will progress into a new sign and/or house. **Since this occurs so few times in a person's life, this change of sign or house is of major importance.** Aspects formed by the progressed Sun to natal planets are of extreme importance!

RELATIONSHIP OF NATAL AND PROGRESSED SUN

I would like to make it clear that the progressed Sun grows right out of the natal Sun. In a sense the natal Sun is expressed through our progressed Sun (and vice versa). A type of marriage is formed. The natal Sun is still the dominating force. The progressed Sun is a further refinement of our natal Sun. The progressed Sun is not an isolated entity completely separate from our natal Sun. It is a step along the way of a very special, delicate, organic process of self-development.

"ELEMENTAL SHIFT"

Astrology books do not talk enough about the tension that occurs when the progressed Sun changes signs or houses. A natural elemental contrast occurs. I am not saying this is bad. It is an awakener for us. The Sun's crossing over into a new element (*i.e.*, from fire to earth; earth to air; air to water; water to fire) as much as into a new sign and/or house makes this a memorable time period. Our consciousness is "pushed" to grow. The element that our progressed Sun moves into represents new dimensions of growth. Our birth element and progressed element combine to intensify our self-expression.

Suppose an individual has the natal Sun in fiery Sagittarius. Her Sun progresses into the earth sign Capricorn at age twenty-seven. The individual may find her lofty ideals (Sagittarius) need to be grounded into practical (Capricorn) self-expression. A similar experience could occur if the Sun progressed from the fiery ninth house into the earthy tenth house. While the Sun is progressing through the ninth house the individual may seek numerous life options and many changes of direction. Life seems like it will last forever. When the Sun progresses into the tenth house a more serious life attitude may be born. Time becomes an important factor. The wanderer and philosopher (ninth house) seeks to make visions concrete (tenth house).

The pioneering psychologist Sigmund Freud was born with the Sun in Taurus in the seventh house. He entered medical school at the University of Vienna in 1873 (approximately age 17). He began his first original piece of research in 1876, as his progressed Sun was about to enter the eighth house. His natal Sun moved from the communication-oriented, airy, seventh-house atmosphere to the more introspective and psychologically-oriented, watery eighth house.

Freud's famous book, *The Interpretation of Dreams,* was written while his progressed Sun was in the air sign Gemini and in the watery eighth house. This book is quite symbolic of the 3rd/8th chord combination of the progressed Sun. His theory of the mind is in this book — a strong representation of the 3rd/8th chord (air/water) combination!

The actress Meryl Streep was born with the Sun in the first degree of watery Cancer (June 22, 1949). It was approximately thirty years later (thirty days after birth) that her Sun progressed into the following sign, fiery Leo. It was at this time that she became known through films such as the *Deer Hunter* (1978), *Manhattan* (1979), and *Kramer versus Kramer* (1979). It was as though Streep's instinctual and intuitive sensitivity (Cancer) were projected quite powerfully through her progressed fiery Leo Sun sign.

The famous German author, Herman Hesse was also born with the Sun in Cancer, July 2, 1877. Many of Hesse's novels center around characters having to overcome trying childhood circumstances similar to the author's own early life. His Cancer personality surfaces through his characters often dealing with the conflict created by their roots (and relationships as symbolized by Hesse's seventh-house natal Sun).

Hesse's Sun progressed into the fire sign Leo when he was about 19. He developed the creative insights to produce work that would make him known worldwide. His Sun progressed into the eighth house the same year it entered Leo. This is quite a dramatic shift. The Sun moved from an air house (seventh) into water (eighth house) and from a water sign (Cancer) into fire (Leo).

Hesse's Sun remained in the eighth house approximately forty-four years from 1896 until 1940. Many of his novels were written during this time period: *Demian* (1919), *Siddhartha* (1922), *Steppenwolf* (1927), and *Narcissus and Goldmund* (1930).

In 1919 when Hesse brought out *Demian,* his Sun had progressed into a conjunction with his natal Uranus. This book reflected Hesse's preoccupation with psychoanalysis (eighth house). Hesse studied the works of Freud and later underwent analysis with Jung as well as being a patient in a sanitarium while experiencing the eighth-house progressed Sun. The eighth house, being a water house, offered Hesse a further vehicle to explore his already emotional and introspective watery Cancer natal Sun. He used the deep psychological, mystical, and spiritual sides of the eighth house as a definite part of his self-expression. He was the master in his novels of exploring survival instincts and the deepest recesses of the mind.

Shortly after Hesse's progressed Sun entered Virgo (still in eighth house) the novel *Steppenwolf* was written. This must have been a powerful time in the author's life. His Sun had progressed into a conjunction with his South Node in Virgo (opposing second house North Node in Pisces). The book itself describes a person confronting his alienated feeling from society but his attraction to its creature comforts (second house). A definite understanding of self-destruction (eighth house) is evident in the mystical atmosphere of the book. This may have been a period of time where Hesse was dealing with his own personal conflicts.

The natal Sun symbolism by sign and house is lifelong. It is an organic beginning that is further defined through the progressed Sun. A person born as a Gemini or third house Sun may become more emotional and reflective while experiencing the progressed Sun in Cancer or the fourth house. However, the natal characteristics are still the primary focus. Secondary progressions are secondary. The progressed planets are like a lens through which natal planets operate.

PLANETARY ASPECTS

The aspects formed by the progressed Sun to natal planets last approximately two years. An aspect begins when the progressed Sun moves to within a one-degree orb of making an exact aspect to a natal planet (or angle). The progressed Sun will separate from the exact aspect about one year later. Remember the birthchart is stationary. It is the progressions and transits that move through the birthchart. There is a complete discussion of aspects formed by the progressed Sun to natal planets in Chapter Nine. (Aspects formed by the progressed Sun to the Ascendant and Midheaven are in Chapters Ten and Eleven; aspects to the Moon's Nodes in Chapter Twelve).

INTENSITY PROMOTING ASPECTS

The most significant aspects formed by the progressed Sun to natal planets, Ascendant or Midheaven (or progressed planets or angles to the natal Sun) are the conjunction, square, quincunx, and the opposition. These aspects represent times of challenge, tension, and a test of strength in our lives.

It is important to always consider the particular planets forming an aspect. For instance, the progressed Sun moving into a conjunction with natal Saturn will likely be more intense than a conjunction to Jupiter. There is already a natural intensity about Saturn not found in Jupiter. The Sun/Saturn conjunction could represent the need to rise above one's fears to gain tangible results. There is a natural optimism and lightness in Jupiter's symbolism that would not yield the same concern with stamina, and reluctance to take a risk as in Saturn's symbolism.

Repeating themes found in the natal chart must also be considered. For instance, a person with an already existing natal Sun/Saturn aspect is likely to experience the progressed Sun aspecting natal Saturn in a very deep way. It is a familiar organic process that is taking a different step. This does not say a person will react positively or negatively. It is only that the process is extra important to the individual. Other repeating themes: a heavily aspected natal Saturn, an angular natal Saturn, key planets in the tenth house, or the sign Capricorn. These repeating themes in the birthchart could also intensify one's experience of the progressed Sun aspecting Saturn (or transiting Saturn aspecting natal Sun and other natal planets).

"SOFT" ASPECTS

The lighter or soft aspects are the sextile and the trine. I have found these angles to the progressed Sun do not always register in one's consciousness with the urgency of the more intense aspects. I think perhaps there is such a flow to the soft aspects that they are taken for granted.

An exception to this is where some people with intense aspects formed by natal planets find it easier to express these themes under a more flowing aspect by progression or transit. For instance, a person with the Sun square Saturn (90° angle) natally may experience this as more flowing when the progressed Sun forms a sextile (60° angle) or trine (120° angle) to natal Saturn years later. This could occur sooner when transiting Saturn forms a more flowing aspect to natal Sun. However, the overall process will probably remain intense as natally the individual's Sun and Saturn form a powerful aspect. **Once again, the key birthchart themes must be considered, especially repeating themes. People who have dealt with their difficult-to-handle natal aspects are often more prepared to flow with similar aspects that repeat in the predictive systems.** These same individuals may even be more productive with aspects that occur in time than people lacking the intensity aspect natally.

PROGRESSED ASPECTS TO PROGRESSED SUN

Some astrologers do not consider aspects formed by progressed planets to each other. I feel they can be important. The conjunction is the most relevant, especially if the progressed planets forming the conjunction aspect a natal planet.

My own chart is a good example. I was born with the Sun at approximately one degree Sagittarius in the eighth house. Mercury is located at twelve degrees Scorpio in the eighth house. When my first book was released, my progressed Sun and progressed Mercury were conjunct at approximately twelve degrees Capricorn. Both planets formed an almost exact square (90° angle) to my natal Neptune located at approximately twelve degrees Libra in the seventh house. This was an important aspect for me. Mercury's symbolism (connected to communication and writing) was fused with my self-expression (progressed Sun). The square by both the progressed Mercury and Sun to my natal Neptune represented a strong drive to communicate (Mercury) myself aesthetically (Neptune) to the public (10th house progressed Mercury - Sun conjunction in 10th chord sign, Capricorn).

So I do believe aspects formed by progressed planets to each other can be important. This still seems part of our organic being. Aspects between a progressed personal planet and a progressed outer planet simply lengthen the period of time involved between a progressed inner planet and a natal outer planet. For example, an aspect from the progressed Sun to natal Uranus will last two years. If you also include the aspect from progressed Sun to progressed Uranus, the period stretches another year or two (depending on the age of the individual). I think that it is more important if the particular planets are strongly linked to the birthchart. Are they important birthchart themes? Are they included in repeating themes?

WHERE IS YOUR PROGRESSED SUN NOW?

I can see some astrologers growing worried and skeptical as they read this particular section. They will be saying there is no shortcut to figuring the "exact" position of one's progressed Sun. They are correct. I am going to offer a "quickie" method to figuring an "approximate" position of your progressed Sun.

The progressed Sun may not have changed signs (or houses) as yet for you. If you are thirty-years old or older, then I can guarantee it has at least changed signs. Don't worry! You are still a Gemini, Leo, or whatever Sun sign you were born with. Remember the progressed Sun is an extension of your natal Sun.

As stated earlier, the progressed Sun moves approximately one degree per year. There are thirty degrees in a sign. It takes approximately thirty years for your progressed Sun to move through one complete sign. The Sun is at zero degrees of a sign on approximately the twenty-second day of the month. For instance, zero degrees Aries starts at approximately March 22nd. This will not hold true for every year, but is close enough for approximation.

Suppose a person was born March 29 of a given year. We want to approximate the position of the progressed Sun for the thirty-sixth birthday. If we consider March 22 as zero degrees Aries, then March 29 is approximately seven degrees Aries. Remembering that the progressed Sun moves about one degree per year we would add thirty-six degrees to the natal Sun position of seven degrees Aries. Since there are only thirty degrees in a sign, we see quickly that by the thirty-sixth birthday the individual's Sun has already progressed into a new sign. By adding thirty-six degrees to seven degrees Aries we find that the progressed Sun position would be forty-three degrees Aries. Since Aries stops at thirty degrees, the Sun has progressed into Taurus at approximately thirteen degrees. The progressed Sun entered Taurus approximately thirteen years earlier or at age twenty-three.

A word of caution: This method is to be used for a quick approximation only. If you want to be sure of the exact location of your progressed Sun, give your birthdata (*i.e.*, time, date, and place) to a competent astrologer! He or she can compute this for you.

AUTHOR'S TIP:
REMEMBER SUN, MOON, & ASCENDANT
In the chapters that follow, you will be introduced to the progressed Moon and Ascendant. If you are new to the study of astrology, pay special attention to the Sun, Moon, and Ascendant. These are not the only areas of importance in interpreting a chart. Understanding these three important symbols can help you begin to tune into the basic patterns or themes of the chart. They do help one gain an overall comprehension of the birth and progressed charts.

CHAPTER SEVEN

FAST-MOVING PROGRESSIONS

The Progressed Moon (☽)

Organic Process:	Seeking meaning within change; trusting our instincts.
Life Challenges:	Maintaining an emotional clarity Responding to consciousness changes Tuning into moods and instincts
Key Allies:	Intuition Accepting life's ebb and flow Understanding life's deeper messages Balanced dependency needs
Illusions:	Emotional confusion Subconscious blocks Fear of change
Sign Cycle:	Approximately two to two and one-half years

MIGRATION OF CONSCIOUSNESS

Compared to other progressed movements, the progressed Moon moves swiftly. The progressed Sun moves through a sign in thirty years. The progressed Moon requires only two to two and one-half years to cover the same distance.

The progressed Moon is a special symbolic indicator in astrology of our instinctual and intuitive energies. It represents a rather unique focus of our consciousness: both the sign and house that are currently occupied must be considered. Relocation and feelings about domestic situations are important parts of the Moon's symbolism.

MASCULINE AND FEMININE IDENTITIES

There is a special relationship formed by our solar and lunar identities. The progressed horoscope dramatizes our masculine (Sun) and feminine (Moon) selves. Whether we are male or female in gender makes no difference. Each of us has an outgoing or solar capacity. Likewise each individual has a reflective or lunar nature.

FINDING NEW COMFORT ZONES

The progressed Moon denotes creating a comfortable atmosphere in one's life. A change of sign or house by our progressed Moon often does correspond to inner and outer changes. People often make life adjustments as the progressed Moon makes its change of sign or house. Moving to a new location or residence is quite possible.

ASPECTS

Aspects made by our progressed Moon to natal planets can be symbolic of attitude or comfort zone changes. For instance, an individual with the progressed Moon about to conjunct his natal Mars may go through a period of mood swings. His anger (Mars) may be easily aroused. Perhaps he needs to express hidden anger. This could be a period of two months where new enterprises are about to begin. The progressed Moon in this instance acts as a symbolic trigger focusing the individual toward taking initiative.

Since the progressed Moon moves approximately one degree per month, its aspects to natal planets last about two months (one degree approaching an exact aspect and one degree departing exact). The planet being aspected must be considered as in all planetary aspects. Also, if a particular planet is accentuated in the birthchart, progressed aspects to this planet are more likely to be expressed externally by an individual.

If the natal Moon is involved in a major aspect to another natal planet, an aspect formed by the progressed Moon to this same natal planet will probably be symbolic of a major two-month transition period. One's comfort zones could be tested at this time. Perhaps new energies are flooding one's consciousness. (There is a complete discussion of aspects formed by the progressed Moon to natal planets in Chapter Nine, to the Ascendant and Midheaven in Chapters Ten and Eleven; to the Moon's Nodes in Chapter Twelve.)

PROGRESSED MOON IN THE ELEMENTS

There has already been some great material written on the progressed Moon moving through the twelve signs and houses. Therefore, I have decided to give the reader a chance to understand the progressed Moon moving through the elements. If one considers the element of progressed planets and Ascendant, the greater psychological processes at work can be better defined.

FOUR ELEMENTS

Fire, earth, air, and water are as essential to an astrologer's repertoire as a computer is to an individual who does word processing. In my first book, *Astrological Games People Play,* I discussed the categorizing of the planets, signs and houses according to their corresponding elements.

The elements represent a specific energy attunement. Fire symbolizes the spontaneous call for action. It represents a self-centering energy which accelerates our life rhythms; earth denotes a slowing-down life rhythm. It is a stabilizing energy; air connotes a mental and communicative energy. It is a speeding-up life rhythm; water represents a reflective life rhythm. It is symbolic of intuitive energy. We slow down with water and may gain more intuitive insight.

PROGRESSED MOON IN FIRE SIGNS
(ARIES, LEO, SAGITTARIUS) OR HOUSES (1ST, 5TH, 9TH)

The progressed Moon in fire represents a two to two-and-one-half year season of dramatic energy bursts. If the individual's birthchart is heavily weighted with fire (emphasized fire planets, signs and/or houses), this can be symbolic of a very fast-paced time period. A person may accomplish tasks that before seemed too challenging. It is a time to display courage, initiative and drama.

Progressed fire Moons can denote a new vigor. A person's optimism, humor, and faith can reach new limits. Oversensitivity to circumstances that once held one back may be overcome during this two to two-and-one-half year time period.

One must be somewhat aware to not ignore practical limits and to avoid burnout during this progressed Moon sojourn. A tendency to become too self-centered can be the **shadow of Moon in fire**. Consciousness can be self-serving. A lack of awareness regarding needs of others can occur. One may be in a hurry to do big things. Impatience and a fun loving recklessness can irritate others.

The progressed Moon in fire is a time of exploration, expansion, and envisioning new enterprises. Some moderation may be needed!

PROGRESSED MOON IN EARTH SIGNS
(TAURUS, VIRGO, CAPRICORN) OR HOUSES (2ND, 6TH, 10TH)

The progressed Moon in earth symbolizes a two to two-and-one-half year season of slowed-down energy expression. This is the most grounding placement for the progressed Moon. Much activity can occur! One can often tune into an order that may have been lacking. One can further refine an already organized life.

If one's birthchart is filled with repeating earth symbols (emphasized earth planets, signs, and/or houses), this can symbolize a great stabilization period. A person may become quite efficient in managing time and resources. It may be a time of investment, ownership, and taking responsibility.

The progressed Moon in earth denotes a more serious time period than in the spontaneous and playful fire element. Earth represents taking care of business and integrating the different areas of one's life. It can represent a time of working hard, budgeting, developing new skills, career changes, buying houses, etc.

The shadow of Moon in earth can be workaholism during this progressed Moon visit. Some fire sign humor and travel urges may be needed. The imagination can be too governed by practical concerns. Subjective needs may be ignored. Love can be felt as impractical. A too serious nature can become rigid.

The progressed Moon in earth is a time of developing commitments. Time management and restructuring one's life can be a focus.

PROGRESSED MOON IN AIR SIGNS
(GEMINI, LIBRA, AQUARIUS) AND HOUSES (3RD, 7TH, 11TH)

The progressed Moon in air denotes an approximately two to two-and-one-half year season of a fast-moving mental activity. Progressed air Moons can be indicative of strong social urges. A person may develop new peers, love relationships, and business partnerships. Writing and communications of all types may increase significantly.

This can be a very objective period especially if one's birthchart is accentuated with numerous or key air themes (*i.e.,* heavily aspected air planets, signs and/or houses). The progressed Moon in air can reflect an adaptable nature and developing greater reasoning power. Some folks go back to school or enter correspondence courses during this period. Others get into self-taught learning. Generally it denotes a time of feeding one's intellect and social appetites.

The shadow of Moon in air can be nervous exhaustion due to indecision or trying to accomplish too many goals at once. Some earth focus may be needed or fire sign action to calm jittery nerves and overactive air minds. An overly aloof nature can keep others at a distance. Compulsive needs for space can hurt relationships if not communicated clearly. The progressed Moon in air is a time for brainstorming, developing mental powers, improving communication skills, and satisfying one's drives for relationships. It can be a time of experimentation. New peers and perceptions can develop.

PROGRESSED MOON IN WATER SIGNS
(CANCER, SCORPIO, PISCES) AND HOUSES (4TH, 8TH, 12TH)

The progressed Moon in water connotes an approximately two to two-and-one-half year season of a highly imaginative energy expression. This is the most psychological of the four elements. Water can symbolize one's drive to understand life's mysteries. A person's intuition may grow stronger during a progressed Moon in water placement. This is especially true if the birthchart accentuates water themes (*i.e.*, heavily aspected water planets, signs, and/or houses).

The progressed Moon in water can symbolize a very reflective time. It can be an emotional period colored by grieving, forgiving, self-sacrifice, balancing dependency needs. One may feel emotionally vulnerable while the progressed Moon is in water. I have seen people tap into past lives within their subconscious during this period. It can be a testy period in facing one's Karma especially if the progressed Moon aspects natal Saturn, Neptune, Pluto, or Moon's Nodes. However, this can be a time when a person rises above self-destructive compulsive behaviors (substance abuses, self-hatred, destructive relationships, excessive self-sacrifice, etc.). An individual sometimes becomes conscious of escapist and denying behavior patterns.

The shadow of Moon in water is related to overidentifying with material released from the subconscious. Many of us release repressed material while our progressed Moon floats through water. The spark of fire, the stability of earth, and the mental objectivity of air can be our allies at this time.

A metamorphosis can be symbolized while our progressed Moon is in water. It can be a time of great creativity. One may accomplish a great transformation of identity during this chapter of life. The progressed Moon in water signs or houses is as symbolic of deep psychological processes as transiting Saturn moving through water houses (4, 8, 12). Both move at about the same rate of speed. This two year or longer period can be a very insightful experience. Some people get very frustrated with either transiting Saturn or progressed Moon in water placements. This seems to be especially true of people addicted to logical reality. They do not like the feeling of not being in control.

When the progressed Moon occupies a water sign or house, we often do feel less in control. Our mind can get quite sensitized to the environment with the progressed Moon in water. Many people learn of other realities when water planet are active in their charts. This can be denoted by progressed Moon in water or transits of Neptune or Pluto.

OTHER FAST-MOVING PROGRESSIONS: MERCURY, VENUS, AND MARS

Progressed Mercury (☿)

Organic Process:	Maintaining clear perceptions
Life Challenges:	Staying open to new growth
	Being aware of cultural news
	Thinking for oneself
Key Allies:	Intellect
	Communication skills
	Quick perception of environment
	Versatility
Illusions:	Anxiety
	Fixed reality
	Negativity
	Mental confusion

Progressed Venus (♀)

Organic Process:	Capacity to enjoy world of the senses and the world of people
Life Challenges:	Creating balanced relationships
	Finding peace
	Balanced sensuality
	Expressing feelings
Key Allies:	Sense of love and beauty
	Social grace and intuition
	Sensitivity
	Partnerships
	"Win - Win" attitude
Illusions:	Self-indulgence
	Style lacks substance
	Fear of solitude
	"War - War" attitude
	Relationship addiction

Progressed Mars (♂)

Organic Process:	Expressing assertion and physical energy
Life Challenges:	Staying focused on goals
	Finishing what is started
	Clear sense of identity
	Spontaneous expression of assertion or anger, leadership

Key Allies:	Assertion
	Self-starting
	Inner motivation
	Courage
Illusions:	Self-hatred
	Fear of anger or assertion
	Winning at any cost
	Impatience
	Aggression

The symbolism of the slow transits (Jupiter, Saturn, Uranus, Neptune, and Pluto) discussed in Part Two and secondary progressions unlock the mysteries of life processes. The "fast" transits give us a greater perspective into the pages or days of our lives.

There are three fast-moving progressed planets in addition to the Sun and Moon: Mercury, Venus, and Mars. Mercury denotes our mental perceptions. In secondary progressions, Mercury represents our evolving communication skills and drive to communicate with others; Venus connotes our evolving interactions with others. This includes romantic, peers, or business. This planet can denote one's aesthetic tastes during given time periods as well as drives for luxury, pleasure, and beauty; Mars symbolizes assertion and physical energy. The drive to expand one's identity through action can be represented by progressed Mars.

ASPECTS MADE BY FAST PROGRESSIONS

The aspects made by progressed Mercury, Venus, and Mars are more like those of the Sun in terms of time. Mercury and Venus aspects will last approximately two years. Progressed Mars aspects can last much longer as this planet is the slowest in speed of the fast-moving progressions. Mars can be quite important in symbolizing the assertion and initiative to realize goals. (There is a complete discussion of aspects formed by progressed Mercury, Venus, and Mars in Chapters Nine through Twelve.)

THE SUPPORTING CAST

Progressed Mercury, Venus and Mars act as a supporting cast. The main actors are the progressed Sun, Moon, Ascendant and Midheaven along with the slower-moving transits. (Remember, fast-moving transits act as catalysts as can aspects formed by our progressed Moon.)

Sometimes when looking at the progressed chart it is helpful to know in which directions the person wants to go. For instance, an individual wanting to pursue a career in writing or needing to develop communication skills would be interested in progressed Mercury. Aspects made by progressed Mercury to a natal planet will be very important. (Also, aspects formed by transits or other progressions to natal Mercury.) The focus of an individual has a lot to do with whether the symbolism of progressions such as Mercury will be realized.

Individuals may not act on the symbolism denoted by a progressed Mercury, Venus, or Mars unless it is accompanied by a key progressed Sun, Moon, or Ascendant aspect. Perhaps even more important is if a key transit is occurring for the individual (*i.e.*, a Saturn Return, transit of an outer planet moving across an angle of birthchart, etc.).

I am not saying to ignore progressions of Mercury, Venus, and Mars; only to keep them in perspective. They are important allies. Their symbolism supports other major cycles. Recently a friend of mine with natal Mars in the watery 12th house experienced her progressed Mars entering the fiery 1st house (conjunct her Ascendant). My friend had just made a new and challenging career move. She was now a supervisor for the first time. Her identity (Mars and 1st house) was accentuated at this time. The aspect of the progressed Mars conjunct Ascendant will last about two years for her. This was the first time Mars had changed houses in my friend's chart — age 41. Transiting Saturn and Uranus opposing a 1st house Sun put added emphasis on assertion and identity themes. She has done quite well with the career transition though the energy required is a bit exhausting at times. The challenge is very stimulating.

Another friend five years ago had progressed Venus conjunct his natal Sun for a two year period. This was a vital period concerning relationships (Venus). He had been through some very unfulfilling relationships for years. During the time of progressed Venus conjunct his natal Sun, my friend entered a relationship that later gave him the confidence to seek more balance (Venus) in his future relationships. His confidence (Sun) seemed to grow greatly.

A lot depends on the overall chart in determining how a person might manifest particular symbolism. There are numerous options open to a person. We usually get into more trouble when we forget about options.

One must first master birthchart analysis before attempting to move into predictive astrology. Remember, the birthchart and its primary components (*i.e.*, planets mixing with signs mixing with houses) contains the building blocks for predictive systems.

PROGRESSED MERCURY, VENUS, AND MARS CHANGING SIGNS OR HOUSES

It can be an important energy shift when progressed Mercury, Venus, and Mars change signs or houses. It usually is not as major as progressed Sun, Moon, Ascendant or Midheaven sign or house changes. I **will say though an exception is when these planets progress into a sign that is already highlighted in the chart.** Suppose a person has an Aquarian Sun and other strong 11th chord themes (planets placed in 11th house and/or highly accentuated Uranus). He later has his birthchart Venus in Capricorn move into the next sign, Aquarius. This can denote a great change in relating (Venus) to others. The reserved and cautious symbolism of Venus in Capricorn has now been colored with the more experimental themes of Aquarius. The person may find this motif more compatible with already-existing Aquarian and 11th chord themes.

The same can be said for a change of houses. Suppose an individual has a lot of 9th chord themes such as planets in Sagittarius or an emphasized Jupiter. There may be natal planets occupying the 9th house and heavily aspected. A progressed Mercury, Venus, or Mars into the 9th house might denote the individual will be highly stimulated to possibly travel, go to school, prioritize values, etc. I am emphasizing once again to pay attention to the key birthchart themes. **Do progressed planets in their current movements repeat birthchart themes that are highly accentuated?** This is an excellent question to keep asking when looking at the progressed chart (and transits)!

PROGRESSED MERCURY IN FIRE SIGNS
(ARIES, LEO, SAGITTARIUS) AND HOUSES (1ST, 5TH, 9TH)

Progressed Mercury in fire points to new mental energy. A tired intellect can come alive with enthusiasm. A new direct communication can be exhibited. Progressed Mercury in fire can indicate mental confidence. Individuals may say more of what is on their minds. They may stimulate others to act on their ideas.

People can gain attention through a dramatic display of words. They may think fast and accurately. Assertion and action can resonate to the beat of clear perceptions.

The shadow of Mercury in fire is ego-dominated perceptions. There can be a need for patience with the ideas of others. Individuals could speak before they have the facts. One may hurt others with harsh words. Selfish thoughts can irritate loved ones. People can talk too much, especially about themselves! Hasty perceptions might burn needed bridges.

PROGRESSED MERCURY IN EARTH SIGNS
(TAURUS, VIRGO, CAPRICORN) AND HOUSES (2ND, 6TH, 10TH)

Progressed Mercury in earth denotes a consolidation of the mental processes. One can find a value in thoughts. They can be marketed in the job place or put to practical use. Individuals can stabilize the nervous system. The changeability of Mercury gets grounded in earth. One may have more accurate perceptions when feeling financially secure. One may exercise sound judgment. A commitment to worldly and spiritual concerns can lead to inner strength. A tough and determined mental nature can be displayed.

The shadow of Mercury in earth is rigid thinking with no options. A life with too many routines dulls the intellect. Individuals can lack imagination. A too-grounded mentality blocks imagination. All work and no pleasure gives a boring and uneventful life. Status seeking can block new spontaneous insights. Career and work can become too important. There can be excessive worry over details. The serenity prayer may help!

PROGRESSED MERCURY IN AIR SIGNS
(GEMINI, LIBRA, AQUARIUS) AND HOUSES (3RD, 7TH, 11TH)

Progressed Mercury in air can symbolize mental exhilaration. People can juggle more than one life-style. One may be gifted with words. A capacity to be a great negotiator exists. Individuals can have a sixth sense for timing life changes. Perceptions can pick up the scent of situations. A hunger for company might lead to new peers. One may enjoy the stimulation of a wide circle of friends and allies. Mercury in air is a natural networker.

Mental aloofness is **the shadow of Mercury in air**. A cold heart casts a cold shadow. Individuals hide behind their intellect. Extreme needs for space keep others at a distance. "Thinkitis" can weaken the clarity of Mercury in air. Shutting off the conscious mind is a requirement. There can be a tendency toward nervous exhaustion.

PROGRESSED MERCURY IN WATER SIGNS
(CANCER, SCORPIO, PISCES) AND HOUSES (4TH, 8TH, 12TH)

Progressed Mercury in water is symbolic of the intellect (Mercury) walking the tightrope of intuition (water). Mercury is out of its natural elements (earth and air) in water. Spontaneous fire affords Mercury lots of room to roam the intellectual world. Reflective water challenges Mercury to find its feelings. Individuals can go through remarkable changes when progressed Mercury spends several years in water.

People can perceive life's deepest mysteries. Communicating feelings strengthens relationships. The intellect can get purified by the fine intuitive mist of water. One may learn to have distance and closeness. Past-life intensity could be used creatively. Water can take our thoughts back through time. Individuals may make contact with healing energy. The subconscious can be a friend. A shadowy past now becomes a light of illumination.

The shadow of Mercury in water is a separation of intellect and feelings. One can feel threatened by outer circumstances. Inner roots may be trapped by insecurity and mental confusion. Disoriented perspectives leave one feeling helpless. One may compulsively strive to manipulate life. Words might hide deep emotional pain.

PROGRESSED VENUS IN FIRE SIGNS
(ARIES, LEO, SAGITTARIUS) AND HOUSES (1ST, 5TH, 9TH)

Progressed Venus in fire points to enthusiastic new social urges. Individuals can act on impulses to meet new peers. One may enter social encounters and business dealings more assertively. Confidence can exude. People can act on values. They inspire action in others through belief in self. Interactions with others can broaden value system.

Aesthetic drives or beliefs may be displayed. A shy nature can grow comfortable in showing talents. A subjective personality might bring ideals to reality. A tireless devotion to work and values can take one to new heights. A reserved and cautious person could express more feelings. Love flows naturally. The heart grows less afraid of receiving love. One may truly reward himself.

The shadow of Venus in fire is extreme self-admiration. Being treated like a king or queen is desired for life — not just one day. Wealth and outer styles become more important than authentic identity. Individuals can lack the drive to realize highest values. A loss of identity in relationships and actions might lead to abortive life paths.

PROGRESSED VENUS IN EARTH SIGNS
(TAURUS, VIRGO, CAPRICORN) AND HOUSES (2ND, 6TH, 10TH)

Progressed Venus in earth denotes a practical orientation towards relationships and values. This can be a stabilizing period for those lacking commitment. People may take a stand for values. Individuals can show remarkable endurance. They may be there for others. People can rise quickly to leadership roles. They seem to attract responsibility.

A new career focus might begin. People who waste time and money can learn to conserve. Disciplining the desire nature can be important. Compulsive behaviors for sex, substances, or food may be brought under control.

The shadow of Venus in earth is a surrender of values to a total material focus. Self-indulgence can become all-consuming. A lack of self-esteem and love could be the root of problems. Individuals can try too hard to control others. Love might be too conditional. A cold heart alienates others. Feelings are too reserved and cautious. Wealth can be a compulsive driving force. Getting to the top may be too important.

PROGRESSED VENUS IN AIR SIGNS
(GEMINI, LIBRA, AQUARIUS) AND HOUSES (3RD, 7TH, 11TH)

Progressed Venus in air can symbolize social exhilaration. Individuals can show a remarkable ability to adapt to new situations. A curiosity about life leads to new growth. A desire to know the "why" of situations stimulates new relationships and values.

Versatility may be shown in relations, values, career, etc. People can show multiple ability. Relationships with a wide variety of individuals are possible. Communication is a key ally. People can excel in communication fields.

Peers can stimulate new brainstorms. One may be the catalyst for different perceptions in others. Relationships revolve around shared values. Communication is a strong bond to friends and lovers.

The shadow of Venus in air is a scattered focus. A flighty nature lacks depth. Relating can be superficial. One may be timid about emotional waters. Individuals can lack their own perceptions. They borrow too much from insights of others. An unresolved clash between one's intellect and emotional nature can be disorienting.

PROGRESSED VENUS IN WATER SIGNS
(CANCER, SCORPIO, PISCES) AND HOUSES (4TH, 8TH, 12TH)

Progressed Venus in water is symbolic of finding intuitive clarity in relation to others. Individuals can be excellent at reading body language. They may sense the moods of situations. Emotional sharing deepens relations. The values can be heartfelt. One may express compassion and nurturing naturally. In Venus in earth or water, mother nature may be a valuable friend. Spending time in nature's beauty can bring a feeling of peace.

Tuning into one's own emotional nature brings clarity. The deep emotional waters foster aesthetic creativity. A natural expression of love can attract harmonious relationships. The career can reflect high ideals.

The shadow of Venus in water is emotional isolation. One can have unresolved emotional conflicts. The past becomes a breeding ground for insecurity. One can lack self-love. A fear of rejection blocks commitment or initiating relationships. Individuals may have trouble with closeness. People can give too much of themselves to others. They might try to save others. Some individuals can be too dependent on others. Addictions to people or substances can be dark sides of this shadow.

PROGRESSED MARS IN FIRE SIGNS
(ARIES, LEO, SAGITTARIUS) OR HOUSES (1ST, 5TH, 9TH)

Progressed Mars in fire points to a spontaneous, action-oriented nature. One may thrive on stressful situations. Challenges strengthen willpower. Initiating new situations confirm one's assertion instincts. A clear identity paves the way to a refreshing life. Anger can express naturally.

One may lead by example. Courage can encourage others to stand up for their rights. A decisive nature leads one to be a good negotiator. A tremendous raw focus to accomplish goals is possible. Individuals can clearly sense their own territory. Yet they may excel at making others feel at home. Mars in fire can be generous. A lot depends on the overall self-understanding. One can love deeply and be dedicated to helping others preserve their own rights.

The shadow of Mars in fire is purposeless action. Individuals might be too self-directed. A lack of sensitivity to the needs of others can produce friction in relating. A tendency to express anger to get attention can be aggravating. One may be too pushy and impulsive. A reckless lack of foresight can bring disaster. The life might be filled with extremes. A lack of consistency and discipline comes back later in life to haunt individuals. An angry chip on the shoulder hurts opportunities. People can lack assertion strength. An unclear identity causes over or under use of assertion.

PROGRESSED MARS IN EARTH SIGNS
(TAURUS, VIRGO, CAPRICORN) OR HOUSES (2ND, 6TH, 10TH)

Progressed Mars in earth denotes physical stamina. Mars can be well guided by the wisdom of earth. A greater awareness of consequences of actions is likely. Individuals can find constructive outlets for raw intensity. Actions find discipline and focus. Earth may help define Mars' actions. The identity can solidify through life commitments. Work skills might get more committed.

Individuals can find deeper meaning in responsibility to loved ones. Taking responsibility for welfare of loved ones can be satisfying. The life purpose can deepen.

The shadow of Mars in earth is lack of flexibility. One can direct energies too rigidly. A desire to serve others may go overboard. Individuals can go too far in controlling freedom of others. Taking responsibility for others might get extreme. A failure to delegate can lead to burnout. The drive for recognition and power becomes all-consuming. Career setbacks smash the identity. Attaching too much importance to material success is dangerous. A lack of self-motivation (due to a fear of failing) limits people. One can be "stuck in the mud." A too-serious nature blocks imagination.

PROGRESSED MARS IN AIR SIGNS
(GEMINI, LIBRA, AQUARIUS) AND HOUSES (3RD, 7TH, 11TH)

Progressed Mars in air can symbolize an alliance formed by identity (Mars) and intellect (air). Actions and perceptions can move in harmony. One may be able to change direction suddenly. A graceful flow through life emanates.

One may gain from the stimulation provided by peers. Actions are stimulated by the input of others. This person can be a catalyst for change. He might breathe fresh air into stagnated situations. Feeding the mind may bring a wider perspective and purpose for actions. Initiating new situations allows communication and perceptions to grow.

The shadow of Mars in air is chasing one's own tail. Life is a constant source of frustration. Communication breakdowns occur due to impatience and impulse. One can be burned out by not stopping for a rest along life's way. One may be too open to environmental stimuli. Holding back direct communication can bring a disoriented identity. One may intellectualize anger and bury feelings.

PROGRESSED MARS IN WATER SIGNS (CANCER, SCORPIO, PISCES) AND HOUSES (4TH, 8TH, 12TH)

Progressed Mars in water is symbolic of intuitively understanding motivations for actions. Fiery Mars is definitely out of its element in introspective water. "Wanting something yesterday" may learn patience. A more sensitive nature can develop. The quick, result-oriented Mars is learning to comprehend overall life processes. Water is the essence of "watching" life. Mars can learn to tune into the deepest purpose for its actions. Where earth restrains Mars, water softens the red planet. A need to forgive oneself can be important. Releasing an angry past can free repressed energy.

Self-hatred can be transcended as can a weak identity. One may trust assertion instincts. Establishing meaningful territory can brighten the life. A passion for life might blossom. People can show greater vulnerability. Past life issues regarding loss of identity can be conquered. A purposeless life finds new ideals and faith. Love of self and others heals a tired soul.

The shadow of Mars in water is a confused identity. One may be swallowing large amounts of anger. A direct use of energy is constipated by emotional fears. Unresolved childhood or past experiences get in the way of the present. A moody nature may alienate loved ones and peers. Self-hatred can be devastating. Emotional scars remain unhealed. Running away from problems gives them more power.

AUTHOR'S TIP

Remember repeating themes! Make it your key ally if you want to understand astrology's symbolic language. If themes accentuated in the birthchart **repeat** in predictive astrology, they can be quite important in the present.

For instance, suppose an individual has the Moon in an air sign such as Aquarius. In addition, he has the Aquarian Moon in an air house (3rd, 7th, or 11th). If by progression his Moon enters an air sign and/or house, he can really make use of this energy in the present as this theme is symbolized in his birthchart. This same principle can be applied to aspects. In other words, this same progressed Moon as it occupies an air sign might be aspecting an air planet (Mercury, Venus, Uranus). This would represent another repeating theme.

CHAPTER EIGHT

PROGRESSED ANGLES

THE PROGRESSED ASCENDANT: CHANGING IDENTITY

Organic Process:	Evolving self-image
Life Challenges:	Answering who am I?
	Believing in oneself
	Avoiding an excessive "I am" mentality
Key Allies:	Integrated sense of self
	Spontaneous assertion
	Self-confidence
Illusions:	Hiding behind persona
	Procrastination
	Rigid self-concept

WHAT IS THE ASCENDANT?

The Ascendant is the sign rising on the eastern horizon at one's birth. This "rising sign" or sign placed on the first house of our birthchart colors our identity in a unique manner. It symbolizes how an individual relates to himself. The Ascendant represents our self-image that is often perceived by others. It is for this reason that the Ascendant acts a bit like a persona. It is symbolic of a way of being that surrounds us like an aura.

SELF-CONCEPT IN TRANSITION

The progression of our Ascendant after birth represents a changing self-image. Our natal characteristics seem to alchemize with the new traits we gain by progression. The progressed Ascendant denotes facets of our personality that we need to incorporate into the present.

PROGRESSED ASCENDANT CHANGING SIGNS

One's Ascendant gains speed if moving from the sign Capricorn to Cancer, if the individual was born in the northern hemisphere. When one's natal Ascendant is placed in a sign from Cancer to Capricorn it will move more slowly.

An individual will experience approximately three progressed Ascendant changes into new signs in a lifetime. The first year or two of the change may symbolize the individual adjusting to the shift. If the progressed Ascendant moves into a sign (or element) that is already heavily emphasized in one's birthchart, the individual may already feel a natural affinity for this new focus.

I was born with the Ascendant in late Pisces. My Ascendant progressed into the next sign, Aries when I was still a baby, about age two. I do not remember the change. This brings me to another logical point. If one is still quite young at the time of the progressed Ascendant changing signs or aspecting natal planets, the time period will probably not represent dramatic outward life changes. I have traced health issues in some instances in the charts of infants to these time periods.

My progressed Ascendant was in the fire sign Aries until I reached age sixteen. At this time my progressed Ascendant entered the earth sign Taurus. I have very little earth in my chart. My adjustment period to this Ascendant was not easy. I must say it took many years before I could accept the grounding and stabilizing themes of this fixed earth sign. I have a lot of fire in my chart. When fire and earth work together, it can represent a lot of productive activity. The trick is mastering the patience suggested by earth to channel the raw emotional energy of fire.

My Ascendant progressed into the air sign, Gemini at about age thirty-seven. I felt right at home with an air Ascendant. Fire and air are both projective elements that complement each other. I am not saying that my progressed Ascendant in Taurus was not valuable. It was part of a big life process symbolizing many growth-promoting lessons. I am only saying it took a bit longer to adjust to the earth element. Actually, looking back in time with hindsight twenty-twenty vision at the progressed Ascendant in Taurus period is interesting for me. I did learn a lot about patience, discipline, and some good, old-fashioned, common sense. That period of years was a great life chapter in my learning to better focus my fire and water energies.

I had done very little writing until my Ascendant progressed into the air sign Gemini. This was my third sign change since birth with my Ascendant. I went from watery Pisces to fiery Aries to earthy Taurus into airy Gemini. It will remain in this sign until I reach age sixty-seven.

It is interesting that the Ascendant can act like a persona. I remember that long before my first book was published people started to immediately view me as a writer when my Ascendant progressed into Gemini. I began to think of myself as a writer when my progressed Ascendant moved into Gemini. This air sign is of course greatly associated with communication in all forms.

Writing seemed to be an organic process in my chart that had always seemed foreign. I read other people's books. I did not write my own! I remember when friends suggested I try writing a book. I froze with fear. It took a lot of encouragement from those closest to me and later by my editor to see I could really do it.

So the progressed Ascendant is an organic part of our identity. We must pull ourselves back far enough from its cover to tap into this energy. The progressed Ascendant is a further refinement of our birth Ascendant. Both Ascendants are vital symbolic keys to personal energy.

PROGRESSED ASCENDANT CHANGING HOUSES

My progressed Ascendant entered the second house of my birthchart at about age twenty-two, while in the sign of Taurus. It entered my third house at age forty-three. The progressed Ascendant will spend a varying amount of years in a house depending on the size of house and speed of Ascendant.

When one's Ascendant reaches the earthy second house, it generally symbolizes a solidifying time period. Some folks have trouble with this time period. It can represent a period of time to face reality. A person may question his identity or feel changes in the life are needed. It can be a time of questioning one's values.

If a person has moved ahead in life with a reasonable amount of clarity, this can represent a very satisfying time. The individual feels in touch with life. Ideals and reality appear to be in harmony. As usual, the entire chart must be considered. As an isolated factor, the progressed Ascendant moving into the second house often symbolizes career interests. Sometimes one may feel the need to acquire property or find "meaningful" employment.

The progressed Ascendant moving into the third house denotes one's awareness of life as a process. This can be a bit disorienting if one is not too grounded mentally or extremely shallow in mental depth. Different life options seem to appear. The individual must stay very focused to adjust to this period of time.

I believe this is when some individuals get much insight into how free they really are of cultural myths. It depends on the willingness of the individual to face the power of cultural myths and illusions. One's personal self-concept history (progressed Ascendant time period in first house) and personal values (progressed Ascendant in second house) surface at this time. Sometimes it is not easy to face how foolish we all can be.

If there are important transits of outer planets (*i.e.*, Saturn, Uranus, Neptune, or Pluto) occurring simultaneously with the progressed Ascendant moving into the second or third house, deep consciousness changes could be symbolized. The progressed Ascendant movement into the third house is a time of integration on both the inner and outer planes of consciousness. It can be a very unsettling period. Some people find it a new lease on life. It is a breath of fresh, stimulating air!

PROGRESSED ASCENDANTS OF THE FAMOUS

In Chapter Seven, I mentioned that Los Angeles Laker Kareem Abdul Jabbar experienced his Libra Ascendant at birth progressing into the sign of Scorpio at age six. His progressed Ascendant remains in watery Scorpio through approximately age forty-six at which time it moves into the fire sign, Sagittarius.

Kareem is now in retirement. It will be interesting to see how he will express his progressed Sagittarian Ascendant. (Also, his Ascendant is currently moving through his second house). He may become a lot warmer with the public. I think he will adjust rapidly to a fire Ascendant. This element is accentuated in his natal chart. He had a fiery Aries Sun at birth as well as a Mercury and Mars conjunction in Aries. He had a Saturn and Pluto conjunction in Leo as well as three planets in the fiery fifth house.

At this time Kareem's progressed Scorpio Ascendant conjuncts his natal second house Jupiter in Scorpio. I think he could do well as a commentator with his progressed Sun already in Gemini and the progressed Ascendant approaching Sagittarius. This could just as well be expressed in public speaking engagements.

Alan Alda entertained many of us as the character Hawkeye in the television series *M.A.S.H.*. His Ascendant had already progressed from its birth sign, earthy Capricorn, into the air sign Aquarius before 1972. In 1971, Alda's progressed Aquarian Ascendant entered the second house and perhaps symbolized the coming together of his talents. The *M.A.S.H.* series ran from 1972 until 1983. Alda's Ascendant changed signs for the second time in 1983 as it entered the water sign, Pisces.

THE PROGRESSED MIDHEAVEN: CHANGING AMBITIONS

Organic Process:	Evolving world profile
Life Challenges:	Understanding a life purpose
	Accepting responsibility
	Living within reality
	Finding a meaningful career

Key Allies: Clear cultural roles; humility; determination

Illusions: Career confusion
                     Out of touch with reality
                     Lack of purpose
                     Exaggerated self-importance

The progressed Midheaven moves at the same speed as the progressed Sun. This is approximately one degree per year. The Midheaven is the 10th house cusp of the birthchart. Its symbolism is related to one's interaction with the community or to one's sense of the world. A person's career aspirations are denoted by the Midheaven.

I think of the Midheaven as our game plan. It typifies our strategy to reach a meaningful life purpose. The progressed Midheaven represents our ambition in motion. A change of sign or house by the Midheaven can be indicative of a major life passage. This is our current game plan.

The creator of the motion picture *Star Wars*, George Lucas, offers a good example of a Midheaven changing signs and symbolizing an important life transition. His Midheaven changed signs for the second time since birth in 1975. Lucas was born with his Midheaven in the sign of Capricorn. He was only a year old when his Midheaven progressed into the next sign, Aquarius. It was in 1975 that Lucas' Midheaven entered the sign Pisces, paving the way for the release of *Star Wars* in 1977. The progressed Midheaven in the watery, dreamy Pisces was indicative of his passion for film. His career drives (natal tenth house ruled by Capricorn) were well expressed through the aesthetic symbolism of Pisces.

Jane Fonda was nominated for an Oscar and won the New York Film Critic Best Actress Award in 1969 for her performance in *They Shoot Horses Don't They?* It was at that time that her progressed Sagittarian Midheaven was trine her 7th house natal Moon in Leo. When Fonda's progressed Midheaven conjuncted her natal Sagittarian Sun (11th house), she helped her former husband, Tom Hayden, with his Senatorial campaign. Her progressed Midheaven was about to enter the sign Capricorn. When Fonda won her second Oscar as Best Actress for *Coming Home* in 1979, her progressed Midheaven was about to enter her natal 12th house.

Alan Alda's progressed Midheaven changed signs in 1970 for the second time since birth. His Midheaven progressed into the fire sign Sagittarius. Alda projected through this glib and humorous Sagittarian motif with ease. He has two planets placed in Sagittarius at birth indicating he was already quite familiar with those motifs.

Alda was in a movie that had limited success in 1970, *The Moonshine War*. It was stated earlier that Alda's progressed Aquarian Ascendant moved into the second house (values, possessions, and finances) in 1971. The individualistic orientation of Aquarius (Alda has the natal Sun and Mercury in Aquarius!), along with a Midheaven in Sagittarius, goes a long way in explaining Alda's preparation to assume the role of the rebellious and philosophical Hawkeye in the 1972 entrance of *M.A.S.H.* for TV audiences. I watched a television interview with Alda at the conclusion of the *M.A.S.H.* series. He said that it was a fortunate turn of events that he got the *M.A.S.H.* role. Perhaps it was the luck of the Sagittarian Midheaven!

The Midheaven entering the 11th house can symbolize a period of experimentation. One sometimes feels the need to find new peers or a new tribal sense. A person's goals may clash with those of authority figures. A person may simply feel he has outgrown a particular way of being. This can definitely be a period of going beyond cultural restrictions but for some represents a fear of the future.

One may feel drawn to a particular subculture at this time. The 11th house is a strange house in that it can denote strong individualistic tastes as well as group affiliation. I think of the 11th house as one's desire to interface personal ambitions within a greater world. For some this could translate into IBM while another person may be drawn to a political cause or movement. It is definitely a "growing-up" and sobering experience for many when their Midheaven progresses into the 11th house.

The progression of the Midheaven into the 12th house is a critical time period. It does not symbolize a retreat from the world as much as learning "to watch." I do not mean to say this is not a creative time period. Quite the contrary, for many of us this is when we may find the time to be creative. Time itself is felt more intensely. Many folks are well into their forties, fifties, or sixties, depending on their chart, when the progressed Midheaven enters the 12th house. An individual may no longer be a parent. She could be free of many previous responsibilities at this point in life. A person seeks a greater whole. This can be a period when one finds a deeper faith in self and a higher power.

One's attachment to the outer world can go through a great metamorphosis at this time. A person can sometimes see through past illusions that have limited consciousness. An individual may gain the strength to transcend power, envy, greed, possessiveness, etc. However, if the person is afraid of facing himself, the progressed Midheaven in the 12th house can be symbolic of one who is drunk with illusions, a legend in his own mind.

PART IV
DELINEATIONS

CHAPTER NINE

PLANET/PLANET ASPECTS

Part Three is divided into three chapters. Chapter Nine is a discussion of the aspects formed by planets to planets. Chapter Ten is an interpretation of aspects formed by the planets to the Ascendant and Midheaven. Chapter Eleven is a discussion of aspects formed by planets to the Nodes of the Moon.

It is important to remember that the sign and house placement of two planets must be considered. Learning to interpret planetary aspects is a process in itself. Getting a feel for two planets aspecting each other comes with study and practice. Fiery Mars placed in its home sign of Aries trine fiery Jupiter in Leo is a strong "soft" aspect. There is a key **repeating theme** involving the fire element — two fire planets placed in fire signs. The theme is even more focused on the fire element if Mars and Jupiter occupy fire houses (1,5,9).

Interpreting the birthchart is an art. It is a challenge that requires **patience, practice, contemplation, and determination.** The symbols will unfold themselves to you with practice.

The following interpretation of the aspects is a **guideline**. There are always **exceptions**: It is my hope that my interpretations will at least give the reader a sense of direction in considering the aspects. The aspects are symbolic of dynamic energy patterns.

SUN/MOON ASPECTS

Progressed Sun/Natal or Progressed Moon
Progressed Moon/Natal or Progressed Sun

Process:	Loving the inner and outer self
Ally:	Respect for willpower and intuition
Illusion:	Fear of intimacy with life

In Sun/Moon aspects an individual is making use of outward creative expressions (Sun) and inward security instincts (Moon). Finding comfort with oneself is especially challenging. **Balancing strength (Sun) and dependency needs (Moon) is highlighted.** Procreative urges of the fiery Sun can combine with establishing roots symbolized by the watery Moon. Creative urges can be shown in career expression. Starting a family or giving birth can occur. Residency needs can change.

INTENSE ASPECTS
Conjunction: Progressed Sun Conjunct Natal or Progressed Moon
Progressed Moon Conjunct Natal or Progressed Sun

LIGHT
The progressed Sun conjunct the natal (or progressed) Moon or the progressed Moon conjunct the natal Sun can denote a powerful new energy expression. Individuals may use spontaneous energy bursts. They may fall in love with life. A tired psyche rejoices to find a new life.

A person can find new security. Excessive displays of ego tendencies can be cast aside for a humbler self-expression. People may be more nurturing and admit vulnerability. The two "lights" can indicate a person is seeking to enrich her life. Career changes are possible, as is moving into a new home. Individuals may receive more public recognition. It is not uncommon to find new love relationships being born. Greater love and care for others can occur.

SHADOW
Progressed Sun conjunct natal (or progressed) Moon or progressed Moon conjunct natal Sun can manifest as holding back a spontaneous nature. **One can become too lost within internal struggles.** A feeling of failure or isolation from love can be detrimental.

Individuals can be too afraid of love, neither wanting to receive love nor caring for others. Unresolved moods may diminish the Sun's fiery enthusiasm. Too much investment in a big ego or hiding from a true identity will bring problems. A fear of creating a bigger world can keep one from growing. Intuition (Moon) can be lost in power motives (Sun).

Square: Progressed Sun Square Natal or Progressed Moon
                  Progressed Moon Square Natal or Progressed Sun

LIGHT

The progressed Sun square the natal (or progressed) Moon or the progressed Moon square the natal Sun can denote dynamic energy bursts! Individuals may feel capable of tackling monumental tasks. One can celebrate success.

One may take more chances than usual. The outgoing solar energy stretches the security-oriented Moon beyond playing it safe. A person may be more playful and less fearful. A growing desire to share one's life with others can occur. A crisis between an outer solar world and inner lunar world is being resolved. **A tendency to hide one's true creativity behind too much self-consciousness can be transcended.** Residency or domestic changes are not uncommon.

SHADOW

The progressed Sun square the natal (or progressed) Moon or progressed Moon square natal Sun can result in inaction. One may be too engulfed in unresolved situations. Resisting quiet contemplation can bring confusion. Energies may scatter into numerous distracting activities. Instead of harnessing creative talents, emotional intensity drains the psyche. A longing for what one does not have robs the present. Self-pity or crushed ideals are given too much importance. A new life direction is resisted. Growth is stunted.

Quincunx: Progressed Sun Quincunx Natal or Progressed Moon
                 Progressed Moon Quincunx Natal or Progressed Sun

LIGHT

The processed Sun quincunx the natal (or progressed) Moon or progressed Moon quincunx natal Sun is the "Yoga of finding a sense of security (Moon) in creative self-expression" (Sun). The quincunx formed by the watery Moon brings reflection to the fiery Sun. Individuals can become aware of subjective feelings. A restless and impulsive soul may respond more truly to innermost needs. A private (Moon) person may "warm up" (Sun) to others. This can be a time of taking care of body, mind, and soul. Strengthening physical and psychic energy inspires new insights. Individuals can feel a zest that has been lacking.

SHADOW

The progressed Sun quincunx the natal (or progressed) Moon or progressed Moon quincunx natal Sun can be a futile attempt to change one's life. People may try too hard to force issues the solar way. The more sensitive Moon approach is not trusted. An individual more inclined to follow the way of the Moon excessively may have little energy to find new meaning in life. A clash with outer and inner needs can occur. Not being in the right place at the right time may seem usual. This can be a time of painful frustration. Fear of the future can dominate.

Opposition: Progressed Sun Opposing Natal or Progressed Moon
                     Progressed Moon Opposing Natal or Progressed Sun

LIGHT

The progressed Sun opposing the natal (or progressed) Moon or progressed Moon opposing natal Sun is symbolic of a crossroads. The watery Moon can bring greater sensitivity to the fiery Sun. Individuals may find this an exhilarating time period. A sleepy psyche awakens to new opportunities. Relationship urges might take full fruition. Business and love relationships can both reach a high. Individuals could find security in a relationship. Creative urges may peak. Intuitive impulses can lead to new creative directions. A drive to go beyond current life circumstances is possible. The need for stimulation from others can lead to new peers. A private person can become more sociable; a socialite more reflective.

SHADOW

Progressed Sun opposing the natal (or progressed) Moon or the progressed Moon opposing the natal Sun can be expressed as looking for too much fulfillment in a relationship. Dependency needs can be out of balance. A too dependent type (Moon) can cling desperately to others. An egocentric type (Sun) may not allow others to get close.

Emotional disorientation can cause an abortive life journey. A failure to recognize behavior patterns can be problematic. A loss of the self in relationships can be destructive. The compulsive drive for attention takes away from real needs. A lack of self-confidence can occur. One may not value accomplishments. A tendency to focus on the darkness hides the light. One may feel pulled into extremes that confuse perspective.

SOFT ASPECTS

Sextile: Progressed Sun Sextile Natal or Progressed Moon
               Progressed Moon Sextile Natal or Progressed Sun

Trine: Progressed Sun Trine Natal or Progressed Moon
               Progressed Moon Trine Natal or Progressed Sun

LIGHT

The progressed Sun sextile natal (or progressed) Moon or progressed Moon sextile natal Sun can denote a time of self-satisfaction. Intuition and creativity could be in alignment. Creative potentials may surface. Feelings are communicated and subtle understanding is magnified. Individuals can inspire creativity and hope in others.

Progressed Sun trine the natal (or progressed) Moon or progressed Moon trine the natal Sun may denote a greater ease in expressing love for others. A heavy personality may find joy; a life with no faith discovers a new vision. A narrow belief system widens its horizons. Self-confidence inspires creativity.

The progressed Moon sextile or trine the progressed Sun can be particularly stimulating. **Individuals may feel reassured inwardly and outwardly.** Life responds positively to self-confidence. The soft aspects can symbolize a new spark in the life.

SHADOW
The progressed Sun sextile the natal (or progressed) Moon or the progressed Moon sextile the natal Sun can be a period of nervous energy with little productivity. A lack of organization could keep creativity unknown. Restlessness may cloud common sense. Moods could lead one astray. One may so much desire a change that timing is out of synch.

The progressed Sun trine the natal (or progressed) Moon or the progressed Moon trine natal Sun can denote a lazy outlook on life. One may sit back idly as dreams come and go. Individuals can flow into escapism. Conflict and risk taking may be avoided at all cost. (This is more likely if natal charts show escapist tendencies.)

DAWN
Sun/Moon aspects can be combined into a youthful exuberance. Life is lived to the fullest. **Intuition (Moon) and forceful action (Sun) can be a beacon of light.** Individuals may enjoy the intimacy of love. They appreciate the joy of creative expression. These aspects can symbolize going beyond childhood fears and habits. Maturing emotional intensity can bring a fruitful time period. **Balanced dependency needs (Moon) encourage freedom of self-expression (Sun).**

SUN/MERCURY ASPECTS

Progressed Sun/Natal or Progressed Mercury
Progressed Mercury/Natal or Progressed Sun

Process:	Creative Mental Power
Ally:	Growth Oriented Perception
Illusion:	Mind is Greater Than the Heart

Sun/Mercury aspects are very mental. The fire power of the Sun is cooled by intellectual Mercury. **Creative communication is emphasized.** The Sun and Mercury are never more than twenty-four degrees apart at birth. Therefore, in secondary progressions, one is likely to experience only the conjunction, sextile, trine, and square. (In the birth-chart, only the conjunction aspect can be formed by natal Sun and Mercury).

INTENSE ASPECTS

Conjunction: Progressed Sun Conjunct Natal or Progressed Mercury
Progressed Mercury Conjunct Natal or Progressed Sun

LIGHT

Some astrologers state that having the Sun and Mercury within 5° of each other is unfortunate. This is referred to as combust. I disagree with this philosophy. The Sun/Mercury conjunction, whether in the birth-chart or formed by secondary progressions, can denote a sharp mental nature. Willpower (Sun) and mind (Mercury) can be mutually stimulating.

The progressed Sun conjunct natal Mercury or progressed Mercury conjunct the natal Sun symbolize a dynamic communicator. Forcefulness and tact may make a good salesperson, counselor, diplomat, and lawyer. An intuitive person can find this aspect centering. An already mental individual can find even more confidence. New frontiers are invented for learning. A bored life finds fresh mental vitality. New options come onto the horizon.

SHADOW

The progressed Sun conjunct natal (or progressed) Mercury or progressed Mercury conjunct the natal Sun might symbolize "all intellect and no emotions." **Perceptions could be dominated by one's own selfish desires.** Controlling situations with mental dogma is possible. A failure to change directions can lead to disaster. A lack of intuition blocks spontaneity. Logic may hide feelings. A compulsive analytical nature distracts perceptions away from clarity. Excessive self-criticism and judgment of others can occur. One may find it difficult to compromise. Biased attitudes can block learning.

Square: Progressed Sun Square Natal or Progressed Mercury
Progressed Mercury Square Natal or Progressed Sun

LIGHT

The progressed Sun square natal (or progressed) Mercury or progressed Mercury square natal Sun can denote individuals confident in their perceptions. Since this aspect will occur much later in life, individuals may reflect about their past. People may find new hobbies and interests to spice up their lives. Older individuals might feel mentally young again. People may resolve past conflicts. They can possess a more detached attitude. Choices may feel less pressured.

Emotional conflicts are less distracting. Individuals may find new communication skills. Details are assimilated without losing perspective.

SHADOW

Progressed Sun square natal (or progressed) Mercury or progressed Mercury square natal Sun can be expressed as a lack of mental drive. One may be saturated with worn-out beliefs. Cultural biases can be limiting. Jumping to hasty conclusions can be troublesome. Signing contracts foolishly could lead to financial problems. A lack of common sense frustrates the self and others. Negativity and skepticism block new experiences.

SOFT ASPECTS

Sextile: Progressed Sun Sextile Natal or Progressed Mercury
Progressed Mercury Sextile Natal or Progressed Sun

Trine: Progressed Sun Trine Natal or Progressed Mercury
Progressed Mercury Trine Natal or Progressed Sun

LIGHT

Both the Sun/Mercury sextile and trine can connote excitement over new opportunities. Individuals often enjoy mental stimulation. New perceptions develop. The intellect requires a steady diet of new knowledge. This is an aspect of power-packed communication. People can make themselves understood more adeptly. Life may feel responsive to one's heartfelt needs. The trine can be a time of a new teaching ability. One's ideas inspire thoughts in others.

SHADOW

Both the Sun/Mercury sextile and trine can be expressed as nervous exhaustion. People can overreact to new circumstances. Hasty changes of mind prove irritating. A lack of consistency is disorienting. Indecision can be frustrating. A fickle mental nature might dominate.

DAWN

Sun/Mercury aspects can express as flashes of brilliance. New mental growth can be stimulating. This period may fill with new options. Creative imagination inspires others to new heights. The head (Mercury) and heart (Sun) become valuable allies.

SUN/VENUS ASPECTS

**Progressed Sun/Natal or Progressed Venus
Progressed Venus/Natal or Progressed Sun**

Process: Creative Relating

Ally: Composure and Social Grace

Illusion: Constant Need for Attention

Sun/Venus aspects can typify romantic periods. The nature is more social than usual. **People strive for beauty and peace.**

The Sun and Venus are never more than forty-eight degrees apart at birth. Therefore, in secondary progressions, only the conjunction, sextile, trine, and square are likely to occur.

INTENSE ASPECTS

Conjunction: Progressed Sun Conjunct Natal or Progressed Venus
           Progressed Venus Conjunct Natal or Progressed Sun

Square: Progressed Sun Square Natal or Progressed Venus
           Progressed Venus Square Natal or Progressed Sun

LIGHT

The progressed Sun conjunct natal (or progressed) Venus or progressed Venus conjunct natal Sun can denote a balanced love life. **People may take more initiative in establishing a relationship.** A timid individual can express more confidence. An already outgoing person could become more refined and tactful.

This might be a period of financial aspiration. Venus has a financial connection as the natural ruler of Taurus. The Sun as natural ruler of Leo can symbolize speculation. Taking some extra risk can bring career change. President Clinton was elected November 10, 1992 with his progressed Sun conjunct natal Venus in Libra. One may creatively improve life's abundance. He may achieve more wealth. Individuals can pay more attention to improving their personal appearance. Changes in hairstyle and clothing preferences are common.

The progressed Sun square natal (or progressed) Venus or progressed Venus square the natal Sun can symbolize a dynamic new aesthetic expression. A person may find a second wind in creativity. A desire for companionship might be rekindled. A social type may become leader of a group or find new creative outlets.

An individual could pursue a delayed desire. He could take that trip or buy that item postponed due to financial obligations. An individual may be appreciated for accomplishments. Rewards for hard work finally pay dividends. One may go beyond the past. Releasing people or things frees up psychic space. Past emotional pain might be resolved.

SHADOW

The Sun/Venus conjunction or square can highlight a wasteful period. An individual may have little common sense regarding material things. People may be discarded carelessly. A lack of sensitivity may disrupt relating to others. Greed and forcefulness are too readily utilized. Ego-centered values and desires lack compromise. Sensual fulfillment reaches extreme proportions. Reckless financial investments can be a disaster. The advice of others could be followed foolishly. An inability to make decisions leads to confusing circumstances. **One may stay stuck in relationships or careers that conflict with one's values.**

SOFT ASPECTS

Sextile: Progressed Sun Sextile Natal or Progressed Venus
Progressed Venus Sextile Natal or Progressed Sun

Trine: Progressed Sun Trine Natal or Progressed Venus
Progressed Venus Trine Natal or Progressed Sun

LIGHT
Both the Sun/Venus sextile and trine can denote establishing new social contacts. More versatility and social skills may be displayed. One may more spontaneously initiate relationships. People can become excited by new career options. Multiple outlets for creativity are possible. The love centers might open widely. A sad heart may "lighten up." A life with no hope may find a ray of sunshine.

The sextile particularly indicates social stimulation. This can be a time of new popularity. A person can find a new set of peers that bring out his best. Partnerships may bring new opportunities.

SHADOW
Both the Sun/Venus sextile and trine can express as a tendency to avoid conflict. People can try to "sugar coat" life. A "going with the flow" outlook can keep one trapped in worn-out situations. Indulgence in sensual desires is substituted for finding a true expression of love. People may cling desperately to bad relationships. A lack of emotional clarity could leave one in limiting relationships. A lack of foresight brings shallow experiences.

DAWN
Sun/Venus aspects can denote a fulfillment of emotional needs. Relationship drives become based on inner clarity. One may balance giving and receiving. This can mark a fulfilling time in expressing real emotional needs. **A clear sense of self and an appreciation for life's beauty are the true dawn.**

SUN/MARS ASPECTS

Progressed Sun/Natal or Progressed Mars
Progressed Mars/Natal or Progressed Sun

Process: Raw Energy
Ally: Strength Without Aggression
Illusion: "Might is Right"

Sun/Mars aspects can indicate tremendous bursts of energy. Raw courage and leadership may be exhibited. Insensitive people can become even less caring. There could be a talent for initiating new experiences. Finishing what is started might be a challenge.

INTENSE ASPECTS

Conjunction: Progressed Sun Conjunct Natal or Progressed Mars
Progressed Mars Conjunct Natal or Progressed Sun

Square: Progressed Sun Square Natal or Progressed Mars
Progressed Mars Square Natal or Progressed Sun

LIGHT

Progressed Sun conjunct natal (or progressed) Mars or progressed Mars conjunct the natal Sun can denote a bold new self-confidence. A timid personality may begin Assertiveness Training 101. One may take more pride in identity. Her creative energy pushes forward. She no longer waits for others to initiate experiences.

Since the Sun and Mars are **fire planets**, people may find they have more energy. Building muscles in the physical body can accompany more psychological fortitude. A person can learn how to better channel raw energy. Balancing physical and mental appetites becomes important. Yoga or karate help channel this energy with control and grace. One could find the courage to deal with a dangerous or difficult situation.

The progressed Sun square natal (or progressed) Mars or progressed Mars square natal Sun can connote breaking through an identity problem. **One may forcefully express her true nature.** Releasing anger appropriately can clear the way for the future. A competitive spirit can be born. Assertion rather than aggression is exhibited. A capacity to not quit can be inspiring. One may tap into survival instincts. Courage in the face of danger may be remarkable. This aspect can point to a good salesperson. It is very enterprising for advertising and any career requiring a **dramatic display of energy**.

SHADOW

Both the Sun/Mars conjunction and square can express as self-hatred. Individuals may fight themselves. An inability to resolve internal conflict makes for unstable outer situations. Arguing for the sake of conflict can be draining. Irrational releases of anger are possible. **Some individuals are carrying a lot of explosive anger.** A flashy, egotistical show could hide emotional fears.

One may compulsively strive to outdo others physically or mentally. Being number one can be compelling. It may take physical ailments or accidents to slow someone down. Health may suffer due to burnout. High blood pressure could occur in over- or underdoing self-expression.

Impatience can be a problem. A lack of insight in channeling intense energy can prove wasteful and dangerous. A tendency to act with no plan brings frustration. One may consistently **act first and think later.** Excessive risk-taking may disrupt relationships and careers.

A person could be accident prone due to moving too fast. Some individuals could enjoy the thrill of physical danger. They may have trouble accepting a normal life.

Quincunx: Progressed Sun Quincunx Natal or Progressed Mars
Progressed Mars Quincunx Natal or Progressed Sun

Opposition: Progressed Sun Opposing Natal or Progressed Mars
Progressed Mars Opposing Natal or Progressed Sun

LIGHT

Progressed Sun quincunx natal (or progressed) Mars or progressed Mars quincunx the natal Sun is the "Yoga of creative action." One learns how to curb compulsive impulses. Power can be channeled into many different directions. Getting the most out of each moment can occur. A person may stop relying on others to fulfill identity. A fear of confronting others is overcome. Passivity can be changed into assertion. A fear of one's own intensity is transcended. The time to stop making excuses is here. A chance to heal old scars occurs. Egocentric behaviors no longer rule the life. Self-hatred becomes softened by new self-respect; carelessness is sensitized by love, a warrior finds a creative spirit.

The progressed Sun opposing natal (or progressed) Mars or progressed Mars opposing natal Sun can denote new assertive power in relating. Individuals can be more direct in all life encounters. The potential of the Sun's warmth and Mars' strength can find its way into growth-promoting relationships.

Individuals may desire a more challenging career or life-style. Mars tugs on our pioneering and adventurous sides. Leaving comfort zones behind can be refreshing. A lack of pride in oneself can be transcended. A tendency to lose one's identity in relationships can be overcome. A new behavior pattern emerges. Being dominated by power hungry individuals is no longer a need. A territorial type may let others be themselves; a false "macho-facho" image can be dropped.

SHADOW

Both the Sun/Mars quincunx and opposition can express as a lack of assertiveness. An individual may too often say yes when she means no, with lost opportunities resulting. She lets others fight her battles. An overachiever may find life has little meaning. A feeling of no roots could be haunting. Finding more territories to plunder gets tiring and boring. She feels lonely, with nobody close who knows her.

One may be led by a fiery passion into **reckless abandonment of self**. Life in the fast lane could lead to eventual disaster. Relationships might lack insight. Lovers and friends can be just as blind. One may attract people who are too insensitive. People might be too impatient to let relationships deepen. Consistent conflict keeps relationships from stabilizing. Anger may be used to bully others. This could be a person who is easily threatened by anger. More assertion might bring relationships into balance.

SOFT ASPECTS

Sextile: Progressed Sun Sextile Natal or Progressed Mars
            Progressed Mars Sextile Natal or Progressed Sun

Trine: Progressed Sun Trine Natal or Progressed Mars
            Progressed Mars Trine Natal or Progressed Sun

LIGHT

Progressed Sun sextile natal (or progressed) Mars or progressed Mars sextile the natal Sun can point to great determination. A feeling of excitement regarding the possibilities for growth can occur. One may try a new enterprise. Identity and creative pursuits can flow. People are action-oriented (Mars) yet manage situations (Sun). They can be very competitive, yet do so with character.

Progressed Sun trine natal (or progressed) Mars or progressed Mars trine natal Sun can manifest as **inspiration**. It may be an upbeat time for people recovering from a down period. Individuals learn to put intensity into acceptable outlets such as work or sports. A natural optimism emanates from a trine formed by fire planets. One may feel ready to handle any challenge that comes her way.

SHADOW

In both the **progressed Sun/Mars sextile and trine, haste can lead to waste.** Selfish desires may block insights. These aspects can be problematic in charts of individuals with reckless behaviors or criminal tendencies. Individuals could feel as though no law is sacred. They may believe power is meant to be abused. People with extremely reckless impulses could have difficulty controlling wild desires. **Lack of discipline or focus can lead to disaster.**

DAWN

Sun/Mars aspects can be the answer to reckless self-abandonment. There is a natural courage and moving ahead in this fiery combination. Creative desires may be a reflection of love for self and others. The me-focus of Mars and the power desires of the Sun can be channeled with fairness and clarity.

SUN/JUPITER ASPECTS

Progressed Sun/Natal or Progressed Jupiter
Transiting Jupiter/Natal or Progressed Sun

Process:	Luck Created by Faith and Electric Vision
Ally:	Sound Principles
Illusion:	A Lazy Philosophy

Sun/Jupiter aspects accentuate expansion and faith themes. Creating realistic expectations for self and others can be a key challenge. There is sometimes a generous spirit symbolized. These aspects can denote new soul growth.

INTENSE ASPECTS
Conjunction: Transiting Jupiter Conjunct Natal Sun
Progressed Sun Conjunct Natal or Progressed Jupiter
Square: Transiting Jupiter Square Natal Sun
Progressed Sun Square Natal or Progressed Jupiter

LIGHT
The progressed Sun conjunct natal (or progressed) Jupiter or transiting Jupiter conjunct natal Sun can symbolize travel on both the mental and physical planes. Giving birth to a new life philosophy is not uncommon. A feeling of freedom and a faith in life can occur. One may get lost in new knowledge. It can be an adventurous time. Teaching and counseling talents may be displayed. Professions focused on sales or involving travel can be enjoyed. One's natural confidence can bring abundance.

A negative individual may lighten up; a selfish person becomes more generous. A shy person finds social confidence; an uneducated person may learn through traveling and self-taught knowledge. Electric philosophy may help bring harmony where there is discord. An individual could find the faith to conquer escapist habits.

Progressed Sun square natal (or progressed) Jupiter or transiting Jupiter square natal Sun can symbolize a bold new faith in oneself. Someone lacking purpose might blaze a new path. This can be a time of overcoming negativity.

People may find more confidence in expressing opinions. A teenager may accept challenges of adolescence; an employee may offer advice to superiors; a student may find his major; a seeker his true path. An individual may feel forced off the fence of contentment. He may be asked to **practice what he preaches**. One may discover a less judgmental attitude through generosity.

SHADOW
Both the **Sun/Jupiter conjunction and square** can express as a lack of common sense. **People can leave good situations for greener pastures.** One may ignore consequences of actions. Pushing forward can be carried to extremes. Exaggeration of accomplishments could occur. Sun/Jupiter aspects are usually not too harmful. **Wastefulness and foolish risk-taking can be a problem.**

A lack of follow-through can be frustrating. Endless excuses and rationalization may be mind boggling. All talk and no action is possible. Dogmatism can be extreme. Eclectic reasoning can become a narrow judgmental perspective. People preach too much of their own virtues and morals. One's faith might lack effort and depth. Individuals may be too easily discouraged from goals. Blind faith can lead idealism down the wrong road. Some individuals refuse to acknowledge negative situations. A denial of a problem keeps it lingering.

> **Quincunx:** Progressed Sun Quincunx Natal or Progressed Jupiter
> Transiting Jupiter Quincunx Natal Sun
>
> **Opposition:** Progressed Sun Opposing Natal or Progressed Jupiter
> Transiting Jupiter Opposing Natal Sun

LIGHT
The progressed Sun quincunx natal (or progressed) Jupiter or transiting Jupiter quincunx the natal Sun is the "Yoga of abundance." Individuals learn how to reward themselves. There can be a tendency to be very ascetic. This may be a spiritual time. Individuals might find a deeper faith in life. More common sense can develop. Individuals may find a conscience. Those with little sensitivity can become more conscious of their actions. A wasteful person may learn how to better manage resources. Individuals who are followers can now think for themselves. Blind faith can look for the truth. People who overdo eating, exercise, and pleasure can learn moderation. Trimming down the desire nature brings internal satisfaction.

Progressed Sun opposing natal (or progressed) Jupiter or transiting Jupiter opposing natal Sun can express as generosity towards others. One may attract good fortune with a **positive and friendly attitude**. Relationships could fill with growth. Partners can bring rich eclectic experiences into relationships. There may be a spiritual harmony. This can be a rewarding period. Awards and financial success are possible. Individuals have the faith to follow through on goals.

In birthcharts with **few intense aspects**, this may be an uneventful period. Events are likely to occur more on subjective levels such as a feeling of well-being. This could be a reflective period for study. There can be travel urges. Learning from foreign environments is stimulating. A longing for fresh experiences can lead to travel, education, and new business enterprises.

SHADOW

Both the Sun/Jupiter quincunx and opposition can expect the impossible from others. There can be unfounded idealism. Individuals may foolishly worship others, easily led by flowery words. A person might hide behind humor, pretending life is always sweet. A fear of commitment can be related to not wanting to be tied down. Freedom urges are strong. **Individuals may leave stable relationships (or other situations) due to boredom.** An aimless feeling can be bothersome. A "Jack of all trades" or "all roads lead to Rome" mentality can occur.

Relating to others through cultural biases can be limiting. One may always talk through morals. Self-righteousness can be annoying; sitting in judgment of others alienating. One may let go of a spiritual purpose, or surrender to a material consciousness. A disheartening loss of creative vitality is possible. Deception (lies) may occur.

SOFT ASPECTS

Sextile:	Transiting Jupiter Sextile Natal Sun
	Progressed Sun Sextile Natal or Progressed Jupiter
Trine:	Transiting Jupiter Trine Natal Sun
	Progressed Sun Trine Natal or Progressed Jupiter

LIGHT

Progressed Sun sextile natal (or progressed) Jupiter or transiting Jupiter sextile natal Sun can denote a time of celebration. This can be a soothing aspect. The psyche draws new breath. Life may seem like a blessing. Spiritual and material worlds can be in harmony. People may not be so attached to spiritual concepts. Living one's highest beliefs becomes more important than preaching.

Progressed Sun trine natal (or progressed) Jupiter or transiting Jupiter trine natal Sun can denote a powerful spiritual purpose. The trine is a natural component of both the Sun and Jupiter (see 5th and 9th chord chapters in *Astrological Games People Play*). A person might feel a special flow with life forces. **The momentum of positive energy brings this into fruition.**

One can be a peacemaker - benevolent figure for a family, organization or community. One could face Karmic conflicts. Much depends on the willpower (Sun) and morals (Jupiter) of the individual. An articulate nature can come forward. A power of persuasion might excel in communication fields. One could link together the common attributes of different opinions and philosophies. A giving spirit offers healing power through words and actions.

SHADOW

In both the **Sun/Jupiter sextile and trine** a person can do too much for others. Individuals may not give others enough room to grow. Diarrhea of the mouth can be nauseating. One may go in circles without getting things done. Shallow learning can hold him back. A tendency to push beliefs on others can occur. There may be a narrow belief system. **This is contrary to the expansive nature of this planetary combination.** Simple truths and easy answers block the path to new growth. One may be too eager to swallow false propaganda. Repeating cultural biases seems more enticing than reaching for a more expansive truth. The trine is more prone to exaggerated self-importance. Rigid attachment to a personal belief system can occur. Using others in the name of love leads to tragedy.

DAWN

Sun/Jupiter aspects can be steps to a bigger world. If one tries to become Mr. or Mrs. Big, they may get into trouble. Instead of exaggerating, one could speak with simplicity. **Limited belief systems can move to new heights by eclectic learning.** This is a fiery planetary combination. There is no end to the creative imagination. These aspects remind us of a childlike spirit. Alice in Wonderland perhaps said it right: "Getting more curiouser and curiouser."

SUN/SATURN ASPECTS

Progressed Sun/Natal or Progressed Saturn Transiting Saturn/Natal Sun

Process:	"Consciousness Stretching"
Ally:	Uncompromised Determination
Illusion:	Compulsive Power Drives

Sun/Saturn aspects challenge personal ambitions. Expectations of authority figures can be an issue. Combining creativity and inspiration with reality testing is one of the key challenges.

Saturn aspecting our natal Sun symbolizes a tremendous stretch of consciousness. Growth within the aging process is another key theme. Our creative identity is challenged by the reality of life. Even the softer aspects (sextile and trine) denote one is learning how to accept responsibility and take pride in accomplishments. Our creative potential and self-expression is being redefined. Patience and commitment are resources. Issues related to responsibility, power, wisdom, trust, and self-confidence can be additional themes.

INTENSE ASPECTS

Conjunction: Transiting Saturn Conjunct Natal Sun
Progressed Sun Conjunct Natal or Progressed Saturn

Square: Transiting Saturn Square Natal Sun
Progressed Sun Square Natal or Progressed Saturn

LIGHT

The progressed Sun conjunct natal (or progressed) Saturn or transiting Saturn conjunct natal Sun denotes a person trying to understand ambition. This can be a very fulfilling time. An individual may find the confidence to launch new career goals. A person may conquer a fear of risk-taking. The Sun symbolizes a drive to go beyond limitation. Taking control of one's life may become a joy rather than a burden. Organizing and structuring one's ambitions can be stimulating. A person could rise above self-defeating thoughts.

This aspect sometimes symbolizes new self-growth or a new course of action. One works hard for success, embracing inner strength. An individual may transform previous disappointments into solid building ground. It can feel like part of the old self is dying. A new self is being born. If a person rises above a depressed emotional state, a tremendous deepening of consciousness can occur. This period may feel like an emotional vacuum. If one does not panic during the transition, great emotional strength can be cultivated.

Some individuals are attracted to solitude. The experience feels like a recharge of the psyche. Reflection provides deep insights into inner motivations. Some people really enjoy dealing with crises during Saturn/Sun aspects. Fear is cast aside. Situations that were too stressful for the nerves are now seen as challenges. The last thought is to run away.

Career could be an issue. **A person might find a more creative career expression.** Positions of authority that offer more control over decision making become a focus. The challenge of accepting more responsibility is exciting.

Progressed Sun square natal (or progressed) Saturn or transiting Saturn square natal Sun can symbolize an individual is realistically reaching goals. The timing is exceptional. A person may conquer past limiting behaviors. One might impress others with excellent management skills. A reputation for being a good supervisor or leader can be highlighted. One may be rewarded for accomplishments.

This can symbolize a person accepting the physical laws of the universe. Common sense and realistic goals may be exhibited. One gains disciplined concentration. Individuals can face cultural inhibitions learned during childhood. An opposite insight may occur for someone excessively reckless. This could be a time of trying to join the mainstream.

Forming love, business or stable relationships can be symbolized. A person is eager to share a newfound confidence with others. A person can feel quite centered even while the environment is going through major changes. One's strength holds her together during relationship, career or residence transitions.

SHADOW

Both the **Sun/Saturn conjunction and square** can indicate a person may combine the pride of the Sun with the ambition of Saturn into a ruthless display of **authority and control**. A complete fixation on career success and worldly ambitions can isolate one from friends and loved ones.

Illness may tell the mind and body to slow down. Workaholic tendencies could be compulsive. The person ignores physical limits. Desiring to constantly be the center of attention can be problematic. The underlying issues usually are related to insecurity, lack of trust or just plain fear.

One of the bigger problems is a stubborn resistance to changing behavior patterns. A refusal to be more emotional, affectionate, or trusting can lead to greater problems later. Some individuals fall into heavily depressed states. A too-serious nature sets a person up for repeated negative adventures. A blocked flow of creative energy grows heavy.

Trusting one's emotions is a scary experience. Perhaps one would rather stay isolated in a more tangible world of outer success and exhibition. The compulsive need to control the environment represses consciousness expansion. Dictator tendencies can surface. Power and position are used to keep people at a distance. One gets fixed on a particular view of reality and is afraid to show feelings.

People may find they have little control over their lives. A person may find she is too much at the mercy of circumstances. This can symbolize a crisis in one's life. The creative flow feels smothered by limiting circumstances. One may deny a change of career is needed. The individual may lack the talent of delegating responsibility. This can be due to too much self-reliance or a lack of trust in others. One can feel pressured by obligation and duty. Some leisure time or a creative choice of new options is ignored. Time can seem like an enemy full of stressful pressures.

Quincunx: Transiting Saturn Quincunx Natal Sun
Progressed Sun Quincunx Natal or Progressed Saturn

Opposition: Transiting Saturn Opposing Natal Sun
Progressed Sun Opposing Natal or Progressed Saturn

LIGHT

Progressed Sun quincunx natal (or progressed) Saturn or transiting Saturn quincunx the natal Sun can denote an individual

is **mastering the art of combining work and pleasure**. This stretches our work muscles. It can be a very busy time when one is carefully organizing her schedule.

This aspect is the **"Yoga of Consciousness Stretching."** One is seeking desperately, and sometimes compulsively, to integrate desires for success with the wisdom of worldly experiences. One is learning time management. Establishing priorities makes time for relating, work and fun. An individual can get quite creative at establishing rewards for hard work. She may integrate diet, exercise and rest with hard and consistent work.

This can be a very psychological aspect. Individuals might grow introspective regarding service to others, power instincts and even tuning into Karmic patterns. Someone may gain insight into compulsive addictions to power or giving away power too easily. Much wisdom and soul growth can fill a person's awareness, if they are so motivated.

A person may seek counseling to gain control over destructive thought patterns. A person entering into a dialogue of trust with a friend or counselor can go beyond a painful or limiting past. People may learn new work skills. It is a good time for apprenticeships and taking a skills inventory. A person may leave dead-end jobs or relationships.

Progressed Sun opposing natal (or progressed) Saturn or transiting Saturn opposing natal Sun can symbolize an individual attempting to redefine relating to others. One may gain creative strength in relationships. This can include love, peer, children or business. The opposition can denote more equilibrium in relating to others. A person may rise above past mistakes and create new ways of relating. This is a very **strategy-oriented** aspect. Strength may be derived from meaningful commitments. One may prove she is reliable and able to support the growth of others. A business sense may crystallize into a practical avenue. Relating well to the public and authority figures can be a valuable asset. The individual might attract people willing to invest in her ability and talent.

Credit with financial institutions can be established. Saturn can be a sobering motif. An individual may move swiftly to pave the way for personal ability. A more natural fluidity in communicating ambitions to others is possible. One may drop extreme power urges. A more vulnerable emotional nature might break through. The loss of a relationship or career may create an atmosphere of self-examination. A slowdown and concentration on relating habits can occur.

Some individuals make a new commitment to growth. One may adopt more realistic expectations of others. The individual may feel less compelled to control her relationships. However, an individual may choose to leave a relationship that has proven **unfulfilling and unresolvable**.

SHADOW
Both the Sun/Saturn quincunx and opposition can point to an individual integrating the "me-focus" of the fiery Sun with the power of Saturn. One might block the natural flow of Sun energy. **A fear of trusting others can be the root problem.** This can produce someone over- or underusing control.

An individual can allow others to make all of the major decisions in love relationships. This can be someone who feels undeserving of warm and affectionate relationships. A person can project responsibility onto others. One may blame people and life in general for repeated problems. Being bossy and in control can reach great extremes.

One may submit too easily to pressure from others and accept limiting life roles. A dominating parent or supervisor may hold the individual back from a happier life. One's indecisiveness can frustrate self and others. A person sometimes will face their own unwillingness to develop deep relationships. Heaviness and negativity may undermine self-confidence.

One can settle for humiliating situations. Career blahs may surface. The person is frustrated with a present job, but lacks the confidence to move ahead to a new situation. It is possible there is no clear choice available that allows a person to express ambitious drives. A person could even fear to leave a destructive relationship. One's focus and concentration may need a tune-up. Numerous distractions may exist.

There can be tendencies to compulsively control others. A lack of self-confidence in relating to others may bring out power urges. Someone can seek to be a parent figure for others.

SOFT ASPECTS
>   **Sextile:**   Transiting Saturn Sextile Natal Sun
>   Progressed Sun Sextile Natal or Progressed Saturn
>
>   **Trine:**   Transiting Saturn Trine Natal Sun
>   Progressed Sun Trine Natal or Progressed Saturn

LIGHT
Progressed Sun sextile natal (or progressed) Saturn or transiting Saturn sextile natal Sun can symbolize eagerness to express creativity. The sextile symbolizes a flow of self-expression within the pressures of everyday life. A person can have insights into business dealings. New responsibility is accepted. One may be very stimulating to others. Work and play seem easier to integrate.

Progressed Sun trine natal (or progressed) Saturn or transiting Saturn trine the natal Sun can denote a more relaxed flow of ambition and pleasure. Faith and optimism may reach new heights. Creative self-expression may feel fulfilling. Both the sextile and trine denote times when one may reflect upon past consciousness-stretching experiences and be glad to have survived. There may be an appreciation of one's past. The aging process might flow with one's ambitions. This aspect in later years can reflect humility and wisdom learned.

SHADOW

In the Sun/Saturn sextile or trine, the biggest hurdle is a lack of ambition. The flow symbolized by the sextile and trine can connote lack of concentration. The trine especially can symbolize running away from responsibility. There is a fear of expansion. One would rather not risk a failure.

The soft aspects can show one lacks the determination to set limits. If a person was so motivated, the trine could symbolize a person's disrespect for authority or reality. Such an individual has difficulty with responsibility and defining goals. A person can lack the wisdom to learn from past experiences. Too much can be taken for granted. One conveniently forgets her history in the world.

DAWN

Sun/Saturn aspects can symbolize conquering fears. Taking control of one's life and redefining strengths and weaknesses can bring satisfaction. Self-imposed pressures and demands can be released. The spontaneous flowing themes of the Sun can denote new insight. **Seeing that life needs to be a mixture of pleasure and hard work can help reduce stress levels.**

Circumstances that once held the person in a grip of fear, lack of trust, and emotional blockage can be broken through. **Strengthened willpower and** focused ambition can be highlighted rather than false pride and extreme self-control. The warmth of the Sun is allowed to thaw the freeze of Saturn's caution. One can clearly test the safety of the territory.

SUN/URANUS ASPECTS

Progressed Sun/Natal or Progressed Uranus Transiting Uranus/Natal Sun

Process:	Creative Experimentation
Ally:	Freedom and Individuality
Illusion:	Eccentric Self-Focus

Sun/Uranus aspects point to finding new ideas for self-expression and relating to peers. There is a lot of self-focus in these aspects. One learns to experiment. Many new doors can open unexpectedly. Goals and ego needs often go through amazing transformations. Life seems to get faster. An individual may become quite unpredictable. Key personal transformations can be indicated.

INTENSE ASPECTS
Conjunction: Transiting Uranus Conjunct Natal Sun
Progressed Sun Conjunct Natal or Progressed Uranus
Square: Transiting Uranus Square Natal Sun
Progressed Sun Square Natal or Progressed Uranus

LIGHT
Electricity! A dramatic change of life-style is not uncommon. One learns to fuse together self-expression and individuality. **Progressed Sun conjunct natal (or progressed) Uranus or transiting Uranus conjunct natal Sun** indicates brain waves bombarded with mental stimulation. A person may develop much insight into future goals. An individual who is normally slow and methodical mentally may have flashes of mental genius. He can be inventive. One can find a unique purpose. A person may interpret symbolic languages such as astrology. A person who is too ego-centered may develop a broader vision. This can be a universal energy. One may begin thinking collectively or globally. Some people develop humanitarian consciousness.

An overly dependent individual may develop a more independent life. He may control extreme emotional outbursts. The detachment symbolized by Uranus may bring more balance between mind and emotion. Constant attention is less necessary. A person who normally lives creative energy through others may discover his own gifts. New confidence and originality can be attained. Bonds of friendship can deepen. A person may find a group that supports creative strength. One may become more adept at receiving and giving support for goals.

One can question societal mores and expectations. One may rebel against limited thinking. A new mental intensity may inspire others to question their life direction. A new freedom may be uplifting.

Progressed Sun square natal (or progressed) Uranus or transiting Uranus square natal Sun can denote acting smoothly on mental impulses. An individual may break the shackles of the past. One may stop living individuality through others. A desire for self-recognition may develop. A person can break the hold of limiting societal values fed to him as a child. An individual may fight city hall or authority figures.

Various conflicts associated with freedom and self-expression can be resolved. A person may forcefully argue for rights previously denied. He can experiment with new creative outlets. New peers, hobbies, or goals can become important. One may take a new pride in individuality. A person at war with himself could learn how to channel intensity more creatively. Perhaps an authority figure or institution in the past was limiting and critical of the person. One might work through the conflict in a direct manner now. This dynamic energy may be channeled into one's own creative pursuits. An individual may burn down self-defeating bridges. Rising to a higher level of creative intelligence might spark many years of fulfilling growth. One may find goals to better fit new levels of consciousness.

SHADOW
In the Sun/Uranus conjunction or square a nihilistic mentality can dominate situations. One can be too focused on self and not support the goals of others. Self-focus can be extreme. One may tear down obstacles with no insight where to go next. He moves much faster than life can prepare for him. Disillusionment and frustration await a lack of planning. A constant need for stimulation make one difficult to be around. Nervousness and a rambling mind deplete energy. One may simply go in circles. A lack of listening to others can occur. One may be too attached to unique opinions. A person may never fit into social situations due to changeability and eccentric beliefs. A loss of any middle ground brings isolation.

Quincunx: Transiting Uranus Quincunx Natal Sun
Progressed Sun Quincunx Natal or Progressed Uranus

Opposition: Transiting Uranus Opposing Natal Sun
Progressed Sun Opposing Natal or Progressed Uranus

LIGHT
Progressed Sun quincunx natal (or progressed) Uranus or transiting Uranus quincunx natal Sun is the "Yoga of expressing individuality." One strives to understand self-expression and unique goals. Much soul work can occur. One may tune into inner motivations for extreme needs for attention. Some individuals will work with their inability to pay attention to individual needs.

An individual may conquer an addiction to unstable relationships. A person may overcome an identity crisis. Combining expectations of others with personal expectations can get clearer.

The progressed Sun opposing natal (or progressed) Uranus or transiting Uranus opposing natal Sun can denote one is balancing freedom urges and self-expression. One often seeks new, stimulating relationships. An individual may make important discoveries concerning abilities. Sun/Uranus aspects are accentuated by **experimentation**. One may exhibit creative abilities in communication. A person may enjoy a wider variety of relationships. Attraction to unconventional ideas and people can expand horizons. An individual can be stimulated by people from different walks of life. One may clarify love relationships. He can be excited about achieving more independence. Equality is important to Uranus. A person who gives up individuality too easily may learn to enjoy freedom. An individual too controlling may start giving equal footing to partners.

A person with conservative values can become more liberal. One may discover new options and choices in problem solving. Some individuals become quite active in humanitarian causes. A thirst for knowledge and higher consciousness can exist. When my progressed Sun in Sagittarius (9th house) opposed my natal Uranus in Gemini (3rd house), I traveled thousands of miles over the two-year period. When transiting Uranus conjuncted my Sagittarian Sun in 1981, my desire to do astrological counseling and writing deepened. I discovered a new group of peers that helped support my work.

One needs a lot of stimulation. New mental challenges and a break from limited thinking can occur. **Sun/Uranus aspects can denote tremendous self-discovery**. One may make adjustments that bring new excitement into a relationship. Both people may create more flexibility and freedom for each other.

SHADOW

In the Sun/Uranus quincunx or opposition, one can be easily distracted from goals. Paying too much attention to opinions of others brings indecision. One's peers may not give enough support. A person may be doing all the giving.

One's life may be disorganized due to a hectic pace. Denying body signals for rest can lead to a mental breakdown. One may be compulsively addicted to excessive exercise, work or enjoyment. Individuals may be frustrated with self. Not setting goals may result in procrastination. A lack of assertiveness can lead to frustration. People may settle for much less than they want. Dead-end jobs and limiting relationships can occur.

A person can unpredictably desire space and then want closeness, making for much tension. Relationships can break up due to unclear communication. One's changeability is less threatening, if others understand a need for space. A drive to leave a good relationship for greener pastures can be a mistake. One may react too quickly to situations. This can apply to career situations, too. An individual may leave a limiting situation impulsively. It is important to carefully think changes through. A person can get reckless. Ignoring the needs of others or not paying attention to responsibilities can lead to trouble. Restlessness and impatience not properly channeled lead to burning bridges too soon. A failure to communicate feelings could occur. One can move so fast that quality time for intimacy is ignored. A person can hide behind intellectual arrogance.

Some people fight against progressive thinking. One may have grown up in a conservative cultural setting and have difficulty with new ideas. **This is Uranus working in reverse!** An individual may fear the freedom of others. Also, this can be a person suddenly in a situation that has set him free. Perhaps a lover or spouse has suddenly left the relationship. A very dependent individual may struggle with inherited independence. This can be life's way of saying to get on with one's goals. It can be scary for a person previously supported by a lover or spouse.

It is important not to simply believe in a **"different just to be different"** philosophy. One can display eccentric and extremely uncooperative behavior. He directs this energy at inappropriate targets rather than at truly limiting authority figures or institutions. An extreme lack of stability may ruin productive goals.

SOFT ASPECTS

Sextile: Transiting Uranus Sextile Natal Sun
Progressed Sun Sextile Natal or Progressed Uranus

Trine: Transiting Uranus Trine Natal Sun
Progressed Sun Trine Natal or Progressed Uranus

LIGHT

Progressed Sun sextile natal (or progressed) Uranus or transiting Uranus sextile natal Sun can denote one is eager to explore new territory. This can be an exciting time, perhaps filled with good news concerning one's future goals. A person may establish needed contacts to promote ideas. One's enthusiasm can be contagious. He could brainstorm new options to promote ideas and solve problems. One's environment may be packed with stimulation. Establishing a network to meet new people and to promote goals is possible.

The trine can symbolize a confidence to **rise above conflict or limiting circumstances.** One may establish a new faith in self. He may conquer impatience and lack of responsibility. People may be less distracted by intense environmental conflicts. Dynamic mental energy is directed more productively. One may be more open than usual to support from others. He may balance dependency and freedom needs.

SHADOW

In both the **Sun/Uranus sextile and trine** a person can look too much for positive strokes. Stagnation can result due to low self-motivation. One may lack mental fortitude, never reaching much mental depth. There can be a lack of focusing power or an inability to say no. A person can exaggerate the intensity of situations. Even a little stress provokes the individual. A desire for harmony at all costs can lead to confining careers and relationships.

An individual can be consumed by his own goals. He demands a lot of attention and gives little in return. There can be a need for constant stimulation. Things come too easily. If a person has disciplined himself, this can be a highly productive period. One could exhibit tremendous vision.

DAWN
Sun/Uranus aspects can be expressed as clear vision of future goals. People may inspire others, with clarity in the midst of chaos. A cool, detached perception of situations sets others at ease. One may adeptly regulate needs for space and closeness. Balancing dependency needs and self-expression can be an art. Communicating insights clearly establishes a free give-and-take in all relationships.

An individual may possess a powerful global awareness. Creative works and group participation may offer enlightening stimulation. One might alter behavior related to nihilism, anarchy, emotional coldness, or dependency. The freedom to be oneself emerges powerfully!

SUN/NEPTUNE ASPECTS

Progressed Sun/Natal or Progressed Neptune Transiting Neptune/Natal Sun

Process:	Living Ideals
Ally:	Spiritual Values and Intuitive Faith
Illusion:	Outer Glamour

Sun/Neptune aspects can point to reaching new levels of consciousness. These aspects can denote behaviors ranging from a new spirituality to running away from reality. Inner crisis may satisfy an urge for a "high" feeling. Neptune energy represents the height of divine discontent. One's quest to find perfection or unity may drive her into creative aesthetic expressions.

Sun/Neptune aspects **require careful reality testing**. The denial themes of Neptune can lead to disorienting and self-destructive actions. One can pretend ignorance for compulsive behaviors. A person can transcend difficult situations through **faith and intuition.** One may feel a higher power is guiding her actions.

INTENSE ASPECTS
Conjunction: Transiting Neptune Conjunct Natal Sun
　　　　　　　Progressed Sun Conjunct Natal/Progressed Neptune

Square:　Transiting Neptune Square Natal Sun
　　　　　　　Progressed Sun Square Natal or Progressed Neptune

LIGHT
Progressed Sun conjunct natal or progressed Neptune or transiting Neptune conjunct natal Sun can be expressed as creative inspiration. An individual may find a new faith in self and a higher power. A person can develop great intuitive powers. Devotion to a new creative expression could be relentless. A person may find the energy

and imagination to live highest visions. Charisma is sometimes noted. A person may attract situations that foster success.

Individuals may become involved in a collective movement. Gandhi had transiting Neptune conjunct his natal Libra Sun when India achieved its independence in 1947. He had the natal Libra Sun opposing natal Neptune in Aries at birth. This **repeating theme** accentuated this transit in his life. A person can learn humility and compassion. There is strong spiritual symbolism in Neptune. One can rise above negative thinking. Clear emotional and intuitive energies can resolve conflicts. A stubborn ego may become more flowing. A person can sometimes resolve issues through sacrifice and a more giving nature. An openness to the possibility of a higher power brings new faith. A sense of unity and peace help heal a worn-out consciousness.

An individual may find a deeper personal love. She may for the first time experience love. Personal healing and transformation of dynamic proportions can occur. A person may tune into symbolic languages such as dreams, astrology, or tarot. An individual can have intuitive insights. One's dreams may be filled with subconscious messages. She can find deep inner peace through meditation. A person can develop an aesthetic talent such as art, music, or dance.

Progressed Sun square natal (or progressed) Neptune or transiting Neptune square natal Sun can symbolize a forceful time. One can find faith through self-expression. There is often environmental turbulence. A person can express herself in spite of the odds. A person may use the media to broadcast a message. Jesse Jackson made great advances during the political primaries in 1988 while transiting Neptune in Capricorn squared his natal Sun in Libra. During his famous speech at the Democratic Convention in Atlanta, the television ratings increased by about thirty percent!

People can boldly live ideals. Intuition and clarity may lead to tremendous growth. Karmic patterns related to a big ego or escapism can be transcended. A person may seek out humility and sacrifice. One can work to increase the consciousness of society. A person may volunteer to bring a cause into the public eye. Creative drives can lead one into fields that deal with psychological energy: psychotherapy, social work, prisons, or nursing. Metaphysical or alternative fields can become an interest such as massage, astrology, Neurolinguistic Programming, etc.

An individual can conquer a self-destructive habit. Faith in a higher power may help to transcend drug or alcohol addiction. A new self-confidence may help break away from addictive habits.

SHADOW

In the Sun/Neptune conjunction or square, a person can lack inspiration due to a loss of faith. An individual can excessively deny her natural intensity. She may try too hard to be loved or accepted. A person may have trouble insulating her consciousness from life circumstances. One may not disengage from emotionally intense circumstances until long after the event. She may be too attached to the outcome of situations. A person can merge with her dreams, making no practical plans for action. Extreme idealism and fantasy may lead to disappointment. Life may seem unusually harsh if things do not go perfectly according to plan. Procrastination may be a regular behavior.

An individual may never be satisfied. Standards are set too high for self and others. She can deny problems and escape through sleep, sex, or substance abuse. Individuals might indulge in excessive self-pity and helplessness. People can have unrealistic fears. A too sensitive or impressionable imagination may distort perceptions. One's emotional nature may lead to a lack of mental fine-tuning. A person can weave an imaginative story rather than see objectively. A person may block the intuitive flow. One may be stuck in the conscious mind and fear her imaging power. An individual can exaggerate fame. One may be too ego-centered to notice anybody else. A drive to be center stage can alienate others. A shallow consciousness can be limiting.

Quincunx: Transiting Neptune Quincunx Natal Sun
              Progressed Sun Quincunx Natal or Progressed Neptune

Opposition: Transiting Neptune Opposing Natal Sun
              Progressed Sun Opposing Natal or Progressed Neptune

LIGHT

Progressed Sun quincunx natal (or progressed) Neptune or transiting Neptune quincunx natal Sun is the "Yoga of expressing higher consciousness." An individual may bring emotional intensity more in line with highest values. A person may project less creative potential onto others. An individual may pay more attention to a mental-physical-spiritual balance. One can move with a greater awareness of actions. A true giving nature may replace greed. More selflessness can transcend grabbing for attention. Deeper intuitive insights into motives for actions emerge. Individuals may stop putting too much faith in others. A person begins to trust her own instincts.

Progressed Sun opposing natal (or progressed) Neptune or transiting Neptune opposing natal Sun can be expressed as creative relating. An individual can relate to a wide variety of people. A sixth and seventh sense tunes into the unspoken language of others. There can be harmony in relating. A person may be more adept at expressing compassion and sympathy. A great life transition can lead to inner peace. One may become less manipulative and aggressive, attracting what she needs through a new emotional clarity. A more genuine expression of love and empathy wins the approval of others. One may enjoy periods of romance by trusting intuition.

An interest in the mysteries behind life experiences may enhance one's ability to accept life's ups and downs. Neptune does seem to symbolize the fleeting illusions of life that come and go. Eastern Indians refer to this as Maya. An individual may begin to grasp a greater awareness within the finiteness of physical life. She may tune into the infinite beauty and timelessness of the soul. An individual may become clairvoyant. She may become intuitive when meeting strangers. A greater confidence in interacting with others can result.

A person may find an aesthetic expression or find success after years of striving. It can appear as though a special grace has been showered upon her. Important emotional breakthroughs can dominate this time. An individual can conquer excessive dependency and helplessness. Running away from creative self-expression may be replaced with a new faith. One may forgive those who have caused emotional pain. It can be a time for forgiving oneself. Conquering guilt and no longer trying to be a savior for others can be important lessons. A person may gain greater faith in a higher power. One may achieve a clearer understanding of a lover or spouse, perceiving subconscious motives.

SHADOW

In both the **Sun/Neptune quincunx and opposition,** a person can get deeply into a relationship without realizing it. One's attracting power (or need for a relationship) is accentuated. Too much devotion may occur. Trying to save others can be a bad habit. An individual could run away from problems by escaping into a relationship. A person can deny unfinished business by jumping from one person to another. One may become addicted to sexual fantasies rather than establish meaningful relationships.

One can lose oneself in intimate relating. She may merge too much with the identity of a lover or spouse. A person may have irrational fears of closeness. Everything is fine until the initial passionate attraction settles down into the reality of everyday living together. A person may project her inner qualities and talents upon others. A male could live his inner feminine (or *anima*) out through female partners; a female can project inner masculine (or *animus*), living this out through a male partner. A male can place unrealistic expectations on a feminine partner to do his emotional expressing. A female can expect a male to be her outward expression into the world. Denial of inner potential makes for relationships lacking harmony.

One may have trouble breaking an attachment to past circumstances. Too much nostalgia for "good old days" keep one from moving ahead. An ongoing addiction to a past intimate partner keeps one in a stagnating present. One can put someone on a pedestal. A person's peers could be a bad influence. Gambling, substance abuse, and time wasted through extreme escapism deplete energy. One may be poor at choosing role models or peers. A lack of objectivity in decision making can occur. Too much compromising or pleasing others can be problematic. An oversensitivity to criticism may be exhibited. An individual can deceive others. She may fear equality in a relationship, deliberately misleading those who become attracted or involved with her.

SOFT ASPECTS
Sextile: Transiting Neptune Sextile Natal Sun
          Progressed Sun Sextile Natal or Progressed Neptune

Trine: Transiting Neptune Trine Natal Sun
          Progressed Sun Trine Natal or Progressed Neptune

LIGHT
Progressed Sun sextile natal (or progressed) Neptune or transiting Neptune sextile natal Sun can denote a person is excited about creative opportunities. The environment may flow with a person's expectations. An individual could enjoy new opportunities created by faith and hard work. A person may receive encouragement from peers. One's mental powers may rise to a higher level of intuition. A person with too much me-focus can show more sensitivity.

Progressed Sun trine natal (or progressed) Neptune or transiting Neptune trine the natal Sun can point to a **new faith in self and a higher power**. She may find it possible to be happy. An overly serious life attitude can be dropped. Both the Sun/Neptune sextile and trine symbolize more flexibility in decision making. The trine can denote finding idealism, transcending too much practicality.

A person may cultivate an aesthetic interest that later becomes a career. An individual allows more time to rest her psyche. One may be attracted to living by the ocean or to sites of natural beauty. One yearns for experiences that harmonize the psyche.

SHADOW
In both the **Sun/Neptune sextile and trine**, people can lack the willpower (Sun) to fulfill dreams (Neptune). With intense Sun/Neptune aspects, one feels driven to actualize perfection instincts. With the soft aspects, a person may lack the volition to accomplish ideals. One can feel like time will wait forever.

A person may be too transparent in negotiating. She may give in too easily to demands of others. A lack of self-expression can be frustrating. The individual may dwell in a passive world. This can be a very sensitive individual who lacks self-confidence. An individual may desperately try to avoid conflict. It is too exhausting. An individual can become disoriented due to environmental stress. A person with a birthchart lacking intense aspects and having a history of not dealing well with reality may choose escapism.

DAWN
Sun/Neptune aspects can be expressed as periods of powerful illumination. An individual may achieve new enlightenment. Escapism, addiction, and running from reality can be brought into clear focus. A new faith can be born. New emotional depth can be attained. A guilty nature can find peace. A person can replace impatience with compassion. She can transcend self-denial with self-love; greed can be eliminated by a more giving spirit. A new level of right brain or intuitive intensity can be displayed through creative self-expression. A person may find a place of inner rest.

SUN/PLUTO ASPECTS

Progressed Sun/Natal or Progressed Pluto
Transiting Pluto/Natal Sun

Process:	Creative Self-Mastery
Ally:	The Vitality to Penetrate Through Obstacles
Illusion:	I Need More Worlds to Conquer

Sun/Pluto aspects are penetrating life chapters! Lives can go through a major metamorphosis. This can be a two-year period involving self-mastery. One could tap into personal power. Karmic ties may be broken. Compulsive urges could be brought under control. A release of emotional intensity can free creative energies. **This is a time of knowing oneself on the deepest of levels.**

INTENSE ASPECTS
Conjunction: Progressed Sun Conjunct Natal or Progressed Pluto
Transiting Pluto Conjunct Natal Sun

Square: Progressed Sun Square Natal or Progressed Pluto
Transiting Pluto Square Natal Sun

LIGHT
Progressed Sun conjunct natal (or progressed) Pluto or transiting Pluto conjunct the natal Sun can symbolize a regeneration process. Individuals become acquainted again with emotional intensity. A powerful release of subconscious energies in creative pursuits is possible. Compulsive desires can be surrendered. Life's dark side is not so compelling. A tendency to love danger can be modified. Life in the extreme lane finds a rest stop. The transformation is away from self-undoing.

The death of worn-out roles can be liberating. More self-control in directing energies is satisfying. A sense of rebirth gratifies. A grasp of the subtle forces at work in life is confirming. A life of anger and resentment can be healed. The past is finally forgotten or buried. Emotional and physical loss become the compost material for new horizons. One may excel as psychologist, hypnotist, shaman or business wizard. A grasp of the big picture can allow one management ability.

A capacity to forgive is realized. Emotional undercurrents and shadows come into the light. Strength through psychological insights replaces a forceful nature. One may find a balance of power in life circumstances. Individuals may realize the preciousness of life. Death is accepted as a process. People may tap into the power or gifts of past lives. Irrational behaviors can be remarkably changed. Sexual energy may enhance a bonding process to others. One may exercise more control of passions and desires. Proving sexual potency is less compelling. Ego needs can work for someone rather than steal his show.

Progressed Sun square natal (or progressed) Pluto or transiting Pluto square natal Sun can denote an intense display of survival instincts. A release of vigorous creative energy can make this a key transition period. A dynamic passion for life can bring a new business or lover. A refusal to give up allows one to accomplish difficult tasks. Even a physical or psychological handicap may be overcome.

One may leave behind excess physical or psychological baggage. Sarcasm can be replaced by creative effort. Jealousy and revenge can be transcended through self-honesty. Power urges may find more constructive outlets. Greed can turn to love. A selfish survivalist may share with others. A person who has suffered emotional or material loss can bounce back. The past can be forgiven or transcended. The present becomes a more authentic stamp of one's true identity. A lack of courage can find new symbols to arouse vitality. A passive individual can act out a new spirit. A lost soul can break new ground. A shallow person can express more psychological depth. A compulsive type might relax. One may bring possessiveness and manipulative tendencies under control.

SHADOW

Both the **Sun/Pluto conjunction and square** can be expressed as a fear of personal power. A person can lack the stamina to deal with life challenges. Difficult situations are avoided. Individuals can lash out at life too compulsively. An angry person can blame problems on external factors. An insecure type can be ruthlessly mistrustful of others. An individual may be too attached to people or things. A loss may totally disrupt one's life. An inability to bounce back feels paralyzing. Creative energy seems blocked.

Hiding emotional pain can delay intimacy with others. Individuals may have trouble with closeness. Past emotional pain interferes with the present. Individuals can lack honesty. Manipulating situations rather than dealing truthfully, can occur. People can have ulterior motives for altruism, always expecting a lot more in return.

One's life may be in constant crisis. A lack of self-honesty and insight bring disastrous consequences. People may too hastily tear down solid structures. Individuals may repeat Karmic behaviors. Jealousy, helplessness, dictator tendencies or vindictiveness are all possible. Emotional secrets poison one's creative spirit. Instead of regeneration, the result is stagnation.

Quincunx: Progressed Sun Quincunx Natal or Progressed Pluto
Transiting Pluto Quincunx Natal Sun

Opposition: Progressed Sun Opposing Natal Pluto
Transiting Pluto Opposing Natal Sun

LIGHT

Progressed Sun quincunx natal (or progressed) Pluto or transiting Pluto quincunx natal Sun can express as refocusing personal power. This is the "Yoga of deepening awareness." One can learn valuable lessons in cleaning up the past. A wasteful person learns more respect for time and resources. A person finds emotional strength. Healing a damaged psyche or body is possible. Cleansing the mind, body, and spirit is not unusual. Physical or psychological healing can occur.

A taker may not be so quick to grab. A weak person learns to assume rightful power. A person can conquer desires that are harmful to mental and physical well being. One may tap into healing energy. Bonding with others can bring one into healing professions. A shy person may grow strong in expressing passion. A cold individual may become more loving. A tired person may find new vitality.

Progressed Sun opposing natal (or progressed) Pluto or transiting Pluto opposing natal Sun can denote a great depth in relating to others. Individuals may enjoy bonded relating due to sexual and emotional balance. Emotional intensity strengthens relationships. Partnerships of all kinds are based on trust and mutual respect. An individual may be an artful negotiator. Defending one's turf assertively wins respect from others. A charismatic nature may attract positive allies.

Individuals may find investors in their creative potentials. This can be a highly abundant period. A tremendous concentration on creative pursuits can bring success. One may stop projecting too much power onto others. A drive to express one's own feelings becomes of paramount importance. Being dominated may be a thing of the past. An overly dominating individual may relinquish some power. A person may gain insight into the motives of others. Relationships can be mutually rewarding. One need not provide all of the emotional strength or resources. A person may stop being too needy. Destructive relationship patterns can be ended. Behaviors related to over or under use of power can be transcended. Being shackled to addictive appetites is no longer a primary need. One may realize his finiteness and appreciate the gift of life. People can form a deep spiritual bond with the mysterious forces of the universe.

SHADOW

Both the **Sun/Pluto quincunx and opposition** can denote imbalanced power instincts. Possessiveness can manifest. Enslavement is possible as well. One can be led into the dark side of life. A desire to steal or lie can dominate. Individuals can go bankrupt emotionally or materially. Excess can be a way of life.

An inability to forgive keeps one attached to past relationships. Manipulation can be compulsive. A person may try to rule by aggression. A lack of trust keeps relationships on a superficial level. One may always seek to control situations. A need for simplicity is ignored. Life can be a series of crises. Living on the edge becomes a way of life. A need to leave worn-out behaviors is denied. Subconscious fears or irrational tendencies may lead one in circles. A life with no purpose leaves an empty feeling. An individual may constantly dump problems on others. An inability to change patterns exhausts others. One may need to stop making a lover or spouse his psychotherapist! Sexual odysseys may be substituted for real love. One may try to show self-worth through sexiness. A person may be trying to impress the wrong people.

SOFT ASPECTS

Sextile:	Progressed Sun Sextile Natal or Progressed Pluto
	Transiting Pluto Sextile Natal Sun
Trine:	Progressed Sun Trine Natal or Progressed Pluto
	Transiting Pluto Trine Natal Sun

LIGHT

Progressed Sun sextile natal (or progressed) Pluto or transiting Pluto sextile natal Sun can connote a person who finishes what is started. One may be excellent at repairing broken down things or people. One can help others get back on their feet. One may integrate intensity and enjoyment of life. One works ferociously yet knows when to rest. Individuals may make good managers of time and resources.

This can be a time of emotional fulfillment. The love nature can blossom. A silent positive attitude attracts an abundant life. Individuals may deal with past emotional conflicts. A proud person can learn to ask for help. An individual lacking pride finds confidence.

Progressed Sun trine natal (or progressed) Pluto or transiting Pluto trine natal Sun can denote a charismatic personality. One can be forceful, yet generous. An individual may be protective of others.

A person might be a good supervisor or leader — a dynamo of energy that stays under control. One may prove trustworthy, winning the loyalty of others. A deepening awareness of life's mysteries can emerge. A person can become fascinated with hidden forces. Mysticism and metaphysics could be studies of interest.

SHADOW

Both the **Sun/Pluto sextile and trine** can express as a sly manipulation of situations. Individuals can act helpless to attract sympathy and donations. Some individuals try to get away with crimes. They feel above the law. An all-powerful attitude causes poor assessment of situations.

An overly dependent nature may exist. One can get too attached to more powerful people. People might lack the drive to finish projects. A weak will brings frustration. Individuals may become too content. Boredom dulls the vitality. A big ego can hide emotional insecurity. Doing things to impress others does little for inner needs. Individuals may be emotionally starved, but do nothing to resolve loneliness.

DAWN

Sun/Pluto aspects can be dynamic chapters of enlightened consciousness. Hidden issues can be faced. Worn-out behaviors may be transcended. Mastering psychological intensity can regenerate a tired spirit. Creative vitality brings a new confidence. Karmic habits can be better understood. Penetrating subconscious instincts puts light on old conflicts. Unresolved power urges can be released. Personal power soars to new heights. The mysteries of life can be allies, rather than foreign voices in the dark.

MOON/MERCURY ASPECTS

Progressed Moon/Natal or Progressed Mercury
Progressed Mercury/Natal Moon

Process:	Balancing Intellect and Intuition
Ally:	Intuitive Perception
Illusion:	The Mind is Everything

Moon/Mercury aspects are an interesting pair. **Subconscious instincts and conscious perceptions combine.** Past impressions can greatly alter the present. Progressed Mercury can show us finding **new communication skills.** Individuals could find new mental plateaus. Old ideas and concepts may not hold together when challenged by the present. These aspects are a challenge to adaptability. Our intuitive strength can bolster our mental stability.

INTENSE ASPECTS

Conjunction: Progressed Moon Conjunct
Natal or Progressed Mercury
Progressed Mercury Conjunct Natal Moon

Square: Progressed Moon Square Natal or Progressed Mercury
Progressed Mercury Square Natal Moon

LIGHT

Progressed Moon conjunct natal (or progressed) Mercury or progressed Mercury conjunct natal Moon can denote increased feeling in one's thoughts. Intuition and mind can work forcefully together. **The conjunction dramatically brings together instincts and perception.**

Moods may become more objective. Those with sudden emotional outbursts may better channel this energy. A person can express more feelings. One's past can become a focal point. Childhood conflicts can be resolved. People may talk to parents or loved ones more easily. Feelings are discussed more openly. A secretive type can learn not to hide emotions. An overly reserved type can communicate more passionately. An analytical person can rely more on intuition. Practical mindedness can find comfort in a more subjective approach. An intellectual can find emotional clarity.

My father died on Halloween in October of 1989. He had been diagnosed with lung cancer a few months prior to his death. My progressed Moon (family and roots) in Scorpio was making an exact conjunction to my natal 8th house Mercury in Scorpio. (Transiting Pluto was conjunct my natal Mercury as well!) This was an intensely emotional period for me. My research of the death and dying experience helped me to accept my father's death. I still had a powerful grieving process to experience. The funeral was especially meaningful for me with my progressed Moon in Scorpio and in the 8th house, as both the sign and house deal with birth/ death/ rebirth. My mind (Mercury) was definitely in an introspective air space.

Progressed Moon square natal (or progressed) Mercury or progressed Mercury square natal Moon can symbolize a forceful display of intellect and emotion. One may follow through on perceptions. Security drives motivate a person to act. Changes can be stimulating. New learning experiences are attractive. Travel or changes of residence feel refreshing. An earthy type may break loose from too much routine. A watery type can find mental/intuitive insights. A fiery type might display more sensitivity. An air type might reveal her innermost feelings. People can break the grip of the past. Old behavior patterns can be replaced with new insightful tapes. New mental recordings transform worn-out thoughts.

SHADOW

Both the **Moon/Mercury conjunction and square** can manifest as a short memory span. Insights may be blinded by emotional insecurity. Relaxing into experiences can be difficult. A feeling of not being loved might bring loneliness. Emotional isolation due to oversensitivity to others can occur. An inability to communicate feelings creates disorientation. Worry over needless details can be irritating. One may lack concentration. Thoughts can dart from past to future. The present seems a vague mood. One's analytical nature might be too critical of self and others. A lack of intimacy can be disappointing. People fear closeness. Secrets of the past keep doors closed to emotional closeness. One may fear dependency. An overly dependent type could find this a disorienting time. Lovers move further away.

Quincunx: Progressed Moon Quincunx
Natal or Progressed Mercury
Progressed Mercury Quincunx Natal Moon

Opposition: Progressed Moon Opposing
Natal or Progressed Mercury
Progressed Mercury Opposing Natal Moon

LIGHT

Progressed Moon quincunx natal (or progressed) Mercury or progressed Mercury quincunx natal Moon can symbolize reflecting on subconscious thought patterns. This aspect is the **"Yoga of calming the mind."** Learning to channel emotional intensity is important. People can differentiate fact from imagination. Irrational ideas may be surrendered. Healthy affirmations can become a regular diet. Nervous exhaustion finds relief.

People may find security in clearer perceptions. A lack of trust due to misperceptions is overcome. Listening becomes a new skill. Less blaming, accusing and gossiping intensify creative energies. Jealousy can be channeled into more fruitful directions.

Progressed Moon opposing natal (or progressed) Mercury or progressed Mercury opposing the natal Moon can symbolize new lovers or intimate communication. Perceptions can be filled with intuitive clarity. One may attract what she needs. **One may better understand inner motivations**. New peers can be stimulating. Teachers and peers can help one find her way. Relationships may be mutually growth-promoting and full of cultural exchanges. An individual can excel in communication. Sensing the mood of an audience makes for a great speaker. One can make a good counselor. Talking and listening can be nicely balanced.

SHADOW
Both the **Moon/Mercury quincunx and opposition** can manifest as poor perception of others. One may attract the wrong people. Dependent individuals may attract cool and unfeeling people. Relationships may lack emotional stability or honesty. People may hear only what they wish to hear. Poor listening becomes a bad habit. Insecurity may keep conversations on an intellectual level. One may have trouble separating love and business. She may work too hard on changing people.

Poor concentration could interfere with listening. Day dreaming may distract one from everyday details. Worrying can deplete energy. Criticism can be compulsive. One may not trust her ability to communicate. A fear of criticism can repress ideas. A too passive nature may keep people emotionally isolated.

SOFT ASPECTS
Sextile: Progressed Moon Sextile Natal or Progressed Mercury
             Progressed Mercury Sextile Natal Moon

Trine: Progressed Moon Trine Natal or Progressed Mercury
             Progressed Mercury Trine Natal Moon

LIGHT
Progressed Moon sextile natal (or progressed) Mercury or progressed Mercury sextile natal Moon can connote awakening to new experiences. Individuals can seek new living situations and opportunities. People can show more flexibility. There can be less tension or conflict in life.

Progressed Moon trine natal (or progressed) Mercury or progressed Mercury trine the natal Moon can symbolize an ease with the environment. Feelings and thoughts flow harmoniously. A moody person may learn to relax; a serious person sees life has its ups and downs; a realist allows her mind to dream; a type "A" personality may find time for rest. The mind's new information is not fed with the force shown by hard aspects. People may tune into deep security needs. A person may get busy writing and creating. Intensity might find a natural flow.

SHADOW
Both the **Moon/Mercury sextile and trine** can indicate a false pretense of feeling secure. One may hide natural intensity. A lack of drive could occur. People can settle for situations that do not challenge intelligence. One may cling to old ideas. One could fear emotional intensity in others and overreact to tension in relationships. A person could misperceive the intentions of others. An individual might be easily deceived by compliments or surface appearances. One could lack insight.

DAWN
Moon/Mercury aspects can denote new emotional and mental comfort. A person may possess excellent listening skills. Her words put others at ease. Communication can be dynamic. Writing and speaking may excel. Conquering old self-defeating habits improves perceptions. One may relax into life. A person's home can be used as a place to share ideas.

MOON/VENUS ASPECTS

Progressed Moon/Natal or Progressed Venus Progressed Venus/Natal Moon

Process:	Inner Harmony
Ally:	Social Ease and Sense of Emotional Balance
Illusion:	Compulsive Desires

Moon/Venus aspects can be socially stimulating. Both planets indicate emotional themes. **The internal feminine is symbolized by these aspects**. Aesthetic impulses can awaken. Romantic longings can occur. A key theme is finding emotional security through finances or love.

INTENSE ASPECTS
Conjunction: Progressed Moon Conjunct Natal or Progressed Venus
Progressed Venus Conjunct Natal Moon

Square: Progressed Moon Square Natal or Progressed Venus
Progressed Venus Square Natal Moon

LIGHT
In both the **Moon/Venus conjunction and square**, a person can begin satisfying relationship urges. Relating needs may change. One may become more adept at expressing emotions. Passion can be expressed through the arts. One may tune into deep internal beauty. Self-satisfaction may result. An individual may feel in harmony with life.

A lonely individual may find love. A social type may find a special love relationship. A novice discovers a creative opportunity. A poverty-conscious individual creates a new abundance. A romantic can find true love in people and life in general. A person may reward herself for a life of hard work. Relationships with family can become closer. A more genuine caring is displayed. One may become more appreciative of support from others.

Karmic relationships can be indicated in this particular planetary pair. One could make peace with the past of this life. We can attract people with some of the same challenges and Karmic themes. This can be a great opportunity to find emotional clarity. We can begin understanding motives for relationships. Decorating a house or office can occur. Wearing more colorful clothing may brighten one's moods.

SHADOW

In both the **Moon/Venus conjunction and square**, a person can push too hard to satisfy relationship drives. Emotional confusion can lead to vague relating. Dependency needs can be out of balance. A person may depend too much on the emotional and physical resources of others. Aesthetic frustration may occur. One might have the talent but no audience. A place to market abilities is not available. Individuals may dwell too much on what they don't have.

One may ignore loved ones due to career motives. He may lack the depth to appreciate a solid relationship. Fixation on luxury and outer appearances seems more important than inner harmony. People could refuse to resolve past emotional problems. One may fear closeness. A desire to hide one's fears in sensual satisfaction can be limiting.

Quincunx: Progressed Moon Quincunx Natal or Progressed Venus
            Progressed Venus Quincunx Natal Moon

Opposition: Progressed Moon Opposing Natal or Progressed Venus
            Progressed Venus Opposing Natal Moon

LIGHT

Progressed Moon quincunx natal (or progressed) Venus or progressed Venus quincunx natal Moon can denote an individual making important adjustments in relating. A tendency to get lost in relationships can be overcome. This is the **"Yoga of finding emotional clarity."** Individuals can curb a compulsive need to cling to others. A fear of independence can be faced. People can confront a childhood fear of abandonment. People may take more care of their emotional well-being. Expectations of self and others become more reasonable. Individuals can find contentment and accept life at face value. One can work hard. A person may overcome obstacles to happiness in a career or business.

Progressed Moon opposing natal (or progressed) Venus or progressed Venus opposing the natal Moon can be a time of entering balanced relationships. Some tension is typical of an opposition. **Emotions can be charged! This can be a significant period in understanding one's deepest motives for a relationship**. One may become easier to know emotionally. People can get more intuitive. Individuals can learn to not be so sensitive; the callous individual can find a softer heart. This is a good aspect for business. Dealing with the public can flow with a sociable nature. Moods may become less volatile. A very intense individual may enter counseling. Forming friendships or allies outside of a primary relationship can be helpful. Intensity is spread out over many people. Feedback from others can give insights. One may forgive the past. A broken heart can find a new love. A courtship may become a marriage.

SHADOW

The **Moon/Venus quincunx or opposition** can be expressed as emotional pain. **One may make poor relationship choices.** A person may run away from himself. Relationships could result from emotional disorientation. A true bond is not formed. Neither partner is honest.

A past of not facing problems catches up. A person may smother others. He does not give the emotional distance needed. One could attract people with emotional problems. People can have difficulty believing they are lovable. Self-criticism dominates the inner voice. Individuals may waste resources. Overindulgence in food and drink can substitute for love.

Individuals can project their own finer qualities onto others. The partner must express beauty and emotion for the relationship. One may feel others have all the creative talent. Relationships can be based too much on appearances or sexual pleasure only. The depth needed to work through problems is lacking. A blaming attitude assumes that problems are caused by others.

One may live for their aesthetic abilities and have trouble caring for others. This could cause a feeling of separation in a relationship. A refusal to compromise is the real problem. Individuals can be restless. An eagerness to explore relationships could lead one away from an already fulfilling situation. Sexual fantasies could grow compulsive and block intimacy.

SOFT ASPECTS

Sextile: Progressed Moon Sextile Natal or Progressed Venus
Progressed Venus Sextile Natal Moon

Trine: Progressed Moon Trining Natal or Progressed Venus
Progressed Venus Trining Natal Moon

LIGHT

Progressed Moon sextile natal (or progressed) Venus or progressed Venus sextile natal Moon can be new social encounters. One may satisfy creative talents. A new objectivity regarding relationships is possible. This can be a productive period. Business enterprises could be quite successful. A versatility in relating can increase social circles. Residing in different locations could bring contact with many new peers.

Progressed Moon trine natal (or progressed) Venus or progressed Venus trine natal Moon can mark an appreciation for the little things in life. One who overlooked receiving or giving affection can change attitudes. A softening of the love nature is possible. A low spirit finds a new high. One may attract harmony with intuitive ease.

Emotions can fill with a powerful idealism. One may be a good counselor. Tuning into moods of others is an art. People may find harmonious places to live. Peace of mind and creative expression are fulfilled.

SHADOW
The Moon/Venus sextile or trine can denote a lunar type lost in a solar world. One may lack the willpower to fulfill dreams. Subjective ideals may be hidden from the world. People may fear rejection or criticism. Individuals may give up on relationships or careers too soon. An inability to cope with conflict causes one to quit. People may always wear a happy face. They might mask true feelings. A refusal to deal with situations openly can be frustrating.

One could be a hopeless romantic. Infatuation could lead to strange relationships. One may be looking for folk heroes and heroines rather than real people. People may give too much energy to others. Their lunar nature is called upon constantly to be a parent. Being the helper leads to emotional exhaustion.

DAWN
Moon/Venus aspects can denote a highly intuitive nature. One can have both a home and harmony in the world. Relationships can be emotionally balanced. Our emotions get reflective in these aspects. Life can fill with deep abundant experiences.

MOON/MARS ASPECTS

Progressed Moon/Natal or Progressed Mars
Progressed Mars/Natal Moon

Process:	Acting on Intuition
Ally:	Embracing Sensitivity and Courage
Illusion:	Emotional Outbursts

Moon/Mars aspects can denote emotional outpouring of energies. There is an element of tension in these aspects. The inner self can fight to take action. Struggles can be more with the self than outer challenges. Assertion can be an attempt to find clear reflections of the self in the world.

INTENSE ASPECTS
Conjunction: Progressed Moon Conjunct Natal or Progressed Mars
Progressed Mars Conjunct Natal Moon

Square: Progressed Moon Square Natal or Progressed Mars
Progressed Mars Square Natal Moon

LIGHT
Progressed Moon conjunct natal (or progressed) Mars or progressed Mars conjunct natal Moon can denote a deeper sense of

one's identity. When Mars combines with any water planet (Moon, Neptune, or Pluto), hidden emotional undercurrents can be at work. A passive person can become more assertive; a moody type more willing to act than brood. Unfeeling types may become more emotional. The macho tendencies of fiery Mars are softened by the nurturing qualities of the watery Moon. A person with repressed anger may release it. Blocked energy is freed and directed more creatively. Progressed Mars square natal (or progressed) Moon or progressed Moon square natal Mars can point to a warrior becoming a leader of a family, community, or nation. A follower may question cultural or role models. Sexually fearful individuals can become more adventurous. The taboos taught by family or culture no longer shackle. One may confront others more directly. Anger is no longer a feared emotion. Intuition can be forcefully released. Love and passion for life bring success, joy, and fulfillment. In both the conjunction and the square, an athlete may enjoy popular appeal. Courage and meeting life directly are natural instincts.

SHADOW

The **Moon/Mars conjunction or square** can indicate a bullying energy. One may try to dominate others. Physical and emotional force may get too aggressive. Moods may lack logic. One may jump quickly to wrong assumptions. Emotions may be angrily attached to the past. The past is blamed for problems. A lack of childhood support can be a painful, unresolved memory.

There can be self-hatred. One may see life as empty. A lack of closeness with others is painful to face. One may sit in a helpless mindset. Insights seem lacking. Emotions are drained. People can waste energy. They may compulsively move into new situations. Bridges are burned too hastily. A lack of emotional stability frustrates opportunities. A territorial consciousness can block out others. Insecurity may drive people crazily to prove they are winners. Individuals can have an identity crisis. A lack of reflection keeps one a stranger to herself. Impatience with self and loved ones can be tremendous. Angry outbursts may create tension on the home front. A lack of sensitivity and objectivity makes a "mountain out of a molehill." A failure to talk out problems adds fuel to the fire.

Quincunx: Progressed Moon Quincunx Natal or Progressed Mars
Progressed Mars Quincunx Natal Moon

Opposition: Progressed Moon Opposing Natal or Progressed Mars
Progressed Mars Opposing Natal Moon

LIGHT

Progressed Moon quincunx natal (or progressed) Mars or progressed Mars quincunx the natal Moon can denote a new courage in relating to others. Romantic relationships can have a rich balance of give-and-take. Each partner can show a mutual respect. The Moon/Mars quincunx is the **"Yoga of finding emotional intensity."** One consciously strengthens identity. Intuition and assertion become powerful allies. One may overcome emotional problems. A need for constant protection by stronger mates is transcended. A person may conquer irrational fears. A person desperately clinging to others finds freedom. Someone tied to parental strings may take the initiative to follow a new path. People no longer dwell on the past.

Progressed Moon opposing natal (or progressed) Mars or progressed Mars opposing the natal Moon can indicate a secure identity. One is not threatened by closeness. A good listener can be indicated. An individual may know how to deal with angry people. Body language can be read well. Relationships can share nurturing, passion, and new circumstances. Problems are cleaned up through listening and hard work.

Anger may be expressed spontaneously. Reading situations as they unfold can help avoid problems. One may deal well with pressure situations. One may express more compassion. A short-tempered individual can develop sensitivity. A selfish individual expresses more support for others.

SHADOW

The **Moon/Mars quincunx or opposition** can express as a lack of continuity. One may be unreliable. A poor finisher can be indicated. A lack of initiative can rest on emotional fears. One may give too much power away. Clinging to the identities of others limits growth. Illnesses due to emotional confusion are possible. A person may waste a lot of impulsive energy. A lack of inner stability is reflected in a chaotic outer life.

Individuals may leave behind a trail of broken hearts. Selfishness and impatience disrupt relationships. One may take too much anger out on loved ones. Holding onto anger can interfere with situations. One may lack insight into present relationships due to unresolved anger. Passive people can be dominated. Strong dependency needs can keep one in limiting relationships. One may allow others to do either all of the asserting or nurturing. A person can move too quickly, with little understanding. Instant gratification brings a shallow existence. A person may have trouble settling down, constantly digging up the roots.

SOFT ASPECTS

Sextile:	Progressed Moon Sextile Natal or Progressed Mars
	Progressed Mars Sextile Natal Moon
Trine:	Progressed Moon Trining Natal or Progressed Mars
	Progressed Mars Trining Natal Moon

LIGHT

Progressed Moon sextile natal (or progressed) Mars or progressed Mars sextile natal Moon can denote ease in releasing emotional intensity. Intuition and assertion combine harmoniously. A shy individual can more spontaneously show his true nature. A hardened person may learn to feel again. A down individual may reach a new emotional high. One's past may be resolved in the present. Past fears no longer hold one back. A loner can find room for others. A self-centered person can take more notice of others.

Progressed Moon trine natal (or progressed) Mars or progressed Mars trine the natal Moon can indicate a greater internal security. Personal identity and security drives become mutually reinforcing. Risks can occur. One may courageously support loved ones. A person can feel especially at home with himself. An acceptance of the past can heal old wounds. A moody and angry person may lighten up. A less serious life attitude creates new options.

SHADOW

In both the **progressed Moon/Mars sextile and trine**, one may expect too much from others. One may need excessive support. A tendency to take and not give can be limiting.

One may not save for a rainy day. Ignoring security needs can be a problem. "Let's live for today" could be extreme. An inner restlessness can keep one from settling down. Individuals might carelessly take love from others. People may be unable to commit or "tied to parental strings." Dependency needs keep one from finding new growth-promoting situations. One could smother others.

DAWN

Moon/Mars aspects can be a time of self-assured identity. Intuition and assertion promote growth. Family and individual identity combine in a whole person. One may tune into anger patterns. A passion for life is expressed clearly and lovingly. One may know when to be passive and when to take charge.

MOON/JUPITER ASPECTS

Progressed Moon/Natal or Progressed Jupiter Transiting Jupiter/Natal Moon

Process:	Expanded Comfort Zones
Ally:	"A Past Full of Wonderful Memories"
Illusion:	Life Requires No Effort

Moon/Jupiter aspects can have a dreamlike quality. One may live many visions on inner levels. A writer or someone with a good sense of the public can emerge. There can be a longing to live in new locations.

An innate sense of justice can make one fair minded and even-tempered.

INTENSE ASPECTS
Conjunction: Progressed Moon Conjunct Natal or Progressed Jupiter
Transiting Jupiter Conjunct Natal Moon
Square: Progressed Moon Square Natal or Progressed Jupiter
Transiting Jupiter Square Natal Moon

LIGHT
Progressed Moon conjunct natal (or progressed) Jupiter or transiting Jupiter conjunct the natal Moon can denote emotional comfort. The faith to answer a life challenge can occur. Relocation for learning purposes and to find new opportunity is not unusual. There can be a new spiritual conviction. Finding roots may bring emotional security. Individuals might go back to their past. A new understanding of past conflicts can be freeing; creating roots with a meaningful past brings a new understanding.

Progressed Moon square natal (or progressed) Jupiter or transiting Jupiter square the natal Moon can denote a passion for challenges. New learning possibilities can occur. In the Moon/Jupiter conjunction or square, **travel can soothe the soul.** A person lacking reflective qualities may find more sensitivity. An individual lacking principles may find more self-honesty. Individuals lacking self-confidence can believe in themselves. Individuals may go beyond current security zones. A new enterprising spirit could lead to financial success.

SHADOW
In both the Moon/Jupiter conjunction and square, a lack of focus can be exhibited. People can recklessly move in and out of situations. Restless impulses can lead to constant change. One may lack the courage to follow through on commitments. People can hide in a fantasy world.

Individuals may have fixed opinions. Old biases learned as a child may dominate the present. Loyalty to worn out ideas can be limiting. A person may live freedom on the inside only. A passive attitude may leave one in stagnating situations. Security could be foolishly gambled away. One may lack common sense. Individuals may disregard the property of others. One may use people. This can point to a con artist.

Quincunx: Progressed Moon Quincunx
Natal or Progressed Jupiter
Transiting Jupiter Quincunx Natal Moon

Opposition: Progressed Moon Opposing
Natal or Progressed Jupiter
Transiting Jupiter Opposing Natal Moon

LIGHT
Progressed Moon quincunx natal (or progressed) Jupiter or transiting Jupiter quincunx natal Moon can denote a new optimism in relating to others. An individual may express feelings. A lighter life attitude can calm an oversensitive nature. This quincunx is the **"Yoga of gaining emotional understanding."** This can be a period of settling down. A wanderer may search for roots. A stay-at-home type can look for more terrain to explore. An overly type "A" personality can learn to slow down. A serious individual finds a sense of humor. A gambler takes fewer risks.

Progressed Moon opposing natal (or progressed) Jupiter or transiting Jupiter opposing the natal Moon can point to a good counselor. Empathy and sound judgment can be shown. People can help others find confidence. One may put others at ease. Relating can become more spontaneous. Individuals share more of their emotional wealth. A closed person may open to new encounters. More expansive relationships can occur.

Individuals may attract relationships that strengthen faith. Security through honest communication is possible. People may allow themselves the freedom to fall in love. Travel to inspiring places makes people feel more positive. Learning experiences are exciting!

SHADOW
In both the Moon/Jupiter quincunx and opposition, individuals may have trouble with real issues. Living life on a romantic level seems more convenient. Excuses and rationalizations mask insecurities. A fear of losing freedom causes one to run from commitment. One may display a short attention span. Forgetting friends and lovers could become a continuous pattern. Individuals can be too compulsive for attention and acceptance.

SOFT ASPECTS
Sextile: Progressed Moon Sextile Natal or Progressed Jupiter
Transiting Jupiter Sextile Natal Moon

Trine: Progressed Moon Trining Natal or Progressed Jupiter
Transiting Jupiter Trining Natal Moon

LIGHT
Progressed Moon sextile natal (or progressed) Jupiter or transiting Jupiter sextile natal Moon can indicate overcoming worries. New enthusiasm for the present and future are possible. New areas of study can lead one into growth-promoting situations. Spiritual

well-being can manifest. One may find a new security. Material wealth and property ownership can occur. This can be a very resourceful aspect. Positive attitudes can attract success.

Progressed Moon trine natal (or progressed) Jupiter or transiting Jupiter trine natal Moon can denote a greater faith in self. Security instincts may feel insulated by positive attitudes. Love and compassion flow naturally. A person with a narrow life philosophy might discover a more eclectic approach. A depressed person may find a ray of hope. A person with no faith develops a belief in a higher power. Travel can be enlightening. Leaving the local environment can bring insight and new understanding. The trine is Jupiter's natural aspect. Security through expansive approaches could lead to new faith. People can inspire confidence in others.

SHADOW
In both the Moon/Jupiter sextile and trine, people can act on blind faith. Intuition may lack common sense. Individuals may surround themselves with too much external wealth. A lack of spiritual or intuitive understanding brings insecurity. A shallow life understanding can lead to narrow opinions. People may exhibit a lack of discipline. Ambition may go to sleep. **The trine can be especially passive. The sextile can be a scattered display of energies.** Individuals may have a lot of unfocused emotional excitement.

DAWN
Moon/Jupiter aspects can reflect an inner certainty. Security instincts can rest safely upon an emotional calm. If one can overcome too much passivity, great things can be accomplished. Positive attitudes can attract a rich life full of emotional and material security. **A key to Moon/Jupiter aspects is not taking too much for granted.** Individuals can draw energy from a love-filled past.

MOON/SATURN ASPECTS

Progressed Moon/Natal or Progressed Saturn
Transiting Saturn/Natal Moon

Process:	Stretching Comfort Zones
Ally:	Stable Emotional Nature
Illusion:	Negative Consciousness

In Moon/Saturn aspects one is testing the waters of her comfort zones. One is challenged by the sometimes turbulent demands of **life's realities**. Combining security instincts with challenges in the growth process is a basic theme. **Developing inner strength and trusting one's intuition can be key allies.** Issues related to intimacy, emotional expression, sensitivity, and parents can be accentuated.

INTENSE ASPECTS

Conjunction: Progressed Moon Conjunct Natal or Progressed Saturn
Transiting Saturn Conjunct Natal Moon

Square: Progressed Moon Square Natal or Progressed Saturn
Transiting Saturn Square Natal Moon

LIGHT

Progressed Moon conjunct natal (or progressed) Saturn or transiting Saturn conjunct the natal Moon can symbolize a person is learning to trust intuition. One can make an important life commitment. The focus may be on home, parents, children, relationship and even career. **The underlying focus is often associated with trust.** One may conquer a fear of relating to others. A healing or reconciling of past wounds can occur.

One can direct this very intense emotional energy into solid accomplishments. This can be a person who is facing a life of too much dependency. An individual sometimes can break into feelings of self-confidence previously lacking. **Moon/Saturn aspects have a serious nature.** It can be a sobering experience. A new self-respect can occur. **The element of one's natal Moon** is important to consider if aspected by transiting Saturn (or the **element of progressed Moon** aspecting natal or progressed Saturn). A fire Moon may gain focus for its enthusiasm. An earth Moon may gain wisdom for its practicality. An air Moon may obtain increased depth for ideas. A water Moon may find roots for its ideals.

Progressed Moon square natal (or progressed) Saturn or transiting Saturn square the natal Moon can denote an individual learning to focus emotional intensity. She can forcefully mold her life to meet intuitive insights. Individuals may deal with childhood situations. The Moon is indicative of a person's childhood memories. Working through past childhood encounters can become a strong drive. A person can successfully deal with pain produced by past relationships with parents, friends, or lovers. Moon/Saturn aspects can be very therapeutic. Insights into one's self-destructive habits can occur. Compulsive energy can be directed into productive goals. Business sense is heightened. Starting new cycles is indicated.

SHADOW

In both the **Moon/Saturn conjunction and square**, an individual can lack inner security. She can assume too much responsibility. Parenting others can be extreme, as can being too dependent. An individual may grow cold and difficult to understand. Clear reflective insights are sacrificed to self-hating thoughts. One may feel depressed and out of options.

Intuition may be blocked by fears. This can alter perceptions of reality. Imagination misperceives people and situations. A lack of trust is often the underlying problem. An individual may compulsively control the environment. One may feel life is a punishment. Instead of experiencing life as a challenge, it is felt as an imposed set of conditions.

Quincunx: Progressed Moon Quincunx Natal or Progressed Saturn
              Transiting Saturn Quincunx Natal Moon

Opposition: Progressed Moon Opposing Natal Or Progressed Saturn
              Transiting Saturn Opposing Natal Moon

LIGHT

Progressed Moon quincunx natal (or progressed) Saturn or transiting Saturn quincunx natal Moon can symbolize deep mood changes. A person may solve a personal crisis. This aspect is the **"Yoga of comfort zone stretching."** One may tolerate more stress and hard work. Tasks that previously tired the individual seem less taxing. Karmic material may surface from one's subconscious. An ability to intuit limiting past-life themes can occur. A person may use this insight to balance a current life pattern.

The **progressed Moon opposing natal (or progressed) Saturn or transiting Saturn opposing natal Moon denotes redefining intimate relationships.** Also, learning how to flow with **authority figures** is indicated. This can feel like a Karmic time period linked to repeating past life themes. Relationships with others may help a person break through old, destructive patterns. An individual can strengthen intuitive power. She may be more balanced in **taking responsibility in a relationship.** She can become more adept at working through conflict in relationships. One may truly recognize the need for a committed relationship. Fear of relating intimately can be conquered. Relationships with parents can be resolved. This aspect can remind one that a parent is getting older. Time is running out to resolve a conflict or past wound. One may gain a great appreciation for her parents or the elderly.

One can form a different relationship with career. More time relaxing away from work demands can occur. Delegating responsibility to others is accomplished. Some individuals can enjoy the rewards of hard work. Patience and endurance finally pay dividends. Profits create more free time to explore other creative areas. **One may feel driven to change careers in any of the intensity-promoting aspects of Moon/Saturn**. A person may seek either more challenging situations or a position that offers more security or even less pressure.

SHADOW

In the **Moon/Saturn quincunx or opposition,** an individual can interface the security themes of the watery Moon with the control themes of Saturn. **There can be extreme worry.** Intimacy issues may arise. A person's fear of closeness can keep meaningful relationships from continuing. Saturn can symbolize blocking the flow of feelings. Unresolved internal conflicts concerning past relations with others are often the source of the problem. One may project old issues onto new partners.

An individual may misuse authoritarian urges. Control rather than equal footing is sought. A person can be afraid to take responsibility. The individual may fear failure or making decisions. She can project capabilities onto a partner perceived as wiser and stronger. A person can be a hermit. She only feels comfortable in isolation. Her feelings can be denied. Mistrust of authority figures can arise. Sometimes people get impatient with those closest to them. One can grow too sensitive to criticism or opinions of family members.

A person may feel peers, authority figures, lovers, or spouses are taking up all of their time with demands. One may have trouble separating the truth of the situation due to emotional exhaustion. A person may become too self-critical. A fear of growing old and undesirable may be a compulsive problem. One may be very sensitive to cultural attitudes. One's overall insecurity may lead them into limiting decisions. A person can be still attached to a relationship that already has ended. The individual fears letting go of the past. Memories of the relationship are unrealistic, only the good times are remembered.

Individuals can experience conflict between home and career. Avoiding personal problems through work can occur. One may ignore the home front.

SOFT ASPECTS

Sextile: Progressed Moon Sextile Natal or Progressed Saturn
            Transiting Saturn Sextile Natal Moon

Trine: Progressed Moon Trining Natal or Progressed Saturn
            Transiting Saturn Trining Natal Moon

LIGHT

Progressed Moon sextile natal (or progressed) Saturn or transiting Saturn sextile natal Moon symbolizes accomplishing much success. One may be active in community affairs.

A person may conquer a stressful situation and enjoy the psychological freedom to move ahead. She can follow through to bring a much needed change. One's everyday life may be rewarding. A feeling of accomplishment may stimulate one to even greater heights. Responsibility which previously seemed limiting or confining now seems enjoyable.

Progressed Moon trine natal (or progressed) Saturn or transiting Saturn trine natal Moon suggests finding the confidence to be more affectionate. A new faith in one's intuition and ability to be intimate may occur. A person may feel safer than usual.

Instead of fighting for new situations, an individual learns to be persuasive. Tuning into life's flow is more natural. Organizing one's time may seem effortless. One may conquer a depressing mood or feelings of inadequacy. A more positive feeling can dominate. A person trusts individuals rather than always suspecting an ulterior motive. Comfort and responsibility may hit an all-time high. An individual may work smarter. One can let go of a compulsive drive for control.

SHADOW

In both the **Moon/Saturn sextile and trine**, a person may lack a deep enough intuitive nature. She may be confused by new situations. Too much indecision or procrastination may result. Timing can be terrible. Limits may be hard to define. An unreliable nature can be exhibited. The person could be forgetful. She could be very nervous and unable to deal with deadlines.

An overdependence on parents can exist. The parents may provide too much care for the individual. She still looks for peers and lovers to be parent figures. The passiveness associated with the softer aspects can be particularly **frustrating in Moon/Saturn aspects**. The softer aspects can denote a sleeping nature that finds conflict too emotionally upsetting. A person can fear dealing with new endeavors or tense situations.

DAWN

Moon/Saturn aspects can be expressed as a dynamic polarity. Trusting our intuition can lead to good timing. Painful memories that block feelings of intimacy can be conquered. Life can be a balance of imagination and responsibility. Small successes can be the roots of great accomplishments.

MOON/URANUS ASPECTS

Progressed Moon/Natal or Progressed Uranus Transiting Uranus/Natal Moon

Process:	Independence vs. Closeness
Ally:	A Secure Vision
Illusion:	Emotional Roller Coaster Rides

Moon/Uranus aspects have strong emotional undercurrents. One may combine emotional intensity with mental perception to tune into future goals. A person often confronts security issues. Developing emotional clarity in relationships and dealing with dependency needs are potential themes. An inner restlessness may be the stimulus to seek a higher awareness.

INTENSE ASPECTS

Conjunction: Progressed Moon Conjunct Natal or Progressed Uranus
Transiting Uranus Conjunct Natal Moon

Square: Progressed Moon Square Natal or Progressed Uranus
Transiting Uranus Square Natal Moon

LIGHT

The **progressed Moon conjunct natal (or progressed) Uranus or transiting Uranus conjunct natal Moon** can denote balancing dependency and individuality. **One may have an especially clear intuition about future goals.** Individuals can act on impulses. A person may trust instincts and more easily adjust to changing situations. An individual can gain objective awareness concerning a particular situation. **The sobering and detached mental themes of airy Uranus can balance the watery emotional Moon.** Extreme mood swings may be avoided.

One may feel a refreshing flow in life. A person may communicate emotions more spontaneously. One may resolve confusion concerning childhood. Breaking through an emotional block may lead to clarity. Integrating past memories helps alleviate mental confusion. Relocating may fit the needs of future goals.

Progressed Moon square natal (or progressed) Uranus or transiting Uranus square the natal Moon often symbolizes resolving an emotional/mental conflict. One may find a new security in making decisions and initiating actions. One may work through intense emotional outbursts. She can let go of the past and stop holding grudges. A person may break away from limiting habits. The objectivity of the mentally alert Uranus can denote a person is more secure with her surroundings. One may boldly leave existing comfort zones and explore new territory.

SHADOW

In both the **Moon/Uranus conjunction and square** individuals can be emotionally unpredictable. Sudden outbursts can occur. Emotional distance and closeness may struggle. People can lack insight into feelings. A separation from oneself may be reflected in a scattered existence. Eccentric tastes can alienate others. Extreme independence makes cooperation difficult. Caring for others may be a struggle.

Insecure individuals can lack self-confidence. Clinging to secure situations can hurt growth potential. A fear of change creates tension. Nerves can seem uncontrollable. Perhaps a need to tune into emotions is ignored. People can be difficult to understand. Mood swings could be extreme. Lows and highs appear intolerant of a middle ground.

Quincunx: Progressed Moon Quincunx Natal or Progressed Uranus
Transiting Uranus Quincunx Natal Moon

Opposition: Progressed Moon Opposing Natal or Progressed Uranus
Transiting Uranus Opposing Natal Moon

LIGHT

Progressed Moon quincunx natal (or progressed) Uranus or transiting Uranus quincunx the natal Moon is the "Yoga of mood awareness." A person may instinctively tap into moods before emotional upsets. One can be more reflective and intimate with oneself. One may stop overintellectualizing feelings.

Progressed Moon opposing natal (or progressed) Uranus or transiting Uranus opposing the natal Moon can denote a warmer emotional expression. The cold exterior of Uranus is softened by the Moon. **Balancing vulnerability and individuality can become a key theme.** A person can display a new depth in **communicating feelings.** Selfishness may be transformed into an awareness of others. A global or collective intuition may develop.

An individual may become adept in being true to needs for dependency and freedom. A new cooperation can occur in a relationship that has been plagued with emotional confusion. One may get better at anticipating the moods of partners. He may communicate and act to avoid unnecessary upsets. This is usually an aspect full of emotional surprises! Rebellious urges are strong. One's private life is intensified.

SHADOW

The **Moon/Uranus quincunx or opposition** can be expressed as extreme emotions. A person can move constantly on raw impulse. This period can feel totally draining. Emotional upsets bring instability into the domestic environment.

One's soul can awaken to new growth. One can gain insight into emotions and even Karmic patterns. However, a person may experience paranoia, fear and exhaustion rather than growth. A fear of intimacy can ruin many good relationships. **Intense aspects formed by any planet to Uranus can denote experimentation.** Moon/Uranus aspects can be quite sensual with a fondness for sudden romances. The excitement of the initial sparks attract the individual to relationships. Stability can be a challenge as both the Moon and Uranus denote changeability and impulsiveness. One can get bored with stability and make numerous changes. It can be problematic if one is often digging up the seeds before they have a chance to come to fruition.

Individuals can attract interesting but difficult relationships. One might fall in love with married partners, ensuring that the relationship has limited intimacy. The individual may find it difficult to concentrate on one person for a great length of time. A nihilistic nature can be exhibited. Individuals can need too much emotional intensity. Moods and emotional outbursts may be compulsive addictions which prevent closeness. One may avoid dealing with past emotional problems, but new relationships bring up the same unresolved issues. A person may grow too dependent upon others. A tendency to smother the freedom of others can occur. One may fear his own space.

SOFT ASPECTS
Sextile: Progressed Moon Sextile Natal or Progressed Uranus
Transiting Uranus Sextile Natal Moon

Trine: Progressed Moon Trining Natal or Progressed Uranus
Transiting Uranus Trining Natal Moon

LIGHT

Progressed Moon sextile natal (or progressed) Uranus or transiting Uranus sextile natal Moon can symbolize exciting new security. Living in a new environment or feeling excited by the challenge of new situations can take place. An individual may feel a new mental clarity. In the soft aspects, one may enjoy an invigorating mental flow.

Progressed Moon trine natal (or progressed) Uranus or transiting Uranus trine the natal Moon can point to excitable future plans. One's imagination and goals may spark new ideas. One may slow down in pace and still accomplish much. Learning to relax into situations can be an experiment. One can sense the soul and deep reasoning powers. There can be a drive to communicate visions and feelings. One may be popular amongst various subcultures. He is eager to understand their needs and inner motivations. One yearns to understand the primal roots that make a group have certain beliefs and goals.

SHADOW

In both the **Moon/Uranus sextile and trine**, a person can be too dependent on attention from others. One may expect more than others can deliver. One may be too attached to parents, spouse, children, or other family members. A person can be afraid of making decisions without family approval. A "going with the flow" mentality can make one weak on making decisions.

A person may make a great socializer. The emotional depth that naturally permeates the intense aspects may be lacking. One may grow uncomfortable with deep discussions. One may lack insight into thoughts. A person may not have the sensitivity or courage to give support to others. A timidity may limit one's spontaneous interactions with people. A person may restlessly move from one friendship, career, or relationship to another. A lack of focus or discipline can drive one to escape the present. A life with no ties may be lonely.

DAWN

Moon/Uranus aspects can express as spontaneous intuition. One may clearly envision the future. These aspects represent a heightened emotional intensity. One can feel driven to new horizons. **Vulnerabil-**

ity and mental detachment can be balanced in one's relationships. A person can experience the best of both worlds. One could tap into the collective pulse rate of one's culture. By working on resolving emotional conflicts and fears, a tremendous depth in self-understanding can be attained.

MOON/NEPTUNE ASPECTS

Progressed Moon/Natal or Progressed Neptune Transiting Neptune/Natal Moon

Process:	Search for Perfection
Ally:	Intuitive Faith
Illusion:	Living in a Dream World

Moon/Neptune aspects denote the most intuitive combination in planetary aspects. Each water planet (Moon, Neptune, and Pluto) is associated with our deepest subjective thoughts. The water planets, signs and houses symbolize many of our past-life memories. The Moon points to childhood experiences such as relating with family members, especially the mother.

A divine discontent can drive one to aesthetic accomplishments. The sensitivity of the Moon combined with the intuitive vision of Neptune can symbolize unusual talent in music, art, dance, etc. The meaning of symbols (as in dreams or astrology) can be translated.

Relationship awareness seems to play a big part in Moon/Neptune aspects. The security strings of the Moon are played by the romantic love images of Neptune. Individuals may form romantic attachments to creative works or hobbies. One can embrace both personal and universal love. Some people devote much time to spiritual interests or collective causes.

There may be self-deception. A person can hide within the walls of a fantasy world. One might deny reality. Escapism can reach extreme levels.

INTENSE ASPECTS
Conjunction: Progressed Moon Conjunct
Natal or Progressed Neptune
Transiting Neptune Conjunct Natal Moon

Square: Progressed Moon Square
Natal or Progressed Neptune
Transiting Neptune Square Natal Moon

LIGHT
The progressed Moon conjunct natal (or progressed) Neptune or transiting Neptune conjunct the natal Moon can indicate a

flowing expression of love. A person can comfort others. An aloof person can learn sensitivity. An individual may go beyond disorientation to a higher awareness. She can sense the mood of others with unusual skill.

An individual may establish a deeper relationship with herself. There can be soul searching. A person can look for deeper meaning and purpose. A very inwardly-directed individual may tune into past-life themes. One may consciously begin changing Karmic behaviors. Too much dependency may be balanced by spending time alone. An insensitive individualist may show more caring. Escapism may be transcended by establishing roots. A person may decide to express more creativity in her life.

A person may create a more harmonious home environment. A restless soul may tune into her inner motivations. She could direct emotional intensity more consciously.

Progressed Moon square natal (or progressed) Neptune or transiting Neptune square the natal Moon may symbolize breaking through addictive habits. A person might find a new faith in herself. One may pour emotional intensity into a new inspiration or become emotionally clear and strong. An individual may break through an emotional conflict by meeting real challenges.

Individuals can go beyond a personal love attachment. The forcefulness of the square can indicate an intense spiritual search. One may express aesthetic talents. A keen interest in alternative health practices is possible. Moon/Neptune aspects can highlight the child in us with an urge for spontaneity and simplicity. Communication is more with bodily language than verbal. In leaving a rigid or too familiar old self behind, a person may find this an exciting time period.

SHADOW
In both the **Moon/Neptune conjunction and square**, a person can feel life is useless. She can see through situations before they develop. One may miss creative options by not following through with intuition. **Divine discontent can keep one from trying.** One's standards may be too high. A too-universal outlook blocks a commitment to any one focus. A person can be dissatisfied due to self-criticism. She can turn to self-denial. The emotional waters are subtle but powerful. People may do anything to silence these feelings: substance abuse, sleep, or food can be used as escapes. People can resist a higher consciousness.

One's imagination can run away from her. Discipline and focus are greatly needed. A person can feel pulled into too many directions. One may have too many lovers, dreams, or escapes happening simultaneously. A powerful magnetism can attract relationships and the muse gods. Be careful what you ask into your life!

Quincunx: Progressed Moon Quincunx Natal or Progressed Neptune
Transiting Neptune Quincunx Natal Moon

Opposition: Progressed Moon Opposing Natal or Progressed Neptune
Transiting Neptune Opposing Natal Moon

LIGHT

**Progressed Moon quincunx natal (or progressed) Neptune or
transiting Neptune quincunx the natal Moon can be a deep inner experience.** One learns to love despite physical circumstances.
This can be a season of gaining faith. Intuitive clarity emanates from
emotional harmony. This is the **"Yoga of one hand clapping."** One
learns to leave the past behind and to see deeply into moods. A person
can be spiritually strong. An intuitive strength may help resolve a crisis.

One can stop depending excessively on others. A person might experience higher values without a lot of advice from peers. She may need
more space than usual to explore new insights. A person could gain
control over a compulsive drive to be protected or loved. She may become more conscious of moods that throw reasoning out of balance. Self-
defeating relationships and experiences may be transcended.

**The progressed Moon opposing natal (or progressed) Nep-
tune or transiting Neptune opposing the natal Moon can denote conquering escapism.** One can relate on exceptionally deep levels. An individual can develop new relating skills. A more compassionate and sensitive nature can be exhibited. **People can find new dimensions of romantic love.** They may be more understanding of others. A deeper level of intimacy may be desired. One may transcend a
fear of relationships through new faith.

An unusual intuition about people or events is possible. Sensing
the moods and needs of others can become an art. A person can show
versatility in relating. One can become an excellent counselor or teacher. One's sensitivity could be attractive to others. An individual may be
pulled to people who inspire growth. An attraction to musicians, artists, or individuals in the metaphysical field may open up new understanding. A highly aware person may experience life as a play. A less
serious attitude may develop. An individual can become more aware of
thoughts and feelings in relationships. A capacity to watch or reflect
may develop.

One's tolerance for conflict can go much higher. Imagining a greater situation keeps one working through present difficulties. Love for
others may deepen. One can see through everyday hassles and capture
the real person. One can let go of compulsive fears. A person may interact with people who challenge her escapism. She may balance emotional intensity with a more stable perspective. Deep insecurity can be transcended.

A person can feel as through she is in a movie. One can see how finite is her physical form, sensing how infinite is the soul. Individuals can feel they have found their way home. It can be a turbulent and disorienting time period. People can sense a new depth. **The Moon/Neptune aspects are some of the deepest soul-felt journeys experienced!**

SHADOW
In the **Moon/Neptune quincunx or opposition,** a person can experience emotional confusion like never before. One's energy centers can totally open. An individual may put too much devotion into another person. Her own growth could be neglected. She may overprotect others or be the helpless individual. Emotional energy can be denied. A fear of intuition or closeness can occur. People may fear experiences that cannot be explained rationally.

In a male's chart this opposition can be a denial of his inner feminine (known in Jungian psychology as the *anima*). A person can expect female partners to be the ideal embodiment of beauty. Partners are expected to express all emotions in the relationship. Either sex can project their own talents onto others. Such relationships are way out of balance. One feels used and not respected. Escapism can be center stage. Commitments appear as enemies. Endless excuses and avoidance behaviors continue. One can fall in love repeatedly with substance abusers and escape artists. Relationships can be draining.

Idealism could be a problem. One's dreams may be too easily shattered. Expectations can be impossible to fulfill. A person's idealism for lovers and peers can lead to frustrating circumstances. Finding contentment with self and others can be testy. Moods may be unstable. A person could jump to conclusions about others. There can be criticism. People do not fulfill unrealistic expectations.

SOFT ASPECTS
Sextile:	Progressed Moon Sextile Natal or Progressed Neptune Transiting Neptune Sextile Natal Moon
Trine:	Progressed Moon Trining Natal or Progressed Neptune Transiting Neptune Trining Natal Moon

LIGHT
Progressed Moon sextile the natal (or progressed) Neptune or transiting Neptune sextile the natal Moon can symbolize a person inspired by new transitions. The soft Moon/Neptune aspects lack much of the stress caused by divine discontent found in the intense aspects. A person can still feel bothered by perfection urges but usually is more in touch with impulses. There can be more **objectivity** in the Moon/Neptune sextile than in the other aspects. Instincts and imagina-

tion may blend nicely together. Perception can be highly attuned to new awareness. A person can sort out emotional confusion. There could be flexibility. A rigid mentality may give itself a break. One may make time for herself rather than devoting all energy to others. Exploring new interests can be simulating.

Progressed Moon trine natal (or progressed) Neptune or transiting Neptune trine the natal Moon can point to new idealism or faith. Universal principles can be grasped. One can forcefully express aesthetic talents, particularly if the natal chart has key intense aspects. There can be a drive for higher consciousness. One may strive to understand the hidden unity of life. A person can make previously-lacking connections concerning Karmic behavior. One may want to "clean up her act."

One's compassion and caring for others may make her a role model. The mysteries of life with its often unexplainable accidents may become a reality for the individual. The conscious mind is quieted.

SHADOW
In the **Moon/Neptune sextile or trine**, a person can avoid conflict. It is possible to stay in nongrowth-promoting relationships, careers, and identities by denying problems. There can be a lack of stability. Individuals can float from one relationship or home to another. A person might have dulled or sleepy consciousness and indulge in laziness or procrastination. An individual may lack focus on any one thing. She may escape into a universal philosophy rather than deal with specific circumstances.

One might lack logic. She may become a devout follower of a different spiritual philosophy every month, each time convinced she has found "the way." A person can get quite intense and moralistic about convictions. A person may be too sensitive, overreacting to criticism. An individual could also be insensitive if totally sold on a particular belief. In the intense aspects a person usually cannot afford to sit on the fence. Life demands a decision. **The lack of environmental conflict in soft Moon/Neptune aspects can prolong escapism and addiction.**

DAWN
In **Moon/Neptune aspects, individuals may experience the relaxing whisper of the inner voice.** There is a pull to higher consciousness. One must exercise caution, discipline, and awareness. **Ignoring reality and inner stability during Moon/Neptune aspects is a sure ride into an endless fog.**

One may develop a new sense of beauty. An appreciation for harmony and intuitive clarity can be enlightening. Relationships may take on a deeper meaning. An equal give-and-take in emotional sharing is possible. One may allow herself to love deeply and to be loved.

MOON/PLUTO ASPECTS

Progressed Moon/Natal or Progressed Pluto Transiting Pluto/Natal Moon

Process:	Emotional Intensity
Ally:	Intuitive Bond with Life's Mysteries
Illusion:	Don't Trust Anybody

Moon/Pluto aspects reflect a penetrating awareness of life situations. Individuals with emotional problems may find these aspects unsettling. Both the Moon and Pluto are water planets. Deep moods can be displayed. One may tap into intuitive power. Emotional intensity can pour passionately into relationships, family, work, and all creative endeavors. There is an underlying compulsive need to find security.

INTENSE ASPECTS
Conjunction: Progressed Moon Conjunct Natal or Progressed Pluto
Transiting Pluto Conjunct Natal Moon

Square: Progressed Moon Square Natal or Progressed Pluto
Transiting Pluto Square Natal Moon

LIGHT
Progressed Moon conjunct natal (or progressed) Pluto or transiting Pluto conjunct natal Moon can denote tremendous emotional intensity. A person may more adeptly express feelings. Nurturing and receiving love can occur. One can develop intimate relationships based on trust. An insecure person can tap into personal power. A materialistic individual can find a deeper life purpose. Individuals can overcome great obstacles in accomplishing tasks.

A person can gain insight into ancestral history. Compulsive family habits can be identified and resolved, giving way to security. An individual could begin a new way of life. Individuals can find hidden emotional strength. A dependent person can find emotional power. An arrogant individual may learn to feel. Grieving a loss can free locked energies. A release of subconscious energy might bring new creative insights. Moods can be more balanced. Passions are channeled smoothly.

A dramatic rebirth can occur. A self-healing of old emotional scars soothes a troubled time. People penetrate beneath the surface of situations. One may excel at reading moods and body language. One comforts others during a crisis. Individuals may stay calm during conflict. A period of research and study is possible. Individuals can passionately embrace new beginnings.

Progressed Moon square natal (or progressed) Pluto or transiting Pluto square the natal Moon can symbolize transcending

insecurity. People express their passion for life with emotion and sincerity. People may respond to challenges by personal transformation. Individuals may find a deeper experience of life in an unexpected manner. There is "magic" in Moon/Pluto aspects. The conscious mind cannot penetrate alone where the deep instinctual waters of Moon and Pluto flow. A person can go to the roots of the inner self.

There can be a symbolic burying of the past. One learns to surrender fears of the unknown. A new inner voice can be born. One can bond with intuition, leading to bold new transitions. Rather than run away from emotional challenges, one embraces their intensity. An alchemy can occur. Intuition joins with invisible life forces. A person can concentrate and penetrate deeply to find spiritual strength. Material and physical loss, though painful, build character. In both the Moon/Pluto conjunction and square, people can show remarkable business savvy. Investment can be important.

SHADOW
Both the **Moon/Pluto conjunction and square** can be times of emotional blindness. Individuals can stubbornly fight intuitive understanding. One can suffer emotional pain. A failure to face inner conflicts can ruin the present. Jealousy and revenge can dominate. One may have little trust. Hatred pollutes the consciousness. Emotional secrets abort the bonding process.

One may be stuck in low gear. Life can be fixated on the past. Insecurity keeps one inert. Past-life karma can run the show. One may feed on "old" compulsive habits. Addiction to substances or people is possible. Emotional fears can be irrational. Old childhood pain keeps one from the safe light of the present. A fear of death or the loss of a loved one causes severe emotional despair. A failure to accept the grieving process could keep a person silently suffering. One may lack the intuitive or psychological depth to get beyond a loss or crisis.

Quincunx: Progressed Moon Quincunx Natal or Progressed Pluto
Transiting Pluto Quincunx Natal Moon

Opposition: Progressed Moon Opposing Natal or Progressed Pluto
Transiting Pluto Opposing Natal Moon

LIGHT
Progressed Moon quincunx natal (or progressed) Pluto or transiting Pluto quincunx natal Moon can denote a gain of intuitive power. This quincunx is the **"Yoga of psychological depth."**

A person can find emotional strength through metaphysical studies. One may attain self-mastery through a metaphysical discipline. Concentration and meditation can bring emotional clarity. One may stop giving away power. Extreme dependence may be overcome. Intuition may lead one to motivations for insecurity. A power-oriented person can learn sensitivity. One chooses caring rather than dominating; sharing feelings rather than guarding emotional secrets; mutual trust rather than possessiveness.

A person may discover the importance of privacy or space. Taking time alone brings emotional strength. Quiet reflective moments bring trust in oneself. Progressed Moon opposing natal (or progressed) Pluto or transiting Pluto opposing the natal Moon can symbolize understanding the motivations of others. Relationships can be bonded together by trust, emotional sharing, and a joint passion for love. Caring can flow deeply. Anticipating situations helps elicit appropriate emotional responses. Individuals can display remarkable poise during a difficult crisis.

Resources can be managed. An individual could help others organize confusing lives. One may be an artist in helping others to survive emotional and physical loss. People may forgive the past, leaving behind a loss or emotional scar. Self-transformation can occur.

Individuals may find new personal power. They may stop projecting strength and emotional clarity onto others. An individual may realize his own emotional intensity. Those who depend too much on others can find financial or emotional independence. Space may bring clarity. Emotionally or physically abused people can find the strength to go on. A deep intuitive insight may bring emotional clarity. People fearing intimacy may find new trust. Closeness no longer seems so threatening. The need to control or dominate others is no longer required.

SHADOW

Both the **Moon/Pluto quincunx and opposition** can express as excess dependency. Individuals may rely heavily on others for emotional and material support. Psychological and emotional intensity are lived through others. One may fear space or privacy.

Addiction to sexual appetites can keep relating imbalanced. Intimacy may be denied. One can strive to prove worth through sexual performance. Individuals can reenact old scenarios. Jealousy, revenge, lack of trust, and physical appetites can dominate. Subconscious desires can be difficult **shadows** in one's life. A failure to confront emotional fear feeds compulsive desires. Manipulating others due to greed and control can occur. Lying at all costs hurts intimacy. Individuals can foolishly allow others to deceive them.

Moods can be childish. One may brood to get his own way. The silent treatment might be used. One's fears cause disorientation and emotional confusion. A person may have difficulty turning off emotional intensity. It can be a constant source of conflict. Simplicity and calmness are lacking. One may stay stuck in emotionally destructive situations. A person can lack the insight to withdraw from problems. Refusing to listen to outside advice does not help.

SOFT ASPECTS

Sextile: Progressed Moon Sextile Natal or Progressed Pluto
             Transiting Pluto Sextile Natal Moon

Trine: Progressed Moon Trining Natal or Progressed Pluto
             Transiting Pluto Trining Natal Moon

LIGHT

Progressed Moon sextile natal (or progressed) Pluto or transiting Pluto sextile the natal Moon can denote a masterful expression of feelings. Dramatic transitions occur with ease. An insecure person may find more confidence; a negative individual some hope; a grieving person some peace; a lonely heart some company; a painful life some relief. Emotions may be easier to communicate. An individual may meet people who draw out his secrets. The past can be integrated into the present.

Progressed Moon trine natal (or progressed) Pluto or transiting Pluto trine the natal Moon can symbolize a far reaching vision into the mystery of life. One may feel a special rapport with invisible forces. Personal power may emanate naturally. One's giving nature attracts support from others. Individuals may maintain hope against difficult odds. No task seems too difficult.

Nurturing qualities may attract love. One may provide for the welfare of others. Affinity for a particular cause can bring out one's altruism. Individuals may have tremendous patience. Listening promotes closeness with others. People may indulge in reflection. One could appear passive as a fiery spirit is growing deep within. An individual can make peace with the self or with the past. Forgiving transgressors can take place.

SHADOW

The **Moon/Pluto sextile or trine** can translate into a subtle manipulation of others. Individuals can be smooth operators. A tendency to hold onto feelings can block communication. Emotional confusion keeps others at a distance. A lack of emotional depth can occur. People may have trouble handling crises. Avoiding problems creates negative consequences.

People may lack self-insight. They can be pulled into extremes. Following needs dictated by insecurities creates problems. Individuals can lack trust in intimacy. Jealousy and possessiveness may destroy relationships. One may depend too heavily on power people.

DAWN
Moon/Pluto aspects can indicate an individual stops focusing on what is lacking. A quiet yet passionate emotional outpouring can quench a thirsty life. A life with no purpose can find new symbols that bring a rebirth. One may cross a bridge over Karmic waters. Compulsive habits that take away from life purpose can be transcended. The past can be a valuable ally. The present becomes a confirmation of inner security. Intuition may penetrate into the deepest of life's mysteries. A recognition of invisible forces can strengthen the psyche. One may bond with personal power. Difficult circumstances can be illuminated and a drive to survive dominates.

MERCURY/VENUS ASPECTS

Progressed Mercury/Natal or Progressed Venus
Progressed Venus/Natal Mercury

Process:	Balanced Perceptions
Ally:	Thoughts that Refine the Intellect
Illusion:	Impressing Others with Verbal Cunning

Mercury/Venus aspects are social. There can be a career or business slant to these aspects as both planets rule an earth sign as well as an air sign. People can make new important social contacts. One can learn and appreciate harmonious thoughts. Individuals may communicate and perceive clearly in the face of adversity.

Due to the proximity of natal Mercury and Venus in the birthchart, only certain aspects are possible through secondary progression. The conjunction, sextile, square, and trine are more likely to occur than quincunx or opposition.

INTENSE ASPECTS
Conjunction: Progressed Mercury Conjunct
Natal or Progressed Venus
Progressed Venus Conjunct Natal Mercury

Square: Progressed Mercury Square Natal or Progressed Venus
Progressed Venus Square Natal Mercury

LIGHT
Progressed Mercury conjunct natal (or progressed) Venus or progressed Venus conjunct natal Mercury can symbolize a sharpened intellect. One may not be as easily distracted by others. A keen perception of social situations can be shown.

One may find new career avenues. Multiple tasks can be simultaneously handled. An overly intellectual person may find time for emotions. The love nature can blossom. An emotional person can find mental balance. People may learn quietly by observing the behavior of others. One can relate to a wide variety of people. One may display a great sense of situations. Careers in communication and dealing with public can manifest. A special ability to put others at ease can be exhibited. One may objectively settle disputes. Perceiving facts can be a talent.

Progressed Mercury square natal (or progressed) Venus or progressed Venus square natal Mercury can show communication through aesthetics. I had progressed Venus in Aquarius square natal Mercury in Scorpio when my first book, *Astrological Games People Play*, was released.

One can communicate more with emotion. Life can become more passionate. A dull mind may enjoy new people. One may become more attracted to beauty. A person lacking social grace may develop new behaviors. She may grow more accepting of her inner and outer beauty.

Individuals can be excellent negotiators. They may deal with others in a professional and businesslike manner. A serious type may "lighten up." Life may be challenging yet filled with pleasurable experiences.

SHADOW

In both the **progressed Mercury/Venus conjunction and square**, a person can become a social climber. The substance of life is lost in a display of social glitter. The artist may become commercialized. Spirit is traded in for dollars. One may twist the truth to win approval. Outer admiration brings a shallow mentality. A love of luxury and sensuality bring disillusionment.

People may become too critical of what has brought them success. The past becomes an excuse for a bitter present. Some individuals indulge in self-pity or denial. Self-hatred may follow a lack of rewards. The mind could be poisoned by the negative opinions of others.

SOFT ASPECTS

Sextile:	Progressed Mercury Sextile Natal or Progressed Venus
	Progressed Venus Sextile Natal Mercury
Trine:	Progressed Mercury Trining Natal or Progressed Venus
	Progressed Venus Trining Natal Mercury

LIGHT

Progressed Mercury sextile natal (or progressed) Venus or progressed Venus sextile natal Mercury can denote a talent with words. One may be a mental artist, expressing thoughts clearly and concisely. A wide variety of professions are available. Work related to communication, people, travel, aesthetics, or dealing with finances is possible. Gregariousness brings many social contacts. One may network, linking the services of others.

A person whose birthchart has intense natal aspects may find this a relaxing time. The environment may not seem as demanding. The pace of live can still be fast. Conflict is more recessive. Individuals may resolve internal conflicts.

Progressed Mercury trine natal (or progressed) Venus or progressed Venus trine natal Mercury can connote mental happiness. Life's generosity rewards perceptions. One may attract harmonious relationships through optimism.

Since the trine would come late in life, a person may have fond memories. One may feel abundance. Good people may surround him. Perhaps a hobby is a key form of self-expression. Individuals may discover a special interest later in life that inspires them.

SHADOW

Both the **progressed Mercury/Venus sextile and trine** can express as gullibility. People can be fooled by others. Individuals may be poor negotiators. They get talked into losing propositions.

People may have poor perceptions of situations. They may lie to themselves. A refusal to deal with conflict may alter perceptions. A love of convenience and luxury keep one on the surface of life. A fickle nature that cannot focus is possible. One may change decisions constantly about work and relationships. Promising too much can disappoint others. Running away from intensity can be disorienting.

DAWN

Mercury/Venus aspects can reflect a new horizon. Thoughts and social instincts might mingle in a flowing manner. Ideas may express through aesthetics. One can excel in the business world. A keen sense of people and finances can bring material abundance. One may communicate concisely and accurately. A peacemaker or arbitrator can be born.

MERCURY/MARS ASPECTS

Progressed Mercury/Natal or Progressed Mars
Progressed Mars/Natal Mercury

Process:	Mental Fortitude
Ally:	Thinking Decisively
Illusion:	Impulsive Thoughts

Mercury/Mars aspects have mental intensity. Perception combines with assertion. Individuals can become more decisive in acting on ideas. Thoughts and speech can travel fast. Jumping to conclusions is possible. New ideas can be initiated.

INTENSE ASPECTS

Conjunction: Progressed Mercury Conjunct Natal or Progressed Mars
Progressed Mars Conjunct Natal Mercury

Square: Progressed Mercury Square Natal or Progressed Mars
Progressed Mars Square Natal Mercury

LIGHT

Progressed Mercury conjunct natal (or progressed) Mars or progressed Mars conjunct natal Mercury can symbolize a more decisive nature. Timid individuals can walk taller. Those doubting their own intelligence can find confidence. Procrastinators may move from thoughts to actions. Individuals might move rather than dwelling on worries. Communicating anger might help improve relations with others. Assertion can open up a whole new life. One may incite others into creative thinking and to act on ideas. Competing with others on mental and physical levels is stimulating.

Progressed Mercury square natal (or progressed) Mars or progressed Mars square natal Mercury can denote fighting obstacles. An individual may reach for extra psychic energy in a crisis. One can display remarkable poise in the midst of adversity. The conflict associated with fiery Mars can be calmed by objective Mercury. Anger can be poured into creative expression. One may need to confront others or life issues. A release of anger or bitterness could be freeing. Individuals may learn how to appropriately get attention.

SHADOW

The progressed Mercury/Mars conjunction or square can express as blatant verbal (or physical) attacks on others. People may lack the verbal skills to communicate clearly. A **lack of patience** can bring frustration. A bossy and arrogant attitude could alienate others. One may be demanding, displaying a "me first" nature. Individuals can burn bridges too quickly. A "hit and run" mentality leaves many unfinished projects or situations. People might fear acting on impulses. Opportunities can be missed. A lack of initiating energy can leave one waiting. Unresolved conflicts present an identity crisis.

Quincunx: Progressed Mercury Quincunx Natal or Progressed Mars
Progressed Mars Quincunx Natal Mercury

Opposition: Progressed Mercury Opposing Natal or Progressed Mars
Progressed Mars Opposing Natal Mercury

LIGHT

Progressed Mercury quincunx natal (or progressed) Mars or progressed Mars quincunx natal Mercury is the "Yoga of mental strength." Individuals can change compulsive habits and redirect self-destructive thoughts. A self-hating individual may find a new purpose. One who hesitates can enjoy new spontaneity. Assertion instincts can become clearer. A new health regimen of diet and exercise can help give focus. Studying or education may sharpen mental skills. People can be good problem solvers.

Progressed Mercury opposing natal (or progressed) Mars or progressed Mars opposing natal Mercury can symbolize a new directness in communicating. One may become more eager to interact and share information. People can excel at negotiation. A shy person can gain courage and an outgoing spirit. A self-centered person can find greater perception of others. An impatient type can learn to listen. Reckless actions can become more reflective.

A person can stop depending excessively on others. People can leave relationships with dominating or self-centered partners. One may start looking inward for an identity. Opinions may not be so easily influenced. Self-centered individuals may need to consider the opinions or ideas of others. Cooperation can be learned. Angry people may stop dumping problems. Important insights into anger could be gained.

SHADOW

Both the **Mercury/Mars quincunx and opposition** can express as impulsive actions. One may carelessly rush into situations. An argumentative nature wins few friends. A "must win" attitude makes compromise difficult. One may jump to hasty conclusions. A lack of patience with self and others can occur. One may be always in a rush. A need to slow down is ignored. A lack of consistency in actions can be a problem.

Individuals can dump anger onto others. A person may explode unexpectedly due to repressed anger. Some individuals have difficulty communicating anger. A fear of intensity or direct communication can bring vagueness into relationships. One may talk about problems but do nothing about them. People may rely on others to fight their battles. Strength and assertion might be lived through a partner. One may be too concerned about the opinions of others.

SOFT ASPECTS

Sextile:	Progressed Mercury Sextile Natal or Progressed Mars Progressed Mars Sextile Natal Mercury
Trine:	Progressed Mercury Trining Natal or Progressed Mars Progressed Mars Trining Natal Mercury

LIGHT

Progressed Mercury sextile natal (or progressed) Mars or progressed Mars sextile natal Mercury can denote mental sharpness. Individuals can express enterprising ideas. Perceptions and ideas may be in synch. The mental ingenuity of Mercury is in a sharp focus. The actions of Mars are channeled through Mercurial perceptions. A lazy person can become self-motivated; a reckless individual can gain awareness of actions. Numerous tasks are handled simultaneously. Communication skills might be accentuated. Exciting new inner strength can occur.

Progressed Mercury trine natal (or progressed) Mars or progressed Mars trine natal Mercury can symbolize a more energetic spirit. A person lacking initiative may find confidence. Mental Mercury and forceful Mars may denote a greater vision. Individuals can find a more positive life approach. A person with a lot of intense aspects at birth can find this trine rewarding. One who is accustomed to fighting for ideas may find a calm assuredness. Individuals may move quickly without losing sight of details. They may have unusual perceptions even in crisis.

SHADOW
In both the **Mercury/Mars sextile and trine** an individual can be too timid. A lack of energy can miss opportunities. People can wait for a flow that does not come. A too-passive approach could invite more dominating types to take advantage. One may be afraid to cause conflict. A "tip toe around problems" attitude results. Mental drive may be lacking. A self-starting energy may short out. Ideas and actions could be out of synch. People may be impatient. One may assume everyone agrees with him. One might dominate others with little awareness.

DAWN
Mercury/Mars aspects can denote a quick mind. Individuals can bounce back from adverse circumstances. Impatience can turn into listening; hasty judgments into reflection; angry outbursts become clear communication; a lack of initiative embraces assertion. Perceptions and actions can reflect keen insights into situations.

MERCURY/JUPITER ASPECTS

Progressed Mercury/Natal or Progressed Jupiter Transiting Jupiter/Natal Mercury

Process:	Expansive perception
Ally:	Eclectic Insights
Illusion:	I Know all I Need to Know

Mercury/Jupiter aspects symbolize one's mind being exposed to new experiences. Both planets point toward travel and education. Elevated consciousness is possible.

INTENSE ASPECTS
Conjunction: Progressed Mercury Conjunct
                    Natal or Progressed Jupiter
            Transiting Jupiter Conjunct Natal Mercury

Square: Progressed Mercury Square
Natal or Progressed Jupiter
Transiting Jupiter Square Natal Mercury

LIGHT

Progressed Mercury conjunct natal (or progressed) Jupiter or transiting Jupiter conjunct natal Mercury can symbolize a greater ease in making big decisions. One may not take life as seriously. A lighter mental approach makes transitions easier. People can be excellent communicators. Jupiter shows confidence and Mercury quick insights. Together this is a nice mental blend. A child can find happiness through learning and exposure to new scenery; an adult can find humor and new knowledge.

Individuals can find new life beliefs. The truth sets one's mind free. People can go back to school. The mind needs new learning. This is a good time to promote oneself. Speaking, teaching, selling, and traveling all are in high focus. One may enter into lucrative financial investments.

Progressed Mercury square natal (or progressed) Jupiter or transiting Jupiter square natal Mercury can show one rising above a lack of confidence. Individuals may educate themselves on how to solve problems. A narrow mind can expand. Environmental conflict can bring out one's soundest judgment. A generous disposition can win friends. A person may offer advice to others during a crisis.

Individuals can take a broader perspective. One may jump into new learning experiences. Excitement about the future can bring more enthusiasm for the present. A chronic worrier may surrender fears. Negativity can find more positive outlets. Nagging details can find meaning in seeing a more total picture.

SHADOW

The Mercury/Jupiter conjunction or square can manifest as jumping to hasty conclusions. A lack of focus brings no accomplishments. An overly expansive nature leaves many unfinished tasks. One may be a procrastinator — waiting for that right moment rather than initiating actions. Wasting time and resources is a bad habit.

Eclectic insight can be trapped by narrow opinions. A self-righteous attitude blocks clarity. The present becomes muddled with superficial ideas. Too much useless information blocks natural perceptions. People may resist new learning and rely on yesterday's truths. A lack of order is disorienting. Excess and extravagance become a way of life. Perceptions are clouded by a compulsive avoidance of shortcomings. One may exaggerate problems. People can promise more than they deliver. A person may depend too much on changing situations. Restlessness leads one to leave good situations.

Quincunx: Progressed Mercury Quincunx
                       Natal or Progressed Jupiter
                   Transiting Jupiter Quincunx Natal Mercury

Opposition: Progressed Mercury Opposing
                       Natal or Progressed Jupiter
                   Transiting Jupiter Opposing Natal Mercury

LIGHT

Progressed Mercury quincunx natal (or progressed) Jupiter or transiting Jupiter quincunx natal Mercury is the "Yoga of wise judgment." Individuals can stop their wasteful ways. Perceiving danger in advance can be helpful. A pattern of entering reckless situations can be conquered. A person lacking self-confidence can find more faith. One may attract abundance through positive thinking. People filled with negative thoughts may find more fulfilling beliefs.

Progressed Mercury opposing natal (or progressed) Jupiter or transiting Jupiter opposing natal Mercury can denote more confidence in relating to others. One may develop tremendous persuasive techniques. A dream may feel within one's grasp. The power of positive thinking may attract rewarding relationships. One may find a spiritual group that enhances growth. A teacher may help master an area of study. A person could act as a teacher for others.

Individuals may break through karmic darkness. One who exaggerates his talents may go through a more honest self-examination. Those who twist the truth straighten out their perceptions. A person lacking humor can discover a lighter side to life. One may view life more objectively. Traveling to foreign or new places can stimulate new insights. This can be a time of finding freedom through options.

SHADOW

The progressed Mercury/Jupiter quincunx or opposition can manifest as stupidity. One may refuse to see the light in situations. A naive outlook on life can cause people to be used. Jupiter's generosity could be taken advantage of by others. People can be too trusting. They only look at the good. Individuals may fail to create boundaries or limits for children, lovers, parents, etc. One may follow too many paths. Nervous exhaustion is the result. Choices may need to be limited. Someone loses the forest for the trees by ignoring details.

The dreamer may never settle into a real life. Gypsy, dreamy philosopher, and traveler may have no real purpose. Rather than a lifestyle focused on expansive exploration, one is running away from himself. Relationships can lack depth. Avoidance of conflict keeps emotional content shallow. A cold, intellectual, or arrogant attitude keeps others at a distance. An argumentative nature is possible. Bragging may be a key feature. People may project too many of their good qualities onto others. One may see others as more intelligent, spiritual, and knowledgeable of the world. Too much dependence on the ideas of others can be limiting.

SOFT ASPECTS

Sextile: Progressed Mercury Sextile Natal or Progressed Jupiter
Transiting Jupiter Sextile Natal Mercury

Trine: Progressed Mercury Trining Natal or Progressed Jupiter
Transiting Jupiter Trining Natal Mercury

LIGHT

Progressed Mercury sextile natal (or progressed) Jupiter or transiting Jupiter sextile natal Mercury can explore new avenues of self-discovery. The sextile suggests an even more mental nature to Mercury/Jupiter aspects. Mental sparks fly in learning new skills. No challenge seems too difficult. Thoughts may be spontaneous. Solutions to old problems come fast.

This can be a soothing aspect for someone coming out of hard times. Worries are cast to the wind. A person taps into faith. A hunger for knowledge can occur. One can be especially adept at communication. Long-awaited news may arrive. Enjoying the little things in life becomes important.

Progressed Mercury trine natal (or progressed) Jupiter or transiting Jupiter trine natal Mercury can denote new mental horizons. The trine with its natural expansiveness complements the enthusiasm of fiery Jupiter. Courage to think new thoughts is possible. One may envision more spiritual and material abundance. One may more truthfully perceive life situations. Morals and honesty become important. One may inspire others to seek their highest good. People may relieve the burden of others. Individuals generously offer their ideas. Advice and counseling flow naturally. A warm attitude puts others at ease.

SHADOW

The Mercury/Jupiter sextile or trine can manifest as giving unsolicited advice. One may try to be godlike. Self-righteous attitudes turn others off. Limited ideas can block new learning. One can be a legend in his own mind. Individuals may hide anger and intensity, "an everything is okay" face cloaking strong emotions. Spiritual convictions may stifle emotional relating. One may view everything through an exclusive, all-knowing vision.

An individual with many soft aspects natally may exhibit inertia. Too much of the good life weakens ambitions. A fool may become a bigger fool. Those prone to gambling and reckless actions may now feel they cannot lose.

DAWN
Mercury/Jupiter aspects can be expressed as far reaching vision. Life can be exciting, merciful, and full of fruitful lessons.

MERCURY/SATURN ASPECTS

Progressed Mercury/Natal or Progressed Saturn Transiting Saturn/Natal Mercury

Process: Learning to Concentrate

Ally: Determined Intellect

Illusion: Self-Doubt

Mercury/Saturn aspects can point to thinking logically and with discipline. The conscious mind combines with a getting-down-to-business nature. This family of aspects is rather serious in nature. One may compulsively seek a more organized existence. Concentration and endurance can be key allies. Issues are often related to negativity, fear of loss, and rigid thinking.

INTENSE ASPECTS
Conjunction: Progressed Mercury Conjunct
                 Natal or Progressed Saturn
                 Transiting Saturn Conjunct Natal Mercury

Square: Progressed Mercury Square
                 Natal or Progressed Saturn
                 Transiting Saturn Square Natal Mercury

LIGHT
Progressed Mercury conjunct natal (or progressed) Saturn or transiting Saturn conjunct natal Mercury can connote learning to discipline mental energies. One may be challenged to endure a situation with much patience. I signed my first book contract in 1984 while transiting Saturn was conjunct my natal Mercury in Scorpio. It began a long process of sitting to write in a very focused manner on a daily basis for several months. Writing on a regular schedule became a habit after overcoming my initial resistance. The mind can be a tricky instrument to train. Concentration comes amazingly fast once the first step is taken.

Individuals can gain confidence in communication, business dealings, studying, and undertaking difficult tasks. A mental toughness can be born. An indecisive person can learn to make precise decisions. A fear of studying or learning can be overcome. A time waster can become a good time manager. A person fearing responsibility may enjoy leadership challenges. One may identify the initial steps to action. Excuses that previously held one back are transcended. More attention is paid to detail.

Saturn aspects sometimes are even more meaningful as we age. This aspect can symbolize a new hobby or career for a retired person. One is never too old to learn something new.

Progressed Mercury square natal (or progressed) Saturn or transiting Saturn square natal Mercury can denote becoming aware of self-destructive thoughts. Face your reasoning powers. This aspect symbolizes "putting on the brakes." The slowing-down theme of Saturn can guide the swiftness of Mercury. Details come into focus. One's mental perceptions may get quite clear.

There can be an energy conflict in a person's life between the focus symbolized by Saturn and the Mercurial urge to scatter. One can be more determined despite adversity. One's mental persuasiveness in politics, business, or career can be especially highlighted. **Dealing with a situation that seems out of one's control can be accentuated** (*i.e.*, death of a loved one, loss of job or relationship). An individual may gain a mental fortitude previously lacking or unused. Mercury can soften the controlling tendencies of Saturn. A need to always be in control can get reasonable. An individual who is too expansive can learn how to focus. Often the assuming of responsibility dictates the focus. Dealing with conflict develops powers of concentration.

SHADOW

In both the Mercury/Saturn conjunction and square, a person's objectivity and clear mental perception can be hijacked by fear of commitment. One may feel too confined by life's realities. All duties and obligations are perceived as painful or too demanding. A fear of failure can be the underlying issue. Rather than take a chance on the outcome, all situations are avoided. A stubborn resistance to change arises. One loses sight of options. A person chooses not to communicate openly.

A negative mental nature may be a defense mechanism, an excuse not to take a risk. One may engage in self-talk that sabotages career and relationship goals. One may run away from conflict. A tremendous nervous disposition can be a problem. Not resolving a problem or physical ailment could produce extra tension. One's attention to left-brain details can become a rigid habit. Conscious mind "burnout" is the result. It is like driving on an interstate highway in first gear — much wear and tear on one's mental nature. A person can fixate on lack of success. A career setback leads to depression. Failing one class leads to dropping out. A good mantra here is "Don't stop trying," at least until you are absolutely sure it is for the best. Some will compulsively not change course even though all signals are saying to do so.

Quincunx: Progressed Mercury Quincunx
Natal or Progressed Saturn
Transiting Saturn Quincunx Natal Mercury

Opposition: Progressed Mercury Opposing
Natal or Progressed Saturn
Transiting Saturn Opposing Natal Mercury

LIGHT

Progressed Mercury quincunx natal (or progressed) Saturn or transiting Saturn quincunx natal Mercury is the "Yoga of developing mental concentration." One may reprogram the conscious mind. Negative thinking is channeled into a more positive approach. One may develop a schedule. Diet and exercise may become important ingredients in daily life. Mental perception and reality are brought into harmony. Previous self-destructive thoughts may be transcended.

Insecurity and fear could be converted into positive action. Paranoia and hypochondria now seem unrealistic. One learns from past mistakes without feeling too responsible. A person may slow down and think logically. One may lower standards to more reasonable expectations for self and others. He can expel poisonous thoughts that limit growth.

Progressed Mercury opposing natal (or progressed) Saturn or transiting Saturn opposing natal Mercury connotes adjusting one's perception of others. A person can become very determined to improve communication. One may develop an expertise in making business deals and networking.

An individual may find deeper communication. One's ability to listen can sharpen. Saturn symbolizes slowing down the conscious mind (Mercury). A restless, scattered mind gives way to penetrating concentration. A fast talker slows to listen more.

Seeing a counselor can alleviate personal problems, even for those who have difficulty asking for help. A new confidence in communicating clearly in all relationships is possible. Sometimes a push from a partner provides the impetus to better define one's ambitions. One may receive encouragement from peers, parents, authority figures, spouses or lovers concerning cherished goals.

SHADOW

In the **Mercury/Saturn quincunx or opposition,** an individual can integrate the mental perception themes of Mercury with the caution of Saturn. Suspicions of others can occur. A blaming attitude may dominate. An individual might accuse others of never listening. A fear of losing control or of failure can be the problem. A person can easily find fault with others. Arguments with superiors or with those lower in rank can occur. A bossy disposition alienates people. The individual may refuse to listen to reason.

An individual may grow envious of the success of loved ones, co-workers, or peers. Insecurity buttons are pushed. The person avoids communication because he really is not interested in working through problems. Communication breakdowns in important relationships may occur. A negative outlook can attract a lack of success. Individuals can freeze in self-doubt. A lack of organized thoughts yields confusion. The life may be in chaos, lacking discipline and logic.

SOFT ASPECTS

Sextile: Progressed Mercury Sextile Natal or Progressed Saturn
                Transiting Saturn Sextile Natal Mercury

Trine: Progressed Mercury Trining Natal or Progressed Saturn
                Transiting Saturn Trining Natal Mercury

LIGHT

Progressed Mercury sextile natal (or progressed) Saturn or transiting Saturn sextile natal Mercury symbolizes enjoyable **new perceptions of one's environment**. Reality flows. An individual often feels more in control. Even a lack of control is not as threatening. A person may feel more flexible than usual. His ideas are accepted more readily by others. Perception and ambition simultaneously reinforce each other. One may work within a system more easily than usual. He does not war with the work environment or daily responsibilities.

Transiting Saturn trine natal Mercury or progressed Mercury trine natal (or progressed) Saturn can denote **new confidence in ideas** expressed to peers and superiors. One may be well liked in the community. Individuals can conquer past fears. A new attitude regarding past mistakes can occur. A more flexible nature may result.

One may do well as a counselor, understanding the problems of others. Active talking and listening combine here. Tapes that have plagued the conscious mind can be changed. More desire to change old behavior patterns exits.

SHADOW

In both the **Mercury/Saturn sextile and trine**, the psyche can be too easily invaded by outside stimuli. Information flows in with no filtering. Focusing or setting priorities becomes extremely difficult.

Laziness avoids learning new methods. A complacency with the present is less than fulfilling. An individual could work in a job much below his qualifications. He lacks the ambition to make a more challenging change. Subtle manipulation can occur. A controller can be a very smooth performer. Nobody suspects him until later. He knows just what to say to get what is needed.

DAWN
Mercury/Saturn aspects can express as clear perception of reality. Our conscious mind needs some discipline and focus. These aspects denote organization and carefully defined ambitions. There can be flexibility in Mercury/Saturn aspects. One must not lose sight of the options!

MERCURY/URANUS ASPECTS

Progressed Mercury/Natal or Progressed Uranus Transiting Uranus/Natal Mercury

Process:	Mental Ingenuity
Ally:	Independent Thinking
Illusion:	Lack of Insight

Mercury/Uranus aspects symbolize sparks in one's intellect. These are some of the most stimulating mental aspects possible. Mercury denotes left brain or conscious mind reasoning; Uranus symbolizes flashes of mental insight. Aspects formed by these two mental planets indicate a drive to learn. Issues are often related to hasty perceptions and communication breakdowns.

Traditional astrology states that Uranus is the higher octave of Mercury. Both planets deal with the intellect. Mercury is more associated with digesting details while Uranus denotes tuning into mental processes.

INTENSE ASPECTS
Conjunction: Progressed Mercury Conjunct
                       Natal or Progressed Uranus
                       Transiting Uranus Conjunct Natal Mercury

Square: Progressed Mercury Square
                       Natal or Progressed Uranus
                       Transiting Uranus Square Natal Mercury

LIGHT
Progressed Mercury conjunct natal (or progressed) Uranus or transiting Uranus conjunct natal Mercury can express as mental brilliance. Left-brain Mercury with its analytical focus is given deeper insights by Uranus. This conjunction fuses together two potent mental planets. A dynamic awakening to new life potentials can occur. A person may show a keen perception of her surroundings. One may tackle a new field of study. Avid interest in reading, traveling, and unique communication is likely.

One can digest information at a faster pace. She can sort through details more quickly. Reflexes can be more spontaneous. A conservative person may enjoy new recklessness. One's rigid concepts become more flexible. A person may gain confidence in her ability to learn. One may be excited about new studies or inventions. A more adaptable nature may occur. A deeper perspective can develop. One can go beyond societal opinions. Thinking for oneself becomes important.

Progressed Mercury square natal (or progressed) Uranus or transiting Uranus square natal Mercury can denote using mental force to overcome an obstacle. One may discover new goals. One's environment can challenge her to make an important transition. Not taking life so seriously could be appropriate. Conflict and pressure could bring out new awareness. New reasoning powers can be discovered. Tension and challenges to the intellect may be strengthening. In both the conjunction and the square, people can enjoy using computers and other new technologies of communication.

SHADOW
In both the **Mercury/Uranus conjunction and square**, a person can get trapped by the fixity of Uranus. She can develop rigid concepts. Perceiving another point of view may be difficult. A selfish preoccupation with one's own ideas can dominate. A person can feel like she is having a nervous breakdown. Dynamic mental electricity can block clear expression. If one experiences indecision or too much speediness, she could have nervous exhaustion. This can be a scattered time.

One may regress into safer thinking that is not challenging. Boredom can create nervous tension. A fear of new challenges can cause self-doubt. A lack of adaptability can occur. One can stubbornly resist change or new ideas. A person may hold onto conscious-mind thinking rather than moving into new growth.

"Different just to be different" can become a mantra. Extremely eccentric behavior can lead to leaving the mainstream. One may purposely make herself difficult to understand. She may make snap judgments that leave out needed facts. A person can resist input from others. Extreme impulsiveness becomes a way of life.

The intense Mercury/Uranus aspects can lead to intellectualizing emotions. A person may not trust anything but thoughts. There can be a stubborn resistance against talking about feelings.

Quincunx: Progressed Mercury Quincunx
Natal or Progressed Uranus
Transiting Uranus Quincunx Natal Mercury

Opposition: Progressed Mercury Opposing
Natal Or Progressed Uranus
Transiting Uranus Opposing Natal Mercury

LIGHT
Progressed Mercury quincunx natal (or progressed) Uranus or transiting Uranus quincunx natal Mercury is the "Yoga of directing mental energy." One may discover freedom of thought. The underlying themes for mental anxiety or a failure to set priorities can surface. Some Uranian detachment might be discovered. The conscious mind becomes steady and free of too much debris from environment. One may learn how to turn the mind "on" and "off" creatively.

People may finally make time for their own goals or interests. Maybe they have sacrificed mental interest to please others. Taking a stand about beliefs or perceptions can occur. One may organize thoughts in a clearer manner. Mental closets filled with procrastination, self-doubt, or negativity can be cleaned out.

Progressed Mercury opposing natal (or progressed) Uranus or transiting Uranus opposing natal Mercury may symbolize communicating more clearly. One's perceptions may grow. A person makes mental associations on a different level. One's mind may contact collective trends, ideas, and words to stimulate those around him. Concepts can formulate faster. If one can channel the restlessness of the Mercury/Uranus opposition, she can enjoy creative relationships. One's desire for new peers may reflect a new consciousness. One may outgrow limiting situations. A person may listen better to others. Existing relationships can deepen.

One may question the thinking of peers. She may question authority figures like never before. Sudden impulses to think freely and to initiate new ideas occur spontaneously. Cultural perceptions may change. An individual could become more of an individualist. She may no longer passively live life according to cultural expectations. The Vincent van Gogh or Joan of Arc within us may emerge. A person can fight for equality for self or others. An individual wants to be heard. Experimentation and new enterprising ventures are possible.

SHADOW
In both the **Mercury/Uranus quincunx and opposition,** people can become quite attached to their personal visions. They may get too self-centered. Arguing incessantly to prove a point can occur. Sarcasm can dominate. Criticism of others can be timed and aimed precisely where desired. Fixed opinions can be obsessive. People may grow headstrong in a relationship. The other side of the coin is possible. One may be in a relationship where she is subjected to excessive criticism and receives little support for goals.

People might choose to stay in limiting situations even though all messages are saying to move ahead. They may deny perceptions that point to making changes. A fear of transition can keep one stuck in limiting situations. A fear of one's individuality can keep one locked into unfulfilling experiences.

A person's mind can be so accelerated that mental perception is distorted. Rash and impulsive thinking can lead to disastrous actions. An individual can become mentally drained. Too much thinking can overload the brain. A person can get too worried over details. One may refuse to slow down, leading to physical and mental collapse.

A person may anger or annoy others by being a terrible listener. Others are ignored. An individual can become quite opinionated or rebel excessively. Stability may be difficult to find. Getting bored can reach ridiculous proportions. A person can ruin good relationships quickly through careless behavior. A person's thoughts can leave the mainstream. One may join a group with a limited dogma. One can easily swallow propaganda or new illusory symbols.

SOFT ASPECTS

Sextile: Progressed Mercury Sextile Natal or Progressed Uranus
Transiting Uranus Sextile Natal Mercury

Trine: Progressed Mercury Trining Natal or Progressed Uranus
Transiting Uranus Trining Natal Mercury

LIGHT

Progressed Mercury sextile natal (or progressed) Uranus or transiting Uranus sextile natal Mercury can denote new stimulating experiences. There is an urgency to communicate information. One may excel at teaching or counseling others. One can gain insight into problems. An individual may adopt more flexible attitudes. She may feel less disturbed by outside stimuli. An individual may change negative thought patterns. One may gain a lighter attitude. She can find new mental objectivity.

Progressed Mercury trine natal (or progressed) Uranus or transiting Uranus trine natal Mercury can indicate confidence in acting on ideas. A person may display excellent timing. Adaptability may be much stronger than usual. Nervous energy can be less distracting. Acting on impulses may resolve tension. A person may establish new peers, hobbies, or serious studies. New levels of communication can be attained.

SHADOW

In both the **Mercury/Uranus sextile and trine**, a person can be prone to gossip. One can lack mental depth and be fascinated by useless details. One can display short attention spans. In the more intense aspects, a person may be more determined to change bad habits. The passivity of softer aspects can indicate little discipline to alter thought patterns.

A person may be too sensitive to outside stimuli. Stress thresholds can be low. One may resist beneficial new ideas. A limited lifestyle follows a resistance to mental stimulation. An individual may exaggerate the truth. In the trine one may so badly want the outcome of a situation to go her way that she sees what she wants to perceive.

DAWN

Mercury/Uranus aspects can express as new and exciting mental vision. One's thoughts may reach new levels. A person may discover ideas ahead of her time. Unconventional thinking is likely. One may stimulate others to change limiting behaviors. A person may develop a global consciousness. One can begin a major life transition. A narrow philosophy or negative thought patterns can be transformed. These can be dynamic aspects. Our conscious mind can be excited and highly charged by anticipating our future goals. One may inspire peers.

MERCURY/NEPTUNE ASPECTS

Progressed Mercury/Natal or Progressed Neptune Transiting Neptune/Natal Mercury

Process:	Mental Imagery
Ally:	Intuitive Clarity
Illusion:	Mental Disorientation

Mercury/Neptune aspects denote highly intuitive perceptions. A person can show remarkable poise due to refined awareness. People not looking inward for answers may feel disoriented. Mental confusion or lack of focus may dominate. An aware individual may feel divinely inspired. New levels of consciousness can be attained. Faith and clarity can lead to new growth. The right brain intuitive flow lifts the left brain or conscious mind to new insight.

INTENSE ASPECTS

Conjunction: Progressed Mercury Conjunct
Natal or Progressed Neptune
Transiting Neptune Conjunct Natal Mercury

Square: Progressed Mercury Square
Natal or Progressed Neptune
Transiting Neptune Square Natal Mercury

LIGHT

Progressed Mercury conjunct natal (or progressed) Neptune or transiting Neptune conjunct natal Mercury can open doors previously ignored. A person can tap into new dimensions of mental perception. One's intuition and intellect flow harmoniously. A person may go from being too analytical to tuning into whole processes. People can develop a greater imagination. An extremely practical person may find a new idealism. A very serious individual could become more playful.

A person may discover new intuitive awareness. One may change behavior patterns by reprogramming the conscious mind with inspiring tapes. A life lacking purpose may find new meaning. An individual can feel a great pull to a metaphysical path. One can begin asking questions that traditional institutions cannot answer. A person can feel driven to subjects serving unity in consciousness. He may excel at translating symbolism in astrology, Jungian psychology, color and music healing, massage, kinesiology, etc. One's mind is knocking on the door of higher consciousness. People may express love and caring more spontaneously. Materialistic individuals could become more concerned with the welfare of others. People might become conscious of hidden healing energy. Neptune can represent subtle and unconscious energies being made known to our conscious thought processes.

Escapism may be converted into creativity. A person may find true compassion. Fear of love may be conquered. Surrender may be experienced. A person may realize life is a gift. He is but a player in a dynamic play. A person who has suffered emotional pain may grieve through a loss. Emotional scars can heal. One can gain emotional strength. The emotional depths of watery Neptune are without end!

Progressed Mercury square natal (or progressed) Neptune or transiting Neptune square natal Mercury can express as dynamic inspiration. A person can pull his life together, rising above problems. One may make dreams known to others. A person can feel like he is awakening from a long sleep. He can wonder why it took so long to realize his potential. Individuals may become more insightful during a crisis. A new faith in self and a higher power may be the catalyst for a creative release of energy. One may communicate more feelings. Interaction on deeper levels of awareness can occur. A person may become aware of life issues related to mental disorientation, addictions, and escapism.

SHADOW

Both the **Mercury/Neptune conjunction and square** can show indecision. The slightest disturbance may create mental confusion. The nervous system may be exhausted by oversensitivity to the environment. Reasoning powers may be quite illogical. Rational excuses for behaviors can be prevalent. A person may try to hide from himself. He does not want to uncover any secrets. One can doubt his intelligence. A person may settle for a life that does not challenge the intellect. A person can stay with a shallow knowledge of the world. Past criticisms of his intelligence could hold him back.

Materialistic people may deny a higher power. Invisible forces are seen as nonsense. A lack of imagination may become even more engrossing. An individual could show poor judgment in setting limits. Common sense can be absent. An individual could lack mental stamina, focus, and initiative. One may hold back creativity due to a fear of not being perfect. Memory loss and a lack of concentration can be problematic. One may resist right-brain intuition. He can stay in a confused mental mess.

People may feel too guilty. Sensitivity can be paramount. Perfectionism can be so accentuated that an individual becomes easily frustrated. A lack of faith or inspiration can point one in the wrong direction. Life may seem a meaningless void. One can find convenient excuses to avoid new experiences. An individual may get attached to addictive habits. Escapism can be accentuated. Substance abuse and other self-defeating behaviors appeal. Staying high to numb the conscious mind becomes an obsession. Running away from problems can occur.

Quincunx: Progressed Mercury Quincunx
                Natal or Progressed Neptune
                Transiting Neptune Quincunx Natal Mercury

Opposition: Progressed Mercury Opposing
                Natal or Progressed Neptune
                Transiting Neptune Opposing Natal Mercury

LIGHT

Progressed Mercury quincunx natal (or progressed) Neptune or transiting Neptune quincunx natal Mercury is the "Yoga of integrating thoughts and intuition." One can gain more control over emotional intensity. A person develops more faith in intuition. Contacting higher psychic energy is a distinct possibility. One thinks more creatively. A person can push himself to the limit to communicate intuitively. He may study how to better use his intuitive energies. A person may take classes, read books, or travel to faraway places to find peace.

A person may sharpen his intellect. Details are better remembered. One may inspire others through humility. A person can go through a powerful personal transformation. An individual can adjust thoughts to match enlightening insights. One may repay a debt or make sacrifice to neutralize his past. A person can transcend mental fantasy to enter the real world. One can rise above everyday hassles to perceive a better world. A lack of imagination can find new inspiring symbols.

Progressed Mercury opposing natal (or progressed) Neptune or transiting Neptune opposing natal Mercury can denote looking at the world through new eyes. A person can see hope where there was despair; faith rather than doubt; inner harmony rather than frustration.

Since the opposition has a natural association with relationships, the Mercury/Neptune opposition involves one's mental images of others. A person can reach new mental heights in communication. An individual may be more intuitive about others. Individuals may display a remarkable versatility in relating. They may become attracted to creative people. A new faith may inspire others to new growth. An awakening to a more collective love can occur. Untapped internal energy can stimulate a person to look for higher consciousness. An individual may travel extensively in search of new knowledge.

A person may adjust his relating style. New levels of compassion and care can occur. A person may find a new depth in giving and receiving love. One can be attracted to collective causes for the needy.

The muse consciousness may be discovered. A person may become highly interested in aesthetics. An artistic or musical expression may be highlighted. Poetry or other forms of writing can be indicated. An individual can sense the mood of a room while speaking. Perceptions of the consciousness in a group can be startling.

This aspect is good for self-promotion or promoting others. There is the power of communication combined with a sixth sense on how to capture the imagination of others. A person may excel at translating symbolic languages. This includes astrology, handwriting analysis, tarot, etc. Individuals may explore creative visualization, meditation, biofeedback, etc.

SHADOW
In both **Mercury/Neptune quincunx and opposition,** a person can misperceive others. One's idealism can lead to relationships with undependable people. A person can see what he chooses to see in others. He may deny their unpleasant attributes. Individuals can be manipulated by guilt. One may grow too easily annoyed with reality. A divine discontent may cause one to leave good situations. An individual may find too much wrong with others due to a highly perfectionistic nature. An individual could ignore his own growth. Talents are projected onto others. A person can feel under the spell of others. They are worshipped as greater in intelligence, spirituality, or beauty. Helplessness and powerlessness are too prevalent.

People can run away from reality. Living in a fantasy world may be tempting. People may fear criticism from others. A person may hide thoughts and real feelings, saying yes when he wants to say no. One can be extremely indecisive. He may wait for perfect moments or have trouble differentiating pros and cons in situations.

People can be miserable trying to keep everything logical and normal. The conscious mind can do with some new intoxicating inspiration. A life void of love is too dry. A mind with little imagination grows dull.

SOFT ASPECTS

Sextile: Progressed Mercury Sextile Natal or Progressed Neptune
Transiting Neptune Sextile Natal Mercury

Trine: Progressed Mercury Trining Natal or Progressed Neptune
Transiting Neptune Trining Natal Mercury

LIGHT

Progressed Mercury sextile natal (or progressed) Neptune or transiting Neptune sextile natal Mercury can express as new imaginative ideas. One's perceptions could be well received by others. A new flexibility can be displayed. **The sextile is already a mental aspect providing a natural home for Mercury in balancing dreamy Neptune.** The flightiness of the intense aspects can be absent in this sextile. More common sense and an ability to market one's aesthetic expertise in business is possible.

Progressed Mercury trine natal (or progressed) Neptune or transiting Neptune trine natal Mercury can show new inspiration and faith. One's ability to look beyond immediate difficulty may increase. A person who previously lacked imagination or faith moves ahead. One's perceptions and imagination could flow nicely. A lot of hard work and waiting finally come to fruition. People may naturally tune into right-brain energies. They may feel more at ease, aspiring to use more creative talent. A hobby such as writing, art, or music could become a profession. An interest in new age subjects for self-growth can occur.

SHADOW

The **Mercury/Neptune sextile and trine** lack the drive of the intense aspects. People can settle for status quo perceptions rather than reach for higher consciousness. One passively goes with the opinions of others. A low threshold for dealing with tension leads to a lot of mental confusion. A person may not trust his intuition. Everything must stay on a rational and predictable level. This can lead to a lack of faith in new thoughts.

The **Mercury/Neptune trine** can denote an individual is poor at setting limits. One may be in the middle of a crisis and ignore the situation. A denial of conflict can prolong negative situations. This trine can express as a self-righteous attitude. A person can judge those who do not have the same puritan standards. An individual may hide behind a spiritual image.

Flights from reality can occur in both the sextile and trine. One can become fanatical concerning devotion to a cause. One's self-promotion to fame could be selfish. A person can lie to others to make himself appear to be a great talent.

DAWN
Mercury/Neptune aspects can express as new ideals. People can hunger for higher consciousness. Neptune can denote transforming the conscious mind. One's perceptions can go beyond a self-focus to a more global perspective. A very intellectual person may develop a more spontaneous emotional flow. A person afraid to love may find the faith for a new relationship. Intuitive clarity can be displayed in communication. Speaking and writing talents may become more refined.

MERCURY/PLUTO ASPECTS

Progressed Mercury/Natal or Progressed Pluto Transiting Pluto/Natal Mercury

Process:	Mental Depth
Ally:	Penetrating Concentration
Illusion:	Extreme Over or Under Use of Power

Mercury/Pluto aspects denote probing thoughts. Perceptions can gain great depth. One may no longer be satisfied with easy answers. The mind can passionately penetrate life's deepest secrets. Nothing may be too taboo to explore. An individual's conscious mind may find refuge in a subconscious filled with knowledge of a glorious past. One may need to guard against compulsive and negative thoughts. Directing mental energy is of the utmost importance!

INTENSE ASPECTS
Conjunction: Progressed Mercury Conjunct
 Natal or Progressed Pluto
 Transiting Pluto Conjunct Natal Mercury

Square: Progressed Mercury Square Natal or Progressed Pluto
 Transiting Pluto Square Natal Mercury '

LIGHT
Progressed Mercury conjunct natal (or progressed) Pluto or transiting Pluto conjunct natal Mercury can symbolize new in-depth perceptions. Life may have more of a process orientation. Thoughts may pierce deeply through obstacles. An individual may be surprised by new insights. A person may inherit a new intellectual intensity. An ability to command attention through words is possible. One may captivate audiences through passionate speech. An interest in symbolic languages can deepen. One may penetrate into the essence of symbols. **Comprehending whole processes may bring one into new creative realms.**

 Individuals may perceptively understand moods. An individual can be a powerful negotiator. Silence may be an ally. One may know which words to use in business dealings. Research of any kind can be a talent. Probing the depths of one's own mind is not unusual. A person can go through numerous consciousness changes. A purification of the conscious mind is possible. Compulsive habits may be dug up from their roots. New perceptions can be born.

Lifetimes of negativity may be dumped. Petty jealousy and possessiveness are no longer allies. One can express a true identity. One's mind can communicate creative intelligence. Self-doubt can turn into trust; self-hatred can become acceptance; imbalanced use of power can turn into shared power. Dealing with a loss or a death is common during this transit. The end of one cycle and the beginning of new cycles often accompanies this aspect.

Progressed Mercury square natal (or progressed) Pluto or transiting Pluto square natal Mercury can be a new passion for learning. **In each of the intense Mercury/Pluto aspects a person can attain a deeper understanding of death.** An acceptance of death can be liberating. A person can become sensitized to the birth and death process. Life can seem like a miracle. Each day is appreciated.

A weak-willed person can find power; an authoritarian can learn that one can't always control situations. Emotional intensity can become more objective. One may masterfully use words to resolve conflicts. People can enjoy using their sexual energies in the conjunction, square and opposition.

SHADOW

Both the **Mercury/Pluto conjunction and square** can express as fixed negative opinions. One can be poisoned by jealousy, possessiveness, and revenge. Thoughts can lack flexibility. A tendency to think situations to death can occur. Letting go and flowing may be difficult. Hypnotic fascination with problems can deplete energy. One may resist looking deeply into life. Staying on the surface can cause lack of insight. A suspicious or doubtful nature can cause one to not perceive life mysteries. A too rational or practical approach takes the magic out of life.

Not trusting can block communication. Individuals may try to dominate communication. Their ideas can be pushed on others. A selfish focus in career or finances can be displayed. Individuals may not perceive situations clearly. Personal biases block clarity. Transitions can be fearful. Compulsive habits can irritate.

Quincunx: Progressed Mercury Quincunx Natal Pluto
Transiting Pluto Quincunx Natal Mercury

Opposition: Progressed Mercury Opposing Natal Pluto
Transiting Pluto Opposing Natal Mercury

LIGHT
Progressed Mercury quincunx natal (or progressed) Pluto or transiting Pluto quincunx natal Mercury can symbolize new focusing ability. Negative programming can be transcended. Perceptions can gain intensity. Inner motivations for compulsive habits can be understood. A healthy respect for irrational thoughts can bring one to new insights. A painful life can be healed.

Individuals may find personal power through communication. Decision making is no longer given away to others. One believes in one's ability to learn. A person may study diligently. An interest in life's mysteries can develop. Comprehending the beginning and end of cycles can bring deep insights. Perceptions may penetrate through previous obstacles. Karmic habits related to compulsive self-defeating actions may be neutralized. A person can redirect a passionate mental energy. Emotions may find more objective clarity.

Progressed Mercury opposing natal (or progressed) Pluto or transiting Pluto opposing natal Mercury can denote deep communication with others. Understanding can manifest on the deepest levels. One's words may command attention. Perceptions may be communicated accurately. One may possess x-ray vision into situations.

Individuals can become more aware of others' needs. A controlling individual may start listening. Sharing of power can replace a dictator. A shy person can gain personal power through communicating ideas. People can stop depending too much on others. One may take control once again of her own existence. A person may recognize the existentialism of life. A greater awareness of life's mysteries can occur. An egotistical person can be humbled by life's infinity. Individuals can gain insight into past-life issues.

Power themes can be balanced. Individuals can work through conflicts in relating. Tension and stress in relationships can be handled. One may be an excellent counselor or therapist with talent for gaining trust and listening. Tuning into the problems of others is an art. Practical advice is at one's fingertips.

SHADOW
Both the **Mercury/Pluto quincunx and opposition** can manifest as suspicion and mistrust. Individuals may fear allowing others to really get to know them. Vulnerability is well hidden. Perceptions may be surfacy. A resistance to penetrating life's illusions can occur. A lack of insight into situations may be exhibited. Individuals can depend too much on the ideas of others. A lack of confidence in perceptions can fog clarity.

Holding onto disastrous relationships can be limiting. A person can be afraid to move out of a relationship. The mind may be enslaved by addictive passions. One can be fooled by lack of perception. She is easily manipulated by her desire nature.

A lack of flexibility in relating can be a problem. Fixed ideas can be hard to compromise. One may be too critical of others. Sarcasm can ruin situations. Hasty judgments can be expressed. A fixation on controlling the resources in a relationship may produce tension. Secret or hidden agendas can be especially destructive of relationships. An individual may not learn from mistakes. Repeating patterns (in controlling others or in becoming enslaved) can occur.

One can be paranoid about death or loss. Insecurity may deplete personal power. Negative thoughts doubt any magic in life. Emotions can be constipated. Hidden resentment and anger distort perceptions. One may project the same relationship problems onto new partners.

SOFT ASPECTS

Sextile: Progressed Mercury Sextile Natal or Progressed Pluto
              Transiting Pluto Sextile Natal Mercury

Trine: Progressed Mercury Trining Natal or Progressed Pluto
              Transiting Pluto Trining Natal Mercury

LIGHT

Progressed Mercury sextile natal (or progressed) Pluto or transiting Pluto sextile natal Mercury can symbolize sharp mental insight. One may deal coolly with difficult tasks. Conflict may be dealt with swiftly. Intellect and emotions join powerfully to communicate passionately. The mind may clear past negative debris. New life transitions are exciting. The past and present combine into a stimulating experience. Ideas flow from the subconscious. A person may retain information as never before.

Emotional upsets can lessen. Problems are faced. Stubborn opinions can be transcended. One may be a good problem solver. Reasoning ability is sharpened. Individuals can make good consultants and negotiators.

Progressed Mercury trine natal (or progressed) Pluto or transiting Pluto trine natal Mercury can overcome negativity. A perfectionist can find that making a mess is not death! Greater patience can occur. One may understand why people think differently. A greater tolerance for opinions is possible. New learning can begin. Metaphysics and life mysteries can be of interest. A new inquisitiveness is born. A power person may give up some power. A weak-willed individual may be in "Personal Power Training 101."

SHADOW

In both the **Mercury/Pluto sextile and trine** individuals can lack reasoning power. An inability to focus scatters mental intensity. Concentrating on solutions seems difficult. A person may give up power too easily. Tension due to conflict can bring an early surrender. One may try too hard to say the right thing. A subtle manipulator can be indicated. One is smooth at deceiving with soft words and unkind motives. An individual may foolishly trust the wrong people. Gullibility is too easily manipulated. One needs to think for oneself. One may have a shallow mental nature. Easy answers cause one to stop before exploring life's deepest questions. A lack of interest in inner motivations can leave many blind spots. The mind may be dull from lack of use or challenges.

DAWN
Mercury/Pluto aspects can point to deep new insights. A person could develop mental strength. Negative habits might be neutralized. Karmic lessons regarding power can be illuminating. Communication could reach new levels. Relationships may reflect honesty and trust. A person might create new opportunities through passionate communicating. Self-mastery through mental focus and emotional intensity can combine into a dynamic self-expression. A deeper set of eyes and ears can be born.

VENUS/MARS ASPECTS

Progressed Venus/Natal or Progressed Mars
Progressed Mars/Natal Venus

Process:	Releasing Social Intensity
Ally:	Fairness and Tact
Illusion:	Satisfying Desires Brings Peace

Venus/Mars aspects denote identity and relating are interdependent. Relationships can be dynamic. One can be dramatic. Sensual desires may be strong. Venus points to harmony and balance; Mars lends itself to a "me-focus." Balance in relationships can occur. Peace vs. war, comfort vs. life in the fast lane, and a shy nature vs. a social being can be issues. Individuals can get more feisty about improving their financial situation.

INTENSE ASPECTS
Conjunction: Progressed Venus Conjunct Natal or Progressed Mars
Progressed Mars Conjunct Natal Venus

Square: Progressed Venus Square Natal or Progressed Mars
Progressed Mars Square Natal Venus

LIGHT
Progressed Venus conjunct natal (or progressed) Mars or progressed Mars conjunct natal Venus can indicate self-satisfaction. A serious individual may discover a fun loving nature. A reserved

person may find new confidence in meeting people. A dead-end career could find a new avenue. An individual may take new pride in appearance and sexuality. A fear of criticism may be transcended. A person may release a hidden passion for life. The love nature can blossom.

Individuals can feel less identified with what they own. A deeper sense of self can be found. Values can become influenced by new peers. An angry person can unlock his hurt; a lonely individual may find a lover; a desperate person some peace.

Progressed Venus square natal (or progressed) Mars or progressed Mars square natal Venus can denote conquering a passion for self-destruction. Extreme sensual urges can be focused more creatively. A person hungry for love finds an aesthetic expression. Individuals can find more self-love, rewarding themselves for hard work and new experiences. One may stop fighting lovers and friends, relaxing into relationships rather than combat.

SHADOW
Both the **Venus/Mars conjunction and square** can express as narcissism. Self-admiration can consume the identity. The outer appearance of life may be too valued. A drive for luxury and attention can be compulsive. One may feel worthless if not surrounded by expensive and beautiful things. The life can be shallow. One may feel unappreciated. Demanding one's own way can occur. Compromise becomes a forgotten word. A warlike nature may emanate.

A self-hating mentality can dominate. One may undervalue self-importance. A self-degrading lifestyle can be exhibited. One may fear owning beautiful things or appearing beautiful. Individuals can allow past emotional hurt to block new relationships. Anger can be expressed unclearly.

Quincunx: Progressed Venus Quincunx Natal or Progressed Mars
         Progressed Mars Quincunx Natal Venus

Opposition: Progressed Venus Opposing Natal or Progressed Mars
         Progressed Mars Opposing Natal Venus

LIGHT
Progressed Venus quincunx natal (or progressed) Mars or progressed Mars quincunx natal Venus is the "Yoga of aligning identity and social instincts." A person may discover self-worth. A lazy person may find self-starting motivation. A procrastinator or overly self-indulgent person may move ahead in life.

Individuals can change relationship patterns. Tuning into needs can clarify relationship desires. One may stop attracting unbalanced situations. Tapping into one's own assertion can terminate a need for dominating partners. Expressing one's own love nature can lessen a relationship based on sensuality alone. People may put an emotionally battered life back together. One can sign a peace treaty with oneself.

Progressed Venus opposing natal (or progressed) Mars or progressed Mars opposing natal Venus can symbolize balanced relationships. A person may be at peace with self and world. One may be assertive yet relaxed. A person may know when to turn intensity on and off. Passion can be depicted. People might be rewarded emotionally and financially. People may be more active than usual. They need to show their abilities. People can get attention without appearing pushy. Individuals may support the work of peers or partners. Financial or emotional support is given vivaciously. People may encourage others to realize their own worth.

SHADOW

Both the **Venus/Mars quincunx and opposition** can denote a loss of initiative. Sensual desires may distract. Relationship and sexual drives could be all-consuming. Values may lack depth. A person could live assertion or sensuality through others. A lack of self-understanding can bring someone to follow the values of others. The identity can be too dependent on acceptance by others. Vulnerabilities may be exploited financially and sexually. A person can be at war with self and others. Individuals may explode when criticized.

One may expect too much affection from others. Admiration and attention can be sought constantly. Depth in relating may be lacking. Individuals may place too much value on sexual intensity. A lack of follow-through in resolving conflict can disrupt relationships.

Individuals may project their own abilities onto others, living aesthetic interests or assertion through a partner. People may shortchange themselves regarding beauty and comfort. Relationships and partnerships may lack stability. Intensity can be too prevalent. Some individuals may seek peace at all costs. Anger could be denied.

SOFT ASPECTS

Sextile: Progressed Venus Sextile Natal or Progressed Mars
Progressed Mars Sextile Natal Venus

Trine: Progressed Venus Trining Natal or Progressed Mars
Progressed Mars Trining Natal Venus

LIGHT

Progressed Venus sextile natal (or progressed) Mars or progressed Mars sextile natal Venus can denote new social ease. A person may make social contacts easily. One's emotional nature can be clear. One may be versatile in changing gears from work to private life. A comfort with one's own identity makes life go smoothly. This time can be exciting for career. One may feel energized by career choices. Relationships may promote self-worth and identity.

Progressed Venus trine natal (or progressed) Mars or progressed Mars trine natal Venus can denote abundance comes easily. One may attract good situations through a positive attitude. A low spirit might fall in love. A reckless person may slow down. A warrior could find peace. A lonely heart may find emotional warmth.

SHADOW
Both the progressed **Venus/Mars sextile and trine** can express as much ado about nothing. Individuals can get intoxicated by earthly pleasures. Too much of a good thing dulls the senses. One may surrender deeper values for easy options. The life could lack real challenge or substance. Relationships may lack emotional depth. Casual affairs may hide vulnerability. A party atmosphere leads to nowhere. A lot of acquaintances are possible but no real friends.

DAWN
Venus/Mars aspects can express as aesthetic beauty. One's life may reflect emotional calm. A competitive spirit filled with generosity may be the highlight. Relationships and love make life more exciting!

VENUS/JUPITER ASPECTS

Progressed Venus/Natal or Progressed Jupiter Transiting Jupiter/Natal Venus

Process:	Understanding Life's Abundance
Ally:	Faith in Highest Values
Illusion:	Eat, Drink, and Be Merry!

Venus/Jupiter aspects can point to an interest in foreign experiences. Curiosity reigns. A person can grow restless with a comfortable present. Expansive relating is desired. One may believe in highest values.

INTENSE ASPECTS
Conjunction: Progressed Venus Conjunct
　　　　　　　　Natal or Progressed Jupiter
　　　　　　　　Transiting Jupiter Conjunct Natal Venus

Square:　　Progressed Venus Square Natal or Progressed Jupiter
　　　　　　　Transiting Jupiter Square Natal Venus

LIGHT
Progressed Venus conjunct natal (or progressed) Jupiter or transiting Jupiter conjunct natal Venus can symbolize a generous attitude. One may find a new spiritual purpose. Peers may encourage growth. A person may feel optimistic about the future. Travel can be educational. An individual may excel at counseling, teaching, or speak-

ing. Finding a more fulfilling existence feels urgent. Individuals may take a broader perspective regarding life circumstances. An eclectic understanding may bring a wider peer group. A bigoted individual may become more tolerant. An overly aggressive type might learn to relax. A serious individual can discover humor. An uneducated person may find new knowledge.

Progressed Venus square natal (or progressed) Jupiter or transiting Jupiter square natal Venus can denote an urgency to practice what is preached. Principles and highest ideals lead one to new plateaus. A miserly person can understand life's abundance. Giving and receiving become a natural flow. People may confidently show affection. Warmth and humor are no longer hidden.

The lifestyles of others may stimulate growth. One may find special meaning in the spiritual beliefs or customs of various cultures. The foreign or different can be stimulating. Travel can be fruitful, healing the psyche. Leaving daily routines is a freeing experience. Travel turns one's past into rich memories.

SHADOW
Both the Venus/Jupiter conjunction and square can manifest as pompous behavior. One may rationalize any situation. Opinions may be careless and lack facts. Bragging can alienate others. The truth may be strictly to impress peers. Biting off more than one can chew can occur. Unfulfilled promises can break the trust of others.

One may be fickle. Decisions might be procrastinated. People may be "penny wise and pound foolish." Wasteful spending of time and money is possible. Common sense about the material world is lacking. Spiritual ideals may lack grounding. One could have an unrealistic imagination. Having a good time can reach extremes. One may not face hard work. Commitment to ideals and relationships is absent.

Quincunx: Progressed Venus Quincunx Natal or Progressed Jupiter
Transiting Jupiter Quincunx Natal Venus

Opposition: Progressed Venus Opposing Natal or Progressed Jupiter
Transiting Jupiter Opposing Natal Venus

LIGHT
Progressed Venus quincunx natal (or progressed) Jupiter or transiting Jupiter quincunx natal Venus can denote taking values to a deeper level. One may begin more self-honesty. The truth brings freedom.

Physical appetites may be moderated. A desire for more balance brings desires under control. Belief in a higher power might bring relief. A more disciplined life can occur. One may find more meaningful work. A dead-end existence may be left behind. A lack of faith could be transcended.

Progressed Venus opposing natal (or progressed) Jupiter or transiting Jupiter opposing natal Venus can express as new positive relationships. One may feel a great self-confidence. Emotional honesty is expressed. An individual may be open to a true and meaningful union. Relationships can be highly stimulating. People may encounter new relating through travel.

One may find a teacher. She may enjoy exchanging knowledge with others. Truth and honesty can be powerful allies. Peers may encourage individuals to be all they can be. People may find a restored faith in relating. A greater belief in self or a higher power can bring self-confidence. Individuals may stop projecting their finest attributes onto others. One may discover her creative resources. A judgmental person may find more tolerance. Dogmatism and narrow attitudes can be surrendered.

SHADOW

Both the **Venus/Jupiter quincunx and opposition** can represent a lack of loyalty or honesty. One may jump from one relationship to another with no real depth desired. One might run away from problems. Individuals may take advantage of generosity without reciprocating. One may charm others to foolishly give their trust. Worshipping others can be troublesome. One may blindly follow guru figures, trying to live faith in a higher power through an idealized person. Following the unsound judgment of others could lead to disaster.

Foolish investing could waste resources. A lazy attitude could bring poverty. One may lack faith in the abundance of life. People may rigidly demand others live according to their own values or standards. A lack of flexibility is contrary to Jupiter's eclectic understanding. Individuals could go to the other extreme. There is never enough love, money, or admiration received or spent. A lack of consistency or balance aborts one's happiness. People may expect too much from others. Idealism or expectations are easily disappointed.

SOFT ASPECTS

Sextile: Progressed Venus Sextile Natal or Progressed Jupiter
Transiting Jupiter Sextile Natal Venus

Trine: Progressed Venus Trining Natal or Progressed Jupiter
Transiting Jupiter Trining Natal Venus

LIGHT

Progressed Venus sextile natal (or progressed) Jupiter or transiting Jupiter sextile natal Venus can express as enthusiasm regarding new financial or relationship opportunities. A restless spirit may search for expansive growth. A desire for financial security can lead to business success. One may be adept at making snap decisions.

Relationships may be less intense than usual. A person may stop forcing situations to happen. She may sense what makes a relationship successful.

One could integrate the mundane and spiritual. A person's highest values spill over into everyday life. An already content person may find a deeper understanding of life. A person lacking faith or self-confidence can discover life's generosity.

Progressed Venus trine natal (or progressed) Jupiter or transiting Jupiter trine natal Venus can denote a generous spirit. A person's natural enthusiasm pours outward. Others are moved to greater faith and confidence. One may enjoy people with the same beliefs. A mutually supportive spirituality might be shared. A hunger for a greater life purpose leads one to creative pursuits. One may be an advisor, counselor, lecturer, or teacher. Individuals may inspire others to learn.

SHADOW

In both the **Venus/Jupiter sextile and trine** a person can be too full of himself! One may pretend to honor the opinions of others. He may be diplomatic with ulterior motives. People can foolishly trust others. One may too generously give resources. A too passive approach to life may lack depth. Individuals may deny problems.

People may be impatient. They could have little time for the problems of others. Seeking easy solutions brings a shallow life. Relationships may stay on philosophical levels, denying emotional depth. Individuals may run away from closeness. One may wear a spiritual facade. A "holier than thou" attitude could be projected onto peers. One may hide insecurities.

DAWN

Venus/Jupiter aspects can represent embracing one's highest values. A lack of faith can become a restored belief in self or in a higher power. A generous spirit believes in life's abundance. Spiritual sharing strengthens relationships. Emotional content can be honest. One may have a natural enthusiasm for knowledge and truth.

VENUS/SATURN ASPECTS

Progressed Venus/Natal or Progressed Saturn Transiting Saturn/Natal Venus

Process:	Establishing Commitments
Ally:	Sound Values
Illusion:	Resisting Change

Venus/Saturn aspects symbolize one is serious concerning relationships. Finding harmony within life challenges is a key theme. Time tests the depth of our relationships and physical attachments. Issues related to expressing affection and developing relationships are accentuated. Learning to share one's resources and warmth can be a focus. An overly serious or reserved nature can be an issue.

INTENSE ASPECTS
Conjunction: Progressed Venus Conjunct
                Natal or Progressed Saturn
                Transiting Saturn Conjunct Natal Venus
Square: Progressed Venus Square Natal or Progressed Saturn
                Transiting Saturn Square Natal Venus

LIGHT
Progressed Venus conjunct natal (or progressed) Saturn or transiting Saturn conjunct natal Venus can connote a deeper appreciation for relationships. One learns to see from another person's perspective. The lasting value of a committed relationship is appreciated. Directing this intense energy into life ambitions brings inner satisfaction. Individuals can conquer fear of rejection. A new confidence may be discovered. Blocked affection may be released. A serious disposition can become more playful.

A person fearing ownership of material items may find it a joy rather than a burden. Venus/Saturn aspects often become clearer as we grow older. Appreciation for things of lasting value can slowly unfold. Receiving recognition for talents and hard work builds confidence.

Individuals might face the reality that there are no perfect people. They may balance too much idealism. Some individuals begin getting over a past rejection. A healing period may ensue. Overcoming a loss can be spiritually strengthening.

Progressed Venus square natal (or progressed) Saturn or transiting Saturn square natal Venus can denote reconciling an inner conflict. A person can tap into a previously lacking peace. This is a forceful aspect. A person can find new self-respect. One may tap into the strength to reverse a depressing economic condition.

One's charisma may attract people of wisdom or authority. A bold step can form important career contacts. One may shake the hold of a past failed business or love relationship. Rejection or lack of support is often the problem. Rising above personal conflict releases new energy. In both the conjunction and the square, starting a business is very possible. Wisdom in business affairs can grow rapidly during this cycle. Putting practical experiences to work is rewarding. Business partnerships can be important. Developing a business, as in establishing clients and getting resources, can occur.

SHADOW
The **Venus/Saturn conjunction or square** can mix the relating drive of Venus with the need to be in control depicted by Saturn. A cold dis-

play of conditional love can result. **A fear of losing control brings a lack of trust.** Any Venus/Saturn aspect may feature this theme. A lack of support for others can ruin relationships. A ruthless, ambitious nature could dominate. A depressed and inflexible nature might block new opportunities. Negativity attracts a lack of happiness or abundance. One may be too insensitive to the rights of others. Power and position become a compulsive passion. Controlling people through power brings trouble. One is just as likely to attract individuals who are dominating and controlling.

Individuals may awaken a karmic pattern. They still misuse power urges. If a person refuses to change, the individual attracts difficult relationships and career circumstances. A fear of losing control or being rejected can be scary. A lack of affection reen received early in life is often related to difficulty expressing warmth as an adult.

Quincunx: Progressed Venus Quincunx Natal or Progressed Saturn
Transiting Saturn Quincunx Natal Venus

Opposition: Progressed Venus Opposing Natal or Progressed Saturn
Transiting Saturn Opposing Natal Venus

LIGHT

Progressed Venus quincunx natal (or progressed) Saturn or transiting Saturn quincunx natal Venus may denote coming to grips with relationship issues. One may show more affection and establish balanced relationships. This aspect is the **"Yoga of trusting commitments."** A compulsive drive to sacrifice power to others can be conquered. One can find a new self-respect and take responsibility for actions. Pleasure and hard work can be balanced. One may find a happy medium, enjoying life's pleasures while satisfying ambitions.

Progressed Venus opposing natal (or progressed) Saturn or transiting Saturn opposing natal Venus can connote wanting harmony in relating to others. **Since Venus is the relationshinet, this opposition has a special focus on defining romantic and business relationships.** Closure with a relationship may be required. Relating issues may undergo reality testing.

The cosmic chiropractor, Saturn, indicates some adjustments may be needed. An individual or a lover may need to better define their relationship. **Communication** is a key ingredient in the opposition aspect. Each person needs to acknowledge their commitment to the other. People may seek more stable partners. An individual who has had unpredictable partners may find someone willing to share responsibility. Roots are sought with a partner. The emotional roller coaster has been too exhausting.

This aspect can point to business ventures. The strategy orientation of pragmatic Saturn interfaces nicely with Venus instincts for the value of things. Sometimes people are wise to focus on their career and serious ambitions rather than worrying about the success potential of a relationship. It is possible for a person to be successful on both front simultaneously! Proving one's self-worth is an especially forceful drive in Venus/Saturn hard aspects.

SHADOW

In both the **Venus/Saturn quincunx and opposition,** the social urges of Venus may interface with a "hard" reality of Saturn. A person may do too much of the work in a relationship. He can receive little in return. A person's adoration for a partner goes to extremes. Compulsive drives for acceptance and love work overtime. A lack of balance in relating is highlighted. The individual sometimes feels not deserving of a relationship.

People can become frustrated with a good situation. A lack of flexibility or ignoring options may terminate an excellent opportunity. Individuals may try too hard to change other people. Perhaps one cannot relax into a relationship. Losing control is agonizing. Too much self-consciousness causes one to miss relationship and career opportunities.

A person can have difficulty in finding time for relationships. A career drive may dominate all other interests. One can be too sensitive to the expectations of others. Everybody seems too demanding. Commitments to a career or personal relationships may be avoided.

SOFT ASPECTS
   Sextile: Progressed Venus Sextile Natal or Progressed Saturn
                        Transiting Saturn Sextile Natal Venus

   Trine: Progressed Venus Trining Natal or Progressed Saturn
                        Transiting Saturn Trining Natal Venus

LIGHT

Progressed Venus sextile natal (or progressed) Saturn or transiting Saturn sextile natal Venus may denote exciting social interactions. One can have new enterprising ideas. The soft aspects indicate people may be less controlling with others. They can feel less threatened or distracted by others. A relaxed atmosphere prevails.

Progressed Venus trine natal (or progressed) Saturn or transiting Saturn trine natal Venus can denote feeling more deserving of abundance. An urge to celebrate one's accomplishments can occur. The trine indicates a lot of confidence. One gives himself permission to give and receive affection. It is okay to be happy. Every moment need not be spent fulfilling the needs of others. It is okay to rest rather than work. One can flow with disharmony.

SHADOW

In both the **Venus/Saturn sextile and trine,** the desire for harmony might be expected to come with no work. A person can take too much for granted. People seem expendable. The softer aspects are not as direct as the intensity-promoting aspects. For instance, in the opposition of Venus/Saturn one may be rather cold and authoritarian in relating, or attract others who are cold and authoritarian. However, in many cases these people are easier to figure out than in the trine. There is such an ease in the trine that a person may actually get away with more! It is harder to set the limits. Usually, in the more intense aspects the limits are well defined, even if negative. A self-centeredness can occur in the softer aspects. One can be too focused on getting recognition to the exclusion of others.

DAWN

Venus/Saturn aspects can express as greater fulfillment. Bringing others into our life can help one achieve happiness. Ambition and recognition come naturally. Our relationships can handle the stresses of modern life. We may acknowledge each other's strengths as well as shortcomings. The social urges and desire for harmony of Venus can reach new heights when combined with the patience and hardworking themes of Saturn.

VENUS/URANUS ASPECTS

Progressed Venus/Natal or Progressed Uranus Transiting Uranus/Natal Venus

Process:	The Freedom to be Oneself
Ally:	Unique Value Systems
Illusion:	Eccentric Tastes

Venus/Uranus aspects awaken relationship urges. These are potentially very exciting aspects. One often encounters people from different backgrounds. One's relationship preferences can change dramatically. Existing love relationships may alter. Traditional astrology often referred to Venus/Uranus aspects as divorce aspects. I think of these aspects more in terms of **experimentation.** One can learn how to cooperate on equal terms.

INTENSE ASPECTS

Conjunction: Progressed Venus Conjunct
Natal or Progressed Uranus
Transiting Uranus Conjunct Natal Venus

Square: Progressed Venus Conjunct
Natal or Progressed Uranus
Transiting Uranus Conjunct Natal Venus

LIGHT
Progressed Venus conjunct natal (or progressed) Uranus or transiting Uranus conjunct natal Venus can symbolize more boldness in relationships. One may become more aware of personal needs. A person previously paying little attention to her own goals may awaken suddenly to new potentials. Individuals may enter relationships more spontaneously. A reserved individual could become more expressive. Falling in love might spark creative imagination. One's aesthetic aspirations may fuse with serious goals.

An individual may discover more dimensions of her personality. Flexibility in relating emotions can occur. One may be exhilarating and inspiring to be around. People may exude a newfound independence. New and exciting relationships can develop. People can sometimes survive a lot of conflict in immediate situations. They may display objectivity while others are emotionally confused. They bring harmony into tense situations. One can be an innovative peacemaker.

A new sensuality can develop. Individuals can choose to be more experimental sexually. They may overcome a shy nature. People sometimes break into entirely new lifestyles. An individual may outgrow existing conditions, including a career. Changing careers for new growth can be a positive move. A person might need a lot of freedom. Existing relationships may need more space to keep harmony. One may get especially creative in relating to others. One may fall deeper in love with a lover or spouse.

Progressed Venus square natal (or progressed) Uranus or transiting Uranus square natal Venus can express as combining harmony and individuality. One may stimulate aesthetic ideas in others. A love for life and an abundance of excitement can lead to success in realizing goals. This can be a very enterprising aspect. One may forcefully challenge the environment. Intense interactions can stimulate people to be more creative. Conflict in relationships can be dealt with. An individual may perceive how to achieve harmony from a unique perspective. Existing relationships may achieve deeper meaning. One may stimulate partners to respect their own independence and abilities. A person may display a new courage in relating on the business, peer or love levels. Overcoming sensitivity with objectivity can aid decision making. The emotions are more balanced. In each of the intense Venus/Uranus aspects, relationships can begin suddenly. Surprise is a desirable experience.

SHADOW
In both the **Venus/Uranus conjunction and square**, a person can be too sensitive to criticism. One may react too abruptly when not given enough attention. Individuals can become emotionally unstable. Change may make one excessively nervous and insecure.

A person may push people away due to a fear of closeness. However, the opposite can occur. One may fear her independence and desire too much closeness. A person may even vacillate to either extreme on an irregular basis, making relationships unpredictable. A failure to communicate clearly can produce tension. One may grow impatient with people. It is possible to leave situations too quickly. Snap decisions could be regretted later. An individual may be emotionally drained. Due to a lack of focus, a person can waste emotional or physical resources. One may spend money carelessly. A person may impulsively buy material things to fill the void of not receiving love and support.

Quincunx: Progressed Venus Quincunx Natal or Progressed Uranus
Transiting Uranus Quincunx Natal Venus

Opposition: Progressed Venus Opposing Natal or Progressed Uranus
Transiting Uranus Opposing Natal Venus

LIGHT

Progressed Venus quincunx natal (or progressed) Uranus or transiting Uranus quincunx natal Venus is the "Yoga of relationship equality." One may experience new humility. She may be more supportive of others. One may transcend a pattern of either not paying enough attention to her own goals, or being too self-centered. Excessive sexual stimulation and unfulfilling relationships may be transformed into more stability. One may make friends with lovers.

Progressed Venus opposing natal (or progressed) Uranus or transiting Uranus opposing natal Venus may indicate valuing friendship. The giving and receiving of support can reach new heights. A new cooperation with others may be achieved. One often desires more freedom and space. She can enjoy both closeness and distance. One may respond to others without emotional outbursts or prolonged separations. Needs and expectations may be communicated. A new sensitivity to others can occur.

An individual may leave relationships or groups that stifle growth. One may gain objective awareness. A person can move ahead to new challenges. One may achieve more depth in relating to others, trying extra hard to find common goals. Cooperation and diplomacy could become allies. A person may allow more harmony into her life. An individual could get involved in collective trends. She might become an important catalyst for changes. Peers may respect her insights into future trends.

A new creativity in relating to others can be exciting. People may tolerate more conflict. One may welcome the challenge of new growth. People may excel at communication. Relating to people of very diverse backgrounds can occur. One may put others at ease during times of change. This can be an exhilarating time. One may accomplish numerous goals simultaneously. Balance fulfills the needs of both self and others.

SHADOW

In both the **Venus/Uranus quincunx and opposition,** a person may be easily talked out of goals. Leaning on others for advice may take away from personal needs.

People could feel too vulnerable when falling in love. Romantic encounters may be kept strictly physical to hide vulnerability. A person might fear individuality. She may seek too much protection. An individual can sacrifice too much individuality. She projects attributes onto lovers and spouses. One may be reckless in relationships. She can be unreliable when you need her most. She may run away from shared support and cooperation.

An individual might compulsively pursue unstable friends and lovers. Both partners may be drained by emotional turmoil. Constant intensity in emotional relationships could be addictive. People may waste material things. They may have little respect for the possessions of others.

SOFT ASPECTS

Sextile: Progressed Venus Sextile Natal or Progressed Uranus
            Transiting Uranus Sextile Natal Venus

Trine: Progressed Venus Trining Natal or Progressed Uranus
            Transiting Uranus Trining Natal Venus

LIGHT

The soft Venus/Uranus aspects do not have an intense drive to satisfy the conflict between personal goals and those of others. **Progressed Venus sextile natal (or progressed) Uranus or transiting Uranus sextile natal Venus can indicate one enjoys stimulating relationships.** She may relax into emotional relating. An individual may feel more supportive of others.

People may learn to relax period! A burned-out individualist can have a cooling-out period and tune into personal goals. New friendships or peers can be stimulating. One may begin a sudden romance. An individual might get closer to people she once did not understand. Groups can support growth.

Progressed Venus trine natal (or progressed) Uranus or transiting Uranus trine natal Venus can symbolize a new faith in humanity. One may feel particularly upbeat. Life seems to flow. Goals may lead to personal satisfaction. The soft aspects may attract relationships with less effort. A sense of harmony attracts new people.

SHADOW
In both the **Venus/Uranus sextile and trine**, a person can be too dependent on group support. One's goals may be surrendered to a group mentality. A person may take too much for granted in the soft aspects. One may not be ready for problems that surface. One may leave a good relationship that merely requires some adjusting. Breaking through one's aloofness can be difficult. A person can be less inclined to deal with emotional coldness.

DAWN
Venus/Uranus aspects can express as new growth in relating. One can enjoy both closeness and distance. A new level of cooperation can be attained. People may enjoy the simple things in life. A person can communicate needs and expectations more clearly. One may branch out into new peer groups. A great curiosity and drive to establish unique relationships exist. The stimulation and excitement in meeting new people can inspire new insights. Unique values can be discovered.

VENUS/NEPTUNE ASPECTS

Progressed Venus/Natal or Progressed Neptune Transiting Neptune/Natal Venus

Process:	Faith in Ideals
Ally:	Compassion and Transformational Love
Illusion:	Blind Faith

Venus/Neptune aspects represent a special romance. One may ignore cultural standards or escape societal pressures through love and romance. One can tune into new spiritual values. New peers and love relationships can begin in strange ways. One may feel as though he has known strangers for years.

INTENSE ASPECTS
Conjunction: Progressed Venus Conjunct
Natal or Progressed Neptune
Transiting Neptune Conjunct Natal Venus

Square: Progressed Venus Square Natal or Progressed Neptune
Transiting Neptune Square Natal Venus

LIGHT
Progressed Venus conjunct natal (or progressed) Neptune or transiting Neptune conjunct natal Venus can symbolize feeling showered by love. The heart can open wide. Self-acceptance may take place. An individual may find a person who knows him on a deep level. Both may see deeply into each other's soul. No barriers or defenses sep-

arate one another. Each instinctively may understand the other's karma.

In traditional astrology, Neptune was said to be the higher octave of Venus. Neptune has connections with a right-brain flood of intuition. It is a planet associated with universal love. Collective trends related to beauty and the arts are additional themes. Venus is a more personal factor. It is our way of expressing affection and initiating relationships.

Both the Moon/Neptune and Venus/Neptune aspects symbolize a powerful relationship with one's own inner feminine. Artists, musicians, poets, writers, and metaphysicians often have these aspects at birth. A person can sense a deeper life purpose. There can be a powerful, soul-felt aesthetic drive. Bruce Springsteen dramatically burst into learning guitar at age 13 while transiting Neptune conjuncted his natal Venus.

A person can sometimes sense a divine intervention. It is as though "the time has arrived." Faith and inspiration can blossom. An individual can display a passion for love and intuitive processes. The conscious mind may be elevated away from negativity. It is like the frog in the well finding out there is an ocean!

A person may develop more sensitivity to life's quiet messages. Nature, dreams, reading, listening to music or creating can take on new meaning. The mind may let go to the heart. A greater affection and warmth can occur. One can become a "bigger" person by going beyond a "me" focus. A person can tune into a collective consciousness. This could point to working in movements to improve the environment, etc.

Progressed Venus square natal (or progressed) Neptune or transiting Neptune square natal Venus can express as newfound faith in self. A person can rise above a fear of falling in love. One may find meaningful relationships. Individuals can boldly face conflicts around escapism. Some individuals can cross karmic roadblocks. One may face past-life patterns related to emotionally unstable relationships, escapism, or addiction.

An individual may strive for perfection. A remarkable intuitive sense may lead to a harmonious relationship with one's entire environment. A true emotional fortitude and sensitivity can attract success. People may live their highest values. They may live an ordinary life but with a deep recognition of a universal harmony. One's presence may inspire idealism, creativity, and faith. He could be a role model for other generations.

SHADOW

In both the **Venus/Neptune conjunction and square**, an individual can lose himself in compulsive desires for sex, television, attention, food, or substances. A fear of knowing oneself can lead to bizarre relating or addictions. Running away from problems can be destructive. One can be filled with self-doubt and be emotionally disoriented. Guilt may be a nemesis. Individuals can fear consciousness-raising experiences. One may retreat to the imagined safety of hiding the true self.

A person can become overly sensitive. An individual may tire easily due to soaking up vibrations of others. He may not disengage from emotions. It becomes important to turn off right-brain flows or highly charged emotional sensitivity. A person can have trouble integrating everyday needs with a flighty imagination. He may let compulsive drives lead to unfulfilling relationships.

One may foolishly lose physical resources. A very trusting or idealistic nature can give into others too quickly. They may not have his best interests in mind. There can be greed. A person can lack a conscience. One can fraudulently represent his intentions.

Quincunx: Progressed Venus Quincunx
Natal or Progressed Neptune
Transiting Neptune Quincunx Natal Venus

Opposition: Progressed Venus Opposing
Natal or Progressed Neptune
Transiting Neptune Opposing Natal Venus

LIGHT
Progressed Venus quincunx natal (or progressed) Neptune or transiting Neptune quincunx natal Venus is the "Yoga of developing a loving nature." This can express as romantic love. Individuals can sense the intricate nature of universal forces. One's balance and gracefulness can be a work of art. One's presence can soothe others. A healing power may come through a compassionate nature.

Individuals can stop projecting creativity onto lovers, spouses, or peers. A person can tune into her own talents. One's personal relationship with the muse consciousness can begin.

A denial of emotion and intuition can be transcended. A person may find a new faith in intuitive powers. A revived love of self may inspire new relating. Individuals may bring spiritual values into focus. Someone can be too devoted to spiritual movements or guru figures. Physical and spiritual levels of awareness may be integrated. Disarray may be put into order. One can face a life of emotional confusion. A person may slowly put a disoriented life back into place.

Progressed Venus opposing natal (or progressed) Neptune or transiting Neptune opposing natal Venus can express as a greater sense of one's presence in the world. Not only personal relationships are highlighted. One's entire way of relating to life through powers of imagination, faith, and inspiration are denoted. An individual can develop deep love relationships. Caring about loved ones can intensify. An awareness of the inner beauty of self can propel relationships to new understanding.

Individuals may take a new attitude regarding romantic love. One may bring idealism and imagination more into balance with the needs of others. A male may stop projecting his inner fantasy of the perfect female (*anima*) onto partners. He may see the real person. An individual could acknowledge his own feelings and intuition. A female could stop blocking this expression of love and emotion, too.

A fear of having inner beauty recognized by others could be transcended. An individual could reach a new level of love and emotional sharing in an existing relationship. Both people could inspire one another to new heights. Consciousness-raising experiences could be explored jointly. An individual may desire more closeness with others. Dependency may be seen as more natural. One may learn about love. A person addicted to "falling in love" may find more of herself within deep emotional relationships.

Venus can denote earning money (due to its rulership of earthy Taurus). A person may develop a career rather than depending on partners for support. Someone too dedicated to work may need to pay more attention to love relationships. A person may make peace with life. An angry type might more appropriately negotiate needs. She can master the art of diplomacy.

One may experience a spiritual renaissance. A stronger relationship with a higher power can occur. The universal love themes of Neptune may appeal. A new faith in oneself could transpire. Personal relating may become more dynamic.

One can more fully express her highest and clearest qualities. An individual may become an excellent counselor. She may find a new age or an aesthetic, creative expression. An openness to the muse consciousness can occur. One may discover how to relate from the right brain. An individual may help others explore their own intuitive potentials.

SHADOW
In both the **Venus/Neptune quincunx and opposition,** a person can be turned off by relationships. An individual can block intuition. She may attract individuals with escapist habits. A person may be quite disappointed by lovers or spouses. This can be due to having very high expectations. A person can be involved with unreliable partners. Individuals may ignore real problems. They may love those who do not love them. They may allow blind faith to lead them. People may hide behind Hollywood performances. They may wear false outer images. The same film keeps rolling. One gives up too much of herself. Some people do this out of guilt. Others are too much of a helper. They lack boundaries of knowing when to stop giving.

A person may deny the existence of a higher power. A fear of intuition may leave one with little faith. One may deny the inner feminine or imaging power. A lack of idealism or romantic intensity could create stale relationships.

SOFT ASPECTS

Sextile: Progressed Venus Sextile Natal or Progressed Neptune
Transiting Neptune Sextile Natal Venus

Trine: Progressed Venus Trining Natal or Progressed Neptune
Transiting Neptune Trining Natal Venus

LIGHT

Progressed Venus sextile natal (or progressed) Neptune or transiting Neptune sextile natal Venus can denote a new love of life. A person can feel stimulated by new peers and opportunities. The soft Venus/Neptune aspects lack the drive to conquer environmental obstacles. A sense of flowing unity can emerge.

One may develop remarkable intuitive ability. She can dodge detours from fulfillment. One's inspiring attitudes can attract fulfilling career, family, and love opportunities. Multiple expressions are possible. One may juggle an intense career and love life harmoniously. Physical and spiritual life are mutually reinforcing. One can fulfill self-growth and be supportive of others.

Progressed Venus trine natal (or progressed) Neptune or transiting Neptune trine natal Venus can indicate new faith in self and/or life itself. The universe may appear more giving. An attitude shifts from feeling lack to abundance. Enthusiasm can be powerful. A spontaneous expression of give-and-take may occur. Pride in one's creative ability may lead to greater accomplishments. An extremely intense emotional individual might find more peace. A greater awareness of the subconscious may ease intensity levels. Life is accepted at face value. Addictions associated with escapism and emotional imbalance may be surrendered.

SHADOW

In the **Venus/Neptune sextile or trine**, one could feel tension due to indecision. Too many doors are opening. A choice must be made. Transitions may be nervous experiences. One could adjust slowly. A lack of inner clarity brings confusion. One may be naive or gullible.

One may appear shallow but be truly capable of deep relating. Too much self-consciousness can lead to unclear perceptions. One may try too hard to save others. Relationships with people who do little to improve self-defeating behaviors can waste a lot of time. A person could feel extremely dependent on others. A desire for a fantasy world with no problems could lead to trouble. People can be Pollyanna types who ignore the faults of others.

DAWN
In Venus/Neptune aspects, a selfish individual could become more sensitive and caring. A reckless individualist could slow down and enjoy life's simplicity. A deeper appreciation for lovers and spouses may occur. An individual may take less for granted. Universal love and collective powers may tune an individual into more consciousness. Awareness of the intangible can occur. This can be a wonderful time in life. Venus/Neptune aspects are the stuff that create dreams and idealism. An intense faith in oneself and life can be expressed.

VENUS/PLUTO ASPECTS

Progressed Venus/Natal or Progressed Pluto Transiting Pluto/Natal Venus

Process:	Deep Intense Bonding Instincts
Ally:	Trusting the Power of Love
Illusion:	Manipulating Power of Love

Venus/Pluto aspects can be filled with intense expressions of love. A passion for life can come through sexuality, values, and warmth. Deeper meaning is sought through relationships. A sharing of values, customs, resources, and love can reach intimate levels. A person can feel trust and loyalty. Issues often center around directing intense emotional energies. Balancing power within relationships is a key theme.

INTENSE ASPECTS
Conjunction: Progressed Venus Conjunct Natal or Progressed Pluto
             Transiting Pluto Conjunct Natal Venus
Square: Progressed Venus Square Natal or Progressed Pluto
             Transiting Pluto Square Natal Venus

LIGHT
Progressed Venus conjunct natal (or progressed) Pluto or transiting Pluto conjunct natal Venus can denote finding one's niche. One may bond with a lover or spouse. A true sharing love can be established. A commitment to each other's welfare and growth is understood.

Values can change profoundly. The same beliefs may no longer fulfill a growing intensity. One may penetrate through the walls of a family, group, or cultural beliefs. The past may truly be put to rest. Grieving a loss (whether material or spiritual) can bring strength. Self-honesty releases hidden emotions. The dam can break.

Personal power may rise through initiating new relationships. Love, friendship, or business can build confidence. Financial independence improves self-esteem. A cold personality could thaw. A type "A" can value relaxation. The austere can appreciate rewards.

Individuals can find sexual expression. Compulsive sex drives could be better directed. Addictive habits may be moderated. Past-life power themes involving relationships can be resolved. Repressed power instincts are born. Extreme power urges learn to share intensity.

Progressed Venus square natal (or progressed) Pluto or transiting Pluto square natal Venus can denote finding meaningful values. Worn-out purposes give way to truer needs. Simplicity can conquer complexity. A serious individual may learn to relax. A passive person finds focus. One can find suitable outlets for emotional intensity. Pouring energy into work or projects takes pressure off of loved ones or peers. A desperate search for a purpose can yield aesthetic expression. One's art may be filled with passion. Aesthetics can be therapeutic. A passion to improve a standard of living can intensify. Helping finance the career aspirations of others is possible.

SHADOW
Both the **Venus/Pluto conjunction and square** can denote extreme mistrust. One may be too protective of resources and emotions. Intimacy might be blocked by a fear of closeness. Individuals can erupt like emotional volcanoes. Anger and resentment are dumped on the nearest targets. One may take and give little in return.

People may go through a values crisis. A life with no purpose can be disoriented. Surviving physical or emotional loss can be traumatic. A person may fear life's mysteries. She may wish to stay ignorant. A lack of emotional depth can keep relating shallow. An individual may attract conflict. Relationships and career may lack consistency. Everyday life can be a constant crisis. Compulsive karmic habits can return. Subconscious thoughts may dictate irrational choices. A person can stubbornly refuse to make good choices. Sensual appetites can ruin happy situations.

Quincunx: Progressed Venus Quincunx Natal or Progressed Pluto
Transiting Pluto Quincunx Natal Venus

Opposition: Progressed Venus Opposing Natal or Progressed Pluto
Transiting Pluto Opposing Natal Venus

LIGHT
Progressed Venus quincunx natal (or progressed) Pluto or transiting Pluto quincunx natal Venus can symbolize a greater life purpose. This is the **"Yoga of focusing emotional intensity."** An individual may realize new relationship needs. Individuals may stop depending too much on the resources of others. Domination by others can be overcome. Emotional imbalance in relating can be transcended.

Individuals can look deeply into their souls and find greater self worth. A person can control compulsive desires. Emotional hatred can find more peace. A self-punishing person can give herself rewards. A weak-willed person can find more personal power. A power-oriented person can learn to share power. A person stuck in the past can discover hope for the present. Individuals may tap into clearer emotional expression.

Progressed Venus opposing natal (or progressed) Pluto or transiting Pluto opposing natal Venus can denote bonding deeply with others. Relationships can feature shared power. A person may understand others on deep levels, tuning into their emotional needs. Forgiving the past can free emotional intensity. Individuals may now accept those who have hurt them. Rising above emotional scars is liberating.

Addiction to people that bring extreme emotional pain can be overcome. Irrational submissiveness to others can be neutralized. One may stop trying to control others. A more authentic self-expression attracts more productive relationships. An individual can enjoy sexual rapport and emotional fulfillment. A desperate need for a relationship can be curbed by increased self-worth. One may learn to enjoy space and privacy.

An individual may find peers with the same karmic habits. The friendship may give both the confidence to conquer compulsive habits. Lack of trust can be transcended. A person may achieve a productive relationship. An individual may stop giving up too much power to others. More insight into relationship patterns can bring fulfillment.

People may find success in business. A person can handle great sums of money expertly. She may have a green thumb for financial success. People can survive difficult situations. The compost of the past brings a fruitful present. Refusing to focus on lack and negatives can bring new growth situations. One may deal constructively with a physical or emotional loss.

SHADOW

Both the **Venus/Pluto quincunx and opposition** can indicate strange emotional states. Individuals may fear trusting others. Moods can be difficult to express. People can choose silence when communication could remedy problems. Past emotional conflicts can block closeness. One may create problems to avoid intimacy. Others are blamed for problems.

A lack of insight into the motivations of others can be troublesome. Individuals may be easy prey for manipulative types, who take advantage of one's resources and emotions. Individuals may not feel worthy of love. Perhaps past emotional scars are not resolved. Low self-esteem thwarts chances for healthy relating.

One may attract individuals out of touch with their feelings. They may be difficult to get to know with unpredictable moods. Power struggles can be a way of life. One may fight with lovers and in business. Compromising can be difficult. Physical desires can be extreme. Compulsive habits throw the life out of balance. Careless business risks can be typical of the intense Venus/Pluto aspects.

SOFT ASPECTS
Sextile: Progressed Venus Sextile Natal or Progressed Pluto
                 Transiting Pluto Sextile Natal Venus

Trine: Progressed Venus Trining Natal or Progressed Pluto
                 Transiting Pluto Trining Natal Venus

LIGHT
Progressed Venus sextile natal (or progressed) Pluto or transiting Pluto sextile natal Venus can denote a new attitude regarding emotional expression. A person may better channel intensity. Rather than adding to her own problems, one may become a solution. A very intense person can start flowing with change. Life's ups and downs may be less upsetting. Extremes can settle into a more natural lifestyle. A wise business sense can emanate. Bold financial decisions may be made with coolness.

   Progressed Venus trine natal (or progressed) Pluto or transiting Pluto trine natal Venus can connote a masterful creative expression. One may bring harmony where there is discord; unity rather than chaos; beauty to situations that lacked meaning. One may attract wealth. A belief in the abundance of life brings material and psychological success. Trusting life's magical and metaphysical laws can bring inner strength. Values reflect a deep inner glow. One may negotiate forcefully but with integrity and character. Manipulation is not required.

SHADOW
Both the **Venus/Pluto sextile and trine** can reveal emotional stagnation. One may lack the volition to break through a crisis. Surface appearances block a deeper comprehension. Facing the consequences of one's actions can be difficult. Values can be compromised. A desire to be accepted or rewarded brings a sacrifice of values. A desire for quick wealth brings out dark qualities, the ends justifying the means. Relationships may lack a real bond. During a crisis, relationships may be destroyed. Lack of emotional insight makes conflict difficult to resolve.

DAWN
Venus/Pluto aspects can symbolize a deep bond. Relationships may reflect mutual trust. Power could be balanced in relationships. One might enjoy sharing emotional and sexual intensity. A capacity to survive emotional conflict gives more permanence to relationships. A penetrating awareness of life's magic carries one through the hard times. Values may bond with appreciation for life's generosity. One may face the deepest secrets in relationships. Self-honesty and forgiveness free blocked energy.

MARS/JUPITER ASPECTS

Progressed Mars/Natal or Progressed Jupiter Transiting Jupiter/Natal Mars

Process: Knocking on Opportunity's Door

Ally: Endless Energy Propelled by Faith and Imagination

Illusion: "I Can Think Later"

Mars/Jupiter aspects can denote not accepting no for an answer. A person can show remarkable faith in times of difficulty. Assertion and faith join forces to bring dynamic results. People should exercise good judgment prior to actions. Twenty-twenty hindsight could leave embarrassing realizations.

INTENSE ASPECTS

Conjunction: Progressed Mars Conjunct Natal or Progressed Jupiter
Transiting Jupiter Conjunct Natal Mars

Square: Progressed Mars Square Natal or Progressed Jupiter
Transiting Jupiter Square Natal Mars

LIGHT

Progressed Mars conjunct natal (or progressed) Jupiter or transiting Jupiter conjunct natal Mars can denote a vivacious spirit. New expansive experiences may be shown. A passion for truth and principles could be important. One may initiate change. Worn-out roles may lift to new heights. A person may inspire others to move ahead. Courage in the face of adversity can occur.

A person may go beyond known territory. A fighter may learn to reason. Individuals too attached to immediate situations may find a broader perspective. Physical strength and eagerness to learn can combine to illuminate dark situations. One may devote self to causes. A helping spirit encourages faith in others. One may find his own faith.

Progressed Mars square natal (or progressed) Jupiter or transiting Jupiter square natal Mars can manifest as fighting through difficult situations. An individual may assertively defend principles. One may champion the underdog. An uneducated person may arm himself with knowledge; a poor person with a better livelihood. An already successful person may find integrity. A person of conviction discovers a cause.

In both the Mars/Jupiter conjunction and square individuals can gain faith in identity. Eclectic understanding can free one of self-hating beliefs. Self-doubt may no longer constipate actions. Belief in a higher power lessens excessive self-reliance. **Moving quickly to take advantage of opportunities is typical of the Mars/Jupiter conjunction and square.**

SHADOW
Both the **Mars/Jupiter conjunction and square** can express as action without consideration of consequences. One may wish he could undo a mess. Rushing to the next red light leaves many unfinished beginnings. Impatience can be extreme. Individuals can expand on situations too quickly. The foundation of an investment or plan could lack reasoning. The "ends" are much more emphasized than "means." People can be too pushy. They can get too attached to opinions. Temper dominates situations. Aggression may lead to a "win at all cost" philosophy.

Individuals may lack the faith to begin new challenges. Impatience with self can undermine ability. People may be too reckless to follow through on obligations. Gambling or a lack of restraints might bring financial disaster. Physical danger could surround those with little common sense. Individuals may have few morals or principles.

Quincunx: Progressed Mars Quincunx Natal or Progressed Jupiter
Transiting Jupiter Quincunx Natal Mars

Opposition: Progressed Mars Opposing Natal or Progressed Jupiter
Transiting Jupiter Opposing Natal Mars

LIGHT
Progressed Mars quincunx natal (or progressed) Jupiter or transiting Jupiter quincunx natal Mars can denote strengthening faith. This quincunx is the **"Yoga of acting on faith."** Individuals can find new positive life directions. Self-hating actions may be transcended. One can bounce back from difficult situations.

A new spiritual awareness can begin. One may find a greater purpose for actions. Finding humor in situations can help. Curbing anger or resentment alleviates stress. Recklessness may be tempered by sound judgment; aggression surrendered to fairness.

Progressed Mars opposing natal (or progressed) Jupiter or transiting Jupiter opposing natal Mars can point to untiring energy. Individuals may be hard on problems and fair to people. People might fight for morals. A vision of truth could lift one through adverse circumstances. Conflict may strengthen faith. A person may handle crises comfortably. Individuals take charge when nobody comes forward to lead. A person might stop relying on others to do their asserting.

Individuals can maintain identity and freedom within the confines of a relationship. One may achieve sharing and freedom. Relationships mutually reinforce spiritual and worldly needs.

SHADOW
Both the **Mars/Jupiter quincunx and opposition** can express as a loss of faith in identity. Individuals can allow others to dictate their

freedom. They may stop thinking for themselves. A failure to believe in ideas undermines confidence. One may offer unsolicited advice. Individuals may grow too angry at those who will not follow their advice. People may try too hard to motivate others. They do not let them grow at their own pace. One may attack people rather than the problem. Hasty accusations alienate others. One might be a terrible listener.

A "grass is greener" mentality may cause people to leave fruitful situations. Some people lack the courage to stay and work through problems. One might hastily leave good relationships. Individuals could be the lone champions of their opinions. A ruthless and self-serving philosophy makes compromise difficult. Pompous attitudes win few friends. One may wish to be worshipped by others.

SOFT ASPECTS

Sextile: Progressed Mars Sextile Natal or Progressed Jupiter
Transiting Jupiter Sextile Natal Mars

Trine: Progressed Mars Trining Natal or Progressed Jupiter
Transiting Jupiter Trining Natal Mars

LIGHT

Progressed Mars sextile natal (or progressed) Jupiter or transiting Jupiter sextile natal Mars can denote faith is rewarded. Doors open for enterprising ideas. An individual may possess an enthusiastic spirit. Excitement concerning new learning opportunities is possible. One may excel at promoting himself or others.

Actions and beliefs can be mutually reinforcing. One may attract support for ideas or projects. An individual can show poise in making difficult decisions. One may adjust well to change.

Progressed Mars trine natal (or progressed) Jupiter or transiting Jupiter trine natal Mars can denote spiritual strength. Charisma may emanate. Understanding future needs dictates solid decisions for the present. A person's optimism may bring good luck. Balanced assertion and knowledge lead to new growth. A person may have remarkable energy with this fire trine.

SHADOW

Both the **Mars/Jupiter sextile and trine** can symbolize senseless actions. A person can lack a clear vision or purpose. He may lazily refuse to grow. Old opinions block a new life. One may let others do the initiating. An individual can take freedom for granted. He may be too much the follower. Some may feel others were born to follow them. A narrow "my way is the only way" philosophy can be exhibited. People could hide their anger. They may choose to ignore trouble. One might lack insight in how to negotiate. Faith may be strong only when the Sun is shining.

DAWN
Mars/Jupiter aspects can symbolize a tireless spirit. One may have unlimited faith in life's abundance. The self-centered tendencies of Mars can be lifted to a broader horizon by expansive Jupiter. The initiating qualities of Mars can get philosophical Jupiter to act on faith.

MARS/SATURN ASPECTS

Progressed Mars/Natal or Progressed Saturn Transiting Saturn/Natal Mars

Process:	Assertiveness Training
Ally:	Disciplined Actions
Illusion:	Acting Out of Fear

Mars/Saturn aspects relate to assertion, strength and taking initiative. Developing a stable identity is another theme. One is often learning how to appropriately express anger. Martian eagerness tests Saturnian patience. Finishing what is started is a challenge. Some display an overly competitive nature. Others lack an assertion drive. Trying to satisfy one's own needs versus expectations of authority figures can be a key challenge. Finding patience can be important.

INTENSE ASPECTS
Conjunction: Progressed Mars Conjunct Natal or Progressed Saturn
Transiting Saturn Conjunct Natal Mars

Square: Progressed Mars Square Natal or Progressed Saturn
Transiting Saturn Square Natal Mars

LIGHT
Progressed Mars conjunct natal (or progressed) Saturn or transiting Saturn conjunct natal Mars can denote fulfilling key identity needs. One fuses courage and ambition. A person can embark on new soul growth. Taking a risk for a new opportunity can be indicated. Sometimes the aging process is a great ally. With maturity, one gains the wisdom to direct forceful energy constructively. People may develop courage in the face of obstacles. They can courageously challenge an authority figure.

A person often learns how to express anger. Timing in using assertion can excel. Being direct with others and pursuing ambitions can be liberating.

Progressed Mars square natal (or progressed) Saturn or transiting Saturn square natal Mars can symbolize breaking through an obstacle. One may rise above a limitation that before seemed impossible to conquer. This is a competitive aspect. One may inspire others with courage and commitment to action. Difficult tasks can be undertaken.

A fast-paced person may economize action. Slow consistent actions replace fast impulsive actions. A steady use of energy replaces unpredictable energy bursts. One may gain a new security in identity through career accomplishments. She may study a new area. A person can feel more in charge of her territory. Rather than complaining about life circumstances, one takes action. Going from thinking to doing may build self-respect.

SHADOW

In both the **Mars/Saturn conjunction and square**, one can combine the "me-focus" of Mars with the defensive themes of Saturn. Problems may be blamed on external causes. One can repeat errors due to impatience. A recklessness causes the individual to repeatedly break the physical laws of the universe. Timing of changes is poor.

An individual can be at war with herself. She blames life for problems. Carelessly dumping anger onto others does not win friends. People can quit a task shortly after starting. An extreme rebelliousness may alienate others. One may fear failing. The intensity aspects can indicate an authority figure hurt an individual's confidence. There may have been too much negative input at an early age. The identity needs a chance to grow.

Some individuals "dig up the seed" too quickly. They will not take the time to watch a project grow. Impatience or lack of confidence can be the root cause.

Anger issues are often symbolized by Mars/Saturn aspects. A person may have had repeated difficulty in expressing anger. Those who keep suppressing anger can suffer headaches and high blood pressure. Emotional frustrations may peak. People can be afraid to leave limiting situations.

> **Quincunx:** Progressed Mars Quincunx Natal or Progressed Saturn Transiting Saturn Quincunx Natal Mars
>
> **Opposition:** Progressed Mars Opposing Natal or Progressed Saturn Transiting Saturn Opposing Natal Mars

LIGHT

Progressed Mars quincunx natal (or progressed) Saturn or transiting Saturn quincunx natal Mars can denote patience and stamina. This aspect is the "**Yoga of mastering assertion strength.**" One is carefully learning how to use force with clarity. A person can pursue extremely difficult goals. She may work harder than usual. The identity can be rounded out. A person may learn about fears that cause procrastination. Ruthless self-examination and deepening inner strength can occur.

Someone who usually is a follower may learn to initiate action. One may release anger. A person can channel forceful energy more appropriately. She may rise above frustrating experiences.

Progressed Mars opposing natal (or progressed) Saturn or transiting Saturn opposing natal Mars can denote resolving a conflict concerning assertion. Individuals can renew commitment to ambitions. They may have enterprising spirits. Fear of responsibility may be overcome. For some this is the first step toward self-fulfillment. One may gain valuable insights into what underlying circumstances have frozen assertive energy.

Dealing constructively with an adversary may occur. Direct and confident steps may be taken against those who have taken advantage of the individual. Some people deal with a controlling authoritarian. A lot of energy may be directed into resolving this relationship.

Love relationships may become a target for one's intensity. A person can overcome a sexual blockage. A more direct entrance into love relationships or more openness in meeting people can be displayed. One might face reality in an intimate relationship.

The cosmic chiropractor, Saturn, may point to changes needed in behavior. Taking more or less control in business and love relationships can be needed. One may be too forceful in relating to others. The energy may need to be buffered into alternative outlets (*i.e.*, sports, hobbies, exercise, etc.). Individuals may no longer stand for being used by someone. If this aspect is in the chart of a strong authoritarian type, she may receive the confronting. An opposition can show a middle ground conflict resolution. One may learn how to treat others with a mutual respect.

SHADOW

In both the **Mars/Saturn quincunx and opposition**, one may combine the assertion and courage of Mars with the self-control of Saturn. The result can be over or under using force. Individuals who are quite forceful can dominate situations. A "macho facho" attitude can permeate all encounters. The individual wants to appear all-powerful and never vulnerable. People are not treated as equals. A bossiness pervades negotiations.

A person lacking assertion may be easily dominated. Bosses, lovers, children, peers, or spouses take advantage. Saying "Yes" when she means "No" creates frustration. A fear of confrontation or an oversensitivity to anger causes one to get into undesirable circumstances.

We do not always like what we see during aspects involving Saturn. The reality of our life can be sobering and at times painful. One may regret having been too aggressive or timid in the past. Selfishness can add tension to situations. This is a time to redirect one's initiating energy.

Some people leave stifling relationships or careers. Others move into one disastrous situation after another. Some continue finding victims to dominate. Others keep getting dominated until they face the reality of their behavior. Anger can continue to be repressed or used as a defense. The physical laws of the universe may signal a time to slow down impulsive energy. Visits to the doctor or other helpers may give the same message.

SOFT ASPECTS

Sextile: Progressed Mars Sextile Natal or Progressed Saturn
            Transiting Saturn Sextile Natal Mars

Trine: Progressed Mars Trining Natal or Progressed Saturn
            Transiting Saturn Trining Natal Mars

LIGHT

Progressed Mars sextile natal (or progressed) Saturn or transiting Saturn sextile natal Mars can connote excitement in initiative. One may identify with the success of an idea or a career. **Mars/ Saturn aspects are good for promoting oneself.** One can enjoy recognition and a good reputation. Assertion can be stimulating. External conflicts may calm down. People move ahead. Procrastination may be transcended. One can be motivated by a new career goal.

A person may welcome the soft aspect of Mars/Saturn. There is a natural intensity formed by both planets. The soft aspects can still indicate strong energy, but without environmental conflict. One may simply ignore adversaries or limiting conditions. Learning from past mistakes leads to new insights.

Progressed Mars trine natal (or progressed) Saturn or transiting Saturn trine natal Mars can reflect new enthusiasm. A person may develop the discipline to take on a bigger challenge. One's openness to new situations may attract promotions and success. An individual may no longer see herself as inferior. Cultural limitations or harm caused by authority figures may be overcome. One gains new solidity in identity.

SHADOW

In both the **Mars/Saturn sextile and trine**, one may be less conscious of the need to direct attention away from ambitions. Paying too much attention to serious goals may cause conflict. One may neglect relationships and responsibilities. One can be too attached to attention and recognition. The individual must be seen as an important person. A person can take too much credit for success. Some people dislike transition periods. They do not adapt. A longing for the past may linger in the present.

DAWN
Mars/Saturn aspects can express as new milestones. Chapters are full of rewarding and growth-promoting circumstances. Assertion can reach new confidence levels. Patience and coolness are learned in the face of difficult circumstances. One learns to finish what is started. Identity can truly become complete. Actions are direct and based on common sense.

MARS/URANUS ASPECTS

Progressed Mars/Natal or Progressed Uranus Transiting Uranus/Natal Mars

Process:	Accelerated Pace
Ally:	Futuristic Actions
Illusion:	Reckless and Thoughtless Actions

Mars/Uranus aspects symbolize moving through life swiftly. An urgency may be felt in a person's daily behavior. One's identity may radically transform. A key issue is developing consistency. An individual's physical energy can become highly electrified. Staying aware of one's direction is important. **Knowing the impact of one's actions on others can be a key theme.**

INTENSE ASPECTS
Conjunction: Progressed Mars Conjunct Natal or Progressed Uranus
Transiting Uranus Conjunct Natal Mars

Square: Progressed Mars Square Natal or Progressed Uranus
Transiting Uranus Square Natal Mars

LIGHT
Progressed Mars conjunct natal (or progressed) Uranus or transiting Uranus conjunct natal Mars can indicate forcefully initiating new goals. Experimenting with new directions of assertion can occur. A reserved person may find a lot of untapped energy. One can be excited by a growing identity. New discoveries about one's intensity can be symbolized. A new boldness in interacting with peers may be displayed. An individual may overcome procrastination. More insight can be shown. People can inspire through enthusiasm and initiating energy.

Progressed Mars square natal (or progressed) Uranus or transiting Uranus square natal Mars can indicate using raw energy to accomplish difficult goals. A person can defend meaningful beliefs. Mars is a territorial planet. A person may fight for individuality, rights, or a cause. This can be a humanitarian, fighting for an underdog. One may release an intensity that has been building for years.

An individual could discover an exciting new identity. People can break away from limiting beliefs.

SHADOW

In both the **Mars/Uranus conjunction and square**, an individual who denies assertion can be explosive. Anger may be poorly timed. One may express anger at the wrong people. He may fail to deal directly with problems. One may be too pushy. Temper tantrums force issues. A compulsive addiction for attention can strain relationships. Individuals may give up at the first sign of conflict. Lack of patience or foresight could lead to abortive plans. A failure to be flexible can lead to setbacks. People may get too fixed in acting out insights. They can be too intense about goals, expecting others to always agree.

There might be accidents. Repressed assertion could lead to accidents. An already fast-paced person may max out time. The famous actor James Dean died in an auto crash with transiting Uranus conjunct his natal Mars in 1955.

One may be especially sensitive to stress. The nervous system can be high-strung. One can overreact to situations. Snap decisions could lack insight. Impatience with self can be problematic. One may be too self-demanding. A person can put too much pressure on himself and others. One wants the future to be here yesterday!

Quincunx: Progressed Mars Quincunx Natal or Progressed Uranus
Transiting Uranus Quincunx Natal Mars

Opposition: Progressed Mars Opposing Natal or Progressed Uranus
Transiting Uranus Opposing Natal Mars

LIGHT

Progressed Mars quincunx natal (or progressed) Uranus or transiting Uranus quincunx natal Mars is the "Yoga of regulating nervous energy." One learns when to accelerate and when to slow down. Understanding inner motivations for sudden actions can be a key. Individuals can create a freer identity. Assertive strength increases.

One may rethink goals to maximize potential. An individual may direct intensity more appropriately. Anger is expressed more objectively and in less self-defeating ways. One drains less energy from self and others by negotiating more objectively. A person can express more assertion in relationships. One may see she is an equal. Support can be mutual.

Progressed Mars opposing natal (or progressed) Uranus or transiting Uranus opposing natal Mars can indicate balancing assertion and freedom. One may go from being too pushy to allowing others to make their own decisions. A person can go from a lack of assertion into more equal territory with others. An individual may overcome temper tantrums and quell emotional outbursts. He may rise above stressful situations. A person may open up to support from others.

One may learn how to reflect before jumping into impulsive actions. A person may consult the opinions of others to gain objectivity. Support from peers may help one relax into his own identity. Giving up extreme control over decision-making in a relationship can become a key theme.

An individual may appropriately express a competitive nature through work, play, sports, or politics. The Mars/Uranus aspects can denote powerful jolts of stimulation from the environment. New relationships may be exhilarating. One can pour tremendous energy into causes or goals, achieving much in a short period of time. One may balance initiating energy and long-range perceptions. Cooperation and a more flexible nature resolve conflict. One may attract the support needed rather than forcing issues. An individual may adopt more patience and wait for situations to develop before acting.

SHADOW

In both the **Mars/Uranus quincunx and opposition**, one may enter relationships or situations impulsively. There can be recklessness. A person could attract unreliable partners. A person can have difficulty finding stability with others. People may seem too demanding. One may lack patience. A life of extremes is featured. One may stay in a relationship with no support for goals. He could depend on others for motivation. People may look for others to complete identity. Relationships can have too much or little assertion. Individuals can fight for limited causes. Serving a group can hide identity.

A person may negotiate too intensely. He may be too aggressive in all relationships. One may lack adaptability. Explosive anger may be out of control. He deals directly with little intelligence.

One may lack staying power. Too much self-absorption can cause a loss of perspective. An individual can be too unpredictable. Others do not know how to please. He may not cooperate with partners.

SOFT ASPECTS

Sextile:	Transiting Uranus Sextile Natal Mars
	Progressed Mars Sextile Natal or Progressed Uranus
Trine:	Transiting Uranus Trining Natal Mars
	Progressed Mars Trining Natal or Progressed Uranus

LIGHT

Progressed Mars sextile natal (or progressed) Uranus or transiting Uranus sextile natal Mars can denote exciting new ideas. Self-promotion may flow. One is enthusiastic about potential. These soft Mars/Uranus aspects indicate excitement without environmental tension. In the sextile, one's mental energy can stimulate others to try new life directions. A new level of cooperation may be attained. A person may slow down enough to really listen to others. An individual may adopt a less aggressive personality. Both the sextile and trine can indicate new opportunities. One may enjoy a new intensity.

Progressed Mars trine natal (or progressed) Uranus or transiting Uranus trine natal Mars means one can move quickly but with more accurate perception. One may develop confidence in initiating actions.

SHADOW

In both the **Mars/Uranus sextile and trine**, a person can shy away from new challenges. A fear of the unknown can cause missed opportunities. One might think rather than act. Uranus is a very mental planet. Waiting and waiting creates tension. Mars grows stale if one does not act with some degree of enthusiasm.

The **Mars/Uranus trine** can be too passive. Others may lead the individual. One can fear being assertive. Tension in relating is possible. One can grow inert if too attached to stability. Another person could get stimulation crazy. In the more intense Mars/Uranus aspects, one often needs limits to survive stress. In the soft aspects a person may forget caution. Stress may sneak into the body. An individual may think he can handle constant conflict. An accident or breakdown may impose limits. A naturally intense individual can get very stimulated. Identity and goals may coexist nicely. Sometimes a person low on assertion strength ignores physical laws and creates nervous breakdowns.

DAWN

Mars/Uranus aspects are charged with powerful voltage. We can get excited about self-discoveries. One can accelerate forward, full speed ahead! Some individuals manage this spontaneous energy without a lot of recklessness. One needs to be responsible for anger and sudden bursts of energy. He may be asked to be more supportive of others. A person may become more assertive in relationships. The Mars/Uranus aspects are often when a person is individualizing identity. **Territorial Mars and visionary Uranus can combine into exciting growth.**

MARS/NEPTUNE ASPECTS

Progressed Mars/Natal or Progressed Neptune Transiting Neptune/Natal Mars

Process:	Imagination in Action
Ally:	Acting on Ideals
Illusion:	Vague Identity

Mars/Neptune aspects can denote identifying with new symbols. A person wishes to become all she can be. Idealism and inspiration combine with an "I am" focus.

A person should exercise care. Mars can recklessly abandon reason for immediate results. Neptune can attract our urges to transcend reality. This is a dynamic combination, sometimes puzzling and disorienting. New horizons may be reached. The assertive strength of Mars enlivens the passivity of Neptune. The vision of Neptune can see through the shortsightedness of Mars.

INTENSE ASPECTS

Conjunction: Progressed Mars Conjunct Natal or Progressed Neptune
Transiting Neptune Conjunct Natal Mars

Square: Progressed Mars Square Natal or Progressed Neptune
Transiting Neptune Square Natal Mars

LIGHT

Progressed Mars conjunct natal (or progressed) Neptune or transiting Neptune conjunct natal Mars can be a desire for new frontiers. The territoriality of Mars inspires Neptune's lofty ideals into new directions. An individual's inner fortitude may lift her above pressing difficulties. One's environment can be stressful. The consciousness-raising qualities of Neptune can symbolize a new patience with oneself. An individual may solve internal conflicts. One may stop running away from herself.

Individuals may have a highly developed awareness. Moving fast may be attractive. A person may make snap decisions. A selfish individual may give more of herself. A greater sensitivity to the world at large can occur. One may be driven by compassion. A person denying her own needs may learn to promote her abilities. Procrastination due to a fear of oneself can be transcended by self-love. An individual may awaken from a life of self-denial. One can rededicate her life to a more fulfilling identity. Transcending self-hatred may begin. Healing old wounds may free one for future roads.

A very angry individual may tune into deep hurts. Emotional scars may be healed by new vistas. A person may see life as a variety of seasons — some filled with conflict and others with fulfillment. A sense of unity may conquer an inner emotional/mental division. One's actions may develop a higher harmony. Right-brain intuition may orchestrate integrating actions. Individuals may seek deeper meaning. A person seeks the "why" of her actions. End results may not be as important as the process. One may stop lying to herself. An individual wants not just to wash the dishes, but to be sure they are clean.

Progressed Mars square natal (or progressed) Neptune or transiting Neptune square natal Mars can express as the faith to pursue ideals. An individual filled with self-doubt can develop more faith. This can be forceful or passive. Much depends on the nature of the individual. A nonreflective individual may chase illusions. A tuned-in person might understand her intensity. Anger can be redirected more sensitively. A nonassertive person may courageously express feelings. One can overcome a too passive nature.

Individuals could take care of unfinished business. Emotional conflicts can be clarified. An illusory self-image might be purged. One can confront self-hatred. An impatience with obstacles may initiate action. Acting on impulses may lift a person to a higher consciousness.

A warrior may use more intuition. A past conflict of action and intuition could be resolved. An overly self-conscious and guilty nature may be transcended. A person might follow through on initiatives. One may stop making excuses for failing to finish what is started. Spontaneous intuitive actions inspire others.

SHADOW

In both the **Mars/Neptune conjunction and square**, one can hunger compulsively for the limelight. The person can become addicted to an outer show, looking too much for applause. Actions can be deceiving. Passive aggressive individuals can thrive better than usual. One may display anger in body language while projecting a happy face. A denial of assertion and anger throw one off balance. Emotional confusion can follow a blocked expression of anger. A person can procrastinate, waiting for the perfect moment, place, or person to appear.

Addictive substances, sex, television, sleep, etc., may be overused. A person may run away from the past or present. A lack of faith in self or a higher power can be displayed. A person can foolishly believe she can do anything. One may take chances others would never attempt. A lack of foresight may put her into emotionally draining situations.

One may sit in a very divided temple! Discontent may constantly irritate. One may not settle into inner peace. Suppressed anger or false pride could weaken the physical body. An individual may neglect diet and health. A person may be alive but spiritually asleep. The doors to higher consciousness are bolted. One may ignore universal laws. Life is seen as coincidences with no cosmic factors. A lack of imagination debilitates flexibility. A person may get scared by self-examination. She would rather chase illusions. A fear of growth can hold one back. An attraction to safe and familiar territory can stunt **growth.**

Quincunx: Progressed Mars Quincunx Natal or Progressed Neptune
             Transiting Neptune Quincunx Natal Mars

Opposition: Progressed Mars Opposing Natal or Progressed Neptune
             Transiting Neptune Opposing Natal Mars

LIGHT

Progressed Mars quincunx natal (or progressed) Neptune or transiting Neptune quincunx natal Mars is the "Yoga of intuitive actions." Individuals may walk with more conscious footsteps.

They can be direct rather than aggressive; assertive rather than too passive; attentive to their own needs rather than devoting their lives to others. A selfish individual can come to care about others. A person lacking self-focus may tune into her own creativity. Initiating new enterprises can lead to growth.

A regrouping of physical and intuitive energies may center one's consciousness. There can be deep self-realizations. Self-denial may be changed into self-appreciation. Self-forgiveness can be practiced. An individual may develop a new patience with self and others. Foresight into situations may relieve stressful experiences. A person may fix past wrong doing through compassion, sensitivity, and self-sacrifice. A non-assertive individual could learn to say "No."

Progressed Mars opposing natal (or progressed) Neptune or transiting Neptune opposing natal Mars can indicate powerful new inspiration. A person may move forward boldly with ideals, highest cultural symbols, deepest visions, and creative art. A shy individual may allow herself to become romantic. Eagerness to know others physically and passionately can occur. Romantic urges may be the catalyst for new enterprises.

One may confront anger and assertion issues. An overly aggressive individual may learn more sensitivity. A person with a past of rejection may find a more accepting partner. A passive nature can learn to risk. Compromise may be important. A female could develop a new relationship with her inner masculine (known as the *animus* in Jungian psychology). She may stop projecting her assertive powers onto male partners and gain new self-confidence. A male or female could tune into the internal feminine. Peers may be supportive and encourage talents. Tremendous faith in oneself or a higher power can bring tireless energy.

A person may grow more self-accepting of her sexual identity. Relationships naturally bring sexual creativity and freedom. Mutual support for growth can occur. An individual could learn more about sacrifice. She does not need to get her own way. A very intense, high-strung person may learn to flow with life's ups and downs. Curbing angry reactions when idealism is thwarted wastes less time and energy.

People may learn to accept love. A show of being tough may be canceled. One may see that expressing vulnerability is not a weakness. A person may slow down and tune into her inner self. An avid interest in metaphysics, psychology, etc. can happen.

SHADOW

In both the **Mars/Neptune quincunx and opposition,** a person can avoid personal confrontation. She may be afraid to cause any ripples. An extreme avoidance of anger or conflict can delay resolving problems. An individual can be hard to understand. Moods may be extremely unstable. One may stay a victim of the past, refusing to communicate needs.

A failure to communicate is perhaps the biggest downfall. One may brood in self pity or feel helpless. This can be used to punish others or make them feel guilty. A person can purposely misrepresent the truth to control situations. One can be extremely argumentative to get her own way.

Some people become addicted to out-of-balance relationships. One can allow herself to be used by others. She may fail to question the judgment of someone for fear of losing the relationship. A person can be out of touch with reality. She may let others direct too much of her life. Devotion can numb one to the truth. A person can feel tired constantly. Sometimes it is from not pacing oneself. With excessive denial, sleep becomes an escape. Running away from self or reality can lead to abusive behaviors.

SOFT ASPECTS

Sextile: Progressed Mars Sextile Natal or Progressed Neptune
                Transiting Neptune Sextile Natal Mars

Trine: Progressed Mars Trining Natal or Progressed Neptune
                Transiting Neptune Trining Natal Mars

LIGHT

Progressed Mars sextile natal (or progressed) Neptune or transiting Neptune sextile natal Mars can express as an exciting new self. Intuition and actions may flow together. One may find options to issues. People may express more of a true potential. More flexibility can relax tension. A person may learn when to follow impulses. An individual could become more conscious of subconscious urges. She can understand self-defeating behavior patterns. An individual could sense unity. She can integrate an action orientation with more intuitive insights.

Progressed Mars trine natal (or progressed) Neptune or transiting Neptune trine natal Mars can symbolize a new faith in self. New ideals and enterprises are exciting. An endless imagination, in both the sextile and trine, can bring new opportunities. In the trine, one's identity may become less self-centered. A person may open to a bigger vision. The self-preservation instincts of Mars can lift to a more collective concern with Neptune. A person may accept self and others more.

SHADOW

In both the **Mars/Neptune sextile and trine**, a person can be motivated one day and inert the next. One may lack focusing power. The intense Mars/Neptune aspects can denote the energy needed to fulfill a vision. The soft aspects do not denote the same determination. The floatiness of Neptune can dilute Mars' actions. A person could desire extreme stimulation from the environment. Too much sex, substance abuse, or other escapes could debilitate body and mind. A person may choose too many directions. A passive individual might simply not move at all.

An individual may not see a reason for ideals or imagination. One could be very limited in vision and desire narrow territory to explore. A preoccupation with physical desires could limit higher consciousness. One needs to watch extremes. A person can be self-serving. A forceful nature may need to always be right. One may lie or cheat to ensure winning. An overly aggressive nature may be displayed.

A lack of self-honesty can be problematic. One may believe she is always the greatest. Recklessness can deny common sense. One may deny mysteries of the universe.

DAWN

Mars/Neptune aspects can indicate self-gratification instincts reach new levels of awareness. One can be forceful with a conscience. A person can tune into underlying causes for angry outbursts or denied assertion. One may move decisively with a very watchful eye. An individual may transcend her anger. One's identity may reach new inspiring levels. Courage may be displayed. A person may alter self-defeating behaviors and stop running away from the self.

MARS/PLUTO ASPECTS

Progressed Mars/Natal or Progressed Pluto Transiting Pluto/Natal Mars

Process:	Territorial Intensity
Ally:	A Competitive Strength
Illusion:	Might is Right

Mars/Pluto aspects can denote a tremendous drive to go beyond limitations. Survival instincts can surmount extreme challenges. A ruthless determination can overcome obstacles. Old-time astrologers called Mars the lower octave of Pluto. Mars is our individual instinct to be assertive. Pluto symbolizes our desire to bond with others. A balanced Pluto energy can lead to a sharing of power. Mars is a personal planet pointing to a self-focus. Pluto, on its highest level, aims at transforming a "me-focus" to a joint focus.

INTENSE ASPECTS

Conjunction:	Progressed Mars Conjunct Natal or Progressed Pluto Transiting Pluto Conjunct Natal Mars
Square:	Progressed Mars Square Natal or Progressed Pluto Transiting Pluto Square Natal Mars

LIGHT
Progressed Mars conjunct natal (or progressed) Pluto or transiting Pluto conjunct natal Mars can symbolize a transformed identity. One may become more aware of one's actions. Impulsiveness may be moderated. A reckless type "A" individual can learn to conserve energy. Anger may be more clearly expressed. One may not be so resentful of his past. Old angry moods may be resolved. Extreme territorial consciousness can turn into more inner awareness. A greater tolerance for different opinions can be displayed.

Self-hatred can be dropped. Self-destructive tendencies can be turned into powerful creative actions. One may help others get back on their feet. A courageous spirit may stimulate others to action. Individuals may overcome personal loss.

Progressed Mars square natal (or progressed) Pluto or transiting Pluto square natal Mars can denote new focusing power. The same energy that led to self-destruction is channeled into more growth-promoting actions. A vengeance for the past can be transcended. A passion to initiate new situations can be born. Old identities can be brought into a more wholesome present. One may survive an identity crisis. A deeper understanding of emotional needs can occur. People may slow down enough to understand their inner motivations for actions.

Individuals may break free of domination by others. Acting on one's own impulses can be freeing. Anger and assertion are no longer held back. People who are explosive may learn spontaneous expression. Anger is released more appropriately.

SHADOW
Both the **Mars/Pluto conjunction and square** can express as extreme self-hatred. Individuals may not give themselves a break. Intuitive comprehension of actions is lacking. A tendency to selfishly push others to action can occur. One is acting for his own best interest. Anger can be used to manipulate or control. One may use anger to hide insecurity. An individual may fear his own intensity. A tendency to block anger can be emotionally disorienting. A lack of identity may keep one separate from others.

Quincunx: Progressed Mars Quincunx Natal or Progressed Pluto
          Transiting Pluto Quincunx Natal Mars

Opposition: Progressed Mars Opposing Natal or Progressed Pluto
          Transiting Pluto Opposing Natal Mars

LIGHT
Progressed Mars quincunx natal (or progressed) Pluto or transiting Pluto quincunx natal Mars can symbolize a new life purpose. This quincunx is the **"Yoga of working on oneself."** Actions

can align with new emotional depth. Fiery Mars and watery Pluto can denote the depths of raw instincts. An apathetic person can find passion for life; an emotionally blocked person more spontaneous expression. An angry person can communicate feelings. Someone stuck in the mud can act again. A power person can let others be themselves.

People may take on a more rounded identity. A narrow path may widen into more exploration. A deeper purpose for actions can lead to more collective affairs. Wasteful and irrational actions can be refocused. Concentration can replace scattered actions. One may find self-mastery through finishing what is started. Identity may deepen through more internal awareness.

Progressed Mars opposing natal (or progressed) Pluto or transiting Pluto opposing natal Mars can denote more intensity in relationships. Assertion may be trusted more. Power in relating can be more balanced. One may attract more equal relationships. Assertion and power are understood. One may establish mutually supportive relationships.

Self-mastery can come through expressing organizational strength. The energy and talent of others can be managed skillfully. Difficult decisions regarding money and business can be made.

Incessant arguing can be overcome. One may learn to listen as well as act. Tuning into an inner voice can keep one from wasting energy and resources. A hasty gambling type may find more creative expression. Timid individuals may become more direct. Individuals can grow more comfortable with sexual identity.

Assertion builds confidence. People may stop projecting hero worship onto others. Finding one's own identity becomes primary. Power instincts are no longer lived through others. Past emotional pain may be released. Establishing balanced relationships heals old scars. One learns not to dump anger on new lovers or peers. Self-criticism may be lessened by feedback from friends.

One may courageously seek help for emotional problems. The psyche may regroup. An individual may see he is not the only person with a particular problem.

SHADOW

Both the **Mars/Pluto quincunx and opposition** can express as giving too much power to others. Individuals can set themselves up for emotional disasters. Years can be wasted serving the selfish goals of others.

One can be the victim of physical and emotional abuse. Partners may lack emotional insight. They kick the dog or a less powerful person when frustrated. Power-oriented types can be too controlling. Their actions invade the rights of others. They search for other lands to plunder. The greedy or overly aggressive take no prisoners!

Emotional scars may cause one to punish others. Insecurities keep relationships from developing beyond sexual or monetary needs. Emotions are kept a secret. Hidden agendas constantly surface. Revenge and jealousy may bring angry outbursts.

SOFT ASPECTS

Sextile: Progressed Mars Sextile Natal or Progressed Pluto
            Transiting Pluto Sextile Natal Mars

Trine: Progressed Mars Trining Natal or Progressed Pluto
            Transiting Pluto Trining Natal Mars

LIGHT

Progressed Mars sextile natal (or progressed) Pluto or transiting Pluto sextile natal Mars can symbolize dynamic confidence. One may ignore the odds through determination and focus. One rebounds strongly from a setback. New enterprising energy is likely. One may regulate his intensity. He may know when to turn on the speed to finish a project. An inner contentment can help channel tremendous energy bursts.

A self-starting person may find this a particularly rewarding period. Skills and self-confidence can bring financial reward. A passive person can reach back for assertive energy previously lacking. An angry person can become more versatile in expressing intensity. Emotional patterns may come into conscious awareness. One may learn his own body signals and mood swings. He can catch anger before it leads to trouble.

Progressed Mars trine natal (or progressed) Pluto or transiting Pluto trine natal Mars can show actions and emotional intensity in harmony. One may show remarkable ability to shift from action to reflection. Vengeance can be put to rest. One buries the hatchet. Letting go of emotional pain gives life.

Knowing oneself deeply can bring wiser actions. One may be less tempted to control others. A more direct, honest approach is adopted. A warrior can find a greater life purpose. Defending the rights of others may take on more importance. A selfish focus can branch out into more awareness.

SHADOW

Both the **Mars/Pluto sextile and trine** can denote a smooth and calculating manipulation of situations. A desire to possess others can occur. One may act benevolent yet have a hidden agenda.

Individuals can get too complacent. They may expect too much. A lack of initiative leads to losing personal power. One may hesitate and never follow through on needs. Identity can be confused. One can avoid new challenges. Boredom may win out over adventure. Assertive instincts become dulled by inaction and passivity. One may give up before the challenge begins. Running away from inner or external conflict hurts stability. Courage may be lacking in career or relationships. Too little or excessive power urges can be ignored.

DAWN

Mars/Pluto aspects can indicate charismatic actions. Decision making can be assertive and clear. Anger may be under control and channeled appropriately. One may accomplish tasks requiring great stamina. Relationships may foster mutual growth of identity. One can enjoy meeting physical and emotional needs. Selfish interests can be transformed into care for others. Reckless actions can turn into intuitive insights. Power can be shared rather than polluted by hidden agendas.

JUPITER/JUPITER ASPECTS

Transiting Jupiter/Natal Jupiter

Process:	Expansive Philosophy
Ally:	Seeing Opportunities
Illusion:	False Assumptions

Jupiter/Jupiter aspects accentuate a restlessness with the present. There can be an eagerness to seek new growth through learning and travel. Faith in oneself might climb to new plateaus.

INTENSE ASPECTS

Conjunction: Transiting Jupiter Conjunct Natal Jupiter

Square: Transiting Jupiter Square Natal Jupiter

LIGHT

Transiting Jupiter conjunct natal Jupiter (Jupiter return) can express as extreme excitement. A love of adventure is easy to feel. A lightness about the present is possible. The philosopher and teacher within a person bubbles forward. One's optimism could be contagious. The gypsy spirit emanates. Foreign thoughts permeate the consciousness. People may exhibit a leap of faith to transcend a major obstacle. Humor can be a great therapy. Reading books is more stimulating than ever.

Transiting Jupiter square natal Jupiter can express as a sudden show of faith. A person might be ready to follow an impulse that leads to new opportunity. Acting on principles brings self-confidence. A negative person may indulge in positive thinking. Conflict is turned into a learning experience.

SHADOW
Both the **Jupiter/Jupiter conjunction and square** can express as
drawing foolish conclusions. A "penny wise and pound foolish" philosophy can annoy others. Running to greener pastures is an escape from
commitments. People may be so expansive that they lack focus. Promises and more promises are never delivered. There could be an inability
to set limits. People can too quickly "throw caution to the wind." Bragging can irritate others. A false show of confidence might mask insecurities. Hiding from the truth prolongs one's problems. A pushy mentality with narrow judgments does not win friends.

   Quincunx: Transiting Jupiter Quincunx Natal Jupiter

   Opposition: Transiting Jupiter Opposing Natal Jupiter

LIGHT
**Transiting Jupiter quincunx natal Jupiter is the "yoga of wise
judgment."** People can express their opinion with a broader perspective. Those lacking self-confidence might tune into a more positive spirit. Too much dependence on others for advice might be converted into
thinking for oneself. Narrow thinking could look for a four-lane highway. People too hasty in judgment or movement could deepen their reasoning powers. A greater faith in the outcome of situations is liberating.

   Transiting Jupiter opposing natal Jupiter can symbolize an
abundant time in meeting new peers. Love relationships benefit from
positive attitudes. Sharing knowledge with others is probably electrify-
ing. People may be more open than usual to one's opinions. Being with
people of like beliefs might be rewarding. Positive thinking enriches all
social interactions. People may find new meaning when practicing spiritual rituals that elevate consciousness. Teaching others can be stimulating as is exploring new subjects of interest.

SHADOW
**Both the transiting Jupiter/natal Jupiter quincunx or opposi-
tion** can express as wasteful actions. Laziness or lack of discipline could
reach new highs. Arrogance may be a turnoff. A loss of faith may be
disheartening. A lack of a deeper life philosophy keeps inspiration low.
People may become overconfident. Exaggeration of abilities typifies a
loss of perspective. Trying to move in too many directions at once leads
to few accomplishments.

   Believing in the wrong people or causes is possible. Projecting too
many virtues onto others could be a mistake. Individuals expecting people to unquestioningly swallow their opinions are making another mistake. Sarcastic judgments may cause separation from loved ones or special peers. A failure to admit mistakes or faults could be the product of
a big ego.

SOFT ASPECTS

Sextile: Transiting Jupiter Sextile Natal Jupiter

Trine: Transiting Jupiter Trining Natal Jupiter

LIGHT
Transiting Jupiter sextile or trine natal Jupiter may denote a love of life. A desire to truly relax can be shown. One may more quickly see the lighter side of life. The environment might feel more friendly. Individuals can express more generosity. Abundance may surround one's thinking.

SHADOW
Both the Jupiter/Jupiter sextile and trine can express as running away from conflict. Following the easy paths could be poor preparation for real challenges. Some people will refuse to acknowledge the opportunity for a new experience. Alternatives to old problems are ignored. Relying on past thinking gets in the way of new understanding. Hiding behind pretended happiness or shallow beliefs may keep others at a distance.

DAWN
Jupiter/Jupiter aspects can begin new optimism and productive thinking. If one avoids the temptation of unfounded confidence and narrow judgments, the current cosmic weather may be full of brilliant sunshine and colorful rainbows!

JUPITER/SATURN ASPECTS

Transiting Jupiter/Natal Saturn
Transiting Saturn/Natal Jupiter

Process: Test of Faith

Ally: Sound Judgment

Illusion: Faith in Fears

Jupiter/Saturn aspects symbolize faith tested by reality. Jupiter denotes expansion while Saturn emphasizes conservation. Issues can relate to philosophical values. Courage to embrace change can be a challenge. These aspects have a sobering tendency. Idealism is melded to practicality. One's spiritual values can be challenged by authority figures or culture.

INTENSE ASPECTS
Conjunction: Transiting Jupiter Conjunct Natal Saturn
Transiting Saturn Conjunct Natal Jupiter

Square: Transiting Jupiter Square Natal Saturn
Transiting Saturn Square Natal Jupiter

LIGHT

Transiting Jupiter conjunct natal Saturn or transiting Saturn conjunct natal Jupiter symbolizes fusing inspiration and ambition. This can be a restless aspect. One may drive toward greater accomplishment. People may become forceful advocates for change. Opinions can be communicated very convincingly. Well-disciplined and benevolent authority figures can be indicated. Faith and principles can be tested greatly. Persevering through difficult situations brings strength. An individual can sense injustices. One may understand eclectic reasoning. Wisdom can be shared through counseling, traveling, and teaching.

People may overcome rigidity. Humor or an expansive life attitude can develop. A judgmental nature can be released. Greed surrenders to generosity. One may have the faith to pursue ambitions. Initiating new plans is exciting. A more abundant life is pursued.

Transiting Jupiter square natal Saturn or transiting Saturn square natal Jupiter can denote faithfully pursuing ambitions. One may struggle through difficult times but grow tremendously. She can outgrow rigid beliefs taught by authority figures and discover her principles and spiritual values.

Excess in life can be reduced. A scattered person may better define goals. An extremely optimistic person may become more realistic. One may achieve sound judgment. Wisdom and principles are integrated naturally. Confidence comes through past successes. One may inspire others to rise above difficult circumstances.

SHADOW

In both the **Jupiter/Saturn conjunction and square**, people can be super difficult to please. They may dislike reality. Procrastination could lead to frustration. The "grass is greener" philosophy can be an escape mechanism. Responsibilities and commitments are avoided. Negative thoughts keep one from growing. A refusal to acknowledge faults keeps one in a vicious cycle of inharmony.

One can strive to be all-powerful. Opinions may lack flexibility. An individual might dominate others through persuasion and tact. One can lose sight of physical laws. Excess eating, exercise, or work could deplete one's health. A life of austerity is another side of the coin. A denial of love, pleasure, or material items may occur. Faith could be at an all-time low!

Quincunx: Transiting Jupiter Quincunx Natal Saturn
          Transiting Saturn Quincunx Natal Jupiter

Opposition: Transiting Jupiter Opposing Natal Saturn
          Transiting Saturn Opposing Natal Jupiter

LIGHT

Transiting Jupiter quincunx natal Saturn or transiting Saturn quincunx natal Jupiter is the **"Yoga of defining faith."** One can trim down excesses. Economizing energy and resources better serves ambition. More deadlines for goals are met. An individual may deal with unfinished situations. Loose ends can be completed. A person may experience much self-criticism. Conversely, a stronger belief in one's own life philosophy can occur.

Transiting Jupiter opposing natal Saturn or transiting Saturn opposing natal Jupiter can symbolize more confidence in relating to others. New ways of relating can be indicated. One can align her aspirations with the expectations of others. Some individuals meet influential teachers or peers. The opposition can denote eagerness to find a suitable role model for wisdom.

Individuals can stop expecting so much from others. More realistic expectations improve relationships. One may become less demanding. Communicating directly and with conviction can increase. Ideas are discussed forcefully. Emotions are less controlled. Jupiter's humor may neutralize an overly serious nature. Politics or one's community can become an interest. This can be a very influential period in one's life. Paying more attention to people and everyday affairs may help ground one's life. Sharing one's ideas and resources may help bond the person to a lover, spouse, employer, etc.

SHADOW

In both the **Jupiter/Saturn quincunx and opposition**, a person can expect others to love unquestioningly. An extreme case was Reverend Jim Jones. He was founder and guru of the People's Temple. Mr. Jones had a natal 7th house Jupiter in Cancer opposing natal 1st house Saturn in Capricorn. Reverend Jones was known for his amazing powers of persuasion. He eventually led almost one thousand followers to a mass suicide in 1978.

An individual can criticize others excessively. Hasty value judgments control others. Inflexible decisions make relationships tense and unstable. One may leave a good relationship without giving it a chance. The idea of commitment is frightening. One could refuse to work through doubts from a past relationship. The individual would rather run away than deal with problems.

A lack of faith in oneself could lead to disastrous relationships. One may choose more powerful people due to a lack of self-respect. People may gullibly trust others. Others take advantage of one's generosity. One needs to balance idealism and generosity with realistic expectations of others.

One may promise too much. The expansion themes of Jupiter can lead to excess. Wasteful actions can deplete energy and resources. A lack of discipline blocks growth. A too passive nature can be problematic. Fearing confrontation, the individual may hide his intelligence and opinions. A loss of faith is the result. One may be too easily talked out of ambitions.

SOFT ASPECTS

Sextile: Transiting Jupiter Sextile Natal Saturn
Transiting Saturn Sextile Natal Jupiter

Trine: Transiting Jupiter Trining Natal Saturn
Transiting Saturn Trining Natal Jupiter

LIGHT

Transiting Jupiter sextile natal Saturn or transiting Saturn sextile natal Jupiter can symbolize exciting growth. The future never looked brighter. A person can be very stimulated by new educational interests or ambitions. A restlessness for knowledge can surface. Exchanging ideas with others can be enjoyable. One's ideas are met with approval.

Transiting Jupiter trine natal Saturn or transiting Saturn trine natal Jupiter can point to new confidence. A refreshing belief in principles and sense of well being revitalizes the individual. Self-appreciation increases. Growth through travel, education, and business enterprises is possible. In the soft aspects, one may appreciate accomplishments. The aging process can strengthen faith in life. A person may feel life is in tune with her expectations.

SHADOW

In both the **Jupiter/Saturn sextile and trine**, expansive vision may have no use for nagging responsibilities. Restlessness can keep one from enjoying the present. One can think too much about the imperfections of the present. Opportunities without a focus drift away.

A tremendous urge to join a movement can occur. A cult or movement directs compulsive devotional energies. A person may passively allow others to direct his life. An individual can exhibit a mental laziness, tending to avoid conflict.

DAWN

Jupiter/Saturn aspects can express as a positive outlook. Faith in self can be enhanced. A deeper spiritual commitment can be aroused. The power of positive thinking combines with determination and endurance to overcome obstacles. Saturn gives purpose and discipline to Jupiter's idealism and search for a new vision.

JUPITER/URANUS ASPECTS

Transiting Jupiter/Natal Uranus
Transiting Uranus/Natal Jupiter

Process:	Individualized Faith
Ally:	Faith in Future
Illusion:	Eccentric Visions

Jupiter/Uranus aspects accentuate a restlessness for new learning. Curious for knowledge, one can be anxious to enter uncharted territory. He can burst with enthusiasm to create a new philosophy. People may struggle with impatience, trying too many goals simultaneously. An individual's optimism and mental nature can go through radical transformations. Cultural views can shift dramatically forward or backwards.

INTENSE ASPECTS

Conjunction: Transiting Jupiter Conjunct Natal Uranus
Transiting Uranus Conjunct Natal Jupiter

Square: Transiting Jupiter Square Natal Uranus
Transiting Uranus Square Natal Jupiter

LIGHT

Transiting Jupiter conjunct natal Uranus or transiting Uranus conjunct natal Jupiter can point to lightning in the distant skies! One may be driven to new exploration. The first civilian astronaut, Christina McAuliffe, who died with other crew members in the tragic explosion of the *Challenger* space shuttle, had transiting Uranus conjunct natal Jupiter in Sagittarius. She was known as the space teacher. Both Jupiter and its natural sign Sagittarius are symbolic of teaching and travel. Uranus is associated with new technology such as space travel, computers, etc.

Jupiter/Uranus conjunctions can represent a new faith in oneself. An individual can discover new interests through travel and education. One is eager to meet people who think differently. People can make exceptional communicators, able to reach the other person's level of consciousness. One can rise above a difficult personal problem. A lighter life perspective can create new options. An individual may discover a unique spiritual awareness. Faith and optimism may inspire others. A more eclectic life approach is sought.

Transiting Jupiter square natal Uranus or transiting Uranus square natal Jupiter can denote fighting for future goals. One can project ahead tirelessly. A conservative type may explore liberal experiences. A free-spirited personality may replace a shy nature. One can suddenly move at a more vibrant life pace. Individuals may be exhilarated by reaching goals. A new faith transcends surface optimism! Individuals can feed their soul and intellect with higher consciousness. They learn to enjoy what comes easily as well as through conflict. Mental detachment allows one to enjoy the little things. In each of the intense Jupiter/Uranus aspects, people can enjoy using new technology.

SHADOW

Both the Jupiter/Uranus conjunction and square can denote instant lessons about cause-and-effect. Actions may come back to haunt one. Excess is often the problem. One can be exhilarated by bigness. One can travel too many paths at once, following a new pipe dream every other day. Egotistical behaviors can irritate others. One can lose faith from being worn-out. A person can exhaust resources and mental energy by shooting at continuous full throttle. He can feel too many divided loyalties. Jupiter can be quite impractical. Uranus can be thinking too far ahead. One may be so overextended that mental confusion results.

There can be an intense idealism to dedicate one's life to a cause. One may fall in love with collective movements. This dedication is not wrong, unless one becomes too removed from reality. One can lose a sense of self in certain groups.

Quincunx: Transiting Jupiter Quincunx Natal Uranus
Transiting Uranus Quincunx Natal Jupiter

Opposition: Transiting Jupiter Opposing Natal Uranus
Transiting Uranus Opposing Natal Jupiter

LIGHT

Transiting Jupiter quincunx natal Uranus or transiting Uranus quincunx natal Jupiter is the "Yoga of enjoying personal growth." A person can find having fun is okay. If an individual is too much into excess, he may learn moderation. Individualistic beliefs and goals can be examined. Individuals may go through deep consciousness changes. They can become aware of affecting others through reckless or impulsive actions. More tact and tolerance in communicating ideas are helpful. A person may overcome rigid concepts. He may discover more positive energy. A lack of confidence in goals can be transcended.

Transiting Jupiter opposing natal Uranus or transiting Uranus opposing natal Jupiter can express as new faith in humanity. One can devote much time and energy into movements or causes. Devotion to a universal or global consciousness can occur. A person may inspire others. His philosophy is not only unique but he practices what is preached. One may be spontaneous with little tolerance for obstacles to freedom. He may make a good debater. He can mediate a problem. One can be persuasive and convincing.

People may leave limiting situations. They can establish more meaningful and in-depth relationships. A greater sharing of one's life can occur. An individual can establish unique relationships based on freedom yet with common goals. A person may be more comfortable with a long-distance relationship. More space may be required. Both partners can need room to expand understanding and experiment. A change in perspective may creatively maintain a present relationship, career, or a goal. A broader perspective or a newfound freedom is exciting. A love relationship may change into a friendship or vice versa. Awareness deepens and growth continues.

A new positive energy regarding one's life can occur. People can be excited about new opportunities. Individuals may enjoy the support of a spiritual group, friend, or lover. People may stop running away from themselves through reckless behavior. People can be champions of freedom and equality for all. Loyalty and trust may be greatly respected. Individuals can highly value friendship.

SHADOW

In both the **Jupiter/Uranus quincunx and opposition**, a person can be extremely rebellious and impulsive. He may be out of control and insensitive to others. Bridges may be burned without carefully planning the future. Hasty and narrow thoughts can cloud perspective. A person can be too demanding. He may be very impulsive and jump to hasty conclusions. This can create tension in relating. A lack of cooperation can dominate. One can ruthlessly fight for narrow, self-serving ideas.

An individual can surrender too much individuality and decision making. One can look too much for another person's philosophy to live by. One can try too hard to please others. A failure to assert one's own principles creates tension. A lack of self-confidence can disrupt relationships. One may have trouble trusting the wisdom and direction of partners or peers. An inflexible attitude and failure to communicate openly can break up relationships.

SOFT ASPECTS
  Sextile: Transiting Jupiter Sextile Natal Uranus
          Transiting Uranus Sextile Natal Jupiter
  Trine: Transiting Jupiter Trine Natal Uranus
          Transiting Uranus Trine Natal Jupiter

LIGHT

The **soft Jupiter/Uranus aspects** can express as faith in goals and a benevolent humanitarian nature. A generosity and very free spirit can be indicated. Individuals may break away from limiting thoughts. Enthusiasm for the future can generate experimentation with new concepts. Ideas flow within a peer group.

Transiting Jupiter sextile natal Uranus or transiting Uranus sextile natal Jupiter can point to new insights in communication. Individuals could experience an electrically charged time period. Philosophy and goals may stimulate others. Unique talents may pay off financially. However, I have noticed that the abundance that astrologers commonly associate with Jupiter is more often related to faith. One may experience sudden good luck in Jupiter/Uranus aspects through optimism and moving ahead despite obstacles.

Transiting Jupiter trine natal Uranus or transiting Uranus trine natal Jupiter can point to a high-flying spirit. Generosity with resources and ideas can make one visible to others. One may find a new study or a new business enterprise. This trine can be quite visionary. One may work well with new technology. People may desire spiritual depth and search for truth. The trine can denote more sensitivity to others and giving more support. Both the sextile and trine can symbolize a more flowing exchange of higher values and ideas with others.

SHADOW
In both the **Jupiter/Uranus sextile and trine**, a person can egotistically feel he is always right. People "should" follow his lead. This is Jupiter and Uranus at their worst. Instead of refreshing new ideas, one grows stale holding onto old perspectives. One merges with his own vision and makes no room for others. Dogmatism persists. A person can lack motivation. One may passively take what he gets. The philosophical level may never get into action. This can lead to wasted time.

DAWN
Jupiter/Uranus aspects can symbolize exciting new growth. Individuals may discover mental abilities. More knowledge and higher understanding can illuminate. Breaking the shackles of confining thoughts is liberating. A broader perspective in living morals and principles can occur. A greater tolerance for the ideas and lifestyles of others can bring harmony into relationships. Jupiter/Uranus aspects have a global perspective. Communication, learning, and travel can be especially exhilarating.

JUPITER/NEPTUNE ASPECTS

Transiting Jupiter/Natal Neptune
Transiting Neptune/Natal Jupiter

Process:	Faith in Highest Ideals
Ally:	Intuitive Faith
Illusion:	Blind Faith

Jupiter/Neptune aspects can denote lofty inspiration. A person may experience divine discontent with current conditions. The expansiveness of Jupiter combines with the perfection of Neptune. A new spiritual orientation may develop. A strong imagination may be felt. New learning through travel or education can occur. One's ideals can get difficult to put into practice. Dissatisfaction often accompanies Jupiter/Neptune aspects. A person can become a purist and quite judgmental of others. One may think one is greater than God. A person with a clear perception of reality can make good use of this idealistic symbolism.

INTENSE ASPECTS

Conjunction: Transiting Jupiter Conjunct Natal Neptune
Transiting Neptune Conjunct Natal Jupiter

Square: Transiting Jupiter Square Natal Neptune
Transiting Neptune Square Natal Jupiter

LIGHT

Transiting Jupiter conjunct natal Neptune or transiting Neptune conjunct natal Jupiter can denote new inner faith. A person may change a negative mental outlook to positive and turn one's life around. An expansive spirit and intuitive vision can lead to new self-discovery. An individual may learn about subjects that inspire growth. An interest in metaphysics can occur. Ideals can be put into motion. Enthusiasm can carry one beyond limiting circumstances.

One may feel as though certain knowledge was a previous experience. One may travel to places that bring back past-life memories. Traveling with a lover or spouse can be especially enjoyable. One's unconscious may reveal inspiring experiences that bring new faith. An individual may find new spiritual strength. Divine discontent with an empty existence pulls a person to go deeper into hidden dimensions. One may outgrow rigid morals or extreme self-denial of material things. An overly materialistic person may learn that money is not everything. A self-serving individual may discover social work, compassion, and more sensitivity.

Transiting Jupiter square natal Neptune or transiting Neptune square natal Jupiter can express as promotion of new intuitive visions. One may rise above obstacles through faith. One awakens from a long sleep into heightened awareness. A person may awaken to her creative being. Jupiter humor may lighten environmental circumstances. An individual may become less critical. A greater overall acceptance may take place.

Individuals can find new options to limiting situations. Jupiter can denote growth while Neptune can symbolize faith and intuition. Flexibility helps life flow more easily. An individual may find the faith to stop running from conflict. A person may communicate more openly. A very aggressive and dominating individual may become more sensitive to others.

SHADOW

In both the **Jupiter/Neptune conjunction and square,** guilt can be problematic. A person might overidentify with the problems of others. One's values can be unrealistic. The expansiveness of Jupiter could combine with the dreaminess of Neptune into unfounded idealism. A search for greater meaning can lead one in endless circles. Common sense may be lacking. A person can be the source of her own problems. A person may have a difficult time with faith. There may be a resistance to changing a Pollyanna attitude. An individual may have to face a negative attitude regarding relationships.

Quincunx: Transiting Jupiter Quincunx Natal Neptune
Transiting Neptune Quincunx Natal Jupiter

Opposition: Transiting Jupiter Opposing Natal Neptune
Transiting Neptune Opposing Natal Jupiter

LIGHT

Transiting Jupiter quincunx natal Neptune or transiting Neptune quincunx natal Jupiter can express as a newfound self-confidence. One may prioritize values. This can be a key turning point in a person's life. Love of illusion can be transformed into love of the higher self. A person may find new sound judgment. This quincunx is the **"Yoga of faith through surrender."** A person can let go of wasteful habits. Consciousness can be dynamically centered. A person may give up ideals that lack vision. A new ideal or image may inspire faith. A person may attract more positive experiences through a consciousness cleansing. Self-honesty may replace self-deception.

A person with a weak identity may stop self-sacrifice. A lack of confidence could become a stronger expression of one's true self. There can be a hunger for truth, honesty, and loyalty. A person may think more of her own opinions. Loyalty and trust in others may become more balanced.

Transiting Jupiter opposing natal Neptune or transiting Neptune opposing natal Jupiter can symbolize new confidence in relating. A person can establish trust and a deep sharing of love in intimate relationships. A stronger bond could form with intuitive wisdom and/or a higher power. Life processes can be understood. People can learn life's hidden messages. An attraction to metaphysics can become strong. People can become adept counselors. They listen and comprehend the deeper needs of others. An individual may adopt an eclectic approach. Walking in someone else's shoes can foster trust and compassion. A person can make an inspiring lecturer. She can excel in broadcasting a message.

A person's life may gain a broader perspective. Materialism may be tempered by spirituality. Philosophy could be balanced by sensitivity to global issues. Knowledge can be stimulated by shared understanding with others. Travel stimulates growth. Filling the right brain with new transformative knowledge highlights this period. Balancing give-and-take with others can occur. A person may conquer a "love is blind" philosophy. Unfounded idealism and worship of others may be lessened. One may still believe in loyalty, but with more self-awareness. Guilt and trying too hard to serve others may be modified.

SHADOW
In both the **Jupiter/Neptune quincunx and opposition,** a person could allow herself to be used by others. Idealism and openness need to be accompanied by common sense. One may project saintly or highly imaginative qualities onto others. The truth may be exaggerated. Unquestioning loyalty needs to be examined. A person can do all of the giving. Guilt can be extremely problematic. A person might be a helper in situations that are best left alone. One may try too hard to reform others. She could be too easily manipulated by addicted people. A person could deny idealism. Life has soured too many times. Expectations may be too high for self or others. Seeking the perfect love leaves one lonely and disillusioned.

An individual may reject the notion of higher consciousness. A lack of faith and inspiration could lead to an empty life. One may try to substitute wealth and glory for ideals. People can promise more than they deliver. They may deceive others. One can be quite a mouthpiece for her own promotion. An individual may be too expansive and unconsciously get into trouble.

SOFT ASPECTS
Sextile:	Transiting Jupiter Sextile Natal Neptune
	Transiting Neptune Sextile Natal Jupiter
Trine:	Transiting Jupiter Trine Natal Neptune
	Transiting Neptune Trine Natal Jupiter

LIGHT
Transiting Jupiter sextile natal Neptune or transiting Neptune sextile natal Jupiter can express as an exciting life flow. Previously negative attitudes may become positive. One may step back from an overly emotional involvement and let situations happen. Rather than forcing circumstances, one may surrender to a higher faith. New learning opens the imagination. Creative confidence inspires a person to share talents with others. Travel on the physical and mental levels could rejuvenate an emotionally depleted mind. A person may alter a negative behavior.

Transiting Jupiter trine natal Neptune or transiting Neptune trine natal Jupiter can express as being guided by a higher power. Jupiter's expansiveness outshines the other planets. Whether natally or by transit, Jupiter and Neptune point to vivid imagination. People can believe in themselves or in a higher power. One can rise above horrible circumstances through a powerful allegiance to her highest values, integrity, and morals. A person can display unusual patience until circumstances improve. She may continue working hard through devotion to a cause.

SHADOW

In the **Jupiter/Neptune sextile or trine**, closeness can be denied. The soft aspects can escape deep emotional commitment. One drifts. Instead of a real search for deeper meaning, one could have no real purpose. Self-deception might occur. The truth can be distorted. Imagination may lack grounding power. Reality can be denied. An "everything is one" philosophy could hide emotional insecurity. An inability to focus on one thing at a time leads to confusion. A person could become unreliable. Her concept of time might be spacey and forgetful. An individual could blame problems on a higher power or bad luck. A vain personality may develop. An individual can get narrow in vision and grow critical of others.

DAWN

Jupiter/Neptune aspects can symbolize a highly refined judgment. A naturally positive outlook may attract abundance and inspiration. People could have a spontaneous faith in self and in a higher power.

JUPITER/PLUTO ASPECTS

Transiting Jupiter/Natal Pluto
Transiting Pluto/Natal Jupiter

Process:	Knowledge is Power
Ally:	Personal Power through Eclectic Learning & Faith
Illusion:	I am Above the Law

Jupiter/Pluto aspects can represent our tested principles and freedom. An individual may make knowledge achieve results. People may excel at handling crises. Thinking wisely during a personal crisis allows one to land on his feet. Individuals may bond deeply with life pursuits. Emotional intensity pours passionately into personal beliefs. A person may be a true survivor. When the chips are down, one may be at his best.

INTENSE ASPECTS
Conjunction: Transiting Jupiter Conjunct Natal Pluto
Transiting Pluto Conjunct Natal Jupiter
Square: Transiting Jupiter Square Natal Pluto
Transiting Pluto Square Natal Jupiter

LIGHT
Transiting Jupiter conjunct natal Pluto or transiting Pluto conjunct natal Jupiter can denote a passion for truth and honesty. One may champion a cause or belief. An unyielding spirit sees goals through to the end. One may teach in a simple manner. Enthusiasm may inspire others to go beyond limiting circumstances. A determination to learn new knowledge can be displayed. One may be very reliable and trustworthy. An uncompromising desire to do the right thing can win admiration.

Expansive Jupiter can find discipline and focus in Pluto. **Knowledge can give one power.** Penetrating to deeper levels of wisdom can bring self-mastery. One may push through life's obstacles. A bonding with the mystery of life can bring strength. An individual may follow an inner light in the midst of apparent darkness. Faith can carry one through times when others would throw in the towel. Spiritual beliefs may be well-integrated into everyday life.

Transiting Jupiter square natal Pluto or transiting Pluto square natal Jupiter can symbolize finding the faith to survive a disaster. One may deal with a personal loss. A deeper appreciation for the gift of life can occur. People may develop a deeper understanding of death. An interest in metaphysics or psychology is possible. Individuals can seek wisdom to penetrate through personal challenges. Travel can heal a troubled psyche. One may need some distance from problems. An individual may keep the faith while dealing directly with conflicts.

SHADOW
In both the **Jupiter/Pluto conjunction and square**, a person can exercise poor judgment. Financial investments may go bankrupt. Foolish optimism can lead to disappointment. Faith may disappear during conflict. One may abandon sound reasoning or principles recklessly. An overly expansive philosophy can cause one to leave good situations. An inability to concentrate can hurt learning. One may regret a life of chasing greener pastures. Individuals can lose everything to achieve instant wealth or power. The illusion of power can bring an inflated ego. One may think he is above the law. A hidden desire for power can cause one to twist laws to fit his truth.

People may lack insight into life's mysteries. A search for the obvious can lead one to a shallow existence. Material greed blinds intuition and spiritual growth. Compulsive excesses can lead to problems. Too much of a good thing leaves one weak-willed. Personal power may be diluted by expecting success to come easily.

Quincunx: Transiting Jupiter Quincunx Natal Pluto
Transiting Pluto Quincunx Natal Jupiter

Opposition: Transiting Jupiter Opposing Natal Pluto
Transiting Pluto Opposing Natal Jupiter

LIGHT

Transiting Jupiter quincunx natal Pluto or transiting Pluto quincunx natal Jupiter can symbolize renewed faith. This quincunx is the **"Yoga of finding lost faith."** A person can stop a life of excess. Self-defeating habits may be overcome. Self-honesty can bring true power. A life of gambling and impulsive moves could be transcended. Knowledge acquired can bring confidence. One may learn to concentrate. Restless energy gets channeled more constructively. A person with negative attitudes may find new hope. A life of emotional or material poverty can find abundance. One may work for his ideals.

Transiting Jupiter opposing natal Pluto or transiting Pluto opposing natal Jupiter can denote a relationship bonded by spiritual beliefs. Individuals may tolerate differing ideals. Relationships can be mutually stimulating. Expansive growth inspires each other's potential. Partners commit to each other's success. One may trust the right people. One's generosity is no longer taken advantage of by others. One may end a non-growth-promoting relationship. Limiting circumstances can be transcended. (One no longer stays too long.)

Individuals may trust their own learning ability. They may gain faith by defending principles against criticism. They break rules in order to stand up for beliefs. People may find self-mastery through the world of business. Individuals can skillfully budget big projects. They get the most out of others. Personal philosophy can deepen through new learning. Peers may stimulate a person to widen horizons. A burning desire for knowledge may lead to travel and studying new subjects. One seeks to understand the essence of life processes.

SHADOW

Both the **Jupiter/Pluto quincunx and opposition** can express as fanaticism. Individuals can dogmatically push narrow beliefs. Giving up any freedom can be difficult. An argumentative nature blocks cooperation in relating. Opinions may be inflexible. One may act as judge and jury. A loss can shatter faith. A divorce, loss of property, end of a job, or a death could be difficult to face. An individual may run away from the pain. Refusing to communicate prolongs the despair.

A life of excess could hide insecurity. One may do things in an extravagant manner. An individual could be difficult to really know. One may deceive others in the name of truth and spirituality. A person may live his faith through others. He may give away his time and money and be manipulated by charlatans.

SOFT ASPECTS

Sextile:	Transiting Jupiter Sextile Natal Pluto
	Transiting Pluto Sextile Natal Jupiter
Trine:	Transiting Jupiter Trine Natal Pluto
	Transiting Pluto Trine Natal Jupiter

Transiting Jupiter sextile natal Pluto or transiting Pluto sextile natal Jupiter can symbolize an enterprising spirit. An individual can rejoice in success. Abundance can be present. A person may accept his own limitations. More tolerance of other opinions is possible. A love of the extreme can be surrendered. Individuals may be inspired by those who share a similar life philosophy. One may arouse faith through enthusiasm for life.

Transiting Jupiter trine natal Pluto or transiting Pluto trine natal Jupiter can symbolize faith bringing a greater vision. Eclectic learning gives insight into handling problems. One may passionately teach and share knowledge. Positive attitudes increase personal power.

SHADOW

Both the **Jupiter/Pluto sextile and trine** can symbolize a "play it safe" mentality. A failure to go beyond safe boundaries can occur. One may rigidly adhere to existing ideas. A self-righteous philosophy can emanate. One can be insensitive. Power itself can be a compulsive drive. One may subtly control others. "Honesty" and "fairness" hide a hidden agenda. One may lead others astray to take their money and energy.

DAWN

Jupiter/Pluto aspects can denote regenerated faith. An individual may understand universal law. Complex problems can be reasoned through. One may transcend revenge and jealousy. A grip on others is relaxed. A need to manipulate is overcome. A person can regain faith in his own personal power. One may share knowledge from a deep life understanding. No stone is left unturned. A person can move others to solve their own personal shadows.

SATURN/SATURN ASPECTS

Transiting Saturn/Natal Saturn

Process:	Wisdom Gained During Aging Process
Ally:	A Determined Spirit
Illusion:	Fear and Rigidity

Whether I am looking at a person's chart in the present or for a future time period, I find myself first looking at transiting Saturn. The relationship of transiting Saturn to one's natal placement of Saturn may be the most important cycle in the chart. Saturn moves with such predictability that simply knowing one's age will tell an astrologer if transiting Saturn is currently aspecting one's natal Saturn.

Transiting Saturn aspecting natal Saturn represents reality testing. These aspects are particularly associated with ambition. They occur approximately every seven years following birth.

INTENSE ASPECTS
Conjunction: Transiting Saturn Conjunct Natal Saturn

LIGHT

Astrologers commonly refer to the transit of Saturn conjuncting natal Saturn as the "Saturn Return." This aspect begins at approximately ages 28, 58, and 88. This is when transiting Saturn **returns to one's birth placement**. I believe a Saturn Return lasts the entire period that Saturn occupies the sign of birth, about two- to two and one-half years.

This major chapter in one's life accentuates **restructuring and redefining**. However, the Saturn Return is more of a "beginning." One may show decisiveness and discipline. Focus on important goals can be highlighted. Maturity and responsibility can be accentuated. This is a crisis point in the aging process.

An individual may display wisdom, making choices that promote growth. One may drop destructive behaviors. He may turn away from the darkness and move into less compulsive behaviors. **Taking responsibility for one's actions is a key theme.** Clarity can be gained about a career. The first Saturn Return is often the time one plants the seeds of ambition. One can adjust time, resources, and goals to fit current needs. Relationships and life purpose can deepen greatly during a Saturn Return. Time seems like an ally if one is experiencing fulfillment. People may rise above society's pressures and expectations. They may become an inspiration for peers, exhibiting wisdom and knowing how to succeed. People may embrace solitude as a way to gain focus and concentration. Socializing can slow down. Working hard seems to be predictable.

SHADOW

Transiting Saturn conjunct natal Saturn (Saturn Return) can indicate a lost purpose. Lack of ambition or shallow self-examination can lead to abortive plans. One may resist learning from past mistakes. A denial of reality can lead to trouble. Individuals may be legends in their own minds. Not defining limits wastes time and energy.

One may fear taking a risk. Someone may leave relationships rather than work through difficulties. A person may look for easy external answers to problems. The same mistakes are acted out. An individual can assume that a high paying job, new car, and owning a house provide ultimate meaning. This illusion can be perpetuated by parents, peers, and society. One's growth may stop. Individuals who experience setbacks may be overly crushed by failure. A fear of future failure can lead to stagnation. Loneliness can be encountered.

Square: Transiting Saturn Square Natal Saturn

LIGHT

Transiting Saturn square natal Saturn occurs at approximately ages 7-8, 21-23, 36-38, 49-51, 63-65, 77-79. These squares are when one may "feel his oats." The famous philosopher-mystic, Rudolph Steiner, believed that a soul did not fully incarnate until age seven. The first square finds many children encountering authority figures, teachers. The classroom helps structure our early identity. We begin to learn how to fit into society. As we mature, the transits of Saturn square our natal Saturn gain in intensity. The stakes get higher. A person's determination to find success and meaning are challenged. Societal pressures and obligations must be balanced with one's own needs. A person may experience much fulfillment. At age twenty, one may feel proud of adulthood. He may feel more in control. One often needs societal approval of his ambition.

The square following the first Saturn return, about age 37, is a key time period. This is often when one launches the full intensity and clarity of his Saturn Return. Saturn can denote a slow-building energy. Decisions at age thirty may be realized at age thirty-seven. Embarking on a new challenge can be particularly meaningful. A person can find new enthusiasm and vigor. One may live meaningful career goals. An individual can exhibit much self-control and expertise in handling worldly matters. Time and resource management excels.

SHADOW

Transiting Saturn square natal Saturn can denote extreme caution. A fear of life can block growth. People may become compulsively ambitious and ignore the needs of others. Selfishness and authoritarian behaviors can become excessive. Bossiness and dictatorial tendencies alienate others. An individual can get too stressed out by external demands. Life can feel like a pressure cooker. There is never enough time to do a quality job. One may ignore body signals to slow down. Undefined ambition can be extremely stressful. A fear of responsibility, conflict, or failure can lead to holding back too much.

Quincunx: Transiting Saturn Quincunx Natal Saturn

LIGHT
Transiting Saturn quincunx natal Saturn is the "Yoga of making time an ally." An individual can handle stress and time pressures. Integrating life experiences gives one new control. One may resolve a major conflict during any of the intensity-promoting aspects. The quincunx can denote resolving self-doubt and compulsive addictions. One may conquer a karmic pattern that has limited abilities over several lifetimes. Confidence in relationships and abilities can increase. A person may recover from a setback whether physical, emotional, or spiritual. He can build resilience. A person can reprogram negative thoughts with positive energy. Individuals can pour a lot of time into learning new skills. They may carefully adjust ambitions.

SHADOW
Transiting Saturn quincunx natal Saturn can symbolize fear of vulnerability. A person refuses to go to doctors when sick, or ask for help when depressed. A false show of strength creates loneliness. Inflexibility rules the day. One's life is out of synch. One can be controlled by extremes: working too hard or trying to hard to please others. An inability to make decisions and manage time can be frustrating. Too much conflict or environmental stimulation can drain the body and mind. All work and no pleasure cause problems. Compulsive worry can be particularly problematic. An inability to draw logical conclusions wastes time and resources. Controlling the spontaneity in life ruins a good time.

Opposition: Transiting Saturn Opposing Natal Saturn

LIGHT
Transiting Saturn opposing natal Saturn occurs approximately at ages 14-16, 44-46, 74-76. Transiting Saturn is moving through the sign opposite one's natal Saturn for about two to two-and-one-half years. One learns to balance personal ambition and growth with societal expectations and important relationships. This is a major life passage. The first Saturn opposition during adolescence is awkward. One is still a child in society's perspective, coming into his own power. A sensitivity to peer pressure often conflicts with advice from parents and teachers. One searches for the middle ground of reality. This cycle is becoming more difficult in Western societies. Choosing from so many opportunities and options can be stressful for today's youth. Consumer society encourages throwing away relationships and goals for new experiences. Fast-moving contemporary society crams too many experiences into one's life.

The opposition that occurs in one's early to mid forties can produce tension yet be very fulfilling. One may successfully cross the civilization bridge. He can satisfy expectations within the structures of society. One may function within a system without sacrificing values.

This powerful aspect is associated with reality testing. A person can stop displaying too much or too little responsibility. One may trust the decisions of others rather than always doubting. A person could confidently influence the decisions of others. Individuals may face a destructive relationship. They might be too much under the control of a person or situation. Needs in relationships may require realistic definition. A new career direction is possible. Serious ambition is accentuated.

SHADOW

Transiting Saturn opposing natal Saturn can express as not taking responsibility for actions. The second opposition formed by transiting Saturn to one's natal Saturn in early to mid forties can denote childish behavior. One can return to adolescence. People may lack flexibility in relating to others. They can create power struggles. They may refuse to admit faults or use others as scapegoats.

An individual can stay stuck in limiting perceptions of others. A lack of trust inhibits committed relationships. A need to always be in control blocks spontaneous flow. A too serious nature can alienate others. One may be perceived as all work and no play. A lack of emotional depth may yield shallow relationships. A person can have too many defense mechanisms. He is too protective of his turf. A person may give up too much power to authority figures and societal expectations. He could try too hard to be liked or respected. One may deny personal ambitions to please others. A person can lose hope. Not giving in to frustration is challenging. Adjusting expectations can be important.

SOFT ASPECTS

Sextile: Transiting Saturn Sextile Natal Saturn

Trine: Transiting Saturn Trine Natal Saturn

LIGHT

Transiting Saturn sextile natal Saturn can denote clarifying ambitions without environmental conflict. One may actually be under just as much pressure as during an intensity-promoting aspect. Perhaps he feels more in control of life. During the soft aspects of transiting to natal Saturn, one can sense he works too hard. One may be more willing to relax.

Transiting Saturn trine natal Saturn can denote leaving a life of austerity and enjoying the modern luxuries of society. An individual may find a new faith or positive attitude. The healing energy of time overcomes a painful past. One may accept the reality of aging. Each life passage or major stage is perceived as meaningful and filled with valuable lessons.

SHADOW
Transiting Saturn sextile or trine natal Saturn can express as
lack of momentum. Soft aspects may denote wasting time. An individual may not self-start. One may take too much for granted. Success is
sought with little effort. People may settle for surface accomplishments.
People may seek to escape conflict at all costs. A passivity or a lack of
common sense can predominate.

DAWN
**The Transiting Saturn/natal Saturn aspects can denote orches-
trating changes that promote growth.** The conjunction (Saturn
Return), square, quincunx, and opposition can especially denote transcending worn-out behaviors. These passages set the tone for success.
One may adeptly redefine goals and responsibilities. People may overcome self-defeating karma habits. **At each seven year cycle, one may
experience time as an ally.** The aging process will bring its pressures and conflicts. When one does not fear the challenging present,
these aspects can be fulfilling.

SATURN/URANUS ASPECTS

Transiting Saturn/Natal Uranus
Transiting Uranus/Natal Saturn

Process:	Defining Freedom
Ally:	Unique Ambition
Illusion:	Stagnation

**Saturn/Uranus aspects denote breaking through cultural restric-
tions to experiment with individuality.** Responsibility and free will
can be themes. One often learns that freedom requires responsibility.
The mental imaging power of Uranus needs the discipline and focus of
Saturn. One can patiently use creative intelligence. She may break
through inhibitions and obstacles.

INTENSE ASPECTS
Conjunction: Transiting Saturn Conjunct Natal Uranus
Transiting Uranus Conjunct Natal Saturn

Square: Transiting Saturn Square Natal Uranus
Transiting Uranus Square Natal Saturn

LIGHT
**Transiting Saturn conjunct natal Uranus or transiting Uranus
conjunct natal Saturn** symbolizes fusing responsibility to others and
freedom urges. One may go beyond cultural inhibitions and fear of authority figures. Some people become very focused. One may time a major change very well. A person can express a new facet of individuality.

A reckless person might gain more control over actions. A conservative individual may experiment in new directions. One can know which path leads to fulfillment.

One may perceive a more collective awareness of society. Some people become more humanitarian and supportive of others. Overattachment to acceptance by society can be transcended. One may join a group that strongly supports identity. A person can leave a group that has limited growth.

Transiting Saturn square natal Uranus or transiting Uranus square natal Saturn can represent overcoming obstacles blocking one's individuality. One can break free of restraints. An individual may make a complete life change. A major life passage is often indicated. Leaving the past behind can be important. Some people deal with past problems and experience a rebirth.

Major career changes are common in both the conjunction and square. New goals fit a new perspective. One may gain more control over decision making. A person may experience more freedom in relationships by better defining needs. Authority figures are dealt with more confidently. A passive individual may grow more vocal. An individual may actively plan future goals. Desire for freedom and space can increase.

SHADOW
In both the **Saturn/Uranus conjunction and square**, an individual can be extremely self-centered. The rights of others are not respected. A very fast-paced person feels people and events move too slowly. Balance can be difficult to achieve. One may grow easily bored with routine and normal events. A quick exit from jobs and relationships could become a pattern. A person can experience frustration. A lack of planning leads to limiting situations. One may lack the logic needed to fulfill insights. Change for the sake of change leads to setbacks.

A fear of decision making can cause missed opportunities. One may be afraid to express individuality. A person can fear disappointing or confronting others. She could constantly repeat "You can't fight city hall." Cultural values can block new ideas.

Quincunx: Transiting Saturn Quincunx Natal Uranus
             Transiting Uranus Quincunx Natal Saturn

Opposition: Transiting Saturn Opposing Natal Uranus
             Transiting Uranus Opposing Natal Saturn

LIGHT
Transiting Saturn quincunx natal Uranus or transiting Uranus quincunx natal Saturn is the "Yoga of defining Freedom." One learns to express independent urges without invading the space of others. A person can carve out future plans. A person may develop inner

strength. Steady steps produce success. A more carefree attitude can aid the overly cautious. One may gain insight as to why she gives up her own ideas too easily. A person may abruptly leave limiting jobs or relationships. Saturn aspects often feel like imposed conditions, situations beyond our control. **If we respond with patience and wisdom rather than panic or revenge, a great learning process can occur.**

Transiting Saturn opposing natal Uranus or transiting Uranus opposing natal Saturn denotes balancing individuality and responsibility. Thinking for oneself can be greatly enhanced. A passive individual may express more ideas. Sharing goals with others can be exhilarating. Breaking the shackles of limited thoughts can be uplifting. Communicating new ideas to a group or superiors can be powerful. An individual may change destructive habits. A new individuality could occur in relationships.

One may find that old cultural values no longer are meaningful. She can find her own values through a broader perspective. An interest in various movements or subcultures may develop. Defining one's own beliefs is strengthening.

SHADOW
Both the **Saturn/Uranus quincunx and opposition** can point to rigid themes. One can attract people with fixed opinions. They are emotionally cold. A person can feel stifled by a work environment, place of residence, or relationship. Failing to brainstorm options or to seek advice creates frustration. An individual may not get the support needed for goals. The self-focus of partners and lack of attention received is felt as rejection. Individuals can depend too much on the decisions of others. One may continue behavior that has produced problems. This may include rebellion against all authority figures, lack of cooperation in relating, emotional aloofness, giving up freedom too easily, or trouble in clarifying goals. Negative anticipation of the future leads to an abortive ride. A fear of the future kills the spontaneity to try a new lifestyle, job, or relationship. One may fear the growth process. She can compulsively hold onto old cultural biases. Transitions make one nervous, with a feeling of no control. Running away from the truth can cause one to seek meaningless options. A person can rebel against commitments, institutions, or authority figures without having something to replace that which one wants to destroy.

SOFT ASPECTS
Sextile: Transiting Saturn Sextile Natal Uranus
Transiting Uranus Sextile Natal Saturn
Trine: Transiting Saturn Trine Natal Uranus
Transiting Uranus Trine Natal Saturn

LIGHT

Transiting Saturn sextile natal Uranus or transiting Uranus sextile natal Saturn can denote new ambitions. A person's individuality and personal goals are being satisfied. A new respect among peers is possible. One's life can speed with exhilarating stimulation. A person could be in touch with collective trends in her culture. Talents can be integrated. Fewer clashes with authority figures occur. An alternative lifestyle may meet with less resistance.

Transiting Saturn trine natal Uranus or transiting Uranus trine natal Saturn can reflect unique ideas. The lifestyle can take on a broad perspective. One may feel a flow between individuality and expectations of others. A person's ideas may meet with less opposition. Responsibility and individuality can become an everyday reality rather than a sudden rebelliousness. One is able to confidently give and take in relationships.

SHADOW

In both the **Saturn/Uranus sextile and trine,** life can have too many options. People may not define goals. With intense aspects, time or the immediacy of a problem dictates a decision. The soft aspects often lack that urgency. A person can procrastinate decisions, waiting until the situation is a disaster before reacting. One can fail to follow through on personal goals. The opinions of others may be too valued or influencing. (The intensity aspects are more self-propelling.) One can get too attached to personal needs. Independence and space can annoy others if they do not get the same right.

DAWN

Saturn/Uranus aspects can express as deciding personal goals. One can feel free of past limitations and cultural restrictions. Responsibility and freedom can be integrated within relationships and other commitments. The conventional and unconventional can work together. Neither extreme is totally needed. Saturn can offer the wise use of free will associated with Uranus. One may elevate the consciousness of her culture through unconventional wisdom.

SATURN/NEPTUNE ASPECTS

Transiting Saturn/Natal Neptune
Transiting Neptune/Natal Saturn

Process:	Making Dreams Real
Ally:	Inspiration and Faith
Illusion:	Confused Ideals

Saturn/Neptune aspects denote commitment to live one's ideals. Neptune themes relate to imagination, spirituality, intuition, and falling in love. One combines practicality and idealism. Realistically living ideals is an issue. The perfection of Neptune is interfaced with Saturn's reality-testing. Neptune is symbolic of ethereal energy while Saturn is related to logic and common sense.

INTENSE ASPECTS

Conjunction: Transiting Saturn Conjunct Natal Neptune
Transiting Neptune Conjunct Natal Saturn

Square: Transiting Saturn Square Natal Neptune
Transiting Neptune Square Natal Saturn

LIGHT

Transiting Saturn conjunct natal Neptune or transiting Neptune conjunct natal Saturn can symbolize combining idealism and reality. Neptune's divine discontent is unlike any other planet's. Neptune represents seeking perfection. This divine discontent can drive one to tremendous accomplishments. A person can possess clear intuition. Ambition and intuition work forcefully together to produce an aesthetic talent. One may excel in a profession such as art, music, or dance. He may be a gifted counselor or massage therapist.

Individuals can have firm spiritual values. They may be attracted to social work or other helping professions. They need a profession that allows them to share emotional intensity. A time of transformative growth and soul searching can occur. One's ambitions seek a deeper meaning. The life can come together in ways that previously were lacking. Change and letting go of rigid behaviors allows for new understanding.

A person may surrender an extreme external focus. He may be attracted to meditation, Yoga, or other relaxation techniques. Merging and unity are soothing, if a person will take the time to explore inner wisdom. One with too much idealism may seek a balance. A regular schedule can help. Defining limits can be important.

Transiting Saturn square natal Neptune or transiting Neptune square natal Saturn can indicate overcoming a tremendous obstacle. A past painful experience can be surrendered. Acknowledging a situation may help resolve a conflict. Getting grounded to reality can balance ideals. One may discover more compassion for others. Neptune symbolizes sensitivity. One might grow quieter and perceive life's deeper mysteries.

Outward control is less necessary. An inner peace establishes a flowing personality. One is at peace with self and the environment. Performing action while "watching" and developing a deeper awareness can occur. Spiritual ideals can be lived. One may seek a career that does not sacrifice spiritual values. He may rise above limited values taught by authority figures.

SHADOW

In both the **Saturn/Neptune conjunction and square**, one can take a bumpy, abortive trip. Authority themes of Saturn can combine with the visions of grandeur of Neptune. A person can get a bit power crazy. He thinks powers are unlimited. One can fraudulently misrepresent himself to gain praise and to fulfill ambition. A person can compulsively evade responsibility. Commitments are frightening. A fear of rejection is the problem. Escaping commitments due to fear of confinement can occur. People can feel disoriented. One's emotional energy can be unpredictable. A person can stagnate. An individual can compulsively switch from one relationship or ambition to another. He can feel confused about his niche in the world. A loss of inspiration can cause one to wander aimlessly.

> **Quincunx:** Transiting Saturn Quincunx Natal Neptune
> Transiting Neptune Quincunx Natal Saturn
>
> **Opposition:** Transiting Saturn Opposing Natal Neptune
> Transiting Neptune Opposing Natal Saturn

LIGHT

Transiting Saturn quincunx natal Neptune or transiting Neptune quincunx natal Saturn is the "Yoga of staying inspired." One can use intuition to satisfy divine discontent. Distancing oneself emotionally from everyday activities can help. One may explore right-brain therapies or intuitive creative expressions.

A more realistic attitude can be adopted. People can adjust high expectations to fit reality. Perfectionism may receive the sobering balance of Saturn. A person can understand why he is easily disappointed by life. Underlying motives for addiction may surface. People can overcome guilt. They might stop sacrificing too much energy. More strength in relating to others can be gained. One may build the faith to be successful.

Transiting Saturn opposing natal Neptune or transiting Neptune opposing natal Saturn denotes balancing ideals and ambition. One may gain a deeper understanding of relationships, sacrifice and responsibility. One may feel a karma relationship to a lover, spouse, or authority figure has been removed. A rigid behavior becomes more flexible. Control over people and situations may be surrendered.

A person may overcome guilt in relating to others. Faith in one's ability to find meaningful relationships can blossom. Someone can become aware of attracting partners with extreme emotional problems. One may gain a deeper appreciation for love and emotional support. Power, sensitivity, faith, and respect for each other are shared. One may break through a conflict in relating to a person or being true to his own ideals. He may forgive himself or another person. He may repay a karma debt through a relationship. Doing selfless service can balance karma.

SHADOW

In both the **Saturn/Neptune quincunx and opposition**, the sensitivity and unity themes of Neptune blend with the seriousness of Saturn. The result can be feeling too responsible for actions. The flow of intuition can be blocked. Limits and boundaries can be fogged by an emotional disorientation. One can give too much out of guilt. A person may carry helping instincts to an extreme, perhaps sacrificing excessively. He can relinquish power too easily. A fear of responsibility could cause missed opportunities. Emotional confusion can push others away. A lack of faith in people might occur. One may be frozen by past memories. A refusal to transcend the past limits the present. Substance may be abused to escape from reality. A loss of inspiration can be self-destructive.

People can get lost in power urges. They may feel their visions are the ultimate reality. They search for helpless individuals who can be dominated. Someone may try to impress others through wealth, power, and fame. He hides behind a worldly identity and does not trust emotional vulnerability.

SOFT ASPECTS

Sextile: Transiting Saturn Sextile Natal Neptune
Transiting Neptune Sextile Natal Saturn

Trine: Transiting Saturn Trine Natal Neptune
Transiting Neptune Trine Natal Saturn

LIGHT

Transiting Saturn sextile natal Neptune or transiting Neptune sextile natal Saturn can denote exciting accomplishments. One could integrate ideals and ambitions. A person may feel mentally fresh and alert. Life seems exciting and intoxicating. In the softer Saturn/Neptune aspects, a person does not feel the same drive to satisfy ambition and idealism. Creating harmony is a strong attraction. A person with a lot of intensity-promoting aspects in the birthchart may find these softer aspects particularly productive. A lack of conflict between reality and divine discontent can mean it is easier to tap into faith and intuition.

Transiting Saturn trine natal Neptune or transiting Neptune trine natal Saturn can point to a more expansive faith. This could be an inspiring period. Negative thoughts may be transcended. Making peace with one's life can occur. An individual could sense a unity that was lacking. A more giving nature can develop. A desire for a close relationship may emerge. Spiritual values are lived. A deeper meaning in life is sought.

SHADOW

In both the **Saturn/Neptune sextile and trine**, one may go too much with the flow. Procrastination waits too long for the perfect opportunity. Unawareness of time and limits can create a spacey life. Changes may be poorly timed. A lack of inspiration or fear of failure can be a problem. An individual can have extreme dependency needs with a constant need for approval or attention. One may feel quite helpless. People may live in a fantasy world. Reality is too difficult to face.

DAWN

Saturn/Neptune aspects can express as revitalized inspiration. Dealing with real-life issues can enhance faith. One may break through old behaviors related to escapism, power, and addictions to substances or relationships. Intuition can become a powerful ally. People may take more responsibility. A new sensitivity and purpose in life could be born. Subtle processes within life's mysteries may be understood. An individual can rise above any limitations.

SATURN/PLUTO ASPECTS

Transiting Saturn/Natal Pluto
Transiting Pluto/Natal Saturn

Process:	Mastering Power
Ally:	Learning from the Past
Illusion:	Fear of Transitions

Saturn/Pluto aspects denote very focused energy. There can be a passion to fulfill ambition. Issues relate to power, control, channeling intensity, and wisdom. One can sense an urgency to take care of unfinished business. The aging process can be beneficial.

INTENSE ASPECTS

Conjunction: Transiting Saturn Conjunct Natal Pluto
Transiting Pluto Conjunct Natal Saturn

Square: Transiting Saturn Square Natal Pluto
Transiting Pluto Square Natal Saturn

LIGHT

Transiting Saturn conjunct natal Pluto or transiting Pluto conjunct natal Saturn can denote a deep personal transformation. Authority and power are fused. One can release an outworn identity. A drastic change of lifestyle may be needed to match a new inner strength. One may forcefully overcome a physical limitation. Changing one's life despite economic hardship and criticism from others can occur. She can be in touch with survival instincts.

Healing an old wound is possible. Forgiving an enemy or someone who betrayed the individual can occur. Making peace with someone dying may be urgent. An old identity can end. Rebirth can be symbolized. This time period may crystallize in clarity years later. Both Saturn and Pluto themes often blossom as we age. Individuals may go beyond past-life fears. People may have given away too much power or abused authority in past lives. They may balance energies that previously led to trouble in relationships.

Transiting Saturn square natal Pluto or transiting Pluto square natal Saturn can denote focusing power. One may master ruthlessness on problems and fairness to people. One's territory can be clearly defined. A person can separate which problems belong to her and which to others. One may feel less responsible for other people's conflicts.

One can forgive self or others. This aspect can be sobering and humbling. One may discover a new purpose, leave behind a problem, or pay off a karma debt. The cosmic chiropractor and cosmic composter can symbolize transforming energies into higher consciousness.

Some of my clients had transiting Pluto in Scorpio square both natal Saturn and Pluto in Leo during 1988. A question of overall life purpose surfaced. Many of these people were in their forties. Previous career experiences were no longer as fulfilling. A desire for more control and deeper meaning emerged.

One may sense an urgency to fulfill ambitions. Life's finiteness can hit home. A passion for a particular creative expression may occur. A previously denied conflict may be dealt with.

SHADOW

In both the **Saturn/Pluto conjunction and square**, individuals can feel their lives have no direction. A crisis is happening. One sees life as meaningless. Not acknowledging life's magic power can lead to frustrating circumstances. One can act as the sole creator of her destiny. A person could worship empiricism as a higher power. Nothing exists that you cannot see or prove logically.

Individuals can fear life. They do little to initiate new options. Rigid habits, limiting relationships, and careers result. A fear of personal power brings frustration. Not recognizing old patterns — whether over or under using personal power — leads to repeated problems. It is like a scratch on a record. The needle always gets stuck or makes an inharmonious sound. A refusal to make behavior changes continues karmic patterns.

A person can combine the power themes of Saturn and Pluto into extreme control of others. Her entire life can be based on becoming invincible. A vindictive nature can dominate. One may compulsively want revenge. Jealousy and manipulation can become a focus. Others are controlled through emotional and physical force.

Quincunx: Transiting Saturn Quincunx Natal Pluto
Transiting Pluto Quincunx Natal Saturn

Opposition: Transiting Saturn Opposing Natal Pluto
Transiting Pluto Opposing Natal Saturn

LIGHT

Transiting Saturn quincunx natal Pluto or transiting Pluto quincunx natal Saturn is the "Yoga of mastering power." A person can question present circumstances to see if she will fulfill expectations. One may better define goals. This can be a very reflective time. One may tune into personal attitudes that limit growth. Transcending addictive and compulsive habits gives more freedom of choice. A more positive life attitude can be adopted.

One may break away from negative role models. A person may have modeled her life after an authority figure who showed little feeling. Individuals may gain emotional depth. Inner conflict can be faced despite fear. Brave new choices transcend karma habits.

Transiting Saturn opposing natal Pluto or transiting Pluto opposing natal Saturn can denote balancing responsibility and power. An individual may transcend extreme power urges whether over or underdone. People can attract dominating partners or those easily dominated. One can learn not to always be a leader or follower. Power may be shared. An individual can deal with a karma pattern of rigidity in relating. Awareness leads to flexibility. Might may not always be right.

One may grieve the loss of a parent or close relationship. This loss can be physical or psychological. She may leave the hold of a past relationship behind. Individuals often consult therapists and astrologers during Saturn/Pluto aspects, seeking clarity and control over their lives. A person may deal with limiting behaviors. A person may control emotional intensity. A clearer perspective on intimate bonding is possible.

Breaking free from cultural biases could occur. One may overcome ethnic hatred, sexism, and a scapegoating mentality. Hatred taught by an authority figure can be surrendered. One may think for herself. A person fearing cultural judgment or persecution might find new pride or strength. Accomplishing life goals and love relationships may bring a new passion for life.

SHADOW

In both the **Saturn/Pluto quincunx and opposition,** one can be too excited by having power over employees, lovers, children, etc. A person could be quite insecure with personal identity and hate certain ethnic groups or races. One desires to control others. Irrational moods can be displayed. A fear of intimacy causes shallow relationships. A failure to deal with emotional problems ruins relationships. Unresolved anger is projected onto others.

A fear of karma patterns leads one into compulsive behaviors. Someone may have a history of control and manipulation themes. Or, a person may give up power too easily. An individual can exhibit either extreme as a karma problem. Both require willpower to change the pattern. A person may stubbornly resist options.

SOFT ASPECTS

Sextile:	Transiting Saturn Sextile Natal Pluto
	Transiting Pluto Sextile Natal Saturn
Trine:	Transiting Saturn Trine Natal Pluto
	Transiting Pluto Trine Natal Saturn

LIGHT

Transiting Saturn sextile natal Pluto or transiting Pluto sextile natal Saturn can symbolize a person aware of her strength. One can enjoy a rich past of hard work. A person can transcend karma patterns. She may be willing to acknowledge problems. One may excel in management of time and resources. Skills in investment or business operation can be shown. A person gains more control through economic independence.

Transiting Saturn trine natal Pluto or transiting Pluto trine natal Saturn can indicate conquering compulsive habits. An individual may overcome tension between personal ambition and the expectations of others. One may transcend emotional fear in relating to others. A person can relax during the softer aspects. Saturn/Pluto aspects are symbolic of stressful time periods. The lessons are deep and can be on the unconscious level. A person may search deeply for spiritual values.

SHADOW

In both the **Saturn/Pluto sextile and trine**, screening out environmental stimuli can be difficult. An oversensitivity to outside influences creates anxiety. One may be too suspicious of others. One may manipulate and control to avoid internal problems. The natural ease and flow of the trine can indicate one has little awareness of limits. She may be ignorant of physical laws. Closed attitudes can be subtly portrayed in the sextile and trine. A person may appear open but in reality be ruthlessly rigid.

DAWN

Saturn/Pluto aspects can express as transcending karma patterns that have limited one's happiness and growth. Saturn points to how a person can block the flow. Pluto connotes where one may be too compulsive and attached to circumstances. This aspect pair can be refocused into determination to do altruistic deeds. An individual may rise above karma behavior related to authoritarianism and manipulation. This combination has intense focus and concentration. One can master power instincts like never before. **Wasteful and negative energies from past incarnations can be composted into the new growth-promoting soil of this lifetime.** People can make great strides in career. Recognition and wealth can be realized. This is not to say that Saturn/Pluto aspects will not confront us to find patience and determination!

URANUS/URANUS ASPECTS

Transiting Uranus/Natal Uranus

Process: Experimental Individuality

Ally: Innovative Vision

Illusion: Separation from Self

It takes transiting Uranus about seven years to move through a sign. Uranus moves through all twelve signs in approximately eighty-four years. People born during the early 1900s experienced a "Uranus Return" in the 1980s.

The transits of Saturn and Uranus overlap. For instance, at age twenty-one, transiting Saturn is sometimes square natal Saturn while transiting Uranus is square natal Uranus. At about age forty, transiting Uranus opposes natal Uranus, just prior to transiting Saturn opposing natal Saturn (age forty-four to forty-six).

Transiting Uranus aspecting natal Uranus is a process of self-discovery. The aspects often represent accelerated rates of perception. One can greatly stimulate her environment and vice versa. One's cultural and global awareness can intensify. A totally new direction can be born.

INTENSE ASPECTS

Square: Transiting Uranus Square Natal Uranus

LIGHT

Transiting Uranus square natal Uranus first occurs at approximately age twenty-one. This square can start before age twenty-one depending on the year of birth. Those of us born in 1947 experienced this square by age 19.

During the square of transiting Saturn to natal Saturn at about age twenty-one, a person is looking for societal acceptance. The square of transiting Uranus to natal Uranus adds conflicting themes. Saturn says follow the rules. Uranus says rules are made to be broken.

The **square of transiting Uranus to natal Uranus** at ages 21 and 63, can express as brilliant insights. Raised consciousness can insulate a person from societal pressures. She sees the interconnectedness of life. A collective awareness may lead one boldly beyond cultural imprints. A person may question the status quo and stimulate growth in others. One's mental intensity and creativity can tackle any subject. She may experience new freedom. An untiring mental spirit may invent new technology. Uranus symbolizes new technology and systems of communication.

SHADOW
Transiting Uranus square natal Uranus can denote an impatient and cold individual. One can feel superior in intelligence with a callous arrogance. Sarcasm could be bitter. Individuals might fear their individuality. One may fear conflict and not stand up for her ideas.

People may become too rigid in thinking, resisting change and new ideas. One may give in to cultural stereotypes rather than develop unique perceptions. An individual may want to break down structures, but have no idea how to replace them. She can focus too much on change and forget stability. One can become addicted to life in the fast lane, later regretting what was passed up.

Quincunx: Transiting Uranus Quincunx Natal Uranus

LIGHT
Transiting Uranus quincunxes natal Uranus at approximately ages 35 and 49. This is the **"Yoga of bringing the light out from under the bushel."** One stops always following the wishes of others. A person can march to her own drum. One may realize she has been asleep. Individuality can become a goal. A person may stop being the pawn of a group or peer. She believes in her own ideas and future potential. A new direction might begin. Exciting new self-discoveries can occur. More refreshing symbols and role models elicit new insights. One may outgrow cultural beliefs fed by authority figures.

An individual may steer away from peers who are a bad influence. A reckless abandonment could be gradually overcome. One might stop projecting talent onto others. People may ask for support. They more clearly lend support to others. An impersonal aura may be dropped.

SHADOW
Transiting Uranus quincunx natal Uranus can symbolize people blind to the rights of others. Personal freedom at all cost can become a slogan. One can surrender to narrow beliefs — her own or the propaganda of others. One can be easily led away from mental objectivity. A person may blame relationships or "the system" for problems. During intense aspects, a person may find deeper awareness. A person may resist this growth and hide in the past. She can close her eyes to the future.

Opposition: Transiting Uranus Opposite Natal Uranus

Transiting Uranus opposes natal Uranus by the age of forty-two. For those of us born in 1947, this opposition began by our 39th birthday in 1986. This aspect can represent a "mid-life crisis." A person can make growth-promoting choices with a new objectivity. Individuals may experiment with new ways of relating. A refreshing awareness of existing relationships excites them. One may be more of a player in life, instead of sitting on the sidelines.

An individual may perceive she has outgrown her niche in the world. She may desire a deeper level in relationships. A person might need more freedom to pursue new goals. She could enjoy periods of being alone to brainstorm new ideas. One may inspire new cultural trends in writing and speaking. She might become an exceptional communicator. Overreactions could be sobered by cool Uranian detachment. Panic attacks and nervous breakdowns may be transformed into creative energy. Mental energy is used wisely. A person finds a more meaningful life purpose.

People may achieve more equality in relationships. An increased awareness of others can lead to clearer communication. Previously existing tensions may be transcended. More mutual respect for individual needs is realized. Individual awareness may lift to a more collective level. A person can become more aware of community, national, and global trends. One's energies may go into humanitarian causes. A person can stimulate new growth in groups of people.

SHADOW

Transiting Uranus opposing natal Uranus can denote intense sarcasm and bitterness. One may feel unusually frustrated with unrealized goals. She may blame others for problems. An individual can recklessly rebel with no purpose. A person can be "different just to be different." She may enrage others with a lack of sensitivity. An individual can be very aloof and difficult to understand, not communicating clearly.

One may leave productive relationships and situations on a whim. A person can suddenly forget commitments and follow impulsive thoughts. She may later regret not thinking decisions through. An individual may become attracted to neurotic and irresponsible people. She may enter unrewarding relationships that drain energy. One may give up too much for little received. Goals may be sacrificed for self-serving partners.

Individuals can allow their environment to make them into nervous wrecks. Not reflecting or taking private relaxing time can result in burnout. An individual may refuse to grow. One could return to adolescent behaviors for attention, going backward instead of forward. Stagnation and a dulled mental perception may occur.

SOFT ASPECTS

Sextile: Transiting Uranus Sextile Natal Uranus

Trine: Transiting Uranus Trine Natal Uranus

LIGHT

Transiting Uranus sextile natal Uranus can symbolize tremendous mental exhilaration. A drive to communicate can lead into new directions. This very energetic aspect occurs the first time at about age 14 (around the time of transiting Saturn opposing natal Saturn). This can indicate an adolescent finding herself. This tense period is filled with numerous experiences such as establishing new peer groups. Transiting Uranus sextile natal Uranus will not reoccur again until a person is about seventy. A person can become very experimental and be an important role model for younger generations. An individual may risk imprisonment for a cause. A person can be an important link between generations. She has several decades of important insights to share. One can be a motivator or teacher.

Transiting Uranus trine natal Uranus takes place about age 28 and again at about age 56. These trines occur near our Saturn Returns. Uranus is our mental link with past generations. A conscious individual may contribute major new ideas to community, nation, or world. A person may see the future clearly, rising above environmental turbulence to share a clear wisdom. The trine can confirm one's goals and emerging growth. One's choices promote fulfillment.

SHADOW

Both the **transiting Uranus/natal Uranus sextile and trine** indicate less intensity to change one's lifestyle. A person can live on the mental plane and not put ideas into action. An individual can become too removed from the mainstream. Ideas can be impractical and eccentric. During the first sextile, shortly before age 14, a child could be prone to getting into trouble. Destructive peers may be influential. The trines that occur shortly before age 28 and 56 could lead one to think she is above the law and can get away with anything.

A person can move too fast. This can be a wild and reckless youth (first sextile) or a highly-driven type "A" mentality at age 28 or 56 (trines). The flowing nature of the sextile and trine can lead to extremes. If one does not set limits, she could get into trouble. A person can intellectualize too much, not expressing feelings. One can be too self-confident to need support. Conversely, an insecure person might find it difficult to find herself. She could too easily try to please others. One may deny individuality.

DAWN

The transiting Uranus/natal Uranus aspects can symbolize dynamic new perceptions. One may be flooded by stimulating insights.

A person's world may be shaken. An entirely new lifestyle can result, especially during the squares and opposition. Even during the Uranus Return at approximately age eighty-four, a person can grow in awareness. One can share knowledge and perceptions gained through life. Benjamin Franklin at age eighty-four was a motivator for the development of America. His words enlightened others.

Excitement and mental exhilaration can lead one to leave limiting situations. Insights may salvage existing circumstances in need of a refreshing perspective. New life can be breathed into one's future outlook. A new optimism and experimentation give one the confidence to grow.

URANUS/NEPTUNE ASPECTS

Transiting Uranus/Natal Neptune
Transiting Neptune/Natal Uranus

Process:	Appreciating Life's Magic
Ally:	Imaging Strength
Illusion:	Helplessness; Savior Complex

Uranus/Neptune aspects can symbolize unique consciousness changes. Not everybody makes use of these themes on a conscious level. Many individuals experience life as a series of unusual or sudden upsets during these aspects, especially the intense ones. Fast mental insights combine with sensitivity. Finding objectivity aids in using highest values. Feelings inspire one to express greater emotion rather than staying too aloof. Uranus is an agent of the intellect (air element) while Neptune points to intuition (water element).

INTENSE ASPECTS

Conjunction:	Transiting Uranus Conjunct Natal Neptune
	Transiting Neptune Conjunct Natal Uranus
Square:	Transiting Uranus Square Natal Neptune
	Transiting Neptune Square Natal Uranus

LIGHT

Transiting Uranus conjunct natal Neptune or transiting Neptune conjunct natal Uranus can denote sudden insights about the future. Individuals may access subconscious, inspiring goals. New peers may mysteriously come into one's life.

Collective causes or movements may appeal to individuals. A person may inspire a group to move in a new direction. Leaving a group may produce a newfound freedom. Alternative healing and counter-cultural thinking can be stimulating.

Transiting Uranus square natal Neptune or transiting Neptune square natal Uranus could denote expressing highest values. Aesthetic abilities may scream to be made real. Overcoming the odds propels one's faith. Innovative individuals may influence one's life. A deeper spiritual awareness can manifest suddenly.

SHADOW

In both the **Uranus/Neptune conjunction and square**, one can get too emotionally distant. The aloofness of Uranus covers the feeling themes of Neptune. Individuals might grow emotionally disoriented. Holding back independent urges can cause confusion. People get mesmerized by their own beliefs. A loss of perspective could kidnap someone's rational thinking. Zealous, extreme beliefs turn others off.

Quincunx: Transiting Uranus Quincunx Natal Neptune
Transiting Neptune Quincunx Natal Uranus

Opposition: Transiting Uranus Opposing Natal Neptune
Transiting Neptune Opposing Natal Uranus

LIGHT

Transiting Uranus quincunx natal Neptune or transiting Neptune quincunx natal Uranus is the **"yoga of inspired vision."** One can go beyond cultural norms to express unique ideas. This is an aspect that requires patience and some action. Thoughts and feelings may elevate a person's consciousness. Going beyond addictive tendencies restores balance.

Relationships could be based on mutual acceptance. Sacrifice is accepted. Equality is a shared need. Communication can bring a person closer to others. Exploration of unconventional beliefs or interests could be exciting.

Transiting Uranus opposing natal Neptune or transiting Neptune opposing natal Uranus can find people magically encountering new peers or lovers. Life can take on a mysterious quality. Sudden intuitive insights about others may be startling. Tuning into one's own relationship patterns is possible. A deep spiritual link to a person or group could occur.

Others may admire one's unique aesthetic expressions. One's mind may fill with constant, intuitive creativity. A special mission or cause may claim a person's attention. Gaining objectivity concerning personal goals is satisfying.

SHADOW

In both the **Uranus/Neptune quincunx and opposition**, individuals can be too unpredictable in relationships, or attract unreliable partners. A need for moderation and stability might be ignored. Listening to others is a wise policy, as is finding partners willing to communicate. A denial of individuality (or freedom) to stay in a relationship is self-destructive. Trying too hard to please others is burdensome. Guilt is imprisoning.

SOFT ASPECTS
Sextile: Transiting Uranus Sextile Natal Neptune
              Transiting Neptune Sextile Natal Uranus

Trine: Transiting Uranus Trine Natal Neptune
              Transiting Neptune Trine Natal Uranus

LIGHT
Transiting Uranus sextile natal Neptune or transiting Neptune sextile natal Uranus can express as stimulating imagination. Individuals can move briskly and yet be quite centered. Moving in new directions is consciousness-raising and sharpens perceptions. One's peers may be from artistic backgrounds. Exchanging ideas is mentally and emotionally invigorating.

Transiting Uranus trine natal Neptune or transiting Neptune trine natal Uranus can point to inner and outer unity. One might be motivated to do altruistic deeds. An interest in helping society grow in awareness is possible. A self-centered individual may become more supportive. A person lacking faith might discover self-confidence.

SHADOW
In both the **Uranus/Neptune sextile and trine** people might get too complacent. Ideas stay on the mental level. Denial of the present can keep people lost in the clouds. Self-starting potentials may go to sleep. Individuals could be too easily persuaded to enter into risky deals. Forgetting to look at the details leads to trouble. Acting out of guilt leads to limiting situations.

DAWN
Uranus/Neptune aspects can express as wonderful changes in consciousness. Freedom and sensitivity work hand in hand. Seeing the bigger picture in relationships or business affairs may be a great gift. Grasping a fast intuitive awareness of situations is exciting. A new life direction could bring new faith and inspiration.

URANUS/PLUTO ASPECTS

Transiting Uranus/Natal Pluto
Transiting Pluto/Natal Uranus

Process: Psychological Freedom

Ally: Power of Invention

Illusion: Love of Danger

Uranus/Pluto aspects denote a sudden desire for mystery. Unusual events can take a person beyond fixed routines. Peers and lovers may share a passion for freedom and self-exploration. Psychology, science, metaphysics and research could be especially appealing.

INTENSE ASPECTS
Conjunction: Transiting Uranus Conjunct Natal Pluto
Transiting Pluto Conjunct Natal Uranus

Square: Transiting Uranus Square Natal Pluto
Transiting Pluto Square Natal Uranus

LIGHT
Transiting Uranus conjunct natal Pluto or transiting Pluto conjunct natal Uranus can symbolize an empowered sense of direction. Individuals can discover a true purpose in life. A passion to break new ground could excite peers. The drive to be different might take people to unique creative heights. Cultural taboos are fun to explore. People can delight in breaking the rules to shock others.

Relationships can be typified by experimentation. Crossing cultural barriers is exciting. An attraction to unusual partners is accentuated. Partnerships are mutual stimulating. Freedom and space are probably needed. Breaking away from controlling partners is liberating. A controlling person can let others be themselves.

Transiting Uranus square natal Pluto or transiting Pluto square natal Uranus can be intensely inventive. People may break out of their shell. Compulsive needs for mental and emotional highs may lead people to transcend limiting situations. A rebirth of an independent spirit is possible. An in-depth study can be satisfying.

SHADOW
In both the **Uranus/Pluto conjunction and square,** individuals may be too attached to compulsive behaviors. Unpredictable emotional explosions may make individuals difficult to understand. The desire for unstable partners could bring disastrous situations. Being drained emotionally is the result.

Eccentric interests could make a person too aloof from others. One might become absorbed in self-destructive habits. A failure to communicate causes emotional isolation. An extreme elitist attitude blocks the heart from opening.

Quincunx: Transiting Uranus Quincunx Natal Pluto
Transiting Pluto Quincunx Natal Uranus

Opposition: Transiting Uranus Opposing Natal Pluto
Transiting Pluto Opposing Natal Uranus

LIGHT
Transiting Uranus quincunx natal Pluto or transiting Pluto quincunx natal Uranus is the **"yoga of empowering insights."** One might embrace a greater psychological freedom. Giving up power too easily may be a thing of the past. Finding a less unstable emotional partner can bring balance. Identifying self-defeating behavior patterns is uplifting. A person could put much energy into fascinating studies. Emotional needs and important goals may be communicated.

Transiting Uranus opposing natal Pluto or transiting Pluto opposing natal Uranus denotes an unusual charisma. Partnerships can be based on a deep trust, a bond that supports mutual acceptance. Friendship may be important to each person.

One could rebel against manipulative or overpowering people. Moving in a new life is exhilarating. A relationship can get shaken into a more giving partnership. Group involvements can open a person's eyes to more options. Becoming more self-reliant might lead to insights.

SHADOW
In both the **transiting Uranus/Pluto quincunx and opposition,** people can get too dependent. Individuality can be surrendered to more powerful individuals. Rebellion with no purpose may burn needed bridges. Partners may have little interest in real communication. The need for emotional intensity and constant stimulation can get too extreme.

It is vital to discriminate between what is possible to change and what is better left alone. Individuals may make bad decisions in choosing new challenges. A love of diving over the edge can be regretted. A fear of communicating feelings or goals needs to be overcome.

SOFT ASPECTS
Sextile:	Transiting Uranus Sextile Natal Pluto
	Transiting Pluto Sextile Natal Uranus
Trine:	Transiting Uranus Trine Natal Pluto
	Transiting Pluto Trine Natal Uranus

LIGHT
Transiting Uranus sextile natal Pluto or transiting Pluto sextile natal Uranus can point to penetrating insights. Individuals can display remarkable poise in difficult situations. Staying cool within the midst of challenges may surprise others. Making use of what is available is a special talent. Communicating abstract ideas clearly is possible. Fast learning may be displayed.

Transiting Uranus trine natal Pluto or transiting Pluto trine natal Uranus might denote a powerful vision of the future. One may help empower others through suggesting alternatives to problems. A passion to blaze a new trail could lead others to follow. Friends and lovers may share in self-discovery.

SHADOW
In both the **Uranus/Pluto sextile and trine**, one might drift into strange and extreme thinking. A person could ignore opinions of others regarding self-defeating behaviors. Self-indulgent behaviors can go too far. A failure to consider alternatives to problems could leave a person stuck. Too great an attachment to a group consciousness stunts growth. Fearing a more intense life direction can cause missed opportunities. People may resist new thinking to preserve a less thought-provoking existence.

DAWN
Uranus/Pluto aspects can express as awakening dynamic individuality. An intense new life direction can be born. Relationships might fill with experimentation and equality. Communication of insights and feelings could be very rewarding. One may offer the world a wonderful inventive energy.

NEPTUNE/NEPTUNE ASPECTS

Transiting Neptune/Natal Neptune

Process:	Intuitive Belief Systems
Ally:	Compassion and Spiritual Strength
Illusion:	Sacrificing Oneself and Others

It takes transiting Neptune about fourteen years to move through a sign. Neptune moves through all twelve signs in approximately one hundred and sixty-eight years. **Transiting Neptune aspecting natal Neptune is a process of establishing clear ideals.** Creating rewarding relationships and making choices worthy of our devotion is challenging! People can tune into a collective awareness of a community and world issues.

INTENSE ASPECTS
  Square: Transiting Neptune Square Natal Neptune

LIGHT
Transiting Neptune squares natal Neptune at approximately age 42. A person's deepest yearnings for love and spirituality may be active. Some individuals find fame at their doorstep. New inspiring symbols might enter a person's life.

Individuals may fully embrace the muse consciousness. Aesthetic appreciation could awaken. Artistic talents might be displayed. Healing energies can intensify. The faith to change a self-defeating behavior may be found.

Relationships may deepen in devotion and sacrifice. Emotional exchanges can be especially meaningful. People may feel driven to serve their society. Giving something back is rewarding. A desire to share one's life could become urgent.

SHADOW
Transiting Neptune square natal Neptune may denote a person lost in fantasy. Denial can keep people in confining careers or relationships. Extreme sacrifices may go unrewarded. Individuals could feel too much self-importance to serve others. Unrealistic expectations of self or others might occur. Divine discontent could keep people from enjoying their lives.

Opposition: Transiting Neptune Opposite Natal Neptune

LIGHT
Transiting Neptune opposing natal Neptune occurs at approximately age 84. This can be experienced as a great spiritual awakening. Individuals might feel at peace with the world. Surrendering worries is possible. The muse consciousness could still enjoy dancing through the minds of people experiencing this cycle. Volunteer roles can be fulfilling. One may find loving companionship. It can be enjoyable to live near the ocean or to embrace life's natural beauty. Being near family members is reassuring and comforting.

SHADOW
Transiting Neptune opposing natal Neptune could find people disillusioned with life. They can feel deserted by loved ones. A loss of faith might be painful. Irrational fears of being deserted or of death might manifest. One's mind may lose memory.

SOFT ASPECTS
Sextile: Transiting Neptune Sextile Natal Neptune

Trine: Transiting Neptune Trine Natal Neptune

LIGHT
Transiting Neptune sextile natal Neptune can symbolize new ideas surfacing. People may acknowledge they need others. Individuals might awaken to more intuition. This aspect occurs at about age 28 (around the time of transiting Saturn conjunct natal Saturn). If one is able to stay grounded, much may be accomplished. Compassion and wanting to give something to society could inspire others. Individuals in touch with higher consciousness may embark on spiritual journeys. Feeding the mind growth-promoting material can be exhilarating. Dreams that come to fruition might accelerate one's faith in self or in a higher power.

Transiting Neptune trine natal Neptune takes place at about age 56. This trine occurs near the second time transiting Saturn conjuncts natal Saturn and transiting Uranus is trine natal Uranus. Embracing a greater mission in life is possible. One's visions of life may make room for expanded consciousness. Individuals could value their closest love relationships even more. A desire to share one's love of beauty and harmony with others may blossom. Feeling grateful for the little things is possible. Giving of oneself could be a natural expression.

SHADOW
Both the **transiting Neptune/natal Neptune sextile and trine** may denote settling for the easy paths. People might grow too passive to enact their highest dreams. Waiting for life to deliver its gift may lead to disillusionment. Individuals can delude themselves into thinking they are serving a greater good when they are only thinking of themselves. Spiritual values might get lost in a life dedicated to material well being. People may deny their intuition. A lack of faith keeps a broader vision muddled. Blocked emotions might be disorienting.

DAWN
The transiting Neptune/natal Neptune aspects can symbolize tuning into inspiring new symbols. One could express emotions fluently. Devotion to higher values could be done with sensitivity toward others. Making sacrifices may win the hearts of others. Finding unity with romantic partners could be a source of joy. Faith can hit an all-time high.

NEPTUNE/PLUTO ASPECTS

Transiting Neptune/Natal Pluto
Transiting Pluto/Natal Neptune

Process:	Intense Faith
Ally:	Intuition and Survival Instincts
Illusion:	Loss of Healthy Boundaries

Neptune/Pluto aspects symbolize a passion to transcend limiting circumstances. Spiritual awakenings are not unusual. An intuitive understanding of life's deepest mysteries can unfold. A fascination with power and wealth could occur. People may identify with collective movements. Establishing romantic relationships could be an intense need.

INTENSE ASPECTS
Conjunction: Transiting Neptune Conjunct Natal Pluto
Transiting Pluto Conjunct Natal Neptune
Square: Transiting Neptune Square Natal Pluto
Transiting Pluto Square Natal Neptune

Transiting Neptune conjunct natal Pluto or transiting Pluto conjunct natal Neptune can denote a dynamic release of hidden emotional material. Finding happiness becomes an urgent need. People may get more relaxed in expressing themselves. A compulsive drive for fame and riches can be converted into enjoying the moment. Emotionally repressed individuals may learn to communicate feelings. Faith could be reborn. Pursuing a dream may empower a person. Forming a business or romantic relationship can bring exciting growth. Forgiving oneself is liberating.

Transiting Neptune square natal Pluto or transiting Pluto square natal Neptune can connote reclaiming one's power. Surrendering the past paves the way for a brighter future. People too attached to overpowering others could trust more. Relinquishing extreme power drives balances relationships. Addictive energies may be converted into more productive expressions. Faith in self or a higher power can bring more peace into one's life.

SHADOW
In both the **Neptune/Pluto conjunction and square**, individuals can be ruled by their compulsive desires. Strange drives for perfection could be self-defeating. Not playing by the rules might get people into trouble with the law. Ethics are greatly needed. Allowing others to control one's life is limiting. Serving undeserving people is a mistake. Giving up too easily on a dream or heartfelt need takes away from faith.

Quincunx: Transiting Neptune Quincunx Natal Pluto
Transiting Pluto Quincunx Natal Neptune

Opposition: Transiting Neptune Opposing Natal Pluto
Transiting Pluto Opposing Natal Neptune

LIGHT
Transiting Neptune quincunx natal Pluto or transiting Pluto quincunx natal Neptune is the **"yoga of reflection."** One can move intensely but with an intuitive eye. A deeper understanding of power motives allows others to interact more freely. Faith in self or a higher power may rise to new levels. Releasing the hold of anger and jealousy frees energy. Meditation and other unifying experiences raise one's consciousness.

Transiting Neptune opposing natal Pluto or transiting Pluto opposing natal Neptune may express as tuning into the inner needs of others. A greater listening ability can manifest. A person may relate to others in a sensitive manner. Establishing clearer psychological boundaries in partnerships yields more clarity and freedom. Spiritual and intuitive links with others can blossom. Wonder and awe could inspire a person to creative heights.

SHADOW
In both the **Neptune/Pluto quincunx and opposition,** people may grow paranoid. A refusal to see issues clearly may confuse others. A

denial of problems prolongs the agony. Repeating the same old relationship patterns (regarding the over or under use of power) is possible. Addictions to emotionally disoriented partners keep relationships out of balance. Refusing to seek solutions to personal problems is limiting.

SOFT ASPECTS

Sextile:	Transiting Neptune Sextile Natal Pluto
	Transiting Pluto Sextile Natal Neptune
Trine:	Transiting Neptune Trine Natal Pluto
	Transiting Pluto Trine Natal Neptune

LIGHT

Transiting Neptune sextile natal Pluto or transiting Pluto sextile natal Neptune points to intuition and emotional intensity working nicely together. Already harmonious relationships can go to even deeper levels of trust. Mystical links to higher energies instill greater faith. Financial investments could pay great dividends. One's dreams may be met with positive regard by others.

Transiting Neptune trine natal Pluto or transiting Pluto trine natal Neptune can express as inner, personal power. One's faith might attract financial and emotional success. Individuals may experience a special grace coming into their lives. New doors could open miraculously. Allowing the concept of more wealth or fame makes it a possibility. Love relationships and spiritual pursuits can be sources of joy.

SHADOW

In both the **Neptune/Pluto sextile and trine**, individuals may chase after illusions. Excessive fascination with power and wealth could derail one's life. Addictions to self-destructive drives may be a problem. Unclear boundaries in relating to others may exist. Keeping emotional exchanges shallow blocks true relationship development. Following powerful people is no better than manipulating blind followers.

DAWN

Neptune/Pluto aspects can express as devotion to one's highest truths. Relationships can thrive on selfless love. Sharing power with trust elevates the possibilities of partnerships. A belief in life's magic frees one to explore fullest potentials.

PLUTO/PLUTO ASPECTS

Transiting Pluto/Natal Pluto

Process:	Self-Mastery
Ally:	Emotional Strength and Rebirth
Illusion:	Overpowering is the Way

Transiting Pluto aspecting natal Pluto points to challenges to our personal power. Individuals can transform themselves. Relinquishing worn-out behaviors makes new options possible. Finding a clear way to empower oneself and forming trusting bonds are part of the Pluto experience.

INTENSE ASPECTS
Square: Transiting Pluto Square Natal Pluto

LIGHT

Transiting Pluto square natal Pluto denotes a great purge from within. Individuals may rid themselves of self-defeating behaviors. A tremendous drive to rise above limiting circumstances can take one onto new highways. Dealing with power issues is probable. People can ferociously seek the resources to become all that they can be. Finding the strength to let go of what is bad is challenging. Being centered is satisfying. Charisma might be strong. A person could be good in business and make things happen. Channeling negative energies into more positive directions is exciting and confirming. Strong bonds with others may deepen trust.

SHADOW

Transiting Pluto square natal Pluto can point to a one-dimensional emotional nature. Greed is the message of the day. Manipulating others is a great temptation. Being controlled by more powerful people is limiting. Not letting go of the past interferes with enjoying the present. Old emotional relationship patterns may be difficult to surrender. Insights into relationships could be ignored. Selfish needs which alienate loved ones can be regretted later.

SOFT ASPECTS
Sextile: Transiting Pluto Sextile Natal Pluto

Trine: Transiting Pluto Trine Natal Pluto

Transiting Pluto sextile natal Pluto can denote insights into power issues. Finding ways to improve one's material and emotional state could be stimulating. Individuals learn to be more honest in dealing with others. Communicating emotions may bring people closer. The seeds of an empowering future might be planted at this time.

Transiting Pluto trine natal Pluto can point to a special period of self-realization. People may feel at the top of their game. Enjoying what one has acquired spiritually, materially, and emotionally might be satisfying. Giving to others could win their admiration. Bonding with collective movements might arouse a new passion for life. The rebirth of creative powers could inspire others.

SHADOW

Both the **transiting Pluto/natal Pluto sextile and trine** may result in having hidden agendas. Power could be used in sly ways. Lack of self-honesty might keep people caught in self-destructive relationships or careers. Balance is hijacked by compulsive desires for control. Limiting behaviors are not transcended. Fighting new growth keeps one stuck in the same life.

DAWN

The transiting Pluto/natal Pluto aspects can denote moving into a more balanced existence. Emotional well being can be wonderful. Relationships are based on mutual trust. Power is shared. A strong rebirth can leave self-defeating habits behind. Personal power is guided by one's clarity and openness to change.

CHAPTER TEN

PLANET/ASCENDANT ASPECTS

Aspects formed by planets to the Ascendant indicate special dimensions of consciousness. The **planet/Ascendant** aspects denote nuances in identity. Soft and intense aspects formed by progressed and transiting planets to the natal Ascendant or the progressed Ascendant aspecting a natal planet points to changes in personal style.

SUN/ASCENDANT ASPECTS

Progressed Sun/Natal or Progressed Ascendant
Progressed Ascendant/Natal Sun

Process:	Creative Identity
Ally:	Embracing the Challenge of Transition
Illusion:	Loss of Self-Confidence or Excessive Confidence

Sun/Ascendant aspects can point to a powerful new self-expression. Individuals may experience freedom. They can show creative energies. The self-image could radiate creative imagination. The love nature can burst open. Life at its fullest may manifest. Joy and humor color this life chapter. One may need to guard against inflated ego. There is a desire for attention. Demanding others live in one's self-image could be a pitfall.

INTENSE ASPECTS

Conjunction: Progressed Sun Conjunct
Natal or Progressed Ascendant
Progressed Ascendant Conjunct Natal Sun

Square: Progressed Sun Square Natal or Progressed Ascendant
Progressed Ascendant Square Natal Sun

LIGHT

The **progressed Sun conjunct the natal or progressed Ascendant or the progressed Ascendant conjunct the natal Sun** can point to a new, dynamic self-expression. Leadership roles are highlighted. Feeling important due to recognition is possible. Advertising and promotional instincts are very much aroused. A desire to make major changes in one's physical appearance often surfaces.

A serious person may relax into creative intensity. An already spontaneous individual cashes in on potential. A child can be playful. An adult may find a child within. **This is a major life transition.** One may enjoy getting to know himself in many different ways.

Actions can fill with happiness. The self can radiate. Creative vitality fuses with identity. One may possess remarkable energy. A tired spirit finds a new reason to shine. A lack of confidence can turn into a more positive attitude. Hesitation can succumb to action. Humor and lightness can carry one through trying times. A love for life keeps dreams alive. One may become a romantic. The heart can open to new love. This can be a chapter colored by self-acceptance.

Progressed Sun conjunct a natal or progressed **fire Ascendant** or a progressed fire Ascendant conjunct natal Sun can yield passion and confidence. Creative candles may burn endlessly. A romantic fire could be lit again. Progressed Sun conjunct a natal or progressed **earth Ascendant** or a progressed earth Ascendant conjunct the natal Sun can be a new career expression. People may go beyond playing it safe and take a creative risk. Hard work may finally pay dividends. A lighter feeling about life could occur.

Progressed Sun conjunct a natal or progressed **air Ascendant** or a progressed air Ascendant conjunct the natal Sun can denote confident communication. An individual may enjoy a multidimensional life. A variety of expressions are at his disposal. Social interactions could stimulate energy. Progressed Sun conjunct a natal or progressed **water Ascendant** or a progressed water Ascendant conjunct the natal Sun can point to swimming into deeper emotional waters. Emotional energy can be shared with family, lovers, friendships, career, etc. One may act on intuitive feelings.

Progressed Sun square the natal Ascendant or the progressed Ascendant square the natal Sun can indicate the confidence to change. An internal conflict may be resolved. One may make identity changes. Roadblocks to happiness might be conquered. Individuals learn to accept what cannot be changed.

Progressed Sun square a natal or progressed **fire Ascendant** or a progressed fire Ascendant square the natal Sun can denote solving an assertion crisis. One may gain insight into a lack of confidence. Some individuals overcome a big ego. Progressed Sun square a natal or progressed **earth Ascendant** or a progressed earth Ascendant square the natal Sun can overcome a serious identity. A heavily structured individual may become more spontaneous. A sense of humor can manifest. Work and pleasure are mixed.

Progressed Sun square a natal or progressed **air Ascendant** or a progressed air Ascendant square the natal Sun can denote discovering the heart. One may express more excitement about life. One may act more and reflect less. Progressed Sun square a natal or progressed **water Ascendant** or a progressed water Ascendant square the natal Sun can indicate conquering emotional fears. One may face old conflicts. A new intuitive burst of energy is released. Dependency needs can be balanced. Emotional undercurrents are channeled into creative actions.

SHADOW

Both the **Sun/Ascendant conjunction and square** can express as a big ego. One may constantly compete for attention. Center stage is the only desirable place. One may be too extravagant. A tendency to impress others can take away from the real self. An individual may hide an insecure identity. Individuals can get stubborn. A refusal to cooperate could occur. Pride can be excessive. A failure to show vulnerability might be a problem. The nature can be bossy. One might try to railroad his needs through others. Not letting others shine makes for a lonely existence. Individuals can lose their humor. Life becomes a series of instant Karmas. A hurried lifestyle produces chaos. A disorganized and undisciplined life leads to frustration.

People can get struck in first gear. **Fire Ascendants** can burn out, stewing in inaction. People may complain constantly, but do nothing to change. **Earth** individuals can get bogged down in needless worry. Negative outlooks keep one from moving ahead. **Air Ascendants** may feel torn between thought and action. Nervous anxiety depletes energy. **Water Ascendants** can get lost in a subjective haze. Actions to make dreams real are lacking. The fiery Sun can turn to steam when watered down.

Quincunx: Progressed Sun Quincunx
Natal or Progressed Ascendant
Progressed Ascendant Quincunx Natal Sun

Opposition: Progressed Sun Opposing
Natal or Progressed Ascendant
Progressed Ascendant Opposing Natal Sun

The quincunxes formed by the progressed Sun to the natal or progressed Ascendant or progressed Ascendant to the natal Sun are the "Yoga of creative transitions." One may wear a new identity that better reflects life in the present.

LIGHT

Progressed Sun quincunx the natal Ascendant or progressed Ascendant quincunx the natal Sun can refresh a tired identity. People may watch health and diet. A person might further creative needs. One can bring talents into fruition in new ways. Identity is no longer lived through others.

Natal or progressed **fire Ascendants** can overcome excessive pride. A lack of awareness can be transcended. One may display a new decisiveness. An insensitive individual may find more heart. Natal or progressed **earth Ascendants** can increase self-esteem. One may work hard to accomplish meaningful goals. A commitment to success can strengthen identity. Adopting a less serious demeanor can stop a fixation on material plane. One may become more aware of life's abundance.

Natal or progressed **air Ascendants** can let go of intellectual arrogance. One may express passion for life rather than hiding behind intellect. A person doubting his own intelligence may attain more knowledge. Ridding oneself of limiting concepts can expose new opportunities. Natal or progressed **water Ascendants** may conquer compulsive or addictive habits. Too much dependence on people or substances can be alleviated. Experiencing a natural high lifts one above escapism.

Progressed Sun opposing the natal or progressed Ascendant or progressed Ascendant opposing the natal Sun can denote radiating love to others. People may choose marriage or begin important partnerships. Proving oneself can manifest as passionately releasing creativity. Confidence has no end. An individual may spontaneously promote himself or others. One may win the admiration of others for courage and leadership. Individuals may take special pride in achievements. Long-awaited recognition may arrive.

A natal or progressed **fire Ascendant** may enjoy a moment in the spotlight. An eagerness to experience life is highlighted. One may cease seeking identity within a relationship. A tendency to push others into decisions may be modified. One no longer needs constant reassurance from others. A natal or progressed **earth Ascendant** may confidently trust hunches. Rather than hitting the brakes, one takes more risks. One may meet individuals who motivate. A person lacking confidence may gain new optimism.

A natal or progressed **air Ascendant** can act on perceptions. Ideas may be stimulated by peers. More honest communication can occur. Individuals may be encouraged by others to grow mentally. A teacher may inspire learning. A person may be a fine communicator or teacher, inciting a passion for learning in others. A natal or progressed **water Ascendant** can display intuitive ability. Dormant self-expression comes alive. Peers or lovers encourage emotional expression. One may find inner beauty through relationships. People modify their tendency to be dominated by others. Identity is no longer lost through dependency. A lost soul can find himself again.

SHADOW

The **Sun/Ascendant quincunx or opposition** can manifest as letting people be too influential. One may exhibit little willpower. Choices are dominated by others.

Natal or progressed **fire Ascendants** may lack courage. Inaction can be disorienting. Hasty actions might disregard the rights of others. One may try to always win by force. Showing off could hide vulnerability. One may lack clear insight into self or others. Natal or progressed **earth Ascendants** can get lost in proving themselves. A person can work too hard on changing others. Individuals may have trouble combining pleasure and work. Relationships may be more like a job than shared experiences of responsibility. A person could feel unworthy of a relationship. People can depend too much on others for security.

Natal or progressed **air Ascendants** can lack mental flexibility. A tendency to be aloof can hide warmth. A war of words may abort closeness. One may be too caring of what others think. A tendency to not think for oneself can occur. Natal or progressed **water Ascendants** can get disoriented by relationships. Dependency needs get confused. Others may need too much emotional support. Relating can drain energy. A tendency to "save" others can be a problem. One may diffuse energies, tending to feel defeated by life.

SOFT ASPECTS

Sextile:	Progressed Sun Sextile Natal or Progressed Ascendant
	Progressed Ascendant Sextile Natal Sun
Trine:	Progressed Sun Trine Natal or Progressed Ascendant
	Progressed Ascendant Trine Natal Sun

LIGHT

Progressed Sun sextile or trine the natal (or progressed) Ascendant or the progressed Ascendant sextile or trine the natal Sun can denote a special confidence. One may feel his time has arrived. Happiness or joy can be powerful.

Natal or progressed **fire Ascendants** can feel stimulated to act on creative impulses. One may exemplify good timing in taking a new risk. Spontaneous action gets results. One may enjoy more leisure. Natal or progressed **earth Ascendants** can become more excited about transitions. Change is not so unsettling. One may be more assured by the present. Creative expression can solidify into meaningful results. A natal or progressed **air Ascendant** can find mental coolness. One may relax into actions. Nervous tension is balanced. Social contacts bolster confidence. One may find multiple creative expressions. Natal or progressed **water Ascendants** may find more emotional balance. One's inner and outer life is more equal. Greater confidence in expressing emotions may occur.

SHADOW

Both the **Sun/Ascendant sextile and trine** can express as a too passive nature. One may not take a stand on anything.

Natal or progressed **fire Ascendants** lack direct actions. Individuals may only initiate actions when directed to do so. Some people can lose sight of limits. Individuals may bite off more than they can chew. Risk taking can occur without common sense. One may feel he can get away with anything.

Natal or progressed **earth Ascendants** can work harder rather than smarter. One may lack a greater vision. Tomorrow's challenges catch individuals unprepared. People may lack the willpower to change identities as needed. Old habits remain limiting.

A natal or progressed **air Ascendant** can lack decision-making power. One may put off important decisions until disaster arrives. Some people become too ego-centered. Their opinions must reign.

A natal or progressed **water Ascendant** can get spaced out. A love of fantasy and pleasure can lead to laziness. An individual may hide emotional intensity. The past may enslave the present. Old compulsive habits may be enticing.

DAWN

Sun/Ascendant aspects can be a dramatic display of creative beauty. A person can show a new self-confidence. Creative actions help one to experience life to the fullest. Love can be shared openly. The willpower and self-image can blend together into radiant and spontaneous harmony.

MOON/ASCENDANT ASPECTS

Progressed Moon/Natal or Progressed Ascendant
Progressed Ascendant/Natal Moon

Process:	Securing Identity
Ally:	Self-Acceptance
Illusion:	Life is Out to Get Me

Moon/Ascendant aspects can point to new intuitive clarity. Individuals may tune into inner motivations for actions. Habits may be adjusted to better fit the present. One may break away from a limiting past. Childhood behavior patterns can be outgrown. One may adopt an intimate, caring way of being. The intense aspects can especially point to changing residency needs to fulfill one's self-expectations. A greater need for family experiences or feeling part of a community manifests.

INTENSE ASPECTS
Conjunction: Progressed Moon Conjunct
Natal or Progressed Ascendant
Progressed Ascendant Conjunct Natal Moon
Square: Progressed Moon Square Natal or Progressed Ascendant
Progressed Ascendant Square Natal Moon

The **progressed Moon conjunct the natal (or progressed) Ascendant or the progressed Ascendant conjunct the natal Moon** can denote emotional intensity surfacing. People may stop hiding their deepest feelings. Identity changes may reflect inner security. Comfort and security fuse with evolving personal style. One may make peace with dependency needs. Individuals can be more spontaneous. A shy person can overcome self-consciousness. Understanding needs allows one to make smoother life transitions. Change may be less unsettling. A person may be perceived as more emotional. Loving qualities can attract support from others. One may feel less dependent. One can be there for others in times of crisis. One may act more on intuition. A deep longing for love and closeness can be displayed. A family can be started.

The **progressed Moon square the natal (or progressed) Ascendant or the progressed Ascendant square the natal Moon** can indicate transcending emotional confusion. A person may act on intuitive insights to bring great changes into the life. One may make more room for love. Too much sensitivity may be modified. A hesitation to express true feelings can be overcome. Emotional risks may occur. A person may go beyond comfort zones to better express a growing identity. The past and present can become friends. Old, self-defeating habits can be brought into the light. Inner clarity yields emotional comfort. One may reflect before acting too impulsively. Finding one's emotional center is enlightening. **In both the conjunction and the square, people may change living situations**. These can be unsettling aspects. A restless urge for new surroundings may manifest.

SHADOW
Both the **Moon/Ascendant conjunction and square** can express as emotional fear. A lack of self-awareness keeps one ignorant of emotional needs. A constant inner restlessness is unsettling. People can be fugitives from self-honesty. Individuals can be too self-absorbed. They might dwell on problems. Emotional isolation and extreme privacy can occur. People may think their problems are worse than those of peers. One may fear intimacy. Perhaps life is in constant conflict. Consistent support of others may be lacking. Identity can be unstable. One may lack the confidence to display real needs.

Quincunx: Progressed Moon Quincunx
Natal or Progressed Ascendant
Progressed Ascendant Quincunx Natal Moon

Opposition: Progressed Moon Opposing
Natal or Progressed Ascendant
Progressed Ascendant Opposing Natal Moon

LIGHT

Progressed Moon quincunx natal (or progressed) Ascendant or progressed Ascendant quincunx natal Moon can be a time of finding a deeper sense of self. This is the **"Yoga of securing identity."** This aspect can point to a need to understand dependency needs. An individual can learn to care about others. A self-oriented individual can find more compassion. Individuals who fear intimacy may resolve emotional tensions. A lack of self-love can turn into self-acceptance. People may find more comfort with identity. One may no longer be a stranger to herself. Mood swings can be modified. Emotional intensity might be channeled into creative expression. One no longer depends too heavily on others for an identity. Relationships can be mutually supportive of growth. A tendency to hide feelings may be transcended.

Progressed Moon opposing the natal (or progressed) Ascendant or progressed Ascendant opposing natal Moon can denote a more secure identity within relationships. Individuals can become more intuitive. Spontaneous interactions can be shown. Extreme dependency on others may be overcome. One can find clarity through interacting with peers. Closeness and space might be nicely balanced. Individuals can offer nurturance without feeling threatened. A private person could find greater love in relating; a social person can learn the beauty of her own identity. karmic problems in relating to others may be corrected. A tendency to be too protective of loved ones becomes less compulsive. People let go and trust the flow of life. A relationship with intuitive forces can be meaningful. Problems with intimacy and lack of roots can be transcended. Marriage and a desire for family can become a reality.

SHADOW

Both the **Moon/Ascendant quincunx and opposition** can express as feeling separated from self. One may lose identity in relationships. Falling in love with the wrong people can occur. A need for more time alone might be ignored. Emotional disorientation leads one into poor decisions. Relationships, home, career, and identity may be in constant turmoil. A very insecure identity could be the source of many problems. One may not deal with the roots of emotional problems. Hopping from one relationship or lifestyle to another avoids answers to problems. Relationships can lack emotional depth. Partners can fail to communicate feelings. Individuals can lack intuitive clarity regarding relationships. People may mistrust the motives of others. Trust may remain superficial. Conflict can end relationships suddenly. Both partners could run from their shadowy pasts.

SOFT ASPECTS

Sextile: Progressed Moon Sextile Natal or Progressed Ascendant
Progressed Ascendant Sextile Natal Moon

Trine: Progressed Moon Trine Natal or Progressed Ascendant
Progressed Ascendant Trine Natal Moon

LIGHT

Progressed Moon sextile natal (or progressed) Ascendant or progressed Ascendant sextile natal Moon can denote a relaxed feeling concerning identity. Individuals can be nurtured by their environment. Feelings are easily communicated. People can make sudden adjustments to unexpected events. Individuals may understand the mood of situations. Mental and emotional balance is exhibited. Give-and-take come naturally. One may resolve inner conflict. The future is no longer threatening. One may be excited about changing behavior patterns. Peers can stimulate insights. Emotional intensity can become more objective.

Progressed Moon trine natal (or progressed) Ascendant or progressed Ascendant trine natal Moon can connote finding new inspiring symbols. Imagination can take one beyond immediate problems.

A person can find peace. Emotional stability can blossom. A passion for life can lead to compassion. A feeling of unity can inspire sharing of love. A person lacking hope may discover a new vision. A lost identity can be found again. Self-acceptance comes by working through inner conflict.

SHADOW

Both the **Moon/Ascendant sextile and trine** can denote a flighty emotional nature. One may be pulled to and fro by childish imaginings. An individual may try to copy the identity of others. A lack of self-understanding causes emotional confusion. Intuition may be a stranger. Insights into new situations are lacking. One may retreat to the comfort of a nonproductive past. A person may be too changeable. People may have a hard time getting a fix on the individual. One may hide discontent and fake the appearance of happiness. A person may not support those in need. One may take emotional or material support without reciprocating.

DAWN

Moon/Ascendant aspects can point to more intuition. One can move through life sharply aware of situations. Emotional support for others can be exhibited. One may be comfortable with closeness or space. A greater understanding of one's own emotional nature can occur. Satisfying residency needs and creating a harmonious living situation is important. Home and family needs are highlighted.

MERCURY/ASCENDANT ASPECTS

Progressed Mercury/Natal or Progressed Ascendant Progressed Ascendant/Natal Mercury

Process:	Perceiving a New Identity
Ally:	Communicating with a Clear Conception of Situations
Illusion:	Self-Doubt

Mercury/Ascendant aspects can reflect clarity concerning identity. One may bring deep perceptions to the present. Self-awareness can be sharp. Communication ability can lead to new growth. A person may spontaneously perceive options to situations. Multiple tasks can be performed. Individuals may need to beware of scattering. One could disperse energies in too many directions. One may never be quite sure of himself.

INTENSE ASPECTS
Conjunction: Progressed Mercury Conjunct
            Natal or Progressed Ascendant
            Progressed Ascendant Conjunct Natal Mercury

Square: Progressed Mercury Square
            Natal or Progressed Ascendant
            Progressed Ascendant Square Natal Mercury

LIGHT
Progressed Mercury conjunct the natal (or progressed) Ascendant or the progressed Ascendant conjunct natal Mercury can indicate a growing self-awareness. Contractual agreements might be signed. Important negotiations could be indicated. A new eagerness to absorb information can occur. Adaptability can be strong. One may be adept at communicating difficult concepts in a simple manner. Self-doubt may be cast aside. People may find positive affirmation regarding identity. Individuals can learn to trust their intelligence. Shy individuals can communicate more directly; nervous people can better direct mental intensity; complicated thinking may find simplicity; extremely emotional people may find objectivity. One may pay more attention to thought processes. Negative self-talk can be reprogrammed more positively. A person can transcend self-criticism. Acting on thoughts can bring confidence. Individuals may reflect before jumping into ac-

tion. A dynamic ability to communicate through writing or speech is possible. Business perceptions can be clear.

Progressed Mercury square the natal (or progressed) Ascendant or the progressed Ascendant square natal Mercury can symbolize resolving mental tension. A person may show more decisiveness. A deeper perception of situations can be exhibited. One may develop more mental coolness during conflict. A greater degree of concentration can be shown. A mental fortitude to solve problems can develop. A greater insight into situations can develop. Individuals may find new hunger for knowledge. Old identity conflicts can be resolved. Communication could help transcend self-doubts. Perceptions may be less bogged down by personal biases. One may break away from those who dominate ideas. Free thinking may help strengthen identity.

SHADOW

Both the **Mercury/Ascendant conjunction and square** can indicate one dwells on problems. "Mountains" may be made out of "molehills." Self-criticism or impatience with the ideas of others can occur. Reckless thoughts might lead to problems. Individuals can break appointments with no notice. Perceptions can reflect a confused identity. Decisions could be based on muddled reasoning. A person may change his mind constantly. One can settle for nongrowth-promoting situations. Individuals can hide behind intellect. Words may communicate ideas but hide feelings. People may have sarcastic tongues. The world may be perceived as a cold place. Intellectual distance keeps others away. People may stop learning and settle for old worn-out ideas which dull the mind. Fresh insights are lost in the ashes of an insecure past. The present is yet another instant replay of self-doubt.

Quincunx: Progressed Mercury Quincunx
                  Natal or Progressed Ascendant
                  Progressed Ascendant Quincunx Natal Mercury

Opposition: Progressed Mercury Opposing
                  Natal or Progressed Ascendant
                  Progressed Ascendant Opposing Natal Mercury

LIGHT

Progressed Mercury quincunx natal (or progressed) Ascendant or the progressed Ascendant quincunx natal Mercury can symbolize a sharper conception of identity. This aspect is the **"Yoga of gaining conscious awareness."** Individuals can put thoughts back in order. A scattered intellect can find direction. Solutions to problems bring relief. A worrier learns to flow. Focusing on the big picture keeps details in place. One who questions himself too much can find trust. Mind and identity can get in synch. One may sustain mental effort despite adversity, keeping a calm head during conflict.

Progressed Mercury opposing the natal (or progressed) Ascendant or progressed Ascendant opposing natal Mercury can point to new clarity in communicating to others. Relationships may blossom through stimulating communication. Individuals excel at selling their ideas. They may enjoy work centering around communication. A constant hunger for information drives a person to make new contacts. A person can meet people who stimulate a clearer self-image. Peers may support mental growth. One can find allies in people or in books. A clear sense of self may attract others.

A person may capture audiences through passionate and excitable speech. One can paint clear images with words.

SHADOW

Both the **Mercury/Ascendant quincunx and opposition** can point to getting over stimulated. A need to slow down may be ignored. Extreme cases can lead to nervous breakdown. Narrow opinions can lead to arguments. People may not be good listeners. Pushy opinions can cause separation from others. Ulterior motives pretend to be honest communication. A lack of depth produces few mental accomplishments. One may be good at reading copy but lack original insights. Depending too heavily on the perceptions of others can leave one in limiting situations. Careers may lack challenge.

SOFT ASPECTS

Sextile:	Progressed Mercury Sextile
	Natal or Progressed Ascendant
	Progressed Ascendant Sextile Natal Mercury
Trine:	Progressed Mercury Trine
	Natal or Progressed Ascendant
	Progressed Ascendant Trine Natal Mercury

LIGHT

Progressed Mercury sextile the natal (or progressed) Ascendant or the progressed Ascendant sextile natal Mercury can denote a new self-appreciation. Individuals may be pleased with new opportunities. Hardworking individuals can find this a flowing time period. One may have a lot of confidence in communication ability. A clear sense of self can attract new contacts. One may be a fast-paced person, yet well organized. This can be a good aspect for business. A gregarious nature can attract supportive people. A shy person may trust his ideas. A lost soul can find a new direction.

Progressed Mercury trine the natal (or progressed) Ascendant or the progressed Ascendant trine natal Mercury can point to ease when communicating. Perceptions may be supported by a clear self-image.

Both the Mercury/Ascendant sextile and trine can accentuate an interest in education. A desire to broaden and sharpen the intellect can occur. Mental enthusiasm can inspire growth in others. An ability to persuade and yet listen can be displayed.

SHADOW
In both the **Mercury/Ascendant sextile and trine** people can be too attached to their words. One can be too sensitive to criticism. A passive nature gets hurt easily. One may lose confidence easily during conflict. The identity can crumble during a crisis. Individuals may imitate the ideas of others, tending not to think for themselves. Concentration can be lacking. Individuals might be fickle and change their minds with the blowing of the wind. Some people may be too agreeable, afraid to differ in opinion.

DAWN
Mercury/Ascendant aspects can denote important new insights. Perceptions can strengthen identity. One's personal style can branch out into multiple expressions. The conscious mind can find assurance in a clear self-concept.

VENUS/ASCENDANT ASPECTS

Progressed Venus/Natal or Progressed Ascendant
Progressed Ascendant/Natal Venus

Process:	A Love of Self
Ally:	Genuine Relating
Illusion:	Self-Indulgence

Venus/Ascendant aspects can denote balancing self-expectations with those of others. Individuals may tap into changing relationship needs. Balance becomes an urgent desire. The person could become versed in social skills. One relates warmly to others. Emotional stability and confidence may emanate. One's work can match identity needs. Self-esteem bolsters self-image. Reality can be faced in relating or at work.

INTENSE ASPECTS
Conjunction: Progressed Venus Conjunct
Natal or Progressed Ascendant
Progressed Ascendant Conjunct Natal Venus

Square: Progressed Venus Square
Natal or Progressed Ascendant
Progressed Ascendant Square Natal Venus

LIGHT
Progressed Venus conjunct the natal (or progressed) Ascendant or progressed Ascendant conjunct natal Venus can denote a com-

fortable personality. One's physical appearance can reflect a happy spirit. A social nature that radiates warmth might win valuable associations. **Marriage can be symbolized by this aspect.** Key partnerships grow in importance. Positive strokes may lift one's identity. One may act courageously on values. Sensitivity to others could be curbed. A heavy heart can find peace; a hard personality can soften; self-worth can blossom; relationships can bring strength and sharing; the passive may defend values; the selfish may share their resources. The art of diplomacy can intensify.

Progressed Venus square the natal (or progressed) Ascendant or progressed Ascendant square natal Venus can reflect relationship urges. A vivacious intensity can pour into aesthetic pursuits. One's values may carry her through hard times. A desire for beauty and balance can bring one to take a career risk. A person may break away from limiting circumstances. A time to step out on one's own can be indicated. Individuals who have hidden in the shadows of others may break away. A lonely person may look for love; an argumentative type may look for peace; individuals can reward themselves; the self-indulgent finds moderation; shallow values are driven deeper by life challenges.

SHADOW
Both the **Venus/Ascendant conjunction and square** can manifest as extreme self-indulgence. People can get lost in outer appearance. Self-worth might be too attached to outer success. Values may be tied heavily to possessions. Individuals can lack self-esteem. A denial of money and possessions could reflect self-punishment. One can be hard on herself or others. A rigid value system may block the flow of relating. A person might be argumentative. Emotional balance can be lacking. A person may hide emotions behind outer appearance. The need for attention can reach extremes. One could react too personally to situations. A desire to be noticed might reach obnoxious proportions. One may move so fast through relationships that emotional depth is lacking. One may lack insight into emotional needs.

Quincunx: Progressed Venus Quincunx
              Natal or Progressed Ascendant
              Progressed Ascendant Quincunx Natal Venus

Opposition: Progressed Venus Opposing
               Natal or Progressed Ascendant
               Progressed Ascendant Opposing Natal Venus

LIGHT
Progressed Venus quincunx natal (or progressed) Ascendant or progressed Ascendant quincunx natal Venus can denote a sluggish personality coming to life. This aspect is the **"Yoga of embracing**

values." An individual may make significant relationship adjustments. One may enter more balanced relationships, transcending relationships that lessen self-worth. One may take more care of emotional stability. Relationship equality and mutuality support a new understanding. Identity and values may be brought into alignment. A tendency to compromise values to please others can be overcome. Being true to oneself can begin. A careless infatuation with others may get more sober. Individuals may enjoy more stable relationships. A pattern of stormy relationships can end. People might enjoy a more harmonious existence.

Progressed Venus opposing the Ascendant or the progressed Ascendant opposing natal Venus can point to loving relationships. **Marriage is a distinct possibility.** Long-term relationships and partnerships are highlighted. Business sense can be well developed. Understanding both sides of an issue can win respect and friendship. Individuals may enjoy making others feel appreciated. A natural self-confidence does not fight for attention. People may attract others who are emotionally and materially supportive. A significant union with one's own self-worth could occur. A person can enjoy meeting others with much in common. This can be a very romantic time period. Joy can stimulate much growth. A diplomatic nature with a true generosity can be displayed.

SHADOW

Both the **Venus/Ascendant quincunx and opposition** can express as difficulty in compromising. Agreements may seem next to impossible. Diplomacy is absent. One may be flirtatious but lack in-depth relating. A person may have trouble separating business and pleasure. Individuals can think of money and possessions to the exclusion of emotional warmth. People can manipulate others. One may pretend to be in love to take their resources.

A lack of self-worth can lead to disastrous relationships. One can be too attracted to the wrong types of people. A fear of rejection can keep one in stale relationships. Individuals may fall in love easily but lack the determination to work through problems. Lovers can be fickle or lack character. One may have problems circulating beyond work peers. The identity and daily life are fixated on the job. One may be too tight with resources, spending little on self or others. Attention needs can be compulsive. One's identity might be attached to being center stage. Self-admiration throws relationships out of balance.

SOFT ASPECTS
    Sextile: Progressed Venus Sextile
                        Natal or Progressed Ascendant
                        Progressed Ascendant Sextile Natal Venus

Trine: Progressed Venus Trine
                 Natal or Progressed Ascendant
                 Progressed Ascendant Trine Natal Venus

Progressed Venus sextile natal (or progressed) Ascendant or progressed Ascendant sextile natal Venus can denote understanding one's own emotional nature. A fast-paced person may slow down and take the time to share feelings; a hurt person can find new love; an egotistical person can recognize the needs of others.

People may understand different dimensions of themselves. They may find multiple creative expressions. Feelings may be communicated.

Progressed Venus trine the natal (or progressed) Ascendant or the progressed Ascendant trine natal Venus can point to feeling harmony with life. Natural enthusiasm can attract relationships. One may learn to appreciate the simple things in life. Tension-filled relationships may be replaced by more balance. Give-and-take surpasses either extreme.

One may be good at combining work and pleasure. An inner calmness makes it not so essential to prove self-worth. An inner appreciation calms a compulsive desire for attention.

SHADOW
In both the **Venus/Ascendant sextile and trine**, a person can be naive. A lack of experience can lead one to foolishly lose money and time. Emotional intensity can be lacking. One may lack the determination to leave nonproductive circumstances. Relating can be kept on the surface. Values may be unclear. A person feels pulled to and fro by the current circumstances. A dependence on others to fulfill identity can occur. Vanity may be exhibited. The inner nature stagnates. Material life is too important. Relationships lack substance. One's identity becomes too focused on style. A lack of discipline can occur. One can be too pleasure-oriented. The good life distracts one from ambitions. A person may undervalue love and those closest to him.

DAWN
Venus/Ascendant aspects can represent a season of happiness. Self-image may shine with the supportive ease of Venus. Relationships can be enjoyed. Mutual support may be evident. Peers can stimulate growth. Finding a soul mate can be exciting. Marriage and key partnerships are highlighted.

MARS/ASCENDANT ASPECTS

Progressed Mars/Natal or Progressed Ascendant
Progressed Ascendant/Natal Mars

Process:	Assertiveness Training
Ally:	Courage and Clear Direct Actions
Illusion:	Excess Self-Focus

Mars/Ascendant aspects can point to new courage. Individuals may answer challenges with clear decisions. They can move ahead in the midst of conflict. Self-hating behavior may be redirected into positive actions. Lack of initiative can be transcended. A me-focus might be moderated. Inner strength can surface through life challenges.

INTENSE ASPECTS
Conjunction: Progressed Mars Conjunct
　　　　　　　　Natal or Progressed Ascendant
　　　　　　　　Progressed Ascendant Conjunct Natal Mars

Square: 　　　Progressed Mars Square
　　　　　　　　Natal or Progressed Ascendant
　　　　　　　　Progressed Ascendant Square Natal Mars

LIGHT
Progressed Mars conjunct natal (or progressed) Ascendant or progressed Ascendant conjunct natal Mars can symbolize a more assertive nature. One may make choices that satisfy personal needs. A bold spirit may be displayed. A procrastinator may get more decisive. A passive individual can get into action. Anger can be expressed rather than denied. Self-hating people may forgive themselves. Energy can be constructively directed outward. Angry outbursts could be channeled into more positive actions. Individuals can show incredible stamina. Leading or supervising might occur. A very territorial individual may relax. One may overcome taking criticism too personally. Dominating or bullying tactics may be replaced by balanced assertion.

　　Progressed Mars square the natal (or progressed) Ascendant or progressed Ascendant square natal Mars can denote breaking through obstacles. A furious energy to overcome the odds may be shown. Individuals may never quit. Competitive spirit might be taken into business enterprises. One may be good at promoting talents. A sense of self could be well developed. This can be a good time to act on impulse. Individuals lacking initiative can find a new courage. Type "A" personalities can channel raw energy into constructive outlets. A need to prove oneself can yield great accomplishments.

A determination to stop a self-destructive behavior could surface. One may find the courage to kick dangerous habits. Reckless behavior can be held in check or channeled appropriately.

SHADOW

Both the **Mars/Ascendant conjunction and square** can express as self-hatred. One may be at war with himself. Love of self seems long gone. Sudden impulsive tendencies can be tragic. Individuals may lack insight into their behavior patterns. Aggression and violence can become a way of life. A "me-focus" could be extreme. Individuals can be very demanding of attention. Getting one's own way is too important. Anger can be too passive or carelessly used. Some individuals may fear being assertive. They allow themselves to be doormats. Others may try to force or coerce with angry threats. An overly competitive nature can take all of the fun out of life. Individuals can be in a hurry. They may leave good situations. A "hit and run" mentality leaves life in disarray. Selfishness can dominate this time period.

> **Quincunx:** Progressed Mars Quincunx
>   Natal or Progressed Ascendant
>   Progressed Ascendant Quincunx Natal Mars
>
> **Opposition:** Progressed Mars Opposing
>   Natal or Progressed Ascendant
>   Progressed Ascendant Opposing Natal Mars

LIGHT

Progressed Mars quincunx the natal (or progressed) Ascendant or the progressed Ascendant quincunx natal Mars can denote a new confidence in self. This aspect is the **"Yoga of acting on impulse."** Individuals can turn compulsive urges around. Personal will can gain strength. One no longer depends on others to fulfill identity needs. One can be himself. Individuals may slow down and truly experience actions. Follow-through can be strengthened. A person may bounce back from a disappointment. The determination to move ahead can be found. Hardened individuals could lighten up. Past emotional hurts can be resolved. A chip on the shoulder might be healed.

Progressed Mars opposing the natal Ascendant or the progressed Ascendant opposing natal Mars can denote more courage in relating to others. An individual may break away from destructive relationships. A person can stop leaning on others for fulfillment. People may learn to share their energy.

A "me-focus" person can learn to pay attention to others. A need to always get one's own way can be modified. Clearer communication of anger can result. One may make needs known more confidently. Individuals can stop losing themselves in partnerships. People may work through problems. Sharing concerns can help rectify situations. A more spontaneous assertion can stop anger from building. A need to control others can be surrendered. Invading the territory of others is no longer a drive. Individuals can overcome impatience. More sensitivity may endear others. A tendency to attract selfish individuals can be stopped. Fulfilling one's own assertive instincts replaces a projection of these needs upon others. Competition may bring out one's best talents!

SHADOW

Both the **Mars/Ascendant quincunx and opposition** can express as losing identity in relationships. Individuals can rush impulsively into destructive relationships. A lack of insight can lead to disaster.

Individuals may lack the patience and sensitivity to sustain a relationship. They may run from conflict. Some people create too much tension in relating. They can't accept a steady give-and-take. Selfishness can ruin relationships. One may only be concerned about his needs. Winning at all costs loses friends. People may carelessly express anger at the wrong time. Forcing issues and making war impulsively can cause difficulties.

People can be afraid to initiate relationships. A too-passive nature leaves them in limiting circumstances. Natural assertive ability is denied. One's identity can be too attached to a relationship. Individuals may not feel useful or fulfilled unless in a relationship.

SOFT ASPECTS

Sextile:	Progressed Mars Sextile
	Natal or Progressed Ascendant
	Progressed Ascendant Sextile Natal Mars
Trine:	Progressed Mars Trine
	Natal or Progressed Ascendant
	Progressed Ascendant Trine Natal Mars

LIGHT

Progressed Mars sextile the natal (or progressed) Ascendant or the progressed Ascendant sextile natal Mars can denote confidence in action. One may have a good sense of self. Individuals do not have to prove anything. Transitions can be made quickly. A person may enjoy challenges. Creative risks can be stimulating. Being assertive flows naturally. One may handle disputes with a calm intensity. An intense person might find this an especially enjoyable period. Hard work may find creative outlets. One could be stimulated by the attention given to talents.

Progressed Mars trine the natal (or progressed) Ascendant or the progressed Ascendant trine natal Mars can bring joy. One may win support through sheer enthusiasm and a tireless spirit. People may confidently tackle a difficult challenge. A competitive spirit with integrity may win admiration and respect. A tired soul can find a burst of energy; a burned out psyche discovers new vigor.

SHADOW

Both the **Mars/Ascendant sextile and trine** can denote fear of a new challenge. Individuals may lack a clear sense of self and act without reflecting. Individuals may not finish what they start. A desire for easy answers can cause missed opportunities. Procrastination can result from a lack of confidence. Individuals may need others to push them to action.

DAWN

Mars/Ascendant aspects can denote spontaneous assertion. Individuals can enjoy a clear sense of self. A passive person can find greater courage. A self-focused person can develop greater awareness of others. One might engage in bold new enterprises. One's competitive spirit can be on fire!

JUPITER/ASCENDANT ASPECTS

Transiting Jupiter/Natal Ascendant
Progressed Ascendant/Natal or Progressed Jupiter

Process:	Expansive Identity
Ally:	Eclectic Knowledge
Illusion:	My Way is the Way

Jupiter/Ascendant aspects can symbolize tremendous faith in oneself. A positive attitude can bring abundance. One can get lucky through an untiring enthusiasm. Issues often center around overconfidence. Trying to do too much can scatter energy. A person can try to be too many different people. Snap judgments based on insufficient evidence may occur.

INTENSE ASPECTS

Conjunction: Transiting Jupiter Conjunct Natal Ascendant
Progressed Ascendant Conjunct
Natal or Progressed Jupiter

Square: Transiting Jupiter Square Natal Ascendant
Progressed Ascendant Square
Natal or Progressed Jupiter

LIGHT

Transiting Jupiter conjunct the natal Ascendant or the progressed Ascendant conjunct natal (or progressed) Jupiter can express as a dynamic faith in self. One can go beyond self-doubts. Knowledge seeking has no end. A person can sometimes learn faster during this aspect. The individual is like a sponge wanting to learn a new way of being. Individuals can attract abundance. A drive to experience many different walks of life can enrich understanding. Eclectic knowledge helps integrate one's life philosophy.

President Bill Clinton was elected on November 10, 1992, when transiting Jupiter was conjunct his Libra Ascendant. His character and principles (each connected to Jupiter symbolism) were brought into question by the Republican party. Perhaps Mr. Clinton had the luck of Jupiter with him! His persona and personality (Ascendant) was filled with a promise (Jupiter) for a better America that captured the vision of the American people.

People make good counselors and teachers. Humor attracts listeners. One can combine enthusiasm with communications. Judgments can be wise and understanding. A person can help others find solutions to problems. A generous spirit can arouse faith in others. One's identity may expand. A narrow background might widen quickly. A greater life plan can be embraced. Travel on mental and physical planes could enrich the person. The art of persuasion is magnified. Legal ability and sales instincts are strong. Honesty and principles are heartfelt. A new career, relationship, or residence is exciting. Education can be valued.

Transiting Jupiter square a natal Ascendant or a progressed Ascendant square natal (or progressed) Jupiter can denote solving a lack of faith in self. A personal crisis may bring one to apply knowledge like never before. Individuals can find new faith in learning. By changing stagnating circumstances, one can strengthen his identity. One may leave behind a confining past.

Passive people may act on principles. A conscience can get individuals involved in social issues. Fighting injustice can be educational. Travel and educating oneself offer options to a troubled life. One may take bold steps to find new options. An already fulfilled person can gain an even greater future vision.

SHADOW

Both the **Jupiter/Ascendant conjunction and square** can manifest as a narrow sense of self. One may follow morals and principles that were handed down. A need to expand on life philosophy is resisted. Individuals may hastily judge others. There can be excessive self-criticism. Fixed or closed attitudes are contrary to Jupiter's natural eclectic spirit. A moralistic nature can alienate others. One may impose puritan virtues on others. Dogmatism can occur. Restlessness can lead to erratic actions. Individuals may lose direction. They can feel pulled into multiple experiences simultaneously.

Individuals can lack a positive attitude. A poverty consciousness attracts no abundance. People can lack the confidence to change negative circumstances. An exaggerated sense of self can be displayed. One may brag about abilities and promise too much. There might be no end to one's self advertising!

Quincunx: Progressed Ascendant Quincunx
Natal or Progressed Jupiter
Transiting Jupiter Quincunx Natal Ascendant

Opposition: Progressed Ascendant Opposing
Natal or Progressed Jupiter
Transiting Jupiter Opposing Natal Ascendant

Transiting Jupiter quincunx the natal Ascendant or the progressed Ascendant quincunx natal (or progressed) Jupiter can symbolize a major transition in gaining faith. This aspect is the **"Yoga of believing in self."**

Spiritual courage might be shown. Individuals can repair broken-down identities. A tendency to believe too much in others may be moderated.

People can seek help with compulsive risk taking. A life of gambling or destructive actions might be transcended.

Transiting Jupiter opposing the natal Ascendant or the progressed Ascendant opposing natal (or progressed) Jupiter can denote sharing spiritual values. Relationships could reward both parties. Mutual support and admiration of each other's qualities may be shown. Individuals can enjoy meeting new peers from various backgrounds. The ways of other cultures or groups can be learned.

A person may be enthusiastic but not dogmatic. She respects the beliefs of others. One may attract positive support for cherished ideals and objectives.

Individuals may stop expecting too much from others. A person can live her own beliefs.

Individuals may show faith when relationships are in crisis. One may care for a partner or peer in need. A generous spirit inspires faith in others. An acceleration of the social life often occurs. Selling ideas comes naturally.

SHADOW

In both the **Jupiter/Ascendant quincunx and opposition,** a person can expect too much support from others. Idealism might be crushed. Reality testing seems absent. A naive nature is easily manipulated. People can get demanding. Individuals may leave relationships hastily. Poor timing can be shown. Self-centeredness could get extreme. People can stay in limiting circumstances. An "everything will get better" philosophy delays needed change. One may get critical of different life-styles. Dogmatic attitudes might be forced on others. A narrow philosophy may cause one to miss new experiences. A fear of transitions can be confining. A lack of faith in self leads to procrastination.

SOFT ASPECTS

Sextile: Transiting Jupiter Sextile Natal Ascendant
Progressed Ascendant Sextile
Natal or Progressed Jupiter

Trine: Transiting Jupiter Trine Natal Ascendant
Progressed Ascendant Trine
Natal or Progressed Jupiter

LIGHT

Transiting Jupiter sextile natal Ascendant or the progressed Ascendant sextile natal (or progressed) Jupiter can connote strong inner faith. One's personality may be warm and friendly. A personal vision with broad perspective lights the way. One can enthusiastically meet new challenges. A versatile nature makes adjustments easily. Travel and education appeal. People hunger for growth and knowledge. Individuals can communicate in an articulate manner, easily making themselves understood.

Transiting Jupiter trine the natal Ascendant or the progressed Ascendant trine natal (or progressed) Jupiter can bring upliftment. A faith in self and in a higher power can occur. A tired spirit can awaken. A more abundant philosophy can develop. Negative tapes are cast aside. A love of truth stimulates growth. An individual influences the moral character of others. A positive vision paves the way for opportunity. Good luck becomes a constant guardian. Faith is a great ally. Spiritual values carry one through a crisis.

SHADOW

Both the **Jupiter/Ascendant sextile and trine** can express as a lack of tolerance. One can get too attached to wonderful opinions. Life can become ego-centered. A "holier than though" attitude alienates others. People can stop growing. Success may be expected too easily. Lack of faith leads to quitting early. A soft approach to life causes retreat from the truth about oneself. A lazy attitude can block new knowledge. One may talk about plans yet do nothing.

DAWN

Jupiter/Ascendant aspects can bring a fruitful season. People may possess a good attitude regarding life's ups and downs. A strong faith in self can bring growth. A natural optimism could yield good luck. Relationships can be based on a shared life philosophy. Individuals may be great counselors and teachers. Difficult concepts are explained in simple, understandable terms. One's broad vision invites new expansive opportunity. Eclectic adventures bring options and solutions to challenges. Going to school and greater learning can accompany these aspects.

SATURN/ASCENDANT ASPECTS

Transiting Saturn/Natal Ascendant
Progressed Ascendant/Natal or Progressed Saturn

Process:	Redefining Identity
Ally:	Realizing Ambition
Illusion:	Fear of Imagination

Saturn/Ascendant aspects solidify one's identity. An identity crisis is possible as Saturn can indicate a reality-testing shock to our system! We feel Father Time gaining on us. Our aging becomes important. Life can suddenly seem finite. We need to get moving to fulfill ambition. The cosmic chiropractor, Saturn, connotes control and focus. **Career and assuming more responsibility are key themes.**

INTENSE ASPECTS
Conjunction: Transiting Saturn Conjunct Natal Ascendant
Progressed Ascendant Conjunct
Natal or Progressed Saturn

LIGHT
Transiting Saturn conjunct the natal Ascendant or the progressed Ascendant conjunct natal (or progressed) Saturn points to strengthening the identity. There is a serious tone to this cycle. One may gain focus and discipline. One can find new ambition and determination. A dynamic new beginning is symbolized. **Career changes and promotions can occur. Dealing with career and other major life challenges are common experiences.**

FIRE
Transiting Saturn conjunct a natal fire Ascendant or a progressed fire Ascendant conjunct natal (or progressed) Saturn can denote harnessing raw energy. Fiery action is disciplined by Saturn. A person could become adept at planning. A careless regard for the outcome of actions can be transformed into taking responsibility. One may take pride in accomplishments. Success builds more success. Fire learns through action. A person could build self-confidence. A new life focus could begin. Inner and outer structures are given new blueprints.

EARTH
Transiting Saturn conjunct a natal earth Ascendant or a progressed earth Ascendant conjunct natal (or progressed) Saturn can denote learning to time life transitions. Earthy Saturn can bring even more determination to the earth element. One may display tremendous strength in crises. One could launch into a stimulating career opportunity. Responsibility and time itself may pressure one to make

decisions. An individual may find new decisiveness. A person may flow creatively. Individuals can realistically assess life. One could achieve a feeling of purpose. Self-doubt could become self-confidence.

AIR

Transiting Saturn conjunct a natal air Ascendant or a progressed air Ascendant conjunct natal (or progressed) Saturn can symbolize focused mental energies. The tension in making decisions might be transcended. One may consolidate diverse talents or energies. A mental toughness may develop. People could impress others with communicative ability. A person may creatively use authority. A fickle individual could become reliable. A changeable person may tap into follow-through. Too much thought may find a concrete form. Hidden ideas may be made known.

WATER

Transiting Saturn conjunct a natal water Ascendant or a progressed water Ascendant conjunct natal (or progressed) Saturn might symbolize getting grounded. Subjective ideas could find a purpose in the objective world. A person can accept responsibility. Denial of problems could be conquered. Individuals can take a first small step in a growth-promoting direction. This could be a quantum leap in conquering escapism. The ghosts of the past may be faced. Childhood problems can be resolved. Guilt and too much self-sacrifice might be transcended.

SHADOW

FIRE

Transiting Saturn conjunct a natal fire Ascendant or a progressed fire Ascendant conjunct natal (or progressed) Saturn can denote a flooded engine. Starting and braking can be frustrating. A person may suddenly burst into anger. One can develop self-righteousness. Rigid dogma and attitudes can be pushed on others. A person can stop growing. He could stubbornly refuse to accept new societal trends. Lack of flexibility can hurt relationships, career, etc. Winning can become all consuming. Competition can become too serious. One may stop having time for pleasure.

EARTH

Transiting Saturn conjunct a natal earth Ascendant or a progressed earth Ascendant conjunct natal (or progressed) Saturn can symbolize extreme status seeking. An individual might ignore subjective life dimensions. A resistance to imagination may manifest. Love may seem a waste of energy. Workaholism can become dominant. People may create rigid emotional defenses. A person's life can become dry. One may be bored silly, resisting new symbols. Following the same routines and thought patterns dulls the senses.

AIR
Transiting Saturn conjunct a natal air Ascendant or a progressed air Ascendant conjunct natal (or progressed) Saturn can symbolize rigid concepts. One can fear sharing ideas. Communication is perceived as a threat. Negativity can be a problem with Saturn conjunct any Ascendant. It can be particularly a problem with the air element. One may resist changing negative tapes. A person can become too sensitive to criticism. Fear of rejection might keep a person from communicating.

WATER
Transiting Saturn conjunct a natal water Ascendant or a progressed water Ascendant conjunct natal (or progressed) Saturn can denote a failure to have ideals. Life might be filled with emotional pain. One may fear risking another ideal being destroyed. Instead of releasing the past, a person may embrace it even more strongly. Repeating karmic behaviors related to escapism can occur. One's outer and inner life can be in conflict. Poor reality-testing can lead to disastrous situations. A person may be too self-conscious. Shyness may keep this person very private. An overly cautious nature can miss opportunities.

   Square: Transiting Saturn Square Natal Ascendant
                  Progressed Ascendant Square
                  Natal or Progressed Saturn

LIGHT
Transiting Saturn square the natal Ascendant or the progressed Ascendant square natal (or progressed) Saturn may indicate dealing with authority figures. One can achieve more control over life. New levels of success can be energizing and confirming. Family and career concerns are in focus.

FIRE
Transiting Saturn square a natal fire Ascendant or a progressed fire Ascendant square natal (or progressed) Saturn can symbolize redefining identity. This can be an important step into new enterprises. One may use knowledge gained from past mistakes. A person with excessive pride may become more reasonable. People who promise too much may learn constraint. A workaholic could find moderation. An individual can transcend a lack of self-confidence. One may make choices that bring success. The wise use of power attracts abundance and creativity.

EARTH
Transiting Saturn square a natal earth Ascendant or a progressed earth Ascendant square natal (or progressed) Saturn

can denote managerial talent. Skill with organization and time management can be displayed.

This is a Mr. or Mrs. Reliable aspect: somebody prepared to do whatever is required to get the job done. Commitment is personified! A person may find common sense. This can be a centering aspect. One could feel good about one's personal history.

AIR

Transiting Saturn square a natal air Ascendant or a progressed air Ascendant square natal (or progressed) Saturn can symbolize a detached mental coolness. A person may display solid reasoning powers. Creative logic can solve problems. A nervous individual may solve stress problems. Self-criticism may be overcome. Negative thought patterns could be surrendered. A person may communicate his deepest fears and free blocked energy. An individual may enjoy space. Being alone does not cause fear. People may educate themselves to organize their thoughts.

WATER

Transiting Saturn square a natal water Ascendant or a progressed water Ascendant square natal (or progressed) Saturn can denote conquering past fears. Disorienting emotional problems may be brought to the surface. Control of one's life can reach new heights. An extremely subjective person may stop procrastinating. Talents are made known. A type "A" individual could learn more reflection. Ideals may not seem so silly and impractical. An individual could realize life needs emotional content. An individual could devote more time to humanitarian causes. One can give more nurturing energy to others. This might be a parent spending more time with family.

SHADOW

FIRE

Transiting Saturn square a natal fire Ascendant or a progressed fire Ascendant square natal (or progressed) Saturn can express as procrastination. A fear of failure may frustrate one. A person may hold back the creative self. A failure to learn from past mistakes is possible. One can ignore physical laws and get into trouble with authority figures or law officials. A lack of fiery humor can be evident; life is taken too seriously. One may harshly expect others to follow his rules. A dictatorial demeanor can occur. A bossy attitude may be exhibited.

EARTH

Transiting Saturn square a natal earth Ascendant or a progressed earth Ascendant square natal (or progressed) Saturn can denote inertia. An individual can express little enthusiasm. A person could stay in nonproductive situations. One could deny himself rewards. Individuals may not feel worthy of receiving. A person may be overly dedicated to work. A private life may not exist. People can express little spontaneity. A person could be too mundane. The mysteries of life are not important. Some individuals get greedy. Material accumulation becomes their god.

AIR

Transiting Saturn square a natal air Ascendant or a progressed air Ascendant square natal (or progressed) Saturn can symbolize rigid thinking. One may resist seeing the truth. Outdated concepts are retained. One can resist new ideas that stimulate growth. A fixation on the present gives no direction to life. Understanding complete processes can be lacking. Subjective reasoning is limited. Too much belief in the tangible can block higher consciousness. Conflict may be extremely stressful. A person may play it safe rather than risk confrontation. One could be an authoritarian, afraid to lose power, or a subservient type only wanting to follow ideas of others.

WATER

Transiting Saturn square a natal water Ascendant or a progressed water Ascendant square natal (or progressed) Saturn can manifest as a loss of ideals. An individual can feel defeated by life. Reality is too harsh. Individuals can deny their shortcomings. One can hide behind an outward show of success. A person may be too private about feelings. Transitions may be difficult. Individuals may have trouble with life passages. One can feel like a failure due to high standards. A person can be too self-critical.

Quincunx: Transiting Saturn Quincunx Natal Ascendant
Progressed Ascendant Quincunx
Natal or Progressed Saturn

The quincunxes formed by transiting Saturn to the natal Ascendant or progressed Ascendant to natal Saturn are the **"Yoga of restructuring identity."** A person can question the rigidity of his self-image.

LIGHT

FIRE

Transiting Saturn quincunx a natal fire Ascendant or a progressed fire Ascendant quincunx natal (or progressed) Saturn can indicate more process orientation. Enjoying and experiencing each step of the journey becomes important. One stops wasting time and energy. A person who is too much into the pleasure principle may become more focused. Saturn can concentrate fire's passion for action. The cosmic chiropractor can show one adjusting ambitions to more reasonable expectations. A new pride in assertion can begin. Negativity may be left behind. Taking oneself too seriously may be transcended.

EARTH
Transiting Saturn quincunx a natal earth Ascendant or a progressed earth Ascendant quincunx natal (or progressed) Saturn can express as ultimate efficiency. One may find a greater self-determination. Individuals can be at the top of their game as organizers. Large complex tasks may bring self-confidence. One may win recognition. A person may build lasting memories. One can build structures for a more creative life. Career transitions can be fulfilling. More responsibility brings accomplishment.

AIR
Transiting Saturn quincunx a natal air Ascendant or a progressed air Ascendant quincunx natal (or progressed) Saturn can denote new perception. A person may not be as affected by the environment. Ideas based on practical experience impress others. Wisdom aids in timing transitions. A serious search for a new direction can occur. An intense hunger for new mental stimulation may crystallize. Courage in expressing ideas is possible. An individual may stop projecting intelligence upon others.

WATER
Transiting Saturn quincunx a natal water Ascendant or a progressed water Ascendant quincunx natal (or progressed) Saturn can symbolize facing self-destructive habits. A person can make a quantum leap through karmic residues. Success in dealing with problems of a painful past stimulates even more effort. The dreamer may become realistic; the dependent type becomes more self-reliant; the perfectionist accepts life at face value. Aesthetic creativity could take form in the real world. Fear of rejection is transcended. The invisible ones want to be visible.

SHADOW

FIRE
Transiting Saturn quincunx a natal fire Ascendant or a progressed fire Ascendant quincunx natal (or progressed) Saturn can denote poor physical health. An individual could defy needs for rest. The "workaholic" might manifest. Gambling and reckless behavior can occur. People may feel as though their life philosophy is the best. A pushy and dominating demeanor can develop. One might desire to be the authoritarian, putting down others. Concentration can be greatly lacking. A haphazard existence can yield poor timing. Opportunities may be missed due to excess pride.

EARTH
Transiting Saturn quincunx a natal earth Ascendant or a progressed earth Ascendant quincunx natal (or progressed) Saturn can indicate extreme resistance to change. One may choose to

stay in harmful situations. Growth can become a stale concept. One may choose poverty over risk taking. The self could be lost in the material world. Too much attachment to status can be self-defeating. The outer person could become a primary goal. Health and family might be sacrificed for career success. A false security (in the world of form) can be destructive.

AIR
Transiting Saturn quincunx a natal air Ascendant or a progressed air Ascendant quincunx natal (or progressed) Saturn can denote negative perceptions. A lack of flexibility can be limiting. A narrow life philosophy blocks different points of view. Eclectic thinking can be an enemy. One may get too attached to mental skies. The water world of emotions seems too vulnerable. Life is kept at a safe nonemotional distance. Intuition is a foreign correspondent.

WATER
Transiting Saturn quincunx a natal water Ascendant or a progressed water Ascendant quincunx natal (or progressed) Saturn can express as confusion. People can drown in repressed waters. A fear of intuition and emotional intensity is possible. A person feels out of synch with reality. Growing up seems a bad memory. Aging follows emotional exhaustion. One longs for a mate, yet is surrounded by isolation. One searches for true friendship, yet attracts unreliable souls. One thirsts for a true career, but lacks ambition. One hurts emotionally, but stays silent.

Opposition: Transiting Saturn Opposing Natal Ascendant
Progressed Ascendant Opposing
Natal or Progressed Saturn

LIGHT
Transiting Saturn opposing the natal Ascendant or the progressed Ascendant opposing natal (or progressed) Saturn points to redefining relationships. An individual may take commitments more seriously. New conditions can seem imposed in existing relationships. Time itself could beckon for decisions in relating. A person may deal with relationship fears. Dependency needs can be an issue. Marriage can become a reality. Business sense can multiply. The ending of a partnership is possible. This is a key aspect.

FIRE
Transiting Saturn opposing a natal fire Ascendant or a progressed fire Ascendant opposing natal (or progressed) Saturn connotes taking more control in establishing relationships. One may exercise more caution before rushing into new encounters. An already reserved person may receive assistance from peers or counselors. An individual may be inspired by the wisdom of others. One may initiate

new business enterprises. Taking a small step can be important. A person could grow more comfortable with his own identity. A negative self-image could be transcended. A tendency to doubt oneself could be overcome. Self-centered fire may become more aware of others.

EARTH

Transiting Saturn opposing a natal earth Ascendant or a progressed earth Ascendant opposing natal (or progressed) Saturn can indicate becoming less authoritarian. Exerting less control can be freeing. Learning to feel can be important. A self-reliant soul may find that depending on others balances relationships. Relationships may be better defined. An individual may accept the views of others. One may confront his own lack of flexibility. Learning to make joint decisions as well as individual choices could aid partnerships of all types.

AIR

Transiting Saturn opposing a natal air Ascendant or a progressed air Ascendant opposing natal (or progressed) Saturn can express as more concrete communication. A person may define goals more clearly. The mind is changed less often. Communication problems are worked through. A person may take responsibility for decisions. An individual may adopt a less forceful nature. A more centered and steady communicator can be born. Relating may go to a deeper level. A new understanding of commitment can manifest. One may be reliable and strong during a crisis. This individual may excel at counseling. One might help others organize their lives.

WATER

Transiting Saturn opposing a natal water Ascendant or a progressed water Ascendant opposing natal (or progressed) Saturn can denote balancing dependency needs. An overly dependent individual may develop more inner strength. A person fearing his own space may learn to appreciate time alone. A person lost in fantasy may experience a dose of reality. An individual may find a deeper love of nature. A fear of commitment can be transcended. New intimacy can be attained. A person may initiate the contacts to make dreams real. One may bring his light out from under the bushel. A private person can overcome fears of public. An individual may deal with the past (of this or other lifetimes). A fear of the unknown can be conquered. A running away philosophy may turn into a coming home. Deeper self-understanding is possible.

SHADOW

FIRE

Transiting Saturn opposing a natal fire Ascendant or a progressed fire Ascendant opposing natal (or progressed) Saturn can express as procrastination. A person may wait for others to initiate actions (contrary to natural fire nature). One can be too controlling. A lack of flexibility (unwilling to consider different opinions) can be a problem. Biased opinions inhibit cooperation. A person may project too much intelligence (airy 7th house) onto others. Others are perceived as wiser and more experienced. People can let partners or authority figures make their important decisions.

EARTH
Transiting Saturn opposing an earth Ascendant or a progressed earth Ascendant opposing natal (or progressed) Saturn can connote little faith in intuition. Life can be shallow. One does not understand the motives of others. A person may care for status and material things exclusively. An individual trusts nobody. Emotional insecurity leads to controlling others. People can project emotions onto others (watery 7th house). They expect others to do the emotional expressing for both. Others are felt to be more sensitive. This person can be afraid to feel. Past emotional traumas left scars. The self-reliant may resist help in working through emotional problems. A person can become a workaholic to hide emotional needs. A subjective or private life is fast asleep while one hustles through a hectic lifestyle

AIR
Transiting Saturn opposing an air Ascendant or a progressed air Ascendant opposing natal (or progressed) Saturn can express as being stuck in the past. A person could have difficulty moving forward. A career or relationship setback may still have one disoriented. An individual could be in the midst of a relationship crisis. An aloof person may face the reality of a situation. Perhaps rationalizations have run out of time.

One may redefine life goals. Saturn symbolism can indicate choosing from options. One can suffer a nervous breakdown due to trying to do too much. Individuals can project their need to create an identity (fiery 7th house) onto others. Partners or authority figures may be relied upon to make choices. One may depend too much on others for inspiration and stimulation.

WATER
Transiting Saturn opposing a natal water Ascendant or a progressed water Ascendant opposing natal (or progressed) Saturn can denote a fear of knowing oneself. An individual may be a stranger to himself. One can be lost in fantasies. An inability to organize oneself can be frustrating. The objective or "real" world may cause one to freeze-up. Not taking a first step can lead to procrastination. A loss of faith in oneself can lead to disastrous relationships. People may project creative abilities onto others. They may depend too much on others for being organized and successful (earth 7th house). One may

be afraid to face the past. The scars of authority figures or dominating parents still leave painful memories. Dreams may be thwarted by fear of failure. Faith in intuition or in a higher power collides with a life full of unresolved issues.

SOFT ASPECTS

Sextile: Transiting Saturn Sextile Natal Ascendant
Progressed Ascendant Sextile
Natal or Progressed Saturn

Trine: Transiting Saturn Trine Natal Ascendant
Progressed Ascendant Trine
Natal or Progressed Saturn

The soft Saturn/Ascendant aspects do not have the same urgency to fulfill identity needs. There is often still a serious focus. However, one usually feels more in control of time and environmental pressures.

LIGHT

FIRE

Transiting Saturn sextile a fire Ascendant or a progressed fire Ascendant sextile natal (or progressed) Saturn can express as pride in accomplishments. One may combine wisdom with actions. A person may enjoy the aging process. One could find more time to pursue interests. Difficult tasks can be accomplished with new vigor. Natural enthusiasm may carry one through a difficult period.

Individuals may inspire others through determination and effort. People might take pride in developing expertise. A person could learn how to control personal intensity.

Transiting Saturn trine a natal fire Ascendant or a progressed fire Ascendant trine natal (or progressed) Saturn can denote harmony with the aging process. An individual may feel at peace with a long history of success. Pride in lasting values can occur. One may appreciate tradition, yet respect the fiery enthusiasm of youth. An individual may express cultural stability. People count on this person in times of trouble. A person may be a good teacher. A fiery vivacious spirit inspires others to serious action. One may be respected for directness.

EARTH

Transiting Saturn sextile a natal earth Ascendant or a progressed earth Ascendant sextile natal (or progressed) Saturn can connote excitement in learning new skills. This aspect could indicate a special management ability. Organization and time management can excel. A person may attract more responsibility and respond to the challenge. This can denote working hard to succeed and receiving recognition. The environment may stimulate one to greeter ambition. An individual may have great clarity in timing transitions.

Transiting Saturn trine a natal earth Ascendant or a progressed earth Ascendant trine natal (or progressed) Saturn can denote ease in accomplishing complex tasks. A person may enjoy support for serious ambitions. Confidence in skills is likely. One may be an authority figure who puts others at ease. One might possess a talent for dealing with authority figures and creating win-win situations.

AIR

Transiting Saturn sextile a natal air Ascendant or a progressed air Ascendant sextile natal (or progressed) Saturn can express as mental excitement about new ambitions. One may use past experience to create a more stimulating present. People may find more career opportunities. An individual may integrate different skills into a marketable package. One may excel at consulting and problem solving. An unstable person may find stability. Commitment to situations could begin. Ideas can be made real. A rigid individual may seek new ideas and options.

Transiting Saturn trine a natal air Ascendant or a progressed air Ascendant trine natal (or progressed) Saturn can denote easy decision making. An individual may possess a calm within the storm. One can be an advisory type. Peers can be impressed with an individual's problem-solving. A person could mediate disputes. People expertly present ideas. They may mix new and old trends.

WATER

Transiting Saturn sextile a natal water Ascendant or a progressed water Ascendant sextile natal (or progressed) Saturn can symbolize a confirming time period. Individuals integrate subjective ideals with objective reality. A person may get free of an exhausting past. Emotional agony no longer drains energy. A person can feel centered and recharged. Emotional growth can be exciting. An individual can find faith in ambition. A less complicated life may be structured.

Transiting Saturn trine a natal water Ascendant or a progressed water Ascendant trine natal (or progressed) Saturn can express as focused intuition. One may really flow with intuition and reality. This can be a compassionate aspect. A person may excel at listening and counseling. An individual may draw energy from childhood memories. One may let go of the past. Making peace with authority figures is possible.

SHADOW

FIRE

The Saturn/fire Ascendant sextile or trine can express as a lot of starting and stopping. One's timing may be poor. An individual could be nervous around authority figures. A person could be too needy of approval.

Individuals may get too attached to results. Steps within the process are ignored or forgotten. A need to be in control can irritate others. A lack of trust in others keeps one from delegating responsibility. One may overwork, loving the feeling of maxing out one's body. People can throw their weight around. An excessive need to be a visible authority figure can be problematic. Not understanding limits wastes energy and resources. Too much identification with career can destroy private life. One may promote one's self forcefully. One may not support others. Individuals may be unreliable.

EARTH

The Saturn/earth Ascendant sextile or trine can denote being too compulsive concerning material needs. Needless worry is possible. A person may push too hard. An individual's mind could bog down with endless details. People can be too serious. A drive for order can be stressful. A fear of letting go is frustrating. People may believe too much in the tangible. They have trouble with intuition. Individuals can be too grounded. An individual could grow lazy, expecting to be successful with no effort. People could become too indulgent. They may lack ambition and discipline.

AIR

The Saturn/air Ascendant sextile or trine can denote a lack of flexibility in thinking. A person may resist input from others. Individuals can display a cold and callous personality. Negative thinking can occur. One can be too controlling. An individual may not give support readily to others. One may use communication for power. Intellect may be sabotaged with authoritarian tendencies. A person may be a loner with difficulty trusting.

Organization may be lacking. Timing may be dull. An individual may not perceive situations realistically. Limited thinking can occur. Cultural biases and stereotypes may be present. Scapegoating can be exhibited. A focus on external things may hide an insecure inner self. A compulsive need for status may dominate. An individual may surround himself with "Yes" people.

WATER

The Saturn/water Ascendant sextile or trine can express as a lack of trust in intuition. A person may constantly second guess his feelings. A very subjective type may become nervous when dealing with reality. Decisions may be stressful. Conflict seems almost unbearable. Self-destructive hatred can occur. An individual can become depressed. Self-pity appears everywhere. Transitions cast long, fearful shadows. One may say yes when wanting to say no. Individuals may let others take too much responsibility.

Individuals might retreat into emotional seclusion. Privacy may reach extremes. One could live in a fantasy world. Worship of authority figures is possible. People may lose time and resources by following the wrong examples. Relationships may be out of balance. Dependency needs attract strange people. An already authoritarian person could look for others to dominate.

DAWN

Saturn/Ascendant aspects can accept life's ups and downs. The conjunction and opposition point to major life chapters unfolding. The time-conscious symbolism of Saturn may bring out the best in people. A dreamer can be grounded by new focus and commitment. A realist could find a creative self.

Natal and progressed fire Ascendants can be focused by patient Saturn; natal and progressed earth Ascendants can be given new ambitions by practical Saturn; natal and progressed air Ascendants can be driven to deeper perceptions by serious Saturn; natal and progressed water Ascendants can be enticed into reality by pragmatic Saturn.

URANUS/ASCENDANT ASPECTS

Transiting Uranus/Natal Ascendant
Progressed Ascendant/Natal or Progressed Uranus

Process:	New Identity
Ally:	Independent Way of Being
Illusion:	Loss of Direction

Uranus/Ascendant aspects can symbolize experimenting with a new personal style. People can go through sudden changes in behavior or appearance. Uranus may denote speeding-up. Individuals can be eager to enter new experiences. An already fast-paced individual might become very reckless and impulsive. A conservative or reserved individual might take more risks. This is often an exciting time filled with innovation, surprise, suspense, and a new vision for the future! Meeting new peers and even lovers often occurs.

INTENSE ASPECTS
Conjunction: Transiting Uranus Conjunct Natal Ascendant
Progressed Ascendant Conjunct
Natal or Progressed Uranus

LIGHT
Transiting Uranus conjunct the Ascendant or the progressed Ascendant conjunct natal (or progressed) Uranus can symbolize being stimulated to new heights. New individuality can occur. **A major**

new life direction is indicated. New careers and relationships often begin. Moving to new locations offers opportunity.

FIRE

Transiting Uranus conjunct a natal fire Ascendant or a progressed fire Ascendant conjunct natal (or progressed) Uranus can connote new mental visions. The fire sign passion for immediate action may be tempered with more detachment. A new pride in self could manifest. New assertion instincts could develop. A person may become more self-reliant. A me-focused individual could become more supportive of others. An individual feeling limited by life circumstances may become happy with a new spontaneity. One may boldly move ahead! A shortsighted "live for today" attitude may be raised to a greater vision.

EARTH

Transiting Uranus conjunct a natal earth Ascendant or a progressed earth Ascendant conjunct natal (or progressed) Uranus can symbolize more excitement about life. An individual may find new dimensions of surprise with self. Breaking away from an excessively safe lifestyle could promote growth. One may more quickly seize opportunities. Self-destructive, negating habits can be transcended. One can rise above rigid rules imposed upon oneself. New answers may appear to very old problems. A life with too much discipline and rigidity could become more flexible. Exploring a different lifestyle could bring growth.

AIR

Transiting Uranus conjunct a natal air Ascendant or a progressed air Ascendant conjunct natal (or progressed) Uranus can denote developing truer perceptions of life. A person may begin following her own goals. Opinions are forcefully expressed rather than letting others lead. One can jump off the mental fence and put ideas into action. Priorities are set more easily.

A self-oriented individual may tap into more collective needs of society. A narrow life perspective can broaden immensely. One may display new dimensions of personality and intellect previously dormant. A person may bring stimulation and new ideas to others. Free thinking can encourage self-growth.

WATER

Transiting Uranus conjunct a natal water Ascendant or a progressed water Ascendant conjunct natal Uranus can indicate more objectivity. Clearer mental perception may develop. One's intense emotional nature may become calmer. A "lightening up" in attitude can occur. Perfectionism could be modified. Expectations (of self and others) become more reasonable.

SHADOW

FIRE

Transiting Uranus conjunct a natal fire Ascendant or a progressed fire Ascendant conjunct natal (or progressed) Uranus can denote an erratic and unreliable nature. One may speak without thinking. A rebelliousness against any restrictions may alienate others. One may blast off into too many directions at once! Nervous exhaustion could bring a sudden halt. Ignoring any routine or practical considerations could waste a lot of time. A habit of starting over could be frustrating when some reflection might have prevented making the same mistakes. A "grass is greener" mentality may yield unpredictable behaviors.

Nihilism can become obnoxious. An intense self-centeredness can be distasteful to others. One might demand too much support. A person may lack the confidence to be an individual. A person can refuse to acknowledge her unique qualities.

EARTH

Transiting Uranus conjunct a natal earth Ascendant or a progressed earth Ascendant conjunct natal (or progressed) Uranus can denote hiding individuality in a show of materialism. This person could be afraid to receive help from others. She wishes to not owe anything in return. A person lacking assertion could hide behind a life with no new challenges or rewards. An individual may resist the forward movement suggested by peers.

AIR

Transiting Uranus conjunct a natal air Ascendant or a progressed air Ascendant conjunct natal (or progressed) Uranus can symbolize a mentally fried person. She may be too bombarded by environmental stimuli. An inability to relax depletes energy. Indecisiveness (due to a resistance to being tied down) could frustrate self and others. A tendency to run away from the present (into the past or future) can occur.

Sitting on the fence (as a spectator) may cause missed opportunities. An aloof mental nature can make accurate perception by others difficult. Intellect may block a feeling nature. A stubborn resistance to new ideas, goals, and cultural changes can hold one back.

WATER

Transiting Uranus conjunct a natal water Ascendant or a progressed water Ascendant conjunct natal (or progressed) Uranus can denote an emotional roller coaster ride. A person lacking intuitive insight may jump to hasty perceptions of self and others. A lack of reasoning power could cause missed opportunities. Waiting for perfect situations keeps one stuck in situations inhibiting growth. One may be too dependent on outside stimulation to initiate new goals. An oversensitivity to criticism could be limiting.

One's intuition might be put on the back burner. Not acting on intuitive perceptions can produce self-doubt and tension. One could be flooded by right-brain impulses, but lack the fortitude to use them. Karmic habits of escapism or imbalanced dependency needs could keep one from greater insights and happiness.

Square: Transiting Uranus Square Natal Ascendant
Progressed Ascendant Square
Natal or Progressed Uranus

LIGHT
Transiting Uranus square the natal Ascendant or progressed Ascendant square the natal (or progressed) Ascendant can denote going beyond cultural concepts. A fresh, new self can be exhibited. New individuality can be reached by transcending limiting beliefs. Experimentation and a new style of living flourish. Less sensitivity to the opinions of others can spark new directions.

FIRE
Transiting Uranus square a natal fire Ascendant or a progressed fire Ascendant square natal (or progressed) Uranus can connote a new enthusiasm. Creative sparks can fly! Procrastinators may leave caution to the past. Thoughts of an enticing future abound. Action and ideas may stimulate individuals to discover new consciousness. One may carefully perceive situations in the midst of actions. Individuals might adopt a more collective perspective. They free themselves from limiting self-concepts.

EARTH
Transiting Uranus square a natal earth Ascendant or a progressed earth Ascendant square natal (or progressed) Uranus can denote greater imaging power. People may eagerly seek out growth-promoting experiences. Play-it-safe individuals may enjoy more risky challenges. One may take goals off the back burner. Promoting new financial enterprises can bring self-confidence. Objective reality can be integrated with perceptions.

AIR
Transiting Uranus square a natal air Ascendant or a progressed air Ascendant square natal (or progressed) Uranus can symbolize exciting mental insights. Individuals may discover new options. Decision-making can be more flexible. New communication confidence can be displayed. A new eagerness to learn may begin. One makes ideas known more boldly. A thirst for knowledge can bring self-discovery. Individuals may establish new peer groups. The drive for mental stim-

ulation could be intense. People desire input from many different directions.

WATER

Transiting Uranus square a natal water Ascendant or a progressed water Ascendant square natal (or progressed) Uranus can symbolize a greater fluidity in communicating emotions. People may express more naturally. The subjective tendency of water is balanced by the airy nature of Uranus. Less dependency on others can begin. This can be a time of great creativity. One's dreams and visions may take root. An individual may stimulate creative growth in others. A person could capture the collective attention of her culture. Karmic liabilities related to escapism may be confronted. One might break away from destructive personal habits.

SHADOW

FIRE

Transiting Uranus square a natal fire Ascendant or a progressed fire Ascendant square natal (or progressed) Uranus can denote reckless actions. One may travel in circles. A loss of direction can be disorienting. One could have a serious identity crisis. A refusal to acknowledge limits could be disastrous. Stubborn pride could alienate others. Individuals may become too egocentric. A need for constant attention irritates others. Self-righteousness attitudes could be displayed. A narrow outlook might cause missed opportunities.

EARTH

Transiting Uranus square a natal earth Ascendant or a progressed earth Ascendant square natal (or progressed) Uranus can symbolize a lack of imagination. People can exhibit a backward outlook on societal trends. People can limit themselves due to a lack of flexibility. An overly material consciousness could block experimentation with new ideas. One may be too defensive of personal ideas. A resistance to new perspectives can occur. Disorganized individuals may lack stability. Negative attitudes could thwart self-expression.

AIR

Transiting Uranus square a natal air Ascendant or a progressed air Ascendant square natal (or progressed) Uranus can express as extreme aloofness. Individuals may have difficulty expressing feelings. They can hide within intellect. Nervous exhaustion can occur. Individuals can be stressed out, flooded by environmental stimuli. Indecision could cause tension. One may be too afraid to communicate ideas. A mind might be too active. An inner restlessness could lead to poor decisions.

WATER

Transiting Uranus square a natal water Ascendant or a progressed water Ascendant square natal (or progressed) Uranus can symbolize an emotional crisis. An individual might be highly explosive. Moods could be very unpredictable. An individual can resist facing past mistakes. Too much self-criticism dominates. One may overly rationalize life situations. Individuals can try too hard to be accepted. Sacrificing goals leads to frustration. A person may fight against higher consciousness. One may hold onto a painful past and fruitless present. Change seems too frightening. This individual could deny emotional ties. She seems impossible to really know. Emotional bonds are not trusted.

Quincunx: Transiting Uranus Quincunx Natal Ascendant
Progressed Ascendant Quincunx
Natal or Progressed Uranus

The quincunxes formed by transiting Uranus to the natal Ascendant or progressed Ascendant to natal (or progressed) Uranus are the **"Yoga of establishing unique identity."** Taking a stand or boldly following beliefs can bring courage.

LIGHT

FIRE

Transiting Uranus quincunx a natal fire Ascendant or a progressed fire Ascendant quincunx natal (or progressed) Uranus can denote pride in individuality. Making decisions becomes more exciting. Newfound freedom is surprising. An individual could become more spontaneous. Changes could be better timed. A person may be more reflective. Actions and perceptions could be in synch. A new zest for life may manifest. Individuals discover new, exhilarating goals. People feel filled with endless energy.

EARTH

Transiting Uranus quincunx a natal earth Ascendant or a progressed earth Ascendant quincunx natal (or progressed) Uranus can denote taking new risks. A person may establish new peers. Worn-out behavior patterns can be transcended. Familiar territory may be integrated with more experimental ground. A slow-paced person may enjoy a new, lively energy. An individual could feel younger. She could tune into future goals, looking beyond the safety of the earthy present. Status-quo individuals could express more independence. Much needed free thinking could be born.

AIR

Transiting Uranus quincunx a natal air Ascendant or a progressed air Ascendant quincunx natal (or progressed) Uranus

can symbolize heightened mental clarity. Airy Uranus is at home aspecting an air Ascendant. One's ideas may come together more spontaneously. She could conquer nervous anxiety. A person could find a refreshing life goal. One may adopt a more flexible nature. New trends could be cultivated. A thirst for knowledge leads to self-discovery.

WATER
Transiting Uranus quincunx a natal water Ascendant or a progressed water Ascendant quincunx natal (or progressed) Uranus can denote making subjective dreams a reality. A person may express more visions. One could transcend a karmic habit of running away from herself. A dependent person may think for herself. One may stop projecting her own unique creativity upon others. A person may stop blaming others for problems. An individual could take more risks.

SHADOW

FIRE
Transiting Uranus quincunx a fire Ascendant or a progressed fire Ascendant quincunx natal (or progressed) Uranus can express as actions with no direction. Individuals could be so "fired-up" that they lack reasoning power. Bridges may be burned. People can become quite unpredictable. Repressed people might become accident-prone. A fear of taking pride in one's actions may be displayed. Individuality can be lived through others.

EARTH
Transiting Uranus quincunx an earth Ascendant or a progressed earth Ascendant quincunx natal (or progressed) Uranus can denote an uninspired life. Boredom and routine stifle one's creative imagination. "Tunnel-vision" causes a limiting lifestyle. A person may fear bringing ideas forward. Familiar and safe ground are desired rather than experimenting with new challenges. A person could be too influenced by peers. Negative attitudes and self-doubt hold one back. Material consciousness could block growth in new directions.

AIR
Transiting Uranus quincunx an air Ascendant or a progressed air Ascendant quincunx natal (or progressed) Uranus can symbolize extreme nervous anxiety. People may be unable to relax. Excess worry can drain vitality. A person can be too concerned about the future. Concentration may be poor. An individual could be too defensive about her ideas. Extreme aloofness alienates others. Intellectual domination of others may occur. Ideas may lack solid foundation. Jumping to conclusions may occur. One may forget the facts or constantly change one's mind.

WATER
**Transiting Uranus quincunx a water Ascendant or a progressed
water Ascendant quincunx natal (or progressed) Uranus** can indicate extreme dependency upon others. A person may fear her own
unique qualities. This individual could be afraid to depend upon others.
She prefers distance to closeness. Relating to others involves emotional
confusion and inconsistency. One could resist transcending karmic habits. Escapism and ignoring reality continue to thwart growth. Running
away from the past keeps one attached to the same old problems.

Opposition: Transiting Uranus Opposing Natal Ascendant
Progressed Ascendant Opposing
Natal or Progressed Uranus

LIGHT
**Transiting Uranus opposing the Ascendant or the progressed
Ascendant opposing natal Uranus is a major life passage!** An
individual will sometimes break free from confining relationships. One
may adeptly relate to a wide variety of people. A person is usually
attracted to increased stimulation from others. An attraction to unconventional people or movements can occur. Building equality, friendship,
and freedom are common themes. Romantic relationships can begin
suddenly.

FIRE
**Transiting Uranus opposing a natal fire Ascendant or a pro-
gressed fire Ascendant opposing natal (or progressed) Uranus**
indicates a person can become more objective in perceiving others. She
may tolerate different opinions more willingly. One is more open to receiving and giving support. An individual may inspire creative actions
in others. Exchanging new ideas can be stimulating. A person may find
new depth in relating. A true pioneering spirit may emerge. A person
could offer a lot of mental and physical energy to group or collective
causes. One may find a new reason to live through meeting new stimulating peers.

EARTH
**Transiting Uranus opposing a natal earth Ascendant or a pro-
gressed earth Ascendant opposing natal (or progressed)
Uranus** can denote a person getting free of cultural myths. A very self-
reliant individualist could learn to share her life. A very reserved and
cautious person finds spontaneity stimulating. An individual could express more emotional intensity. A narrow-minded person could widen
horizons. New peers and groups teach a greater wisdom. An individual
could stop a pattern of self-sacrifice. Satisfying one's own needs becomes
important. A new flexibility in relating is possible. Fixed opinions are

transcended by tapping into a higher mind. Extreme practicality could blossom into exciting new mental directions.

AIR

Transiting Uranus opposing a natal air Ascendant or a progressed air Ascendant opposing natal (or progressed) Uranus can indicate more adaptability than usual. Juggling multiple lifestyles is possible. Communication skills could excel. Others may be impressed with enterprising ideas. A person may more boldly enter relationships. A listener may become an initiator. An individual could release tremendous energy into relationships or groups. A person may need numerous peers to express multiple communication outlets. Energy could speed up greatly when socializing. Long-term goals may be given priority.

WATER

Transiting Uranus opposing a natal water Ascendant or a progressed water Ascendant opposing natal (or progressed) Uranus can symbolize more mental order. A dreamy person may gain new insights. Escapism could be transcended. One may balance closeness and distance in relationships. An overly dependent person may find that freedom is refreshing. An extreme individualist could learn to share her life. A very emotional person can gain objectivity. A person could inspire others to follow their own dreams. An individual could meet new peers who teach her to act on intuition. One can balance dreams with the mental world. A person may take the freedom to tap into feelings.

SHADOW

FIRE

Transiting Uranus opposing a natal fire Ascendant or a progressed fire Ascendant opposing natal (or progressed) Uranus can express as extreme rebellion. A person can move so fast that she misperceives others. Individuals may carelessly leave relationships. Impatience with others can occur. An individual can grow dogmatic and opinionated. One's attention span may be short. Lack of cooperation or compromise can dominate. A lack of respect for discipline and continuity could be a problem. Having to be right at all times alienates others. A selfish need to be the center of attention can be displayed. A person can carelessly rebel with no direction. Lack of forethought could disrupt private and public lives.

EARTH

Transiting Uranus opposing a natal earth Ascendant or a progressed earth Ascendant opposing natal (or progressed) Uranus can denote relationships are too dependent on material wealth. A lack of emotional or intuitive depth can cause break-ups with lovers and peers. An individual may fear the freedom of others if he is a controlling type. A person could be too dependent on others. Perhaps he fears his own freedom. One may not trust bright people. The emotional and intuitive nature may be blocked. The individual may avoid the people who could help break his dam. An individual's perception of others may be fogged by fixed prejudices. One may be attached to cultural myths and expectations. Worshipping tradition seems safer than risking innovative thinking.

AIR

Transiting Uranus opposing a natal air Ascendant or a progressed air Ascendant opposing natal (or progressed) Uranus can symbolize an extremely aloof and unpredictable individual. One's mind may race out of control. She can refuse to listen to others. An individual may be lost in the intellect. She could miss opportunities due to a fear of action. One may lack depth due to a mind flooded with endless bits of information.

WATER

Transiting Uranus opposing a natal water Ascendant or a progressed water Ascendant opposing natal (or progressed) Uranus can denote an unstable emotional period. An individual may overreact to criticism. Finding stability can be tricky. Belonging to a relationship may be difficult. A person could feel emotionally isolated from self and others. A fear of emotional hurt may push people away. Emotional instability could alter perceptions. An individual may depend too much on others. Fantasy is easily projected onto others. Taking the lead in situations could be difficult.

Unstable emotional partners may appeal. One may punish herself by entering relationships with people who do not give affection or support. An enslavement to group philosophies could limit growth. Not thinking for oneself hampers freedom needs. One could be afraid to explore new directions. Childhood behavior patterns and parental attachments might cause internal conflict in adult life.

SOFT ASPECTS

Sextile: Transiting Uranus Sextile Natal Ascendant
Progressed Ascendant Sextile
Natal or Progressed Uranus

Trine: Transiting Uranus Trine Natal Ascendant
Progressed Ascendant Trine
Natal or Progressed Uranus

The soft Uranus/Ascendant aspects can show a person not as passionately seeking a new personal style. These aspects can combine with other intense aspects into a stimulating expression of individual creativity.

LIGHT

FIRE

Transiting Uranus sextile a fire Ascendant or a progressed fire Ascendant sextile natal (or progressed) Uranus can live more in the moment. A person may transcend worrying. One welcomes mental stimulation. An individual may be less nervous concerning personal expectations. People are prepared to handle transitions. A piercing intellect may govern actions. Ideas gain an easier acceptance than usual. A person may be less pushy. Ideas and goals are more easily integrated with those of peers.

Transiting Uranus trine a natal fire Ascendant or a progressed fire Ascendant trine natal (or progressed) Uranus can denote an untiring zest for life. One may be excited about long-range goals. A person could enjoy much support for future plans. A lighter feeling about life prevails. Self-confidence flows naturally. A person may take great pride in a unique identity. New personal charisma is experienced. A selfish individual may broaden her perspective. A new view for giving and receiving support could develop. A procrastinator may learn to act on impulses. Self-starting instincts come alive.

EARTH

Transiting Uranus sextile a natal earth Ascendant or a progressed earth Ascendant sextile natal (or progressed) Uranus can express as new business opportunities. One may combine material security and an individualistic lifestyle. A person may work smarter. More time is available for hobbies and creative outlets. One could transcend cultural myths and stereotypes. Earth can get easily stuck into safe or rigid beliefs. Uranus can lift one's thoughts and perceptions to a higher elevation.

Transiting Uranus trine a natal earth Ascendant or a progressed earth Ascendant trine natal (or progressed) Uranus can denote enjoying material security. This could be someone who has denied herself rewards in the past. A hardworking person may reap rewards. This period can be exhilarating. An individual may find more time for creative needs. A nervous type may relax. An overly serious, practical person could lighten up.

AIR

Transiting Uranus sextile an air Ascendant or a progressed air Ascendant sextile natal (or progressed) Uranus can denote exciting new thought patterns. One may seek out new milestones. Mental energy could be quite powerful. One may discover new communication talent. The mind is saturated with new information. A person may outgrow current peers. A collective cause could contain mental intensity. A person may create new life options. More flexibility in decision making can be displayed. An indecisive individual may more easily make key choices. One may be an excellent networker. A sixth sense could link up the resources of individuals. A person may find true meaning in her life. She could inspire others to think for themselves.

Transiting Uranus trine an air Ascendant or a progressed air Ascendant trine natal (or progressed) Uranus can symbolize a greater ability to reason. One may relax more. An individual may enjoy creative thoughts. One may accidentally discover new life directions. The innocent pursuit of a hobby may uncover a talent.

WATER

Transiting Uranus sextile a natal water Ascendant or a progressed water Ascendant sextile natal (or progressed) Uranus can symbolize excitement over new insights. One may gain clarity concerning the past. A person can comprehend subjective, watery dreams on a higher mental level. A streak of creative genius can break through the subconscious. Communicating deep feelings may set one free from self-doubts. An unusual ability to understand abstract concepts can occur. One may display an unusual talent in translating the subjective world with its symbolic languages. Astrology, tarot, or handwriting analysis may be a new intuitive art.

Transiting Uranus trine a natal water Ascendant or a progressed water Ascendant trine natal (or progressed) Uranus can denote a nice flow between intuition and intellect. Greater self-acceptance can occur. Consciousness can expand through new understanding that reinforces unique qualities. One can embrace new liberating ideals. Conquering escapism may be exciting rather than scary. One may rise above limitations, rather than fighting through frustrating experiences. Universal concepts can be shared. A person could become a vessel for humanity — a voice for her society or culture. She can free the self from false identities.

SHADOW

FIRE

The Uranus/fire Ascendant sextile or trine can express as aloof sarcasm. A person can grow impatient with others. Everything in the environment is a bore. An individual could change directions haphazardly. The drive for excitement makes one a junkie for stimulation. One's mind can be jumpy. The nervous system is maxed out! People can be taken for granted. One lacks appreciation for the little things. Too much starting over leaves no depth or roots. One's philosophy or ideas can be out of touch with the mainstream. A "different just to be different" mentality keeps others at a distance.

EARTH

The Uranus/earth Ascendant sextile or trine can manifest as a lack of discipline and concentration. A person can dig up the seed before it is grown. All structure may be defied. A person could resist new learning. The unknown seems threatening. One may preserve the "good old days." A person could fear freedom. Confidence in material security may be excessive. An individual could have a reactionary mentality. An individual could feel technologically alienated from the culture. One's intelligence could be doubted. A person could be suspicious of intellectually superior individuals.

AIR

The Uranus/air Ascendant sextile or trine can symbolize extremely nervous energy. A person can be too worried about life. Internal dialogues can be bothersome. The individual may be pulled in many different directions. One may become anxious when expressing individuality. One might say what others want to hear. A person may be a great socializer, but lack depth. Individuals can be too fond of eccentric habits. Ideas may not be clearly perceived. A person may copy the identity of others. She could lack the clarity to express her own true nature. One could follow the dictates of a group, too guided by peers.

WATER

The Uranus/Ascendant sextile or trine can denote intellectualizing emotions. One could fail to communicate feelings. An individual may run away from the past. She may hide in socializing. One may rationalize mistakes and unpleasant experiences. A person could get lost in the subjective world. Ideas may never take form. Individuality is repressed. An individual could be extremely dependent on others. She may be too attached to parents. One can fear transitions or sudden changes. A person could reenact karmic behaviors related to escapism.

DAWN

Ascendant/Uranus aspects can symbolize a process in realizing one's full potential. Lack of direction can be transcended by spontaneous decision making. A cold spirit can become a stimulating resource for others. One may achieve new consciousness. Natal and progressed fire Ascendants with their impatience to act can be given deeper perception by airy Uranus; natal and progressed earth Ascendants can be stimulated to think by innovative Uranus; natal and progressed air Ascendants can be lifted to the highest intellectual levels by inquisitive Uranus; natal and progressed water Ascendants can be pulled from their subjective roots by detached Uranus into the objective world.

NEPTUNE/ASCENDANT ASPECTS

Transiting Neptune/Natal Ascendant
Progressed Ascendant/Natal or Progressed Neptune

Process:	Sensitized Identity
Ally:	Acting on Faith
Illusion:	Loss of Self

Neptune/Ascendant aspects can denote imagining how to transcend one's identity. People can get to know themselves on a higher level. These aspects can feel a bit peculiar. Very materialistic individuals may look for more subtle and less objective experiences. They may begin to question the meaning of their actions. This can be a very reflective time.

A person may relinquish excessive self-control. One may find new inspiring symbols and myths. New faith and imagination can be attained. A person can tune into deeper subjective awareness. People must work on themselves. Aesthetic pursuits can intensify. People may exhibit more healing energy. Romantic love or seeking meaningful relationships grows in importance.

INTENSE ASPECTS
Conjunction: Transiting Neptune Conjunct Natal Ascendant
Progressed Ascendant Conjunct
Natal or Progressed Neptune

LIGHT
Transiting Neptune conjunct the natal Ascendant or the progressed Ascendant conjunct natal (or progressed) Neptune can symbolize clearer awareness of personal issues. Staying or getting inspired becomes more urgent. One may discover deeper emotional instincts. Ascendant/Neptune aspects highlight emotional vulnerability. Self-destructive behavior patterns can be transcended. One may passionately put an aesthetic boldness into action. A person's entire being can become a unity of love and emotional clarity. Intuition and actions can work in harmony. Falling in love and a desire for closeness in relationships commonly occurs. A special life mission can manifest.

FIRE
Transiting Neptune conjunct a natal fire Ascendant or a progressed fire Ascendant conjunct natal (or progressed) Neptune can point to more understanding of actions. People may learn to watch themselves move through life. A rush toward the next red light could become tempered with "let me experience the beauty of a moment!" One may become aware of new higher consciousness. Being the center of attention becomes less important. A new humility and giving nature may surface. Excessive fire-sign pride could be surrendered.

EARTH
Transiting Neptune conjunct a natal earth Ascendant or a progressed earth Ascendant conjunct natal (or progressed) Neptune can symbolize transcending an earth-bound consciousness. A very dry nature may learn to feel. A person lacking faith may come to trust in a greater power. One may understand subjective life processes. Ideals and imagining power can be embraced. A person may display more compassion for self and others. One is not too attached to the outcome of actions. A more fluid and spontaneous nature can be exhibited.

AIR
Transiting Neptune conjunct a natal air Ascendant or a progressed air Ascendant conjunct natal (or progressed) Neptune can denote trusting intuition as much as intellect. Ideas and ideals can be passionately communicated. The faith to act on thoughts can be realized. An intellectualizer may express feelings more honestly. A nervous individual may begin to relax. He could be attracted to meditation, creative visualization, affirmations, etc. A person learns to commune with parts of the psyche that the intellect cannot reach.

WATER
Transiting Neptune conjunct a natal water Ascendant or a progressed water Ascendant conjunct natal (or progressed) Neptune can indicate high self-awareness. A sensitive individual lacking conviction could rebirth idealism. A dead spirit may wake up! One may transcend emotional fears. A person could focus on consciousness-raising experiences. An outpouring of blocked emotional energy may free self-expression. A person may forgive self and others. One may feel a tremendous burden has been lifted. A cleansing of the spirit can occur. Even if not pleasant, the cleansing can be purifying and enlightening.

SHADOW

FIRE
Transiting Neptune conjunct a natal fire Ascendant or a progressed fire Ascendant conjunct a natal (or progressed) Neptune can indicate carelessness regarding limits. Living for today, disregarding the past, may lead to a foolish future. One's idealism may never get grounded. One can believe he is above the law. One may lack the patience to explore higher consciousness. Too much self-reliance may alienate others. An "I do not need anyone" attitude may prevail. A self-righteousness could lead to judgmental attitudes or insensitivity to others.

One can foolishly rush into circumstances without any forethought. A tendency to not finish what is started can occur. A disoriented identity, watered down by unresolved emotional conflicts, can block assertive instincts.

EARTH
Transiting Neptune conjunct a natal earth Ascendant or a progressed earth Ascendant conjunct natal (or progressed) Neptune can denote doubting intuition. The right brain may be blocked by an overactive left brain. One may lack the faith to trust ideals. Life can be boring and too predictable. Spontaneity is feared. Transitions in life can be viewed as threatening. One's consciousness can become glued to a material level. Inflexibility may lead to missed opportunities.

AIR
Transiting Neptune conjunct a natal air Ascendant or a progressed air Ascendant conjunct natal (or progressed) Neptune can symbolize a person confused by thinking. One may think situations to death. A divine discontent with self and others is possible. An air Ascendant can grow nervous when unable to rationalize feelings. One may suffer burnout and nervous exhaustion. Missed facts or details can dominate this time period. Many changes of plans can bring frustration. Procrastination can be a problem.

WATER
Transiting Neptune conjunct a natal water Ascendant or a progressed water Ascendant conjunct natal (or progressed) Neptune can denote strange mood swings. A person can escape into silence and gain no illumination. One may become an emotional recluse. A fear of new experiences can produce inertia. One may be flooded by unconscious material, but lack the insight to gain clarity. A person can get lost in a world of fantasy. Escape into substance abuse, excessive sleep, television, or sex sometimes occurs. One's lack of faith in self or a higher power can lead to abortive journeys.

Square: Transiting Neptune Square Natal Ascendant
Progressed Ascendant Square
Natal or Progressed Neptune

LIGHT
Transiting Neptune square the natal Ascendant or progressed Ascendant square natal (or progressed) Neptune denotes blending identity with highest ideals. One may act on ideals rather than stew in the waters of divine discontent.

FIRE
Transiting Neptune square a natal fire Ascendant or a progressed fire Ascendant square natal (or progressed) Neptune can denote a new courage to express oneself. One may find the faith to be all one can be. One's intuition and actions can dynamically stimulate each other. Ideals are eagerly put into action. A person may sense a

greater purpose in life. He may include others in his life. One can sense personal finiteness during this aspect.

One's moods may intensify as ideals and reality become a challenge to balance. The divine discontent of watery Neptune can capture the ferocious action orientation of fire. A person may become more personal and passionate. A self-centered individual may become aware of a more universal consciousness.

EARTH
Transiting Neptune square a natal earth Ascendant or a progressed earth Ascendant square natal (or progressed) Neptune can symbolize a new business sense. One may trust common sense. A very logical individual might learn to trust intuition. The intangible and right-brain dimensions could come to life. Real-life crises may tap into subconscious impulses. One can find a new faith in self. Neptune could combine with the tenacious earth element to conquer escapism. One may find new groundedness. A person might combine hard work and relaxation. Work may become a discipline, rather than only a job.

AIR
Transiting Neptune square an air Ascendant or a progressed air Ascendant square natal (or progressed) Neptune can denote more faith in emotional expression. An individual can discover higher consciousness. An adept ability to interpret symbolic languages can be born. A new versatility of perception and communication could surface. One may rise above the stress of everyday decision making. Greater flexibility can be exhibited.

WATER
Transiting Neptune square a natal water Ascendant or a progressed water Ascendant square natal (or progressed) Neptune can denote overcoming personal escapism. A new faith (in self or in a higher power) may bring ideals into reality. An individual may display an aesthetic passion that inspires self and others. One may accept more confrontation from the environment by finding a higher threshold of emotional intensity.

SHADOW

FIRE
Transiting Neptune square a natal fire Ascendant or a progressed fire Ascendant square natal (or progressed) Neptune can symbolize a fear of oneself. One could act on impulses. One's moods could vacillate quickly from excitement to intense introspection. Projects could be halted in midstream. An individual can get lost in ideals or causes. Converting others to personal beliefs could reach fanaticism. One may become absorbed in impressing others rather than expressing one's self naturally. Avoiding conflict could lead to escapist behavior. A

denial of physical laws could lead to breaking the law, burnout, or deception of self and others. A selfish person may be humbled by falling on hard times.

EARTH

Transiting Neptune square an earth Ascendant or a progressed earth Ascendant square natal (or progressed) Neptune can denote a spaced-out mentality. One may fight against logic, common sense, discipline, and commitment. Irresponsibility could ruin relationships (with lovers, peers, and business associates). Physical-plane mania (such as too much desire for pleasure) could keep one from developing keener intuition. He could be lost chasing illusory wealth and fame. One may achieve fame and realize that life is "sitting on empty"! A disorganized physical environment could reflect a disoriented consciousness. One's values could be set too high; or, they could be too earthbound with little room for inspiration, change, or imagination. A person may fear depending on others or be too attached and dependent.

AIR

Transiting Neptune square an air Ascendant or a progressed air Ascendant square natal (or progressed) Neptune can indicate a confused intellect. One may lack direction. A cosmic fog can persist. One may be out of touch with emotional intensity. Decision making can stagnate. One may guard against closeness with others. Not trusting feelings of love or intuition can push others away. One may feel too good for others. Faulty reasoning could distort facts and make for vague perception of situations.

WATER

Transiting Neptune square a water Ascendant or a progressed water Ascendant square natal (or progressed) Neptune can indicate running away from self. One can repeat karmic behavior and surrender identity to others. A weak or confused self-image could lead to unstable relationships. One may be too sensitive and moody. A lack of assertion could be frustrating. Divine discontent with self and others can be extreme. One may create endless excuses for procrastination. Running away from conflict may delay resolving emotional pain.

Quincunx: Transiting Neptune Quincunx Natal Ascendant
Progressed Ascendant Quincunx
Natal or Progressed Neptune

The quincunxes formed by transiting Neptune to the natal Ascendant or progressed Ascendant to natal (or progressed) Neptune are the **"Yoga of finding faith in identity."** A person may go through an inner and/ or outer tidal wave at this time, but gain strength.

LIGHT

FIRE

Transiting Neptune quincunx a natal fire Ascendant or a progressed fire Ascendant quincunx natal (or progressed) Neptune can indicate more sensitivity. Reckless energy may be raised to a more conscious and refined level. One can show more courage and assertion through unifying action and intuition. One may drop a shortsighted "live for today" attitude. A more farsighted and collective awareness could arise. An individual could become more conscious of life processes and stop getting lost in momentary impulses. A tendency to leap first and think later may be modified. Someone who looks too much to others for stimulation or support could learn to be a self-starter.

EARTH

Transiting Neptune quincunx a natal earth Ascendant or a progressed earth Ascendant quincunx natal (or progressed) Neptune can indicate less self-criticism. One's expectations of self and others (on the physical plane) could become more reasonable. One may find alternative beliefs regarding a negative self-image. A person can conquer cultural myths. A person may take care of personal health. One may desire a more meaningful lifestyle. She may perceive the self through more intuitive vision. Inner beauty may be discovered. One's addiction to unreliable lovers and partners may become more conscious. One could reverse this attachment and find more meaningful relationships.

AIR

Transiting Neptune quincunx a natal air Ascendant or a progressed air Ascendant quincunx natal (or progressed) Neptune can bypass the conscious mind to gain easier access to the unconscious. One learns to quiet nervous energies. Mental and emotional energies are organized. A new confidence in presenting oneself to others may be shown. One may become more aware of the unity inherent in life, rather than only seeing separateness. A person could tap into a higher intelligence. One may stop listening to negative messages from peers. More spontaneous feelings may be expressed. A greater awareness of one's own intelligence and mental gifts may bring illuminating perceptions.

WATER

Transiting Neptune quincunx a natal water Ascendant or a progressed water Ascendant quincunx natal (or progressed) Neptune can symbolize emotional clarity. Previous emotional disorientation could be put in order. Stagnation or procrastination can be transcended. One may awaken to a new emotional intensity. A person can gain a new understanding of intimacy. One may conquer a guilty nature. Too much self-sacrifice can be changed to rewarding oneself. One may put idealism into action. A greater faith in self and in a higher power could yield aesthetic creativity. Karmic patterns concerning escapism could be transcended. An individual could inspire others through compassion and a true desire to be a helper.

SHADOW

FIRE

Transiting Neptune quincunx a natal fire Ascendant or a progressed fire Ascendant quincunx natal (or progressed) Neptune can express as extreme laziness. One could daydream about tomorrow and ignore today. A lack of discipline and follow-through can dominate. One may show a lack of respect for others. A selfish desire to be loved unconditionally can occur. A person may display an arrogance and self-righteousness that attracts few friends. An individual may use the love of others. One may depend too much on the good graces and hospitality of others. A person might display a fear of assertion or extreme timidity. Missed opportunities will result. One could feel too responsible for the failures of others. A person may have difficulty asking for help. Fire can carry the pride principle to the max!

EARTH

Transiting Neptune quincunx an earth Ascendant or a progressed earth Ascendant quincunx natal (or progressed) Neptune can express as lack of faith in success. An individual can settle for dead-end jobs, relationships, etc., due to a poor self-image. One may be too self-sacrificing. She could feel undeserving of love, wealth, and success. Individuals can feel too deserving of these things. People could become too devoted to work, and lose sight of loved ones or relaxation. Pleasure and ordinary life could be undervalued. This person may be difficult to please. The more she receives, the more she desires.

AIR

Transiting Neptune quincunx an air Ascendant or a progressed air Ascendant quincunx natal (or progressed) Neptune can express as a loss of perspective. One could be too worried about endless details. The conscious mind can nag excessively. One may lack the intuitive awareness to shut off inner chatter. An individual could listen to the wrong people concerning mental capabilities. An individual could display poor reasoning. Facts may not justify the conclusions reached.

One may be too sensitive about personal opinions. She could be easily hurt when criticized. A lack of imagination and inspiration could lead to a dull consciousness. A skeptical attitude regarding the intangible (or subjective sides of life) could lead to a boring and unimaginative existence. One could regard symbolism as absurd. She could be unable to reason in a collective manner.

WATER
Transiting Neptune quincunx a water Ascendant or a progressed water Ascendant quincunx natal (or progressed) Neptune can express as unfounded idealism. A person may paint unrealistic pictures of others. One may dream, but lack the tenacity to accomplish dreams. A person could hide behind an aesthetic ability. She may fear showing vulnerability in the real world. An individual might become addicted to romantic images. She may become enslaved to their beauty or expect life to flow ideally. Neglecting one's own creativity to serve other individuals is self-defeating. An attraction to unreliable mates or peers could be costly emotionally and materially. One may foolishly repeat the same mistakes, conveniently denying the past.

Opposition: Transiting Neptune Opposing Natal Ascendant
Progressed Ascendant Opposing
Natal or Progressed Neptune

LIGHT
Transiting Neptune opposing the Ascendant or the progressed Ascendant opposing natal (or progressed) Neptune is a dynamic aspect. The self-image comes under careful scrutiny by others. Many people feel as though they are transparent. Some individuals enjoy this experience, while others have difficulty flowing with it. Romantic love is accentuated. Existing relationships can become vague in definition. It is possible that partners will find new faith in one another.

FIRE
Transiting Neptune opposing a natal fire Ascendant or a progressed fire Ascendant opposing natal (or progressed) Neptune indicates channeling raw, action-oriented, fire energy with more sensitivity and compassion. A person is learning to unify the actions and self-focus of fire with the objective awareness of others (through the air Descendant). One may understand the thoughts and actions of others. A contagious enthusiasm for life helps others achieve unity. An individual may be an excellent counselor and communicator. One's humor and objectivity may put others at ease. Reading body language and the messages behind words can help one interpret the feelings of others. One may enjoy a true emotional depth in intimate relating. One responds immediately to the urgent needs of others. One may prove love and concern through thoughts and actions. Love is shared deeply. An attraction to universal thought can occur. One may excel at interpreting symbolic languages as in dreams, astrology, tarot, parapsychology, etc.

EARTH
Transiting Neptune opposing a natal earth Ascendant or a progressed earth Ascendant opposing natal (or progressed) Neptune symbolizes balancing a practical self-image with intuition in

social encounters. The input of others may stimulate more right-brain consciousness. The individual may ground others. One may express more compassion and empathy (learning to walk in the shoes of others). A hardened self may be softened by the caring of another. An extremely cautious and logical nature may give way to more flowing social inter-action. An unimaginative mind may grow in self-exploration. An individual lacking love may become more romantic. A new appreciation for beauty and harmony may be born. One may be rewarded for years of consistent hard work. A too disciplined individual may learn to flow.

AIR
Transiting Neptune opposing a natal air Ascendant or a progressed air Ascendant opposing natal (or progressed) Neptune denotes flowing from thinking into spontaneous encounters. An intel-lectualizer may learn to feel. One may experience love on a more emo-tional level. Mind and heart might become one. Difficult concepts may be communicated to others. One could help others achieve a mental balance and enjoy the present. A person may experience new ease. He might express feelings more spontaneously. A new action orientation could occur. One may need less attention and stop forcing opinions on others. He may be less accusing, and more accepting.

WATER
Transiting Neptune opposing a natal water Ascendant or a progressed water Ascendant opposing natal (or progressed) Neptune can indicate an illuminating experience. The past may become unified with one's present. A Cancer Ascendant (Capricorn Descendant) could show clarity learned concerning childhood roots and deep security issues. A Scorpio Ascendant (Taurus Descendant) could be insight into past power and bonding issues. A Pisces Ascendant (Virgo Descendant) could be intuitive clarity regarding past dependency and escapism issues. A water Ascendant is particularly sensitive to the watery Neptune, natural ruler of Pisces. One may encounter numerous soul mates or feel as though life is a big play. A person can become aware of dimensions of identity that need to be transcended. A greater faith in intuition gains confidence by acting out ideals in the real world.

Denial or self-hatred (water Ascendant) can be comforted by the support of others (earth Descendant). Divine discontent found in water finds a home in the solid grounding of earth. Complex subconscious impulses can be balanced by the soothing comfort of earth. This is a time to heal old wounds from this life and past lives. One may remem-ber past lives and early childhood experiences. Cross out karmic debts from past lives and free the present. One may have an unusual ability to interpret metaphysical and psychological symbols. Ideals (water) and reality (earth) may merge.

SHADOW

FIRE

Transiting Neptune opposing a natal fire Ascendant or a progressed fire Ascendant opposing natal (or progressed) Neptune can express as lack of self-awareness. One may project identity onto others. Looking outward for approval could be a problem. A person may misperceive situations. One may jump to conclusions due to impatience. One could be led by passions and devotional urges, but lack focus. Scattered energy and burnout are possible. Relationships could be vague. A lack of communication may make commitments difficult. One may have trouble settling into a stable situation. An individual can rush into relationships and later wish he had gone slower. One may deceive others by misrepresenting intentions. A lack of depth in relating is possible. One may be attracted to outward appearances only.

EARTH

Transiting Neptune opposing a natal earth Ascendant or a progressed earth Ascendant opposing natal (or progressed) Neptune can express as resistance to higher consciousness. One may repeatedly try to make one's entire life fit into a neat package. A lack of flexibility may put a severe strain on relationships. A rigid way of being inhibits growth. An individual could depend too heavily on others. One may become a doormat if addicted to controlling people. People may try too hard to help others, rather than helping themselves. An attraction to escapist personalities can be harmful. One's relationships could be out of balance emotionally and materially. A lack of acceptance and flexibility could keep relationships from growing. A compulsive desire for fame and success could dissolve love.

AIR

Transiting Neptune opposing a natal air Ascendant or a progressed air Ascendant opposing natal (or progressed) Neptune can express as blurred perception. One's thoughts may run together in a disorienting manner. An individual could have trouble taking ideas from the mind to the heart. A reckless treatment of others could lead to unfulfilling relationships. A person could be attached to extremely self-centered partners. Ego wars could dominate relating.

A lack of sensitivity or acceptance could cause abortive relationships. One may do fine on the imaging level, but lack the focus to deal with everyday reality. People may view one as intelligent but disorganized. An oversensitivity to the opinions of others could "hide one's light under a bushel."

WATER

Transiting Neptune opposing a natal water Ascendant or a progressed water Ascendant opposing natal (or progressed)

Neptune can express as extreme confusion. One may feel tremendous guilt. An insecure identity can limit assertive power. Relationships may keep the person afloat. An addiction or extreme dependency on others could be a problem. One may live out creative potentials through others.

Unresolved emotional difficulties could cause a troubled present. Cancer rising could still deny painful childhood experiences; Scorpio rising could hide from emotional scars and a bruised psyche; Pisces rising could deny hurt expectations. A lack of faith in self (or in a higher power) could bring stagnation.

One could deny a need for love. Personal love may be avoided by devotion to enslaving collective causes. Denying universal truth could be especially problematic. Watery Neptune has a strong repeating theme when aspecting a water Ascendant. Higher values, idealism, and the need for inspiration become accentuated. A denial or lack of faith in one's ability to seek new stimulating ideals can be frustrating. Escapism through sex, substances, sleep, or television can reach extreme proportions.

SOFT ASPECTS

Sextile: Transiting Neptune Sextile Natal Ascendant
Progressed Ascendant Sextile
   Natal or Progressed Neptune

Trine: Transiting Neptune Trine Natal Ascendant
Progressed Ascendant Trine
   Natal or Progressed Neptune

The soft Neptune/Ascendant aspects indicate one's faith is not tested as intensely by the environment. These aspects can combine with other intense aspects into a visible expression of ideals and intuition.

LIGHT

FIRE

Transiting Neptune sextile a natal fire Ascendant or a progressed fire Ascendant sextile natal (or progressed) Neptune can express as a passion to realize ideals. One can exhibit exciting, new, creative opportunities.

An individual could trust intuition more. A burning excitement could conquer procrastination. One may tap into right-brain energy, learning to rely on intuition rather than leaping first and thinking later. Pride could soften and humility increase. A person may learn diplomacy rather than using aggression.

One may control temper tantrums. Patience may become a virtue. A greater awareness of actions can result. Life's beauty may be accentuated.

Transiting Neptune trine a natal fire Ascendant or a progressed fire Ascendant trine natal Neptune can denote a new faith in oneself. A person may embrace her highest values. A devotion to spirituality, truth, or creativity can be expressed.

A feeling of a unity with all life can occur. One may become more aware that life is a process. Each detail may be more treasured rather than seen as a means to an end. The "little things" in life become more important.

A self-centered individualist may become more compassionate. One's faith may move mountains. A person may find a new dignity and self-respect.

EARTH

Transiting Neptune sextile a natal earth Ascendant or a progressed earth Ascendant sextile natal (or progressed) Neptune can express as a new faith in the world. An unimaginative nature may be lifted to new heights. One may gain more flexibility.

An already productive person may intuit even more avenues for growth. Neptune can be a unifying symbol. A person may integrate more lifestyles and solidify identity.

A logical person may experience more unconditional love. Perhaps he sees that not all experiences need to be defined.

Transiting Neptune trine a natal earth Ascendant or a progressed earth Ascendant trine natal (or progressed) Neptune can symbolize a faith to make highest ideals concrete.

A dull or boring person may reach new creative inspirations. One may see that pleasure and work can be combined. A person may appreciate things and people of lasting values. Deeper love and commitments may occur.

AIR

Transiting Neptune sextile an air Ascendant or a progressed air Ascendant sextile natal (or progressed) Neptune can denote a refreshing mental perception. One may accept self and others more. Nervous exhaustion may be transcended. One's thoughts may become more organized, rather than running like wild horses. Ease may gradually replace a tense nature.

One may trust intuition as much as thoughts. Neptune can pull on the air element to "trust the force." An intellectualizer may learn to act more spontaneously.

A new environment may offer more mental space. A person may read the thoughts of others.

Transiting Neptune trine an air Ascendant or a progressed air Ascendant trine natal (or progressed) Neptune can symbolize a bold new faith in one's intellect. A person may communicate difficult concepts in a clear manner.

New learning can be born. A person may attract subjects that challenge the intuition more than the mind. An aesthetic talent may emerge. Social urges may awaken. A person may need to share more with others. She may more actively seek stimulation from peers.

WATER

Transiting Neptune sextile a water Ascendant or a progressed water Ascendant sextile natal (or progressed) Neptune can denote a very refined intuition. One may sense the mood of situations clearly. One might be a good counselor and listener. One may communicate without invading the space of others.

A person could turn around escapist behaviors. Self-defeating habits can be understood. One can translate dreams and internal body signals with more clarity. Moods are no longer unpredictable.

One may accept personal shortcomings as well as talents. Outside help might be accepted. Childhood memories or past life instincts could provide strength.

Transiting Neptune trine a water Ascendant or a progressed water Ascendant trine natal (or progressed) Neptune can denote a new faith in one's idealism. A greater confidence in imagination could arise. One may have clairvoyant senses. One's intuition can burn brighter than usual.

Divine discontent could inspire one to excel at an aesthetic talent. One may experience life as a gift or spiritual grace. Giving more of oneself may inspire others to do the same.

One's relationships could flow more smoothly than usual. She may be catalyst for love and unity. One might find new inspiring myths. She may be a symbol or example of love.

SHADOW

FIRE

The Neptune/fire Ascendant sextile or trine can express as divine discontent. An individual could exhibit no satisfaction with life. Unrealistic expectations can exist. One can be in too big of a hurry. A lack of consistency may prove frustrating. A person might be indecisive and noncommittal.

One may lack foresight. Trying too much at once could be a problem. Excessive stimulation can occur. A disrespect for the little things in life could lead to big trouble. A person could exercise poor judgment. Impatience and constant complaining bring relationship tension. A shallow urge to impress others could stunt growth.

One may see himself as the ultimate gift to mankind, thinking he can get away with anything. It could be a person with burnout. He sets few limits.

An "all roads lead to Rome" mentality may lead to no accomplishments. One can be too tolerant of others. An "everything will get better" mentality can deny hurt pride and feelings. A person may have difficulty asking for help. One may be a General Custer type at Little Big Horn — thinking nothing can defeat him no matter the odds. This can be a foolish belief in oneself that ignores reality.

EARTH

The Neptune/earth Ascendant sextile or trine can express as an extreme material consciousness. A person could get so stimulated by material ambition that he loses sight of a higher consciousness. One may have difficulty trusting intuition. Too much belief in the logical and obvious could limit growth. A person's love nature could be too reserved. A person could be too attached to physical appetites. Excessive food, sex, and other pleasures could be exhibited. Drowning sorrow in worldly lusts could be self-defeating.

Personal ownership could be denied. One may fail to see the self as worthy of rewards. He might be too dedicated to others. People could feel insecure without a big outward display. Individuals may run away from spiritual emptiness with the accumulation of wealth or material things. One may not appreciate hard work. Perhaps things have come too easily. He may be unprepared for a real spiritual/emotional crisis.

AIR

The Neptune/air Ascendant sextile or trine can express as mental confusion. One may resist intuitive vision. The conscious mind may be flooded with new right-brain energy. A person may panic if lacking awareness and/or groundedness. A person may become forgetful. He may need to slow down and concentrate. This time can be disorienting. A Gemini Ascendant can get distracted by too many options; a Libra Ascendant by expectations of others; an Aquarian Ascendant by vague future goals.

One's thoughts and feelings could get tangled. He may need to communicate feelings more openly. An intellectualizer could be afraid to feel. There can be procrastination. One may rationalize with the best.

A person could be easily disappointed. Expectations of self and others might be too high. A person may fall in love with people who have escapist tendencies. A person may assume others understand his communication. He could be a vague communicator. One may not really say what he is feeling, but more what he thinks people like to hear.

WATER

The Neptune/water Ascendant sextile or trine can express as intuitive confusion. One may be emotionally depleted. He could run away from facing problems. One's moods could be strange and unpredictable. Spending too much time alone or not communicating feelings could be disorienting. Memories may produce fears.

A dreamy nature may keep a person from moving forward. Longing for the past could rock the boat of the present. A denial of inner turmoil may prolong problems.

A person could do too much second-guessing of self. An individual could be too dependent on others. She may fear independence and lack faith in self. One may doubt intuitive ability.

Life may appear meaningless. A lack of trust in others or ideals could lead to difficult situations. Emotional scars could block creative growth. One may lack a clear identity. Self-expression might be blocked by a lack of faith in self or in a higher power. An individual could have unfounded faith. Higher ideals and values may not find a clear foothold on the physical plane. One's relationships could be out of balance. The individual could settle for limited circumstances. He may be hopelessly devoted to unappreciative partners.

DAWN
Ascendant/Neptune aspects can denote an unusual capacity to embrace one's highest ideals. Broken dreams and unfulfilled ideals could be transcended by a dynamic faith in self and in a higher power.

Natal and progressed fire Ascendants can be cooled by watery Neptune into patience and sensitivity; natal and progressed earth Ascendants can be inspired by dreamy Neptune to new ideals and imagination; natal and progressed air Ascendants can be lifted by seductive Neptune to new intuitive horizons; natal and progressed water Ascendants can be intoxicated by romantic Neptune to express feelings and creative powers. Romance and finding harmony in relationships is highlighted.

PLUTO/ASCENDANT ASPECTS

Transiting Pluto/Ascendant
Progressed Ascendant/Natal or Progressed Pluto

Process:	Empowered Identity
Ally:	The Strength to Bond With a True Sense of Self
Illusion:	Holding onto False Identities

Ascendant/Pluto aspects can symbolize transcending an old identity. One can experience a rebirth. A person may experience different layers of identity. A tug of war to break free from old lifestyles and habits may occur.

A new emotional intensity may break through obstacles. Individuals could regress into manipulative behaviors. A very aware person may find this an empowering time period. One's deepest instincts may be confirmed by clear outward actions. An introspective individual must be careful not to go to extremes of self-examination.

INTENSE ASPECTS
Conjunction: Transiting Pluto Conjunct Natal Ascendant
Progressed Ascendant Conjunct
Natal or Progressed Pluto

LIGHT
Transiting Pluto conjunct the natal Ascendant or the progressed Ascendant conjunct natal (or progressed) Pluto can denote new passion for life. An already confident individual may naturally command respect. Bonding with one's deepest instincts may attract others. A person can feel excited by new self-mastery.

This time can be painfully illuminating. A person may learn to forgive. This can be a major life passage, colored by self-healing. During Ascendant/Pluto aspects a person can go through a key metamorphosis. One can shed actions that distract from higher consciousness. A renewed vigor for life can occur. Life may take on a more fulfilling purpose. Dealing with a significant loss or death sometimes accompanies this aspect. **People can be masterful at achieving wealth and fame.**

FIRE
Transiting Pluto conjunct a natal fire Ascendant or a progressed fire Ascendant conjunct natal (or progressed) Pluto can denote a tremendous emotional release. One's external orientation may be tempered with a heightened awareness of the environment. Exceptional tasks may be performed. One may discover a new pride. Self-confidence may transcend a fear of actions. A new patience with oneself may aid self-healing. A new interest in life's mysteries may replace a moment-to-moment impatience with the present. Transcending a rigid ego may begin. One may move away from karmic habits related to ignorance of limitation or misperception of others.

EARTH
Transiting Pluto conjunct a natal earth Ascendant or a progressed earth Ascendant conjunct natal (or progressed) Pluto can symbolize a greater depth on the physical plane. An individual may learn to trust and establish commitments. A person may rise above material success, or lack of it, to realize life's deepest processes. A person may overcome an addiction to physical senses. A stubborn tendency to play it safe may become transcended by a new trust in self.

One may learn to be good to herself. A life of denial (or lack of reward) may be replaced by a new self-respect. Bringing emotional intensity into a boring life may stimulate creative urges. A selfish or hoarding mentality may bond with a more giving consciousness. An urge to share more of one's love and resources may occur.

AIR
Transiting Pluto conjunct an air Ascendant or a progressed air Ascendant conjunct natal (or progressed) Pluto can symbolize a

deepening of one's thoughts. Information can be processed more clearly and efficiently. The mood of situations can be captured. One may communicate more of herself with fewer words. One could rise above the intellect into a right-brain awareness. Concentrative powers may excel. New mental stimulation and communication can bring out creativity. One may desire more depth in life experiences. A heightened perception can be exhibited. A deeper desire to penetrate the surface of oneself and life can occur.

One may feel as though her internal mental tape heads are being cleaned. Pluto can represent a purification of the mind when making contact with an air Ascendant. Conquering nervous anxiety may release pent-up energy. One may need less time to bond thoughts with actions. An intellectual individual may learn to trust highest instincts. A dynamic communicator may be born. One's social urges may lead to altruistic movements. An overly worried person may become empowered by trusting herself. One ceases surrendering to enslaving thoughts; subconscious karmic tendencies may be transcended.

WATER

Transiting Pluto conjunct a water Ascendant or a progressed water Ascendant conjunct natal (or progressed) Pluto can symbolize a dynamic emotional intensity. One may display an unusual awareness of subconscious motivations. New expressions of emotion or intuition may occur. One may awaken new power. Making peace with one's past can occur. One may break the hold of guilt. More self-reliance can manifest. A person can heal. Feeling the pain of others can make one a good counselor. An individual may help others survive loss or suffering. One may be more emotionally vulnerable. Watery Pluto is especially potent when conjunct a water Ascendant as this is a repeating theme. Shadow material or self-defeating behaviors may be transcended.

SHADOW

FIRE

Transiting Pluto conjunct a natal fire Ascendant or a progressed fire Ascendant conjunct natal (or progressed) Pluto can denote a person is too ego centered. Everything must be an extension of personal identity. Hasty judgment and endless argument can be typified. A person may hold anger within. Angry outbursts can come with no warning. Repressed anger may fill the body with toxins. A need to always be the leader may attract few followers. A fear of facing one's shortcomings can produce too much sensitivity to criticism. One may lack empathy for others. Feeling one is above the law can lead to disastrous consequences. One may fail to learn from past mistakes, reinforcing negative karmic history. Blocking the growth of others wins few admirers. Not appreciating one's own creativity can be harmful. One may fear finding one's true self.

EARTH

Transiting Pluto conjunct an earth Ascendant or a progressed earth Ascendant conjunct natal (or progressed) Pluto can indicate people are compulsively insecure unless accumulating tremendous resources. Success on the physical plane can become god. Individuals may chase physical desires in endless circles. Shallowness (lack of emotional depth) is possible. Greed and selfishness can occur. Manipulation to possess the wealth and freedom of others is possible. A callous attitude regarding the emotional needs of others can be exhibited. Ignoring continuity or history can lead to shortsightedness. One may be too hard on herself. The mind may be addicted to negativity. One's instincts for survival could be disoriented. A paranoid fear of failure can occur. One may feel too inadequate to compete with others.

AIR

Transiting Pluto conjunct a natal air Ascendant or a progressed air Ascendant conjunct natal (or progressed) Pluto can symbolize a fear of achieving mental depth. One may hide from self and others in the shadows of the mind. Lacking trust, one fears to communicate directly. One may compulsively fear the perceptions of others. Avoiding emotional pain keeps relationships from developing. One may rigidly adhere to fixed mental concepts. Lying or deceiving others can be a problem. A person's paranoia could distort mental perception. She can rationalize taking advantage of others.

A lack of flexibility can cause one to repeat mistakes. An individual may compulsively worry over situations long behind her. Failing to work through emotional residue keeps one a slave to the past.

An individual could be too spread out. Following too many paths causes mental exhaustion.

WATER

Transiting Pluto conjunct a natal water Ascendant or a progressed water Ascendant conjunct natal (or progressed) Pluto can indicate fear of one's own emotional intensity. This is a repeating theme as Pluto is a water planet (ruler of Scorpio). An individual can be too emotional. Every situation becomes a crisis, rather than a lesson learned. One may hide emotional vulnerability. An excessive dependency on others or emotional isolation is possible. Unfinished business with one's roots or past can disorient the present. A person may blame the past.

One's idealism may cause pain. She could resist love and new growth due to ideals being smashed. An addiction to escapist tendencies can be troublesome. Feeling like a victim leads to stagnation. One may refuse to be realistic about others, opening the door wide for emotional hurt. A denial of frustration with circumstances could keep one stuck in limiting situations.

Square: Transiting Pluto Square Natal Ascendant
Progressed Ascendant Square
Natal or Progressed Pluto

Transiting Pluto square the natal Ascendant or progressed Ascendant square natal (or progressed) Pluto can reflect honesty about identity issues. Individuals may go through intense, soul-searching periods. There is a friction in this aspect as identity and personal power instincts can be at odds, fighting within a person's consciousness for a rebirth. Letting go of relationships may be just as prevalent as starting new ones. A new cycle is indicated (which could involve career or moving).

FIRE

Transiting Pluto square a natal fire Ascendant or a progressed fire Ascendant square natal (or progressed) Pluto can denote raw courage. One may break through obstacles. A new consciousness in action can occur. A person may comprehend the impact of her actions upon others. Impatience and self-destructive tendencies might be mastered. A person may gain self-control to regulate the wildness of the fire element. One's own selfishness may be ruthlessly confronted. Pluto can draw fire back to the past to fix unresolved situations.

EARTH

Transiting Pluto square a natal earth Ascendant or a progressed earth Ascendant square natal or progressed Pluto can denote overcoming a compulsive security consciousness. A person may reach out with emotions. A person in limiting conditions may find new power. An individual's biggest crisis can be moving ahead and leaving the past behind. Bonding logic with intuition may begin healing or regeneration. Pluto can draw earth back to the past to create deep roots that support a road to the future.

AIR

Transiting Pluto square a natal air Ascendant or a progressed air Ascendant square natal (or progressed) Pluto can symbolize a new threshold for tolerating mental stress. A person may watch reality humble her conceptions of life. The psyche moves forward. Emotional intensity may combine with intellect into creative action. One may concentrate more and be more decisive. A person may become more organized and adept at doing complicated tasks. Learning may be stimulated. Communication can bring out one's charisma. Pluto can draw the air element back to the past to reflect upon perceptions.

WATER

Transiting Pluto square a natal water Ascendant or a progressed water Ascendant square natal (or progressed) Pluto can denote a deeper awareness of survival instincts. A person can bounce back from adversity. Environmental stress may drive one into higher consciousness. A person may clean up her past. A disoriented person may gain clarity and deal with reality. In rising above escapism, a karmic pattern may be transcended. A person may let go of emotional pain. Pluto can draw the water element to relive the past from a greater emotional clarity.

SHADOW

FIRE

Transiting Pluto square a natal fire Ascendant or a progressed fire Ascendant square natal (or progressed) Pluto can denote a compulsively ego-centered consciousness. Personal insecurity can cause ruthlessness. Fearing a loss of power may drive one to conquer others. One may tend toward aggression. Every action can be premeditated.

A person can lack self-confidence. A fear of conflict confines one to a life of misery. Self-hatred can be debilitating. Past-life identity issues may be repressed. Hiding from the truth about oneself throws life out of balance.

EARTH

Transiting Pluto square a natal earth Ascendant or a progressed earth Ascendant square natal (or progressed) Pluto can denote a compulsive drive to prove oneself. Accumulation of things and status may kill one's emotional instincts. One may hide behind a very dry persona. One may be paranoid about expressing emotions. An individual may feel unable to achieve success. One may experience a conflict involving self-control. Earthy, sensual appetites can get out of control.

AIR

Transiting Pluto square a natal air Ascendant or a progressed air Ascendant square natal (or progressed) Pluto can symbolize a lack of clear perception. One's thoughts may lack flexibility due to mistrust. Striking out at others and asking questions later can occur. "The best defense is a good offense" may dominate the thoughts.

A revengeful and sarcastic nature can disrupt social encounters. One may seek out vulnerable people to control them. A person may live on the surface of life. Perceptions may be bonded to a painful past. Mind games can be a way of life. One might hide behind a mental wall. Nervous exhaustion can deplete the individual. One can doubt her own intelligence. She may depend too much on outside stimulation. The other extreme is possible. A person could resist input or advice from others.

WATER

Transiting Pluto square a natal water Ascendant or a progressed water Ascendant square natal (or progressed) Pluto can denote a fear of intimacy. One may mistrust the wants of others. One may be driven (by self-conscious tendencies) into addictive behavior. A person may continue a karmic theme of running away.

An individual may be too sensitive to criticism. A need for approval may cause missed opportunities. An individual may become too secretive and reclusive. Strong dependency needs may lead one to stay too long in nonproductive situations. A fear of change may reach extreme proportions. Extreme moods make for inconsistency.

Quincunx: Transiting Pluto Quincunx Natal Ascendant
Progressed Ascendant Quincunx
Natal or Progressed Pluto

The quincunxes formed by transiting Pluto to the natal Ascendant or progressed Ascendant to natal (or progressed) Pluto are the **"Yoga of rebirth in identity."** A new self-image may emerge. One can leave an old self behind.

LIGHT

FIRE

Transiting Pluto quincunx a fire Ascendant or a progressed fire Ascendant quincunx natal (or progressed) Pluto can indicate new positive pride in oneself. An appreciation for one's own self-expression can occur. A person may find strength in showing more vulnerability. A feeling of freedom could occur. One may awaken to more physical energy. A self-centered person may develop a greater perception of others. One may stop finding identity through others.

EARTH

Transiting Pluto quincunx an earth Ascendant or a progressed earth Ascendant quincunx natal (or progressed) Pluto can denote a greater self-reliance. One may balance her own budget. A greater sharing of mental and emotional resources can be displayed. A more collective awareness may develop. An addiction to sensuality or other physical appetites may be transcended. One may reward herself for hard work. She can take more care of body and psyche. A spaced-out person may learn to organize. The "Type A" personality may learn to relax. One can conquer an intense emotional attachment to material things. One may leave dead-end situations.

AIR

Transiting Pluto quincunx a natal air Ascendant or a progressed air Ascendant quincunx natal (or progressed) Pluto can show a more positive self-image. Inner tapes of uncertainty may be erased. One may become more decisive. A dynamic clarity concerning self finds birth.

An overly intellectual individual may listen to instincts. She may finally admit "there is more to life than meets the eye." A greater emotional closeness can occur. One may stop trusting too much in the perceptions of others. Less possessive peers or partners can be found. Concentration improves and compulsive thoughts can be stopped.

WATER

Transiting Pluto quincunx a natal water Ascendant or a progressed water Ascendant quincunx natal (or progressed) Pluto can express as dynamic intuition. Extreme dependency is surrendered. A savior type learns to let others be more independent. Escapism can be converted into a passion for self-fulfillment. Creativity can overcome a fear of the unknown. A new devotion to an ideal or creative art may bring new power. A selfish person may learn to be more serving; a too devoted individual may find her own "piece of the pie." Karma can be dissolved. Escapism and guilt may be overcome through strong willpower.

SHADOW

FIRE

Transiting Pluto quincunx a natal fire Ascendant or a progressed fire Ascendant quincunx natal (or progressed) Pluto can express as a life of extremes. People can waste energy and resources. They may be emotional drains. People can be too optimistic and lack respect for universal laws. Others can be dominated. Or, this person could be easily dominated. Individuals can promise more than they deliver. Too much pride resists a new identity. A lack of assertion keeps one from realizing a new self-expression. Repressed anger can create difficulties.

EARTH

Transiting Pluto quincunx a natal earth Ascendant or a progressed earth Ascendant quincunx natal (or progressed) Pluto can express as a stubborn resistance to change. Holding onto the past may block growth. A person could lack respect for material items. One may be too easily taken advantage of by others. People can be power hungry and very controlling. A fear of failure could keep someone stuck in a rut. An individual may have problems bonding to jobs, people, home, etc.

AIR

Transiting Pluto quincunx a natal air Ascendant or a progressed air Ascendant quincunx natal (or progressed) Pluto can express as a paranoid mind. One may have great difficulty trusting. A suspicious nature may dominate. An individual could get too introspective. Changes may be poorly timed. A person's consciousness can fill with thoughts about power and money. A manipulative mindset could make closeness difficult. Emotions may not be trusted. An individual could be stuck in timid thoughts. A fear of expressing ideas could create imbalanced situations. One's mental nature could be disoriented by emotional conflict. A lack of life direction and unclear perceptions could result from self-deception.

WATER
Transiting Pluto quincunx a natal water Ascendant or a progressed water Ascendant quincunx natal (or progressed) Pluto can express as a fear of intuition. A person could give up power too easily. A tremendous desire to be loved could attract strange relationships. One may be abused physically, mentally, or spiritually. Individuals can fear decision making. People may be out of synch with emotional intensity. They may live their creative selves through others. Helpless victims or saviors can be indicated. One may fail to balance a karmic habit of escapism. Reality may be denied. Mood swings can be tremendous. People may lack the trust to communicate deep emotions. A person may continue to act out irrational past-life themes. One may hide from life.

    Opposition: Transiting Pluto Opposing Natal Ascendant
                   Progressed Ascendant Opposing
                   Natal or Progressed Pluto

Transiting Pluto opposing the Ascendant or the progressed Ascendant opposing natal (or progressed) Pluto can point to major life passages. Relating to others may deepen immensely. Relationships that lack understanding or depth may undergo major transformation. One may find key allies to strengthen self-understanding. The loss of a key partner can occur. Important partnerships might develop. Powerful allies or key power brokers can enter a person's life.

LIGHT

FIRE
Transiting Pluto opposing a natal fire Ascendant or a progressed fire Ascendant opposing natal (or progressed) Pluto indicates people can focus raw energy. They may master an undisciplined nature. Relationships may slow down and deepen. An individual may appreciate being part of a relationship. The independence of a fire Ascendant may learn to communicate and listen (air Descendant).

    More persuasiveness can emanate from a new self-confidence. An individual may mature quickly. A new respect for death or loss can occur. The fiery attitude that life will last forever can be humbled. A person can become more conscious of the rights of others. A nonassertive individual may assume more control. A need to be dominated can transform into sharing power and resources.

    Lasting relationships may replace a history of hit and run situations. One may successfully grieve through a difficult loss or past emotional conflict. A new higher consciousness can bring self-mastery. A person may intuitively tap into a more collective awareness. Peers attracted may contribute meaningfully to one's true identity.

EARTH

Transiting Pluto opposing a natal earth Ascendant or a progressed earth Ascendant opposing natal (or progressed) Pluto can indicate breaking away from a material consciousness. The logic of earth can be alchemized with intuition. An individual can experience a new emotional intensity. One may end a pattern of repressing creativity and emotions. A person may undergo a deep metamorphosis in personal relating. A desire to work amongst new peers is possible. A too self-reliant individual may be more vulnerable. An individual who attracts escapist partners may establish more balance. An individual can feel a debt has been repaid. A relationship may end that was stunting a person's growth.

A person may begin to truly understand others. A painful hurt from the end of a situation can lift one to higher consciousness. A person may release immense healing energy. A need to give and receive love could intensify. An individual may achieve a new identity by leaving behind a rigid and unimaginative self.

AIR

Transiting Pluto opposing a natal air Ascendant or a progressed air Ascendant opposing natal (or progressed) Pluto can express as clarity in perceiving others. Nervous anxiety when meeting people could be overcome. Someone could become a writer or communicator. Life can be understood on a deeper level. One may be an adept counselor, able to communicate the emotional needs of others. A person may help others integrate their lives. One may become more reflective when meeting people. A greater decisiveness may occur. An extreme intellectual type may become more emotional and spontaneous.

WATER

Transiting Pluto opposing a natal water Ascendant or a progressed water Ascendant opposing natal (or progressed) Pluto can indicate forgiving self or others. An individual can sense karmic ties. A very powerful self-transformation may occur. A person's escapism or denial of reality can be purged. A new peace is possible.

Relationships or peers may help foster stability. An individual may learn commitment. An overly dependent individual may express strength. Trust in one's instincts may emerge. An old self dies and a new self emerges. Creative intensity comes forward. An individual may become a more passionate human being. Collective causes may help fulfill highest goals.

SHADOW

FIRE

Transiting Pluto opposing a natal fire Ascendant or a progressed fire Ascendant opposing natal (or progressed) Pluto can express as a ruthless drive for power. A person may lack self-confidence and cling possessively to others. An extremely ego-centered individual may wish to enslave others. He could enjoy dependent people. Alternately, people can compulsively give up power. Individuals may be in constant power struggles.

A need for attention (fire Ascendant) could interfere with perceptions (air Descendant). An individual could be opinionated and judgmental. A tendency not to listen to others could make for reckless actions. One may be adept at manipulating situations. Big business deals could become all consuming. An individual may abuse the ideas of others. One may be led by passions, losing perspective. Losing sight of limits could be emotionally and physically exhausting.

EARTH

Transiting Pluto opposing a natal earth Ascendant or a progressed earth Ascendant opposing a natal (or progressed) Pluto can deny feeling. A person could be afraid of emotion. A compulsive drive for wealth or success could hide a fear of deep love. Trust may be shallow. Love could be conditional. The intuitive instincts may be flat. A person can be truly lonely — separate from self and others — "a stranger in a strange land."

Relationships could be emotional roller coasters. Balance is difficult as the individual seeks to create a life of extremes. A lack of trust may sabotage closeness. One's extreme practicality may alienate more emotional people. This can be someone trying to live emotions through others (water Descendant). Escaping into a relationship could be a disaster. A lack of self-examination does not prepare a person for crises. Feelings and emotions may be too unpredictable. Compulsive physical appetites could be an escape from the bonding process.

AIR

Transiting Pluto opposing a natal air Ascendant or a progressed air Ascendant opposing natal (or progressed) Pluto can express as a drive to get one's own way. A piercing intellect could divide and conquer. An individual may be a social animal but extremely lonely. A shallow perspective masks a fear of honest relating. An intellectual wall may keep others at a safe distance. An indecisive nature could miss opportunities. A person can be quick to blame others for personal shortcomings. A person could fear anger or intense emotions. One may attract unreliable individuals. Trusting the wrong people can occur. An individual may be too easily swayed from goals. The many facets of life are difficult to combine. One may try too hard to please others. She may resist the advice of others, and suffer the consequences.

WATER

Transiting Pluto opposing a natal water Ascendant or a progressed water Ascendant opposing natal (or progressed) Pluto can express as a disoriented emotional nature. One may be flooded by subconscious material. Refusing to go with the flow of higher consciousness can result in limiting life conditions. Relationships may explode in one's face. Looking for beauty in others will not fulfill the need for self-realization. A person's relationships could be parasitic. He could be too dependent or he could attract helpless people. A denial of past mistakes keeps one stuck in a confused self-image.

An individual may compulsively reenact karmic relating situations. One may hide emotional intensity. A too sensitive nature may be problematic. An overly suspicious nature can ruin relationships. A person could become addicted to others. A loss of power is destructive. An individual could be dominated sexually and emotionally. A person could refuse to investigate life mysteries. A fear of intimacy and trust yields a pattern of abortive relationships.

SOFT ASPECTS

> Sextile: Transiting Pluto Sextile Natal Ascendant
>   Progressed Ascendant Sextile
>   Natal or Progressed Pluto
>
> Trine: Transiting Pluto Trine Natal Ascendant
>   Progressed Ascendant Trine
>   Natal or Progressed Pluto

The soft Pluto/Ascendant aspects are not as driving to deepen the identity as the intense aspects. However, an individual with many intense aspects natally may use these aspects to explore life more deeply. New emotional intensity can be visible. A person may seek more self-understanding and inner motivations for actions.

LIGHT

FIRE

Transiting Pluto sextile a fire Ascendant or a progressed fire Ascendant sextile natal (or progressed) Pluto can express as a bond of identity and emotional intensity. One may conquer self-destructive habits.

A person could display a new depth in crises. Selfish interests (when feeling insecure) may blend into a greater awareness of others. A going-it-alone attitude might become willing to solicit advice. A burning excitement about life may awaken. An individual may feel the rebirth of passion for life. Understanding the patterns of one's life helps avoid repeating mistakes.

A person may find more creative ways to express emotional intensity. More direct communication may occur. A nonassertive individual may discover new power. A dominating, self-confident type could learn to compromise.

Transiting Pluto trine a natal fire Ascendant or a progressed fire Ascendant trine natal (or progressed) Pluto can denote self-acceptance. A new trust in life is discovered. A deep bond with creative instincts can occur. A person too driven by extremes can find moderation. Emotional self-understanding is displayed. Survival instincts help people get through challenges. A desire for growth brings new internal strength.

EARTH

Transiting Pluto sextile a natal earth Ascendant or a progressed earth Ascendant sextile natal (or progressed) Pluto can express as deepening one's true role in the world. Extending oneself in life accomplishments breeds excitement.

One may go beneath the surface of life and find new meaning. A fascination with life's mysteries could occur. More expression of feelings is possible. Relaxation and intensity may be combined.

A balance may form between material and emotional needs. An individual may become more self-sufficient. A self reliant type may consider the needs of others.

Transiting Pluto trine a natal earth Ascendant or a progressed earth Ascendant trine natal (or progressed) Pluto can symbolize greater decisiveness. A person can bring logic and intuition into a dynamic focus. Personal skills and resources could be used impressively. People could feel in touch with creative power. An urge for self-control could lead to a new career. Wasteful or fearful people may find a creative spirit. A hard persona could be dropped. Showing emotional vulnerability could attract new relationships.

AIR

Transiting Pluto sextile a natal air Ascendant or a progressed air Ascendant sextile natal (or progressed) Pluto can denote mastery of nervous tension. A person could conserve mental and emotional energy. Concentration can be maintained in the midst of conflict.

A person could develop passionate and charismatic communication. A more honest consideration of others' ideas may occur. An intellectualizer could communicate more feelings. Greater interest in mental processes is possible. Stimulation from new learning can occur. Allowing emotional closeness may attract new peers or lovers.

Transiting Pluto trine a natal air Ascendant or a progressed air Ascendant trine natal (or progressed) Pluto can denote a new depth in self-understanding. One may put plans into order. Mental process can be more instinctual.

A person may establish new peers. Emotional support is given and received more honestly. A person may make courageous changes in reasoning. Compulsive thoughts may become more rational. Negative thinking may be transcended.

WATER

Transiting Pluto sextile natal water Ascendant or a progressed water Ascendant sextile natal (or progressed) Pluto can express as adeptly reading unspoken language. One's right brain may intuit the actions of others. A person could thoroughly grasp the bonding process. One may relate to others on a soul level.

People may overcome a highly suspicious nature. A greater trust in one's emotional intensity may attract good situations. This can be a cleansing of the mind. The cosmic composter, Pluto, can symbolize cleaning up one's act. She may free herself of emotional junk. One may heal from a disastrous past. A person could integrate past-life, escapist tendencies into a more positive expression.

An understanding of death, subconscious tenderness, and life's mysteries could be illuminating. A new personal style could reflect intuitive clarity. A person can direct emotional intensity.

Transiting Pluto trine a water Ascendant or a progressed water Ascendant trine natal (or progressed) Pluto can express as control over emotional intensity. A person could embrace a bigger world, perhaps joining a collective cause. A person might tap into higher consciousness.

A timid individual may gain new confidence. A person may find hidden talent. A spiritual search can awaken. One can hunger for rebirth. A person may gain a great vision of family ancestry. She may have a special purpose to reverse a behavioral trend, such as substance abuse or other escapism. A clarity concerning past-life themes is possible.

SHADOW

FIRE

The Pluto/fire Ascendant sextile or trine can denote a fear of being oneself. A person may lack drive. She may lack follow-through. A person could be emotionally burned out. She may go so fast that exhaustion results. A compulsive need for action or environmental stimulation may throw one's life out of balance.

One may manipulate situations. A person might not listen to others. Dominating the thoughts of others can be a problem. Self-centeredness can be extreme. A person may not see around a big ego. A need to control others can color the personality.

Excessive pride can keep one from getting needed support. A fear of showing vulnerability can be covered by an air of self-confidence. A compulsive drive for power can alienate or enslave others. One may distort his intentions to dominate.

A devotion to extreme causes could be dangerous. Extreme groups may suffocate a person's own power. Ignoring limits leads one into impulsive and reckless situations. This person might never have enough money or pleasure.

EARTH

The Pluto/earth Ascendant sextile or trine can express as too much security-consciousness. A person may resist new growth. An individual may have difficulty trusting emotions. A lack of insight regarding others may occur. A lack of depth may foster a lack of trust. Inflexible communications can be a problem. A lack of imagination or investigative instincts can keep one stuck in limiting situations.

One may totally identify with the physical senses. Compulsive appetites may keep one earth-bound. A denial of a higher consciousness can cause one to repeat mistakes. A wasteful nature may be exhibited. One may slip into crises due to a lack of insight.

AIR

The Pluto/air Ascendant sextile or trine can express as a paranoid individual. One may not think for herself. Irrational fears (due to a nervous nature) are possible. A lack of flexibility in making decisions can be problematic. A person can be so emotionally stressed that thoughts run together. One may lack the discipline or focus to slow down. Too much faith in the intellect could deny intuition. Thoughts may take away from the miracle of life.

A person could keep others at a safe distance. Emotions could seem threatening. Blocked spontaneity could cause missed opportunities. There can be too much privacy. One may be a loner to the point of evading emotions.

A person could suffer from a depressed state. Perhaps high expectations of self or others are not being met. A person could sabotage her happiness. An addiction to negativity could be a problem. Lack of trust in others might be extreme. Jumping to conclusions is possible. Harsh judgments can occur.

WATER

The Pluto/water Ascendant sextile or trine can express as escapism. One can dive into a world of illusion and think it is reality. A thirst for creative expression may throw one's life out of balance. A complete devotion to a spiritual existence may deny physical comforts. A lack of groundedness may lead to irresponsibility.

An individual may deny emotions. A fear of one's past may keep him stuck in an uninspired present. A person might be too dependent on support of peers or partners. A fear of change may occur. Transitions are perceived as threats. One consistently runs from conflict.

A drive for fame and power can be compulsive. People stop at nothing to obtain a goal. Another person can be afraid to express any power. One may be too easily talked out of personal needs. He may listen to the wrong people.

An oversensitivity to criticism may keep a person from showing true feelings. A refusal to open up to others may produce shallow relationships. Passivity can hide emotional intensity. One may be too swayed by an addiction to people, substances, etc. Refusing to face problems could lead to an endless chain of difficult circumstances.

DAWN

Ascendant/Pluto aspects can indicate a tenacious creative spirit. One may experience a powerful rebirth. The cosmic composting of Pluto can raise the identity from the ashes of an old self. People can go beyond apparent roadblocks to new power. Self-mastery can become a powerful tool. A person's subconscious can become a great ally.

The spontaneity of natal and progressed fire Ascendants can be given a focus by steady Pluto; the caution of natal and progressed earth Ascendants can be hypnotized into action by the magnetism of Pluto; the detachment and aloofness of natal and progressed air Ascendants can be transformed into feeling by the bonding instincts of Pluto; the sensitivity and intuition of natal and progressed water Ascendants can be lifted into a new vision by the self-mastery of Pluto.

CHAPTER ELEVEN

PLANET/MIDHEAVEN ASPECTS

Planet/Midheaven aspects point to developing cultural roles, whether it is career, parenting, volunteer, etc. One's game plan can be changing. Progressed and transiting planets aspecting the natal Midheaven or progressed Midheaven aspecting a natal (or progressed) planet can indicate new unfolding ambition.

SUN/MIDHEAVEN ASPECTS

Progressed Sun /Natal or Progressed Midheaven
Progressed Midheaven/Natal Sun

Process:	A Revitalized Game Plan
Ally:	Creative Enthusiasm
Illusion:	False Pride

Sun/Midheaven aspects can symbolize creative growth through cultural roles. The challenge is not getting lost in self-importance. Drives to exhibit talents can be strong. These aspects can denote a new pride. Individuals may find self-confidence. They might shine through cultural roles. The game plan can be a combination of creative enjoyment (Sun) and strong focus (Midheaven).

INTENSE ASPECTS

Conjunction:	Progressed Sun Conjunct Natal Midheaven
	Progressed Midheaven Conjunct Natal Sun
Square:	Progressed Sun Square Natal Midheaven
	Progressed Midheaven Square Natal Sun

LIGHT
Progressed Sun conjunct the natal Midheaven or progressed Midheaven conjunct the natal Sun can denote finding a creative cultural expression. **This is a major aspect!** One may enjoy a creative game plan. People may display leadership ability. They can learn self-confidence. A hidden personality shows talents.

Individuals get more serious about ambitions. Getting recognized professionally commonly occurs. **Career changes are likely.** The pleasure-oriented, fiery Sun is focused by the earthy 10th house. This can be the start of a creative process that culminates years later. A serious person can learn to combine pleasure and work. A public life can be balanced with private life. One may enjoy the dual roles of career and parenting.

Progressed Sun square the natal Midheaven or progressed Midheaven square natal Sun can resolve a conflict regarding self-expression. An individual may put more energy into creative talent. A passion for life is no longer hidden. An overly serious person learns to flow. Combining pleasure and work can be challenging.

A forceful personality can see that always leading is not reasonable. Slowing down and enjoying life brings greater purpose. Individuals may stop getting lost in work. Power motives may be understood. **A new career challenge can give confidence**. Individuals can overcome dependency needs. Extremely self-sufficient types find that some dependency is okay.

SHADOW
Both the **Sun/Midheaven conjunction and square** can express as a dictator-like nature. One can be a controller. Leadership and self-importance seem all-consuming.

Creative self-expression can lose to material greed. One may be a mastermind at accumulating material wealth. Emotional resources can be bankrupt. Career drives could carelessly sacrifice loved ones. One may ask others to compromise their needs to support ambitions. A person can allow a career setback to destroy his life. Too much attachment to success kills other creative expressions. Individuals may fear taking a risk. A lack of vitality can be related to emotional problems.

Real circumstances and hidden idealism can conflict. One may be confused. A person may get frustrated with not enough opportunity or resources available to realize full potential. One may lack the willpower to fulfill deepest needs. Insecurity can dominate the life. A deeper life purpose is resisted. A fixed or stubborn mentality can make compromise difficult. One may be too attached to power. One might avoid making transitions or choosing new options.

Quincunx: Progressed Sun Quincunx Natal Midheaven
Progressed Midheaven Quincunx Natal Sun

Opposition: Progressed Sun Opposing Natal Midheaven
Progressed Midheaven Opposing Natal Sun

LIGHT

Progressed Sun quincunx the natal Midheaven or the progressed Midheaven quincunx the natal Sun can denote blossoming creative intensity. This is the **"Yoga of expressing creative ambition."**

A person lacking pride can find confidence. Those with excessive pride can become less self-important. Individuals in nongrowth-promoting careers can make an adjustment. Those being dominated by authority figures can speak out. Bossy individuals can become less dominating.

A setback in life may deepen willpower. One may show strength and resolve in not losing a creative spirit. A sober understanding of creative potential readies one for new opportunities. A humble attitude attracts love and respect.

The **progressed Sun opposing the natal Midheaven or the progressed Midheaven opposing the natal Sun** can symbolize a more sensitive game plan filled with love and purpose. One's life may deepen significantly. Spiritual discovery can take place. A need for roots (family or emotional sharing) can come forward. **Relocation or moving into a new home can occur**.

A longing to digest the past can occur. A person may find new emotional strength. A more authentic willpower can blossom. Grieving a loss may free emotional energy. One may retreat temporarily from the outer world. Privacy can reveal clarity. An exhausted psyche is repaired. A sabbatical is nourishing.

Family ties can support creative identity. One may reach out with love and a dynamic compassion. An individual may learn self-acceptance. The home can be an inspirational source of energy. **The purchase of a home or property is possible**.

One may reevaluate career goals. The entire game plan may be discarded for a new focus. The slate may be cleared, to courageously start over.

SHADOW

Both the **Sun/Midheaven quincunx and opposition** can reflect a person feeling isolated. Life can be an ego trip. Power drives cover insecurities. Holding onto fears blocks free self-expression.

Overrating the world of form inhibits emotional growth. Proving one's importance to others creates misery. A lack of love for self or others is painful. Vitality could be low. One may do little to change. Worn-out identities still linger in the closet. Creative imagination is overshadowed by self-doubts. One may try to live life through others. This could be children, more dominating individuals, or even more creative individuals. One's own emotional intensity seems lost.

SOFT ASPECTS

Sextile: Progressed Sun Sextile Natal Midheaven
          Progressed Midheaven Sextile Natal Sun

Trine: Progressed Sun Trine Natal Midheaven
          Progressed Midheaven Trine Natal Sun

LIGHT

The **progressed Sun sextile the natal Midheaven or the progressed Midheaven sextile the natal Sun** can denote creative self-expression finding new directions. An individual can be excited about new career opportunities.

One may derive pleasure from ambitions. Individuals can enjoy the support of family and peers for most cherished goals. A person may not take life so seriously. A type "A" can stop forcing issues. Greater spontaneity and pleasure are possible. Individuals can be grateful for the love received in life.

Progressed Sun trine a natal Midheaven or the progressed Midheaven trine the natal Sun can express as joy concerning a life purpose. One may feel in harmony with willpower and creativity. Happiness with environmental surroundings is possible.

Emotional and material abundance can be shared. One may attract good situations through an optimistic spirit. Enthusiasm may create new opportunities. A creative risk may inspire growth. Leadership may be recognized. Promotion may bring new challenges. Confidence can be at an all-time high.

SHADOW

Both the **Sun/Midheaven sextile and trine** can express as self-centered tendencies. One may carelessly tell others how to live. Trying to do too much for others is possible. One may not recognize his own limits. Risks can prove foolish.

People may grow too impatient with present circumstances. Individuals may feel driven to get attention. A lack of confidence can leave one in limiting situations. An individual may wait too long to make changes. A person may fear taking a risk.

DAWN

Sun/Midheaven aspects can indicate creative vitality. Self-respect can reach new heights. Compulsive urges for power and visibility can be surrendered. One may find the courage to express creative potential. Love can be shared with others. Public and private happiness can be a reality. **New career successes and directions are accentuated!**

MOON/MIDHEAVEN ASPECTS

Progressed Moon/Natal or Progressed Midheaven
Progressed Midheaven/Natal Moon

Process: Balancing a Private and Public Life
Ally: Embracing Life Transitions
Illusion: Hiding in the Safety of the Past

Moon/Midheaven aspects can denote changing cultural roles. There is a natural tension as the 4th chord Moon naturally opposes the 10th house. Intuition is challenged by real circumstances. Combining dependency needs with taking responsibility can present interesting challenges. Career and home change can be symbolized. One may desire work and a home life that fit present needs. She may make changes to feel less pressured by everyday life.

INTENSE ASPECTS
Conjunction: Progressed Moon Conjunct
                Natal or Progressed Midheaven
                Progressed Midheaven Conjunct Natal Moon

Square: Progressed Moon Square
                Natal or Progressed Midheaven
                Progressed Midheaven Square Natal Moon

LIGHT
The **progressed Moon conjunct the natal (or progressed) Midheaven or the progressed Midheaven conjunct the natal Moon** can symbolize intuitive clarity regarding cultural roles. Individuals easily combine a private and public life. Moving into a different home can be indicated. Dealing with real estate purchases or selling property is just as likely. Relocating for a job is possible. People may take responsibility as well as being open to help from others.

Sensitivity could make one a good leader. Business sense can develop. Individuals may attract support for their ambitions. A private person may exhibit hidden talents. A follower can become a leader. Individuals too dependent on others can find their own way in the world.

People can become active in community projects. One may work closely with others to promote change. Organizing skills can be displayed.

The game plan may be adjusted to meet security needs. One may find a cultural identity that fulfills ideals and financial needs. Change may free stagnant psychic energy.

Progressed Moon square the natal (or progressed) Midheaven or the progressed Midheaven square the natal Moon can denote solving an emotional conflict. A lack of internal security can be resolved.

One may transcend past emotional problems. A lack of groundedness may be conquered through a regular schedule. Running away from problems is no longer the first impulse. Taking care of business is strengthening.

Individuals can find security through a career. Sharing love or nurturing energy can give the life extra purpose.

SHADOW

Both the **Moon/Midheaven conjunction and square** can express as emotional confusion. People may feel they have no direction. They can be too dependent on others. A person may lack intuitive insight.

Unresolved tension can fill career and home. Individuals may go to extremes in either direction. The career can become a compulsive dream; home a total refuge to hide from the outer world. Security instincts are in disarray. One's past and present make a disorienting kaleidoscope of loose ends.

Responsibility may provoke tension. People can play Mom and Dad for lovers. Taking too much responsibility keeps a relationship imbalanced.

Nongrowth situations may prevail. People may fear making an important transition. Clinging to the past could be limiting. Tradition or familiar territory is selected over a risk.

Quincunx: Progressed Moon Quincunx
             Natal or Progressed Midheaven
           Progressed Midheaven Quincunx Natal Moon

Opposition: Progressed Moon Opposing
             Natal or Progressed Midheaven
           Progressed Midheaven Opposing Natal Moon

LIGHT

Progressed Moon quincunx the natal (or progressed) Midheaven or the progressed Midheaven quincunx natal Moon can connote a new intuitive game plan. This aspect is the **"Yoga of securing an authentic game plan."**

Individuals can achieve emotional stability. Emotional currents are constructively channeled. People put their lives in order. Internal strife is resolved. One may assume more responsibility. One stops running away from life.

One may gain clarity about a painful past. Individuals can courageously live ideals. A fear of authority figures can be surrendered. Security instincts can find strength through taking on responsibility. One may break through excessive dependency needs. A fear of being alone is put to rest.

Progressed Moon opposing the natal (or progressed) Midheaven or progressed Midheaven opposing the natal Moon can

denote new internal security. This is a powerful symbolism as the progressed Moon conjunct the natal (or progressed) 4th house (or progressed 4th house conjunct natal Moon) is a **repeating theme**. Individuals may have different priorities in life. Family may come first now. Subconscious processes can gain importance. Individuals find more emotional depth. Career may deepen in purpose. A life lacking love or roots can dig for emotional content. **People often make major home shifts with this aspect.** Purchasing, selling, decorating or a change in who lives in the home is possible.

Moods can get stabilized. One may face a difficult past. More emotional energy can be shared. One may desire to feel needed. A person with a limited life purpose may get more ambition. One may integrate a public role with a private life. A working parent can spend more time with family.

A hardened individual can learn to love again. Intimacy can become a real need. One may enjoy the closeness of friends or family. Individuals may confront karmic habits. Both the Moon and 4th house are water motifs. This could be a time of conquering shadowy secrets. Compulsive fears may be surrendered. A fear to be loved or express feelings can be released. One can become more at home with herself.

SHADOW

Both the **Moon/Midheaven quincunx and opposition** can express as a life of isolation. Privacy may be extreme. One may fear closeness. Emotional pain can keep individuals disoriented. Running away from good relationships can be a habit. One may be attracted to self-destructive situations.

Insecurity can prevent one from trying new challenges. Career or life purpose can lack meaning.

Individuals can be too attached to public roles. Inattention to private life creates tension. One may selfishly need career support. Individuals can be too self-reliant. They do not delegate authority. A person may manipulate others by appearing helpless.

Moods may be strange and unpredictable. Hiding emotional intensity causes sudden outbursts.

SOFT ASPECTS

Sextile:	Progressed Moon Sextile
	Natal or Progressed Midheaven
	Progressed Midheaven Sextile Natal Moon
Trine:	Progressed Moon Trine
	Natal or Progressed Midheaven
	Progressed Midheaven Trine Natal Moon

LIGHT

Progressed Moon sextile the natal (or progressed) Midheaven or the progressed Midheaven sextile the natal Moon can symbolize an exciting transition. Individuals can find calm within a storm. A more objective approach to life is possible. Individuals may not take themselves so seriously. This period can be highly productive. One may show good business sense. New challenges are welcomed. Intuition may guide one. A secure feeling may confirm life choices.

Progressed Moon trine the natal (or progressed) Midheaven or the progressed Midheaven trine the natal Moon can symbolize a strong intuitive vision. The game plan may be in full glory. A person can enjoy the support of authority figures, peers, or loved ones. A person may feel inner and outer life are in harmony. Cultural roles and private life are both fulfilling. One may adeptly tune into the moods of situations. Transitions can be excellently timed.

SHADOW

Both the **Moon/Midheaven sextile and trine** can express as living in a fantasy world. One may exhibit childish responses to challenging situations, perhaps acting helpless to escape. One may be too accustomed to a soft life. Depending on parents or others creates a spoiled life.

Intuition may be asleep or dormant. Emotional energy may be sluggish. One may lack passion for life ambitions. Workaholics could try to derive too much satisfaction from career. Security could be compulsively attached to a show of success.

DAWN

Moon/Midheaven aspects can connote a nice combination of intuition and serious ambition. One may be firm yet caring; dreamy but responsible; happy at home and in public life.

Subjective and objective reality can be in harmony. One may clean out the closets of the subconscious. The present can be lived with a clear conscience.

MERCURY/MIDHEAVEN ASPECTS

Progressed Mercury/Natal or Progressed Midheaven Progressed Midheaven/Natal Mercury

Process:	Perceiving Cultural Roles
Ally:	Evolving Perceptions Based on Practical Experiences
Illusion:	Concepts Tainted by Fear and Cultural Bias

Mercury/Midheaven aspects can symbolize a deepening life purpose. One may wish to communicate through new structures. Perceptions and thoughts can become very focused. Individuals can move swiftly into new careers. One may be mentally exhilarated by new opportunities.

INTENSE ASPECTS
Conjunction: Progressed Mercury Conjunct
                 Natal or Progressed Midheaven
                 Progressed Midheaven Conjunct Natal Mercury
Square: Progressed Mercury Square
                 Natal or Progressed Midheaven
                 Progressed Midheaven Square Natal Mercury

LIGHT
Progressed Mercury conjunct the natal (or progressed) Midheaven or the progressed Midheaven conjunct natal Mercury can symbolize communication skills being recognized. A person may arouse interest in his life work.

Individuals may develop a solid life purpose. They apply skills seriously. A disorganized person can get his life together. One may accomplish ambitions. Individuals may excel at versatile careers or cultural roles. Perceptions can be grounded. One may be an excellent negotiator.

People may find that new challenges build confidence. Responsibility may bring out one's talents. Ideas may be well received by authority figures. Power may not go to one's head. An ability to lead others can be shown.

Progressed Mercury square the natal (or progressed) Midheaven or the progressed Midheaven square natal Mercury can express as a passion to communicate. One may think quickly in tense circumstances.

Skillfully perceiving details can aid in handling life. One may describe situations well. He may shoot at full throttle toward serious ambitions. People can resolve conflicts with others. Individuals can bounce back from setbacks. One may be ferociously determined to find a deeper life purpose. The mind can be lightning fast!

SHADOW
Both the **Mercury/Midheaven conjunction and square** can express as a lack of ambition. A meaningful purpose is missing. Individuals may have trouble integrating private and public life. One could get too carried away with career ideas. Jumping from one big idea to another could lead to nowhere.

An overly serious disposition can alienate others. One may lack flexibility. Thoughts can get fixated on only one type of success. Worry over meaningless details can lead to trouble. A failure to delegate can create a workaholic, laboring until completely exhausted.

Quincunx: Progressed Mercury Quincunx
Natal or Progressed Midheaven
Progressed Midheaven Quincunx Natal Mercury

Opposition: Progressed Mercury Opposing
Natal or Progressed Midheaven
Progressed Midheaven Opposing Natal Mercury

LIGHT

Progressed Mercury quincunx the natal (or progressed) Midheaven or progressed Midheaven quincunx natal Mercury can denote mental strength. Someone can find confidence through learning new mental skills. This quincunx is the **"Yoga of clarifying ambitions."**

An individual may stop growing nervous with new challenges. Negative thoughts can be neutralized. Small successes build confidence. Thoughts and daily habits gain focus. An individual can program the mind with positive affirmations.

A passive person can take control of life. A haphazard existence can be grounded by a clearer life purpose. Individuals may stop trying too hard to be accepted. Perceptions can be based on mental clarity rather than fears.

Progressed Mercury opposing the natal (or progressed) Midheaven or progressed Midheaven opposing natal Mercury can symbolize a new perspective regarding cultural roles (or a game plan). Individuals may think through ambitions. More emotional content may be pursued. A life is no longer filled with too much routine.

A dry existence can find love; an empty life purpose deeper commitment. A person may allow himself to need others. An intellectual can learn to feel. One may communicate with more feeling and perceive with more intuitive awareness. Constant busyness is modified with quiet contemplation. Thinking only about public visibility is balanced by a private life. Space can bring peace. Organizing a home or work space can be accomplished. **Negotiating to buy a home or searching for a place to live is possible.**

SHADOW

Both the **Mercury/Midheaven quincunx and opposition** can denote a fear of communicating openly. One may settle for nongrowth. People may doubt their own perceptions. Compulsive second-guessing leads to frustration. One's intelligence could be hidden due to a lack of confidence.

A fear of authority figures can be displayed. One may be too sensitive to the opinions of others. Individuals may not learn new skills. Staying in ruts becomes a way of life. A person may be too dependent on the ideas of others. A lack of flexibility in finding options to problems can be shown. One may feel lonely. Broader social contacts are denied. Negative thinking can be destructive.

SOFT ASPECTS

Sextile: Progressed Mercury Sextile
Natal or Progressed Midheaven
Progressed Midheaven Sextile Natal Mercury

Trine: Progressed Mercury Trine
Natal or Progressed Midheaven
Progressed Midheaven Trine Natal Mercury

LIGHT

Progressed Mercury sextile the natal (or progressed) Midheaven or progressed Midheaven sextile natal Mercury can symbolize a more versatile nature. New challenges might be enjoyed. One may initiate ideas that stimulate growth in others. Perceptions may be quick and accurate.

The life purpose can awaken. A bored mentality can shine with brilliance. One may stimulate others to new mental heights. This is a good aspect for business. One may have the mental clarity to make the right moves.

Progressed Mercury trine the natal (or progressed) Midheaven or the progressed Midheaven trine natal Mercury can denote mental confidence. One may make others feel at ease. A gentle but firm approach to life may lead to accomplishments. Individuals may possess the broad vision not to be distracted by details.

Fairness can be displayed. One may be businesslike and sensitive to needs of others. Individuals can prove to be trustworthy and reliable.

SHADOW

Both the **Mercury/Midheaven trine and sextile** can express as shallow perceptions. One can consistently look for easy answers. A lazy mental nature may not take advantage of opportunities. Individuals may be unreliable. They may fear responsibility. One may be forgetful and lack concentration.

A nervous nature may cause one to skim through life. Getting trapped by endless details distracts one from a broader vision. Individuals may be too influenced by authority figures. Thinking for oneself can be denied.

DAWN

Mercury/Midheaven aspects can indicate deepened mental perceptions. This can be an interesting life chapter filled with new learning ability. One may focus more mental energy into serious life pursuits. This time can be exhilarating. New challenges test one's ability to think for himself.

Progressed Venus/Natal or Progressed Midheaven Progressed Midheaven/Natal Venus

Process:	Determining a Value System
Ally:	A Drive for Excellence
Illusion:	Too Much Emphasis on Style

Venus/Midheaven aspects can point to a deepening value system. Needs that will bring pleasure or reward can manifest. One may reassess one's career and financial situation. A desire for physical comfort can bring a change in career drives. The aesthetic themes of Venus might combine with the career-oriented 10th house into artistic expression.

INTENSE ASPECTS

Conjunction: Progressed Venus Conjunct
Natal or Progressed Midheaven
Progressed Midheaven Conjunct Natal Venus

Square: Progressed Venus Square Natal or
Progressed Midheaven
Progressed Midheaven Square Natal Venus

LIGHT

Progressed Venus conjunct the natal (or progressed) Midheaven or the progressed Midheaven conjunct natal Venus can symbolize bringing the life into harmony. People may find a meaningful career. Social urges can lead one into contact with supportive individuals.

A person may be talented aesthetically. She can make creative expression known. Individuals may be rewarded for hard, dedicated work. Values or needs may be put into a hierarchy of importance. One may passionately express highest values. One could help others manage their lives. One may be a good supervisor or manager. One can deal with people using sixth sense. One may be firm yet sensitive to needs of others.

Counseling ability can blossom. Others relax in one's presence. A peacemaker, consultant, or arbitrator can be exhibited. Buying property can occur.

Progressed Venus square the natal (or progressed) Midheaven or the progressed Midheaven square natal Venus can symbolize overcoming career obstacles. One may leave a work identity behind. A serious relationship can be indicated. One may be in the midst of multiple expressions. A new career, or creative expression can take place.

A commitment to values can be shown. One may resolve a conflict between work and relationships. A person can find time for both. Desiring a more suitable living situation could occur.

SHADOW

Both the **Venus/Midheaven conjunction and square** can express as extreme vanity. One may not be authentic with people. Joviality could mask inner confusion. Emotional emptiness is hidden by a show of happiness. Career drives may throw life out of balance. Home and relationships are neglected. One may compulsively seek attention from others. A desire for social stimulation can keep one from facing emotional problems.

People may not reach for highest values. Apathy could abort a chance to show creative gifts. One may fear being rejected, causing career or relationships to suffer. A lack of inner understanding regarding emotions can occur. One may be more attracted to jobs and relationships that offer glamour. Substance can be denied by extreme desire for outer style.

Quincunx: Progressed Venus Quincunx
Natal or Progressed Midheaven
Progressed Midheaven Quincunx Natal Venus

Opposition: Progressed Venus Opposing
Natal or Progressed Midheaven
Progressed Midheaven Opposing Natal Venus

LIGHT

Progressed Venus quincunx natal (or progressed) Midheaven or progressed Midheaven quincunx natal Venus can connote making values more realistic. This aspect is the **"Yoga of fine tuning a value system."**

Individuals may overcome self-indulgence. Sensual and relationship urges may be brought under control. One may understand one's underlying motives for extreme attention and sensual pleasure.

Very reserved individuals can find more confidence. One may learn to market abilities. Social instincts may become more spontaneous. An emotionally hurt person can recover. Life gains a new focus.

Progressed Venus opposing the natal (or progressed) Midheaven or the progressed Midheaven opposing natal Venus can symbolize balancing dependency needs. Being a follower can end. One may leave behind childish fears. A war with a parent can be resolved.

Individuals may ground emotional intensity. Emotional energy can be channeled into creative expression. One may find stability and confidence through a successful job.

Home and career can be balanced. An outer show can be surrendered. One may find greater self-honesty. Intimacy needs can grow strong. Real love and emotional sharing strengthen the spirit. Love itself and affection may become as valued as a career. One may move towards emotional growth. Decorating a home is enjoyable. Living with new partners or peers is possible.

SHADOW
Both the **Venus/Midheaven quincunx and opposition** can express
as sacrificing values to the highest bidder. One can lose self-respect.
Career can focus too much on money. Relationships may be pursued for
status and power only.

Emotional disorientation can be denied. Relationships can lack commitment or balance. One may be taken advantage of materially or emotionally. A fear of loneliness can keep a person enslaved to limiting
relationships. A fear of failure can keep one in a dead-end job.

One's idealism may lead to unrealistic expectations. One may enter
new situations with no realism. Values may be set too high for self or
others. One may try to climb impossible mountains. People may lack a
balanced private and public life. One may be too addicted to limelight.
Emotional loneliness can be a reality.

SOFT ASPECTS
Sextile: Progressed Venus Sextile
              Natal or Progressed Midheaven
              Progressed Midheaven Sextile Natal Venus

Trine: Progressed Venus Trine
              Natal or Progressed Midheaven
              Progressed Midheaven Trine Natal Venus

LIGHT
**Progressed Venus sextile the natal (or progressed) Midheaven
or progressed Midheaven sextile natal Venus** can symbolize important contacts whether business or romantic. A person may move
into a new career direction. This may be a flowing time period, full of
emotional well being. A shy individual may find social confidence. An
emotionally reserved person learns to express feelings. A serious person learns to enjoy life.

**Progressed Venus trine the natal (or progressed) Midheav-
en or the progressed Midheaven trine natal Venus** can connote
emotional ease. One may feel good about the present and future. A positive disposition may attract harmonious situations. One may attract
support for ambitions. A hardworking individual may enjoy rewards
for labor. A creative flow can express through aesthetics.

SHADOW
Both the **Venus/Midheaven sextile and trine** can express as a shallow value system. One may be too interested in saying what others want
to hear.

Individuals may fear hard work. They want life to come easily with
little effort. A material consciousness may dominate. One may feel unimportant without rich status symbols.

Relationships may lack depth. One may avoid showing true emotions. She may jump from one relationship or career to another, avoiding commitments.

DAWN

Venus/Midheaven aspects can denote an evolving value system. One may tune into deepest needs. Individuals can enjoy self-satisfaction.

Peers may stimulate career goals. One may reap the benefits of hard work. Greater confidence in decision making can be shown. One no longer fears rejection by others.

MARS/MIDHEAVEN ASPECTS

Progressed Mars/Natal or Progressed Midheaven Progressed Midheaven/Natal Mars

Process:	A Competitive Spirit
Ally:	The Courage to be Oneself
Illusion:	Always Having to be Number One

Mars/Midheaven aspects can symbolize a dynamic expression of identity. This can be a high flying time. One can initiate many new experiences. Directness and decisiveness can be shown.

Important career decisions can occur. One may courageously take on a new challenge. The shackles of limiting ideas can be broken. Identity and ambition can be powerful allies.

INTENSE ASPECTS

Conjunction: Progressed Mars Conjunct
                Natal or Progressed Midheaven
                Progressed Midheaven Conjunct Natal Mars

Square: Progressed Mars Square
                Natal or Progressed Midheaven
                Progressed Midheaven Square Natal Mars

LIGHT

Progressed Mars conjunct the natal (or progressed) Midheaven or the progressed Midheaven conjunct natal Mars can symbolize a new intensity regarding career. One may courageously pursue a new challenge. Work or activities that involve danger can be appealing.

People can overcome fear of failure. Shy individuals can more assertively forge ahead, taking charge of situations.

Parents can relate to their children more directly. A new burst of energy is put into parental and career roles. Individuals may break away from dominating others. They may become more assertive in negotiating business deals. One may impress authority figures with leadership ability. Others can be inspired to action.

Ambitions are followed through. A procrastinator can get moving; a quitter can work harder; a type "A" personality may learn to delegate.

One may learn patience. Focusing power can be tremendous. Selfish interests can blossom into a greater awareness. Shortsighted energy bursts can mature into solid, responsible action.

Progressed Mars square the natal (or progressed) Midheaven or progressed Midheaven square natal Mars can denote forcefully accomplishing desired aims. One may learn a wiser use of power — letting others be themselves rather than being bossy. One may tap into the cause of rebellious behavior. Past authority figures may still bring pain and frustration. One may learn to not take anger out on innocent people.

A person with destructive tendencies can learn to channel anger. Control of intensity can become an art. One may stop bullying. A too-passive individual can make needs and assertion more visible. Actions can attract respect. One may learn a little self-admiration is okay.

Overreaction and angry outbursts can be modified. One may learn to think about consequences.

SHADOW

Both the **Mars/Midheaven conjunction and square** can express as frustration for self or others. A person may lack conviction. Childish rebellion to get one's way can occur. Irresponsible behaviors can ruin opportunities.

One may pursue career goals too selfishly. Loved ones can be neglected. Family obligations may be ignored or forgotten.

Ignoring intimacy needs can alienate others. One may be in too big of a hurry, not completing things. Individuals may not face root causes of anger. A "macho-facho" behavior covers insecurities. People may rebel without understanding hidden anger.

A lack of assertion can keep one frustrated. Following the herd instinct dilutes one's personal identity. One may fear his own intensity.

Individuals can get too big-headed. The need for power and new worlds to conquer becomes a compulsive drive. One may lack an indepth life purpose. An identity totally focused on outward success may be totally fractured.

Quincunx: Progressed Mars Quincunx
Natal or Progressed Midheaven
Progressed Midheaven Quincunx Natal Mars

Opposition: Progressed Mars Opposing
Natal or Progressed Midheaven
Progressed Midheaven Opposing Natal Mars

LIGHT

Progressed Mars quincunx natal (or progressed) Midheaven or the progressed Midheaven quincunx natal Mars can symbolize a more uplifting game plan. Individuals can express a newfound passion for life. This quincunx is the **"Yoga of a resurrected game plan."**

A tired spirit can find sudden inspiration. A new enthusiasm can be displayed. A lack of ambition can find new directions. A boring life can reach for new challenges. More initiative can be displayed. A person afraid of taking control can show courage. Self-starting instincts get ignited.

An angry individual can gain insight into power needs. A warrior type can find a greater vision for actions. One may become more humanitarian rather than exclusively self-serving. A forceful person may allow others to lead once in a while. A "haste makes waste" mentality can learn to conserve energy and resources. A passive person can gain confidence and make talents visible.

Progressed Mars opposing the (natal or progressed) Midheaven or the progressed Midheaven opposing natal Mars can symbolize a greater awareness of actions. An individual may improve at showing feelings.

One may resolve a lack of cooperation with authority figures. Greater reflection makes actions more productive. One may assume more responsibility for behavior. A greater need for emotional support and love can be displayed. Angry moods can be resolved. A painful past can be released.

A poor finisher can learn completion; those lacking motivation can find more initiative; hidden assertion can be brought to the surface.

Parenting and career drives can be mutually satisfying. One may find focus through being needed. An individual may learn that dependency is not a bad thing. Extremely dependent types may find the courage to act alone.

SHADOW

The Mars/Midheaven quincunx and opposition can express as hidden anger. One may experience a confused identity due to suppressed anger. Individuals can become too dependent on others. One may be afraid to make a decision. A life purpose may be unresolved.

A person may operate with hidden agendas. One may play on the weaknesses of others. A person can be too bossy in private and public lives. One could be difficult to live with due to career frustration.

Moods can be strange. Sudden outbursts disrupt the life. One's actions can be erratic. Concentration and focus are lacking. People may have a problem showing vulnerability. A drive to appear strong may block emotional needs. One may avoid taking responsibility for his life. Running away from confrontations delays solutions.

SOFT ASPECTS

Sextile: Progressed Mars Sextile
Natal or Progressed Midheaven
Progressed Midheaven Sextile Natal Mars

Trine: Progressed Mars Trine
                  Natal or Progressed Midheaven
                  Progressed Midheaven Trine Natal Mars

LIGHT

Progressed Mars sextile natal (or progressed) Midheaven or the progressed Midheaven sextile natal Mars can denote decision-making power. One may make a new career direction. Independence can be reassured.

Impatient individuals can learn to think ahead. One need not be so forceful. Pushiness can be moderated. One may find better options. A too-direct approach may be tempered by delayed gratification. Extreme win-or-lose situations can be toned down.

Progressed Mars trine the natal (or progressed) Midheaven or the progressed Midheaven trine natal Mars can show more self confidence. One may be enthusiastic about new career opportunities. A lack of enthusiasm can be turned around.

One's hard work may be appreciated. Individuals may be generous to others. They may show by example how to accomplish life ambitions.

A very intense person may slow down and enjoy life. A person may be more conscious of loved ones. Individuals can feel secure without a show of power. Inner satisfaction makes an outer show no longer vital to identity.

SHADOW

Both the **Mars/Midheaven sextile and trine** can denote a lack of initiative. People can be too complacent. A serious purpose never manifests. Individuals try to hit the big jackpot. An "all or nothing" mentality rarely pays off.

A lack of confidence can hide talents. Insecure people lack the energy to find real success. Laziness can create missed opportunities. Individuals may resist new challenges, taking too much for granted. Individuals may hide power motives. Smooth operators can take advantage of others.

DAWN

Mars/Midheaven aspects can point to a courageous game plan. One may possess an inner security. Actions can be direct and yet not intrude upon others.

A competitive and enthusiastic spirit can be displayed. One may ferociously pursue serious goals. Assertion can be well-tuned. One may enjoy new challenges.

JUPITER/MIDHEAVEN ASPECTS

Transiting Jupiter/Natal or Progressed Midheaven
Progressed Midheaven/Natal Jupiter

Process:	Faith in a Life Purpose
Ally:	A Positive Approach
Illusion:	Lack of Commitment

Jupiter/Midheaven aspects can symbolize a greater faith in a life purpose. These aspects can point to new enthusiasm for cultural roles. Individuals can attract good luck through positive attitudes. Abundance can fill the life. The pitfall can be overconfidence. One may reach out into too many directions. These are rather lighthearted aspects. In charts with more intensity, these aspects may point to material success.

INTENSE ASPECTS

Conjunction: Transiting Jupiter Conjunct Natal Midheaven
Progressed Midheaven Conjunct
Natal or Progressed Jupiter

Square: Transiting Jupiter Square Natal Midheaven
Progressed Midheaven Square
Natal or Progressed Jupiter

Transiting Jupiter conjunct the natal Midheaven or progressed Midheaven conjunct natal (or progressed) Jupiter can denote a refreshing life purpose. A down spirit can rise. Enthusiasm can lead to a new career direction. Individuals can attract abundance through positive attitudes. One can leave stagnating situations. Eclectic learning leads people to seek options.

A hardworking person may find this a flowing time. Recognition may be earned. Individuals may excel as teachers and counselors. A happy spirit can inspire faith in others. Individuals can attract attention through fiery communication.

Transiting Jupiter square the natal Midheaven or progressed Midheaven square natal (or progressed) Jupiter can point to acting on faith. One may demonstrate sound judgment during a conflict.

Multipurpose cultural roles can occur. Individuals can be driven to careers offering expansive growth. One may conquer lack of faith. The courage to take on new challenges brings confidence. A serious individual may learn to relax. A narrow focus can broaden in purpose. One can learn to value life's intangibles.

SHADOW

Both the **Jupiter/Midheaven conjunction and square** can manifest as a lack of purpose. One may lack focus, wandering from one path to another. Restlessness can make follow-through difficult. Discipline is nothing to brag about. People may exaggerate their capabilities. They can promise too much. Individuals can be unreliable and not trustworthy.

Too much fun and no work can occur. Individuals may procrastinate and miss opportunities. People can remain in nongrowth-promoting situations much too long. Indecision and lack of direction can occur.

Quincunx:　Transiting Jupiter Quincunx Natal Midheaven
　　　　　　　Progressed Midheaven Quincunx Natal Jupiter

Opposition:　Transiting Jupiter Opposing Natal Midheaven
　　　　　　　Progressed Midheaven Opposing
　　　　　　　Natal or Progressed Jupiter

Transiting Jupiter quincunx natal Midheaven or progressed Midheaven quincunx natal Jupiter can denote a deepening life purpose. A person can express high spiritual values in public life. A passion for truth and honesty can be exhibited. This aspect is the **"Yoga of faith in cultural roles."**

Individuals can learn to value their own opinions. One may stop running away from responsibility. A person may accept her own potential. Excessive dependence on authority figures for guidance can be transcended. An overly opinionated person can listen to others.

Transiting Jupiter opposing natal Midheaven or progressed Midheaven opposing natal (or progressed) Jupiter can symbolize a deep desire to live ideals. Individuals may be self-confident. Security instincts are tied to a clear conscience. Family life can be strengthening. A person enjoys the support of loved ones. One's private and public life reflect integrity and character. People can make good educators, speakers, or lawyers.

A braggart can achieve more self-honesty; a reckless individual can learn to care about her actions; one of low moral character can find new values. A spiritual rebirth could occur. A more reflective life helps give clarity to actions. One may not be as serious. Rest and relaxation yield clarity.

One may find the courage to challenge authority figures. A person may trust her own opinions and insights. One may break away from a limited life purpose. New ideas can be born. Relocation or moving into a new home often occurs. Going on retreats can be rewarding.

SHADOW
The Jupiter/Midheaven quincunx or opposition can express as a lack of conviction to a true purpose. One may lack the determination to achieve goals. An inability to find options can leave one in stifling situations. One could try too hard to please authority figures. An inability to express opinions can occur.

A restless spirit may have few roots. Roaming from one experience to another causes instability. One may fear being tied down. Emotional problems are not faced.

Individuals may get attached to guru figures who promise much and deliver little. Excessive dependency on authority figures is limiting. People may try too hard to help others. They may go far beyond the call of duty.

SOFT ASPECTS

Sextile: Transiting Jupiter Sextile Natal Midheaven
Progressed Midheaven Sextile
Natal or Progressed Jupiter

Trine: Transiting Jupiter Trine Natal Midheaven
Progressed Midheaven Trine
Natal or Progressed Jupiter

LIGHT

Transiting Jupiter sextile the natal Midheaven or progressed Midheaven sextile natal (or progressed) Jupiter can reflect an optimistic spirit. A person could feel that life is confirming hard work. One may attract abundance through a positive attitude.

Transiting Jupiter trine the natal Midheaven or progressed Midheaven trine natal (or progressed) Jupiter can symbolize a benevolent nature. One may have a tremendous faith to succeed. Individuals may display a natural enthusiasm for life. Supportive people may surround the individual.

SHADOW

The Jupiter/Midheaven sextile or trine can express as apathy. Individuals may not have enthusiasm for growth. New challenges are ignored. Laziness can dominate. One may expect others to do all the work. A lack of self-confidence paves the way for failure. Individuals may lack the willpower to reach goals.

Judging situations in a biased manner is possible. Individuals may lack broad-mindedness. Loyalty to limiting concepts of the past can impede progress. Skimming through life can lead to a shallow existence. Individuals can lack the faith to take a stand. One may run away from conflict. An overly expansive nature may lack focusing power.

DAWN

Jupiter/Midheaven aspects can point to a new, energizing life purpose. Cultural roles can stimulate growth. People may live their highest principles. A generous spirit can inspire growth in others. Eclectic learning can enrich the life.

SATURN/MIDHEAVEN ASPECTS

Transiting Saturn/Natal Midheaven
Progressed Midheaven/Natal or Progressed Saturn

Process:	Redefining Cultural Roles
Ally:	A Tenacious Spirit
Illusion:	I Can't Climb High Enough!

Saturn/Midheaven aspects focus on career, authority, visibility in society and assuming responsibility. One can feel pushed by societal demands and environmental pressures. Since Saturn is the natural planetary ruler of the 10th house, this is a strong repeating theme. A person can face the reality of a lack of ambition or unclear career goals.

INTENSE ASPECTS
Conjunction: Transiting Saturn Conjunct Natal Midheaven
Progressed Midheaven Conjunct
Natal or Progressed Saturn

LIGHT
Transiting Saturn conjunct a natal Midheaven or a progressed Midheaven conjunct natal (or progressed) Saturn can express as pride in leadership. **This cycle marks a major life transition!** One may be recognized for inspiring action. An individual may display steadiness during crises.

People may deepen commitments as parents or citizens. An individual may emerge as a leader or organizer. People take charge of their lives. One might gain a focus. **A new career direction is possible.** One might redefine ambitions. Promotion can begin.

People can have tremendous follow-through. Organizing difficult or complex tasks may be a talent. Years of hard work may pay dividends. An individual may start a business enterprise. Years of real experience are integrated. An excellent reputation may lead to successful career endeavors.

One may be a pillar of strength in the community. Determination might be marked. A deep understanding of karmic lessons related to power and control can be shown. Individuals may achieve a new humility.

One's ideas may be concise and direct. Serious goal planning can begin. A fear of making ideas visible could be confronted. An individual may bring people together. An interest in the community could be shown.

Peace can be made with authority figures. A person may assume new responsibility. Escapist attitudes are transcended. An individual may find that a small step toward more responsibility builds self-confidence. One may stop depending on parents or authority figures.

An individual may achieve the focus and discipline to make an important career transition. One may make time for work and relaxation. One understands that work is not everything.

SHADOW

Transiting Saturn conjunct a natal Midheaven or progressed Midheaven conjunct natal (or progressed) Saturn could express as a compulsive drive for recognition. An individual could sacrifice his private life for status.

One may hide behind a false show of power and wealth. An obnoxious, dictatorial attitude may be exhibited. One's outer world can be all-consuming. A need to always be right alienates others. A compulsive fear of losing gives rise to winning at all costs. One may take more credit than deserved. One can be addicted to work. The intense Saturn/Midheaven aspects are prone to workaholism.

A person may believe in rigid cultural roles. He may lack flexibility. Parental upbringing may dominate common sense. A person may forget to trust his own judgment. People may grow too critical of others. Their own standards are used to measure others. An individual may try too hard to become a success. He could force situations to happen, ignoring life's natural flow. A narrow focus may kill spontaneity. One may fight against the new. Progress is viewed as threatening.

An individual may be a social climber, stepping on others to reach selfish goals. A person may strive to control others. Concentration could be poor. A person may lack discipline. Responsibility can be feared. One may be too dependent on others for decision making.

An individual may miss opportunities due to a fear of risk taking. An individual could stay devoted to an unrewarding career or situation. A lack of self-respect is possible. Individuals could fear leadership and fail to promote themselves. People may be too busy promoting others. A lack of organization is possible. One may lack focus.

Square: Transiting Saturn Square Natal Midheaven
Progressed Midheaven Square
Natal or Progressed Saturn

LIGHT

Transiting Saturn square the natal Midheaven or progressed Midheaven square natal (or progressed) Saturn indicates a person can strive for a more visible identity. Overcoming conflict in manifesting ambitions can occur.

People can show new commitment to ambitions. They may lead courageously, and make decisions confidently.

People may tenaciously complete what they started. They can work with enthusiasm and determination. One's cultural roles may bring pride. Authority figures could be supportive. A self-starting energy could lead to business enterprises. One may have excellent timing for a career change.

Practical answers to life can be found. Individuals may be a steadying influence on others. A person may break through an obstacle to growth. One may rise above limiting cultural beliefs or biases. Responsibility for decisions may get clearer. Defining ambition may be important. The reality of one's concepts can be tested.

SHADOW

Transiting Saturn square a natal Midheaven or a progressed Midheaven square natal (or progressed) Saturn can express as being consumed by public roles. One's private life may be frustrating. Friction with authority figures may be a problem. One may adopt a "must win" attitude without considering the needs of others. The ladder of success may be climbed too ruthlessly.

One may be disappointed in lack of support from authority figures. (The father is often denoted by Saturn and/or 10th house.) One may try too compulsively to win parental approval.

Individuals can preserve tradition at all costs. They forcefully oppose new thinking. A fear of change can occur. Inherited "shoulds" and "oughts" can blossom.

Material consciousness could dominate. People can deny intuitive qualities. Self-reliance may be extreme. One may not be good at delegating.

An individual may not see the forest for the trees. A narrow sense of community can miss opportunities. One may be stuck in the mud. Fear of failure causes lack of ambition.

A need to slow down could be denied. An individual could ignore self-nurturing. People can feel too responsible for the problems of the world. They may deny their own needs.

Quincunx: Transiting Saturn Quincunx Natal Midheaven
Progressed Midheaven Quincunx
Natal or Progressed Saturn

LIGHT

Transiting Saturn quincunx the natal Midheaven or progressed Midheaven quincunx natal (or progressed) Saturn is the "Yoga of growing-up." New challenges confirm ambition. Time can become an ally.

Transiting Saturn quincunx a natal Midheaven or a progressed Midheaven quincunx natal (or progressed) Saturn can denote more centered actions. A person may commit to ambitions. One may stop being his own worst enemy. A new self-respect may occur. People may leave behind negative imprints from authority figures.

One can stop projecting decisions onto others. One may take control of life. A tendency to fight growth can be overcome. People stop fearing new challenges. Self-criticism and negativity can be surrendered.

An indecisive individual may find steadiness. Focus replaces changeability. People can face reality. Emotional disorientation can be conquered. One could let go of the past.

A karmic tendency to deny reality may be transcended. Escapism can be turned into higher consciousness. A surrender to authority figures can be terminated. Believing in oneself becomes a new possibility.

SHADOW

Transiting Saturn quincunx the natal Midheaven or the progressed Midheaven quincunx natal (or progressed) Saturn can express as repeating the same mistakes. One may fail to learn from personal history.

A "haste makes waste" attitude can be present. Individuals can lack initiative. Fear of making a mistake holds one back. A past emotional hurt may be the root of problems. One may depend too much on others for motivation and decision making.

Personal ambition can become ruthless. A desire to be number one can alienate others. People may portray a false show of confidence.

Low self-esteem can be problematic. Individuals may make choices out of fear rather than clarity. Workaholism can dominate.

One may block the flow of creative impulses. Excessive control over self and others can frustrate growth. One can be fixated on status quo opinions. He is afraid to "buck the system."

A person could rely too much on the perceptions of others. Authority figures may be too controlling. One may doubt his own ability. Negative self-talk can be difficult. A failure to resolve negativity creates a bigger problem. One could attach too much importance to status.

Opposition: Transiting Saturn Opposing Natal Midheaven
Progressed Midheaven Opposing
Natal or Progressed Saturn

LIGHT

Transiting Saturn opposing the natal Midheaven or a progressed Midheaven opposing natal (or progressed) Saturn is an important aspect for balancing private and public lives. Finding time (Saturn) for public and private lives can be a source of tension. Finding an inner security can be challenged by the reality-testing of Saturn.

Individuals can reflect on an action-packed past. They may work more wisely. A new focus on private life can occur.

One can control inner resources. A person could face an inner restlessness. The home may become a source of strength. Family may support outward and private lives. An individual may pay more attention to loved ones.

A new objectivity in dealing with authority figures may manifest. One could confront a karmic tendency to concentrate too much on public identity.

The security of home could reinforce the outer life expression. One's subjective ideals can find a concrete home in the world.

Dealing with a disorienting past could ground the present. One's worship of a culture, tradition, or parents could be visited by a dose of reality. One may shake off the internalized opinions of others. Being true to oneself can be accentuated.

One may experience a key life passage in adopting new inspiring symbols. One could transcend worn-out myths. **Starting over in a new physical or psychic location is possible.** One could conquer a karmic tendency to strangle intuitive energy.

A new objectivity in dealing with the past is possible. People can draw mental strength from resolving inner emotional turmoil.

Loved ones may be supportive. They could inspire ambition. The home life may provide the structure for individuals to go forward.

People may become organized. They stay centered during actions and thoughts.

Individuals can balance dependency needs. People may stop devoting all of their time to public roles. A person could be less influenced by societal pressure and expectations.

Individuals can find creative careers. Inner security can be grounding. Going beyond fear of rejection or making a mistake is possible.

SHADOW

Transiting Saturn opposing a natal Midheaven or a progressed Midheaven opposing natal (or progressed) Saturn can denote a dictator. This person could be afraid to lose control. One may procrastinate due to lack of self-confidence. Perceptions are too glued to the opinions of others. One may feel not worthy of recognition.

Lack of flexibility causes problems on public and home fronts. Fixed opinions hide insecurities. Early childhood programming could be filled with negativity. A fear of going beyond normal cultural beliefs is limiting.

One can hide one's "light under the bushel." An individual may have disorienting, subconscious fears. Unfinished business with parents (or authority figures) can be ghosts in the closet. One may refuse to work through problems. Intuitive energy may be blocked, leading to instability in the objective world.

A fear of change can cause missed opportunities. Dependency needs may be out of balance. One could provide too much for others, or be too dependent. One may not listen to reason. One could stay in stagnating situations. A person can be too committed to loved ones, neglecting personal needs.

Individuals can forget their options. Fixation on a goal may lead to compulsive worry. A consuming desire for public recognition can throw the private life out of balance. People can worry too much about fitting into society. They may not express their deepest ideas due to a fear of criticism. An individual may not receive support from loved ones. He could be too demanding and nonsupportive of others.

A failure to organize life priorities may cause frustration. An individual may settle for dead-end jobs. One may fear taking responsibility. An individual could be a "sad sack" with a negative outlook on the world. One may shut off emotions due to oversensitivity.

An individual may be too protective of others. He may need to let go. A person may overidentify with the problems of others.

SOFT ASPECTS
Sextile: Transiting Saturn Sextile Natal Midheaven
Progressed Midheaven Sextile
Natal or Progressed Saturn

Trine: Transiting Saturn Trine Natal Midheaven
Progressed Midheaven Trine
Natal or Progressed Saturn

The soft Saturn/Midheaven aspects can have a serious focus. The events surrounding this symbolism are usually not as dramatic as in the intense aspects. It can be a time of flowing ambitions. One can excel in management, business, and leadership.

LIGHT
Transiting Saturn sextile a natal Midheaven or a progressed Midheaven sextile natal (or progressed) Saturn can express as excitement about new growth. One may have worked hard during more intense aspects to relax into abundant rewards. Ambitions come into fruition.

People may focus much energy into public life. They may attract attention through expertise and enthusiasm. Time may seem an ally during these soft aspects. One may stop working against himself.

An individual may provide a good example of reliability and hard work. He may motivate loved ones to pursue their own ambitions.

Transiting Saturn trine a natal Midheaven or a progressed Midheaven trine natal (or progressed) Saturn can denote new confidence in leadership. The trine's harmonizing nature can symbolize individuals enjoying overcoming obstacles. Each environmental test stretches consciousness into even greater accomplishments.

One may exercise authority with an ease that inspires others. One's own enthusiasm is contagious. This person can provide stability for others. Creative expression may inspire loved ones.

SHADOW

Transiting Saturn sextile a natal Midheaven or a progressed Midheaven sextile natal (or progressed) Saturn can denote a lack of focus. An individual could grow impatient before finishing what he starts. A frustration with reality is possible. One may be very disoriented, working harder rather than smarter. People can feel pushed by time.

A person could need too much recognition. He could pay little attention to others. Support for loved ones is lacking. The private life could be ignored.

Transiting Saturn trine a natal Midheaven or a progressed Midheaven trine natal (or progressed) Saturn can symbolize trying too hard to be accepted. One can desire too much applause. Individuals can allow a parent or authority figure to live through them. One may be too loyal to others to win acceptance.

An inability to set limits can be a problem. Individuals may have trouble following through on vision. Laziness may occur. Enthusiasm wanes shortly after the real work begins.

DAWN

Midheaven/Saturn aspects can express as a focus on choosing a career or cultural roles. One can show much dedication as a parent, employer, employee, citizen, leader, etc.

One can outgrow irresponsible behaviors learned as a youth. An individual may gain the wisdom and determination to provide a good role model for others. An entirely new definition of reality (regarding all major life interests) can surface.

URANUS/MIDHEAVEN ASPECTS

Transiting Uranus/Natal Midheaven
Progressed Midheaven/Natal or Progressed Uranus

Process:	Experimenting with Cultural Roles
Ally:	Breaking through Cultural Restrictions
Illusion:	Nihilistic Vision

Uranus/Midheaven aspects symbolize new consciousness regarding cultural roles. Breaking new ground in a career can occur. People may break from cultural tradition suddenly.

Midheaven/Uranus aspects bring a dynamic electricity to one's societal roles. Environmental stress may spark new insights. A person can be a symbol of freedom to his peers. This period can be irrational and unstable. Freedom of choice can present interesting options.

INTENSE ASPECTS
Conjunction: Transiting Uranus Conjunct Natal Midheaven
Progressed Midheaven Conjunct
Natal or Progressed Uranus

LIGHT
Transiting Uranus conjunct the Midheaven or progressed Midheaven conjunct natal (or progressed) Uranus can point to a new visibility in the world. This is a powerful aspect! Breaking free from the shackles imposed by inner and outer forces can begin a new life passage.

People could experience new pride in individuality. A leader of new societal trends can emerge. Courage and spontaneity make ideas visible. People may bring innovative energy into the community. They may spark a group consciousness.

Individuals might deal with authority figures (10th house) as equals. People may give support as authority figures. One may attract attention through inventive genius. Charisma through surprising others with insights is possible.

Safety and routine can be left behind for bold new directions. One's ambitions may speed up. It can feel like a time warp. Tomorrow's promise has arrived! **Sudden career changes with new opportunities are not uncommon.**

One may assume a new societal role. This could be as parent, authority figure, or explorer. Accomplishments may give the freedom to explore other lifestyles.

There can be mental genius. An individual could network for subcultures within her society. Communication skills may be adept. People may boldly challenge authority figures with fresh ideas. Perceptions may be individualistic. A person may be a role model of free thinking.

One may enjoy fighting inequality. An ability and determination to speak for the underdog can occur. People may be the catalysts for movements. They can be trendsetters for societal change. This can be an authority figure who makes friends easily. She treats others as equals. One may break down bureaucratic walls.

Individuals can break away from dependence on authority types. They dramatically stand up for rights. They stop trying to be accepted by dominating parents (or power figures).

SHADOW
Transiting Uranus conjunct the Midheaven or a progressed Midheaven conjunct natal (or progressed) Uranus can denote purposeless rebellion against authority figures. A aloof and eccentric reputation is possible.

An individual may have a difficult time finding a satisfying vocation. Erratic behavior patterns may ruin opportunities. Changing directions too quickly may abort goals. One's behavior could be explosive. A lack of communication could cause private and public explosions. People can get too attached to their own philosophy.

An individual may have trouble bringing creative genius to a level that others can use. Frustration with the slowness of the present can interfere with common sense. Individuals may resist all structure.

A person can fear freedom. Freedom may be too foreign a territory. A retreat into a status-quo mentality may lead to inner tension.

A rebellious type might have even more trouble concentrating. Fast-paced Uranus can indicate an undisciplined mind. An individual's life could be disorganized. A lack of order could produce a lot of tension.

People may be too fixed on getting support from authority figures. A need to break free from societal or peer pressure is possible. One's direction may be too glued to public opinion.

People can get overwhelmed by stimuli. They resist deepening perceptions of societal roles. One may perform actions without a deep purpose. A nervous anxiety regarding career and responsibility can occur.

A lack of communication could disrupt public or private life. A drive for constant stimulation in the world may cause one to ignore home life. People may not compromise or negotiate. They may hold onto outdated concepts when confronted by change.

A refusal to reason through a painful past may cause emotionally crazy behavior. An individual may blame society (or authority figures) for problems. One may run away from her inner visions. She may retreat to the safety of the past. Dependency on parents and friends could be extreme. Listening to bad role models may reinforce disruptive behaviors.

Square: Transiting Uranus Square Natal Midheaven
Progressed Midheaven Square
Natal or Progressed Uranus

LIGHT

Transiting Uranus square the natal Midheaven or the progressed Midheaven square natal (or progressed) Uranus can point to breaking through obstacles to goals. Thought processes may become stimulated by ambition. New spontaneity in decisions can occur. A person can be enthusiastic in regard to major life transitions.

Alliances may be formed. One may combine forcefulness with perception. One takes advantage of new opportunities more speedily. The hold of dominating people can be broken. Boredom may be replaced with new challenges. Stunted growth may become a thing of the past.

A traditionalist may become excited by innovative ideas. An anarchist could find more middle ground. Responsibility could be a centering point.

Individuals can communicate themselves into public visibility. People may find that conflict sharpens perceptions. Individuals may experience a more collective consciousness. Society's needs become their own cause. Communication can be creatively elevated by interaction with numerous segments of society. One's futuristic insights win respect. Not being distracted by everyday stress accentuates clarity.

SHADOW

Transiting Uranus square the natal Midheaven or the progressed Midheaven square natal (or progressed) Uranus can express as a dynamic recklessness. One may react too suddenly to conflict. Explosive emotional outbursts are possible.

A lack of perception in dealing with authority figures may occur. One may be too determined to push her own ideas. A need for compromise is ignored. An individual may win battles, but lose the war. An inability to communicate causes needless separations. Preoccupation with public life causes tension at home.

A person can deny a need for change. The square's friction may become divorce from reality. One may hold back insights when she should speak out forcefully. One's society and leaders may seem slow to react. An inability to accept life's realities can yield compulsive behaviors. One may lose reasoning power.

Quincunx: Transiting Uranus Quincunx Natal Midheaven
Progressed Midheaven Quincunx
Natal or Progressed Uranus

LIGHT

Transiting Uranus quincunx the natal Midheaven or progressed Midheaven quincunx natal Uranus is the "Yoga of gaining freedom." This can be a time of loosening ties to cultural expectations. One may become a freer parent, citizen, etc.

Enthusiastic sparks can arouse the future. Excuses for procrastination can drop. Spontaneous actions reinforce individuality. A blocked mental nature is transcended.

One may stop projecting unique talents onto others. Fitting into someone else's future is not important. Individuals can find unique purposes. One could follow her own destiny.

One's mental fortitude may develop through leadership. Rising to meet new challenges solidifies individuality. Breaking away from limiting authority figures (or situations) could bring objectivity. One may develop ambition free of societal pressure. She may move forcefully ahead into freer turf.

SHADOW

Transiting Uranus quincunx the natal Midheaven or a progressed Midheaven quincunx natal (or progressed) Uranus can denote an unpredictable person. People may lack patience. One may be too erratic. Public identity could be in constant crisis. Impatience can frustrate future goals. One may ignore those who care about her.

A disrespect for all authority could be problematic. One may have trouble following the direction of others. Arguing needlessly alienates others. Difficulty in accepting advice or criticism causes repeated mistakes. Common sense can be absent. One may not finish goals. Responsibility does not seem important. A "can't slow down" individual may want success without effort.

Reserved people may fail to move toward growth. A desire to be part of the crowd could retard individuality.

Opposition: Transiting Uranus Opposing Natal Midheaven
Progressed Midheaven Opposing
Natal or Progressed Uranus

LIGHT
Transiting Uranus opposing the natal Midheaven or the progressed Midheaven opposing natal (or progressed) Uranus can denote a dynamic change in dependency needs. Individuals may discover a freer mental framework. One may transcend excessive dependency. Negative cues from parents (or authority figures) can be overcome. A new pride in one's own person is possible.

A change of locality can release new energy. The psyche enjoys the stimulus of new surroundings. Perception ignites actions.

One may gain more objectivity as a nurturer or provider. A friendship with loved ones can be formed. Communication clarifies family roles. A deeper inner security can be found. Going beyond cultural norms, a person may discover a deeper awareness. The sudden birth of intuition can be exhilarating.

One may release subjective dreams concretely and forcefully. A commitment to a freer and exciting future leads to self-illumination. One may break away from emotional confusion. Mind and emotions are separated.

One may stop having to be the father (or mother) of humanity. Taking care of personal goals becomes a priority. Receiving as well as giving is a new reality. Facing life's highs and lows becomes easier. Roots and individuality come into balance.

Individuals may hunger for societal roles that fill the intellect. A new confidence in making ideas known is possible. One may deal objectively with authority figures. She may lend more support to others in need. A person may stimulate her society or culture to higher consciousness. Loved ones may support individual growth. An individual may perceive public and private lives more clearly. Clear communication avoids emotional conflict. A need to be noticed is modified.

SHADOW
Transiting Uranus opposing the natal Midheaven or a progressed Midheaven opposing natal (or progressed) Uranus can

express as running away from one's goals. A fear of the future can occur. Unique perceptions can be locked away. Emotional closeness could be avoided. A nervous insecurity keeps people at a distance. An individual could be too impatient in building career goals. She could lack the discipline to succeed.

A fear of being tied down could abort promising situations. Individuals could move so quickly they have no time to develop depth. Individuals may lack the confidence to challenge the ideas of others. They may fail to act on new ideas. People may be stuck in yesterday's reality. A change of menu is stubbornly resisted. One may fight for limited beliefs.

Strange addictions could be substituted for a complete life. A failure to deal with past emotional problems could delay a solid present. People may still live with negative impressions received as a child. Dependency on strong authority figures can take away from growth. Decisiveness can seem like foreign territory. Indecisiveness is a constant nemesis. Procrastination is a familiar parasite. Nervous breakdown could be a reality.

Cultural heroes may have extremist values. An individual could be lost in the words of groups promising much, but delivering little. The identity could be enslaved to cults or rigid beliefs. One may be pulled easily away from ambitions, too changeable.

A bitter sarcasm concerning society and love is possible. This may be a hurt and moody time period. Scapegoats and "it's your fault" are perceived.

Denying unique qualities yields emotional confusion. Running to stronger people for quick answers is not a long-term solution. Shortsightedness causes sudden life disruptions.

SOFT ASPECTS

Sextile: Transiting Uranus Sextile Natal Midheaven
Progressed Midheaven Sextile
Natal or Progressed Uranus

Trine: Transiting Uranus Trine Natal Midheaven
Progressed Midheaven
Trine Natal or Progressed Uranus

The soft Uranus/Midheaven aspects indicate excitable anticipation of the future. The challenge of fighting adversaries and environmental upsets is generally not as dramatic as the intense aspects. A person may not have to fight for beliefs. The environment may be more accepting than usual. Insight into individual and collective ideas may be born.

LIGHT

Transiting Uranus sextile the natal Midheaven or a progressed Midheaven sextile natal (or progressed) Uranus can express as spontaneous perception. Ideas may emerge quickly. Enthusiasm may attract support for goals. Individuals may find a subculture or group that excites creative growth. An individual may accelerate the growth of a group through insights. A person could leave a group behind. She may experiment with a new individuality.

A new objectivity regarding authority figures is possible. Clear perception can replace raw rebelliousness. One fixes problems rather than being the source of them.

Transiting Uranus trine a natal Midheaven or a progressed Midheaven trine natal (or progressed) Uranus can denote ease in planning future goals. The present may inspire new learning experiences. An aloof personality can become more expressive. An isolated person may become more active in society. People can fulfill their own needs. One's vision may encompass more people. A greater openness to the needs of others can be displayed. One could join a collective movement.

SHADOW
Both the **Uranus/Midheaven sextile or trine** can denote a restless spirit with no direction. Private and public lives can be disorganized. One's goals can be in constant flux. A desire for too much attention can be a problem. Opinions lack reasoning. Enthusiasm may block logic. Impatience thwarts forethought. Ambition may be more focused on action than perception. One's life can lack follow-through. An argumentative nature antagonizes others.

DAWN
Midheaven/Uranus aspects can express as becoming one's own person. New insights transcend negative or limiting cultural messages. Individuals may be at the cutting edge of societal changes. They can inspire others to think freely. Finding new ways of being unique and alert are the height of Midheaven/Uranus aspects. Stimulating careers can become a reality. Living in new locations offers a breath of fresh air.

NEPTUNE/MIDHEAVEN ASPECTS

Transiting Neptune/Natal Midheaven
Progressed Midheaven/Natal or Progressed
Neptune

Process:	Faith in Cultural Roles
Ally:	Inspired Game Plan
Illusion:	Living a Lie

Neptune/Midheaven aspects might denote higher consciousness through cultural roles. One may tap into new societal symbols that inspire faith and creativity. These aspects indicate imagination and idealism. Some people become collective symbols of their society. One can make ideals real. Accepting one's imperfections may be especially challenging.

INTENSE ASPECTS
Conjunction: Transiting Neptune Conjunct Natal Midheaven
Progressed Midheaven Conjunct
Natal or Progressed Neptune

LIGHT
Transiting Neptune conjunct the natal Midheaven or a progressed Midheaven conjunct natal (or progressed) Neptune can symbolize a dramatic change of strategy in the world. An individual may be guided by imaginative forces. The need for absolute control is modified.

An extremely self-reliant individual may include others. Excessive pride can be converted into humility. A higher purpose may lift one beyond selfish success. One may repay a karmic debt to society. This can be a time of considerable self-sacrifice. Selfless service is possible. Some individuals succeed in the healing arts.

A tendency to dominate may become a yearning to understand. One may relax into responsible societal roles. Tuning into higher consciousness yields a clearer overall purpose. A new faith in oneself could fulfill business or career dreams. A greater belief in a higher power and humanity can occur. Inflexible cultural roles may change. Expressing oneself can begin. One may be known publicly through a difficult role.

A greedy person can learn to share; a hard individual to be more compassionate; a staunch realist to dream. One can more sensitively present a game plan. Individuals may derive greater emotional satisfaction from life. Work may include more ideals.

Mental outlook can lift to new heights. The world appears a happier place. An individual's ambition may ally with invisible forces. One's imagining power may blossom. An individual could capture the collective or individual imagination. Faith may inspire others to reach for something greater.

People can rise above escapism. Self-destructive tendencies are overcome by facing the music. Irrational fears of responsibility (or societal expectations) are transcended. A lost soul may feel rediscovered. Illumination can occur. One may feel a special calling. He may hear his inner voice. Societal roles may more accurately express one's true nature.

Especially appealing could be careers that involve emotional intensity. Finding a deeper life purpose inspires faith. Collective movements capture imaging power. One may inspire others. Artistic careers are possible. Fashion and design can be talents.

SHADOW
**Transiting Neptune conjunct the Midheaven or a progressed
Midheaven conjunct natal (or progressed) Neptune** can express
as illusory fame; legend in one's own imagination.

A desire to lead others to a promised land can bring fanaticism. A
leader may not practice what he preaches. People may enjoy only extreme highs. They run from conflict to greener fantasies. One may fool
others through false sincerity, deceiving to gain power. Secret agenda
are hidden by a front of directness. Individuals may fool themselves.
One could stay attached to smothering societal roles. An outer show of
success keeps one enslaved, sad and disillusioned. Private life may be
filled with emotional pain.

An individual could become discontent with a good life and leave
behind solid relationships, hard work, and potentials. One may become
too critical. Perhaps he only needed to modify present circumstances.
Inner motives for change may not be clearly understood.

One might feel worthless. Self-criticism could be devastating. One
feels too responsible for situations, trying too hard to be a provider. One
could drown sorrow in substance abuse. A lack of faith in self or in a
higher power brings on the lows. Ambitions can be unclear. One may be
undependable. He could disappoint those counting on him.

Intuition and perception might blur. Individuals may lose purpose,
becoming too near or farsighted. People can experience a right-brain
flood. New intuitive insights are denied. Individuals may resist higher
consciousness. Individuals may fear guidance from higher life processes.

An individual can feel singled out by life. Cosmic forces, parents,
etc., are blamed for shortcomings. Denying responsibility prolongs personal issues. One may have trouble facing problems. He may let others
solve his problems.

One may save others. One may try too hard to help. He may need to
let others fix their own problems. "Tough Love" could be required.

Individuals may have extremely high standards (for self and others). Success could have impossible conditions. One may secretly fear
showing his true ambitions. He may see the world as too limited a place
to fulfill dreams. Procrastination can result. People may attach too much
importance to public life. One may hide in work and sacrifice a private
life.

   Square: Transiting Neptune Square Natal Midheaven
                Progressed Midheaven Square
                     Natal or Progressed Neptune

LIGHT
**Transiting Neptune square the Midheaven or a progressed Mid-
heaven square natal (or progressed) Neptune** can denote illumined

actions. One may find clarity of vision. Less confrontation can occur. Individuals may attract what they need rather than being aggressive. One may know when to be assertive and when to be passive. Conflict is avoided by tuning into situations. One may glide steadily rather than rush foolishly.

Individuals may face escapism. Unity and peace can replace a "divide and conquer" mentality. Creative imagination may bring aesthetic talent. Endless enthusiasm could inspire determined ambition. A new career opportunity may catalyze creativity. Years of hard work might be rewarded.

Some individuals find a new lease on life. A new consciousness could begin. Material shortsightedness may be refined by passionate intuition. One's life may encompass greater beauty. Life is experienced as a process. The "means" are as important as the "ends." Ideals and reality join in a symbolic crisis. One may make ideals a reality.

One may balance public and private lives. An aloofness may become more emotional; an apathetic person could find a meaningful mission in life; a depressed individual may find the energy to unify his life; a highly sociable individual looks for inner answers; a dreamer could develop clearer perceptions; a realist falls in love with life.

SHADOW
Transiting Neptune square the natal Midheaven or a progressed Midheaven square natal (or progressed) Neptune can symbolize a passive approach to life. One may be afraid to say what he needs. Missed opportunities result.

People may follow impulses too rapidly. A lack of reflection may lead to disastrous circumstances. An individual's devotion may lead to limiting paths. He may be used by authoritarian types. One may depend too much on power figures for identity.

A person could lack the stamina to make dreams concrete. He could live in a world of fantasy. Hard work causes him to find greener dreams.

People could be in love with recognition. They may feel unimportant unless showered with attention. This time could feature big ideas but no sincere game plan.

There can be career crises. One could seek a career as though looking for the holy grail. It can become an illusive chase for the impossible. One's high standards guarantee frustration.

The game plan may be disoriented. One could refuse to see the truth. One may hold onto people and things that bring pain. A denial of new inspiration keeps people in a rut. Running away from responsibility could abort growth. Faith in self or in a higher power is denied.

Quincunx: Transiting Neptune Quincunx Natal Midheaven
Progressed Midheaven Quincunx
Natal or Progressed Neptune

LIGHT

Transiting Neptune quincunx the natal Midheaven or progressed Midheaven quincunx natal Neptune is the "Yoga of intuitive purpose." Reality and faith are the co-actors. Idealism and compassion are the supporting cast.

There can be a burst of faith in oneself. An already confident individual may creatively manifest deepest values. One may tap into unconscious forces that strengthen faith. Career confusion may be sorted out. Individuals may finally pursue their heartfelt dreams. Substance abuse and other escapism can be conquered. An enslaved present may be transcended. Belief in authority types may be adjusted. An individual may begin believing in himself. A little success in accomplishing ideals ignites enthusiasm.

SHADOW

Transiting Neptune quincunx the natal Midheaven or a progressed Midheaven quincunx natal (or progressed) Neptune can express as false pride. Self-importance reaches the extreme.

Individuals may be afraid to realize their full potentials. They would rather live a life of illusion. Deception may conquer honesty; theft steal from creativity; misguided game plan ignore higher values. A hurry to get to the top is followed by an empty past. A lack of meaning brings despair. There can be a "fear to leap."

Individuals may cling desperately to illusions. Wealth seems more tangible than faith; outer beauty appears more enticing than inner understanding. A disintegration of discipline can frustrate dreams. A loss of ambition can wait for a new life. One's heroes may be grounded in the material plane. New inspirational role models are thwarted by yesterday's beliefs.

> **Opposition:** Transiting Neptune Opposing Natal Midheaven
> Progressed Midheaven Opposing
> Natal or Progressed Neptune

LIGHT

Transiting Neptune opposing the natal Midheaven or a progressed Midheaven opposing natal Neptune can denote a direct release of idealism. The courage to imagine a new, creative game plan can inspire new growth.

One may find faith by taking control. Dependency needs may be well balanced. One may nurture spontaneously. Personal pride brings security. Subjective or private ideals are made public. Shared beauty inspires the game plan of others.

"Life is not all work" can become a new philosophy. Symbols that transcend cultural beliefs can bring illumination. A zest for life brings commitment to one's highest values. Outer success alone is no longer inspiring. The game plan needs emotion to keep growing.

A sharing of wealth reflects a need to be needed. A bigger world than self begins. New symbols are found through a collective movement. A person may selflessly give to loved ones. Power is relinquished to receive more love. Turning within for answers brings a new understanding. Asking for help becomes a possibility. Self-reliance is raised to new heights by emotional strength. Dependency needs are balanced.

The past and present can become unified. Resolving a painful past releases creative symbols in one's subconscious. Transcending a disorienting past allows one to meet reality. People may stop overplaying their lives. Letting life happen becomes important. One may communicate more from the heart. Appearing sophisticated is less important. Love and unity may inspire a collective change in a group (or society). Imagination may inspire thinking in others.

Deep creative energy may bring a new career. One may need a more emotionally intense career to inspire growth. Seeking a deeper purpose can lead to different societal roles. Adding more color to the home or a decorating spirit can manifest. Spending time in places of natural beauty soothes the soul.

SHADOW

Transiting Neptune opposing the natal Midheaven or a progressed Midheaven opposing natal Neptune can denote too passive an approach to life. Decisions may go unmade. One may be too sensitive regarding approval of actions. Emotional struggles dilute forceful self-projection.

Individuals may move ahead with no purpose. The game plan is in chaos. One needs to slow down and reflect. The private life may be unsettled. Inner clarity is denied. Perceptions are in a fog.

One may be too much of a parent or savior for others. Attachment to parental figures blocks creative expression. One may try too hard to follow in the footsteps of others. An allegiance to parents may crush ideals.

Deeper intuition may be feared. One may stay on the surface of life. Workaholism (or a compulsive devotion to causes) may substitute for a private life. Idealism may be out of touch with reality. Individuals may close their eyes to stagnating situations. Maintaining yesterday's dreams sacrifices today's promises.

Individuals can seek escapism. A fatalistic game plan results. People may enact public and private extremes. Inconsistency in both worlds is disorienting. Social stimulation may become a silent retreat. Guilt can be tremendous. A person can take life too personally. Idealism may be thwarted by reality. One may live in a fantasy world. Unconscious forces may be blocked. Irrational fears leads to confused actions. A lack of discipline is frustrating. Faith in self or in a higher power is needed.

Individuals may try too hard to be perfect. Relaxing into life processes is important. Self-acceptance is a must.

SOFT ASPECTS

Sextile: Transiting Neptune Sextile Natal Midheaven
Progressed Midheaven Sextile
Natal or Progressed Neptune

Trine: Transiting Neptune Trine Natal Midheaven
Progressed Midheaven Trine
Natal or Progressed Neptune

The soft Neptune/Midheaven aspects can denote wonder. The game plan may incorporate more intuition.

LIGHT

Transiting Neptune sextile the natal Midheaven or the progressed Midheaven sextile natal (or progressed) Neptune can denote a greater ease in expressing creativity. Imaging power combines with a serious focus.

Life's mysteries may be brought into one's profession. The career itself may become a consciousness raising experience. (This can be true in all Midheaven/Neptune aspects.)

Transiting Neptune trine the natal Midheaven or the progressed Midheaven trine natal (or progressed) Neptune can reflect a more compassionate attitude toward humanity. People may find unity in life. Spiritual strength may push one into new territory. A leap of faith may occur.

SHADOW

Both the Neptune/Midheaven sextile and trine can indicate a haphazard life. Reality may be lacking. One could be distracted easily from ambitions. Life purpose may get fogged out by hasty emotions. Indecision can cause missed opportunities. Dependency needs can be confusing. A very emotional individual could be disoriented by change. An impatient person can lack the sensitivity and patience to perceive the overall game plan.

Individuals may purposely mislead others. They can appear sincere though fraudulent. Helplessness may be used to deceive others.

DAWN

Neptune/Midheaven aspects can express as creating new, inspiring dreams. The life purpose may lift to clear, intuitive levels. Individuals can inspire change in their society. Higher values can inspire growth. New symbols can unify one's life. Working hard builds a life of dreams, ideals, and faith. A more inspiring career and home life can be realized.

PLUTO/MIDHEAVEN ASPECTS

Transiting Pluto/Natal Midheaven
Progressed Midheaven/Natal or Progressed Pluto

Process:	Intensified Cultural Roles
Ally:	Transcending Worn Out Roles
Illusion:	Unclear Power Instincts

Pluto/Midheaven aspects connote emotional fixation associated with cultural roles, whether a person desires a new job, to be a civic leader, parent, etc. One's game plan may become bonded to a deep commitment. Power over one's own destiny can become a focal point.

A desire for ownership can become important. An individual can break away from confining situations. Societal roles may be reborn. True personal power can be freed. A reputation can fill with charisma. The down side is a game plan aborted by manipulation and compulsive power urges.

INTENSE ASPECTS
Conjunction: Transiting Pluto Conjunct Natal Midheaven
Progressed Midheaven Conjunct
Natal or Progressed Pluto

LIGHT
Transiting Pluto conjunct the natal Midheaven or a progressed Midheaven conjunct natal (or progressed) Pluto can symbolize a passionate search for meaning. One may give up an empty existence. People can gain control over a mismanaged life. Actions can become clear and powerful. One may begin projects that take years to complete.

A selfish type may support others emotionally. A waster may learn to conserve. A lack of self-respect can transform to healthy pride.

One's work may reflect instinctive power. Public and private lives may be bonded. An individual may transcend limiting fears. Envy is dispelled by self-realization. Old destructive karmic patterns associated with power or violence can be conquered. Strong allies can lessen the burden of going it alone. Individuals may courageously help remove ignorance in their community.

Providing for others can bring a sense of being needed. Taking control of one's life can foster self-confidence. Mastery of skills generates emotional excitement. Difficult tasks can be managed. One may win the confidence of authority figures. Crises can bring out survival instincts. Individuals may embark on new game plans that leave old roles in ashes. New concepts might be made public.

One instinctively perceives beneath the surface of life. One adeptly counsels and helps others survive emotional crises. One can help society raise consciousness. She can fuse together different cultural groups. Individuals may have a deep understanding of symbols. Metaphysical symbols can be powerfully interpreted. Self-transformation may lift one above self-destructive thoughts. One can regenerate her own suffering consciousness.

Balancing dependency needs can be a key theme. Independence fosters new emotional clarity. One leaves excessive dependency to focus on new ambitions. Starting a business and working with large companies sometimes accompanies this aspect. Major financial investments can be in focus.

SHADOW

Transiting Pluto conjunct the natal Midheaven or a progressed Midheaven conjunct natal (or progressed) Pluto can express as compulsive power drives. One may do whatever it takes to control situations (or people). Competitiveness may have few scruples. Individuals can create power struggles. A show of power wastes energy. Insecurity can be at the root of power shows.

A lack of emotional intensity highlights a dry life. A person may doubt herself. Negating success can be self-defeating. A dependency on authority types limits growth. One may be financially and emotionally trapped. Living the game plan of another is enslaving. A need to shape emotional intensity could be smothered. A bold new step to find personal power might abort. The safety of the past is confining. The present could be an emotional mess. Imagination and intuition are overpowered by material security. A lack of insight into emotional depths limits options.

One may blame the system (or authority figures) for problems. One can try to dominate others. Flexibility seems a foreign word. Ethics and integrity might be at an all-time low. Creating win-lose negotiations hurts others. One's lack of trust is clear in one's game plan. Ambitions can be twisted. A hidden agenda uses others for power. People may be faced with bankruptcy or financial loss. The death of a parent can occur with the intense Pluto/Midheaven aspects. This may be painful and yet offer a person an empowering experience in dealing with death.

Square: Transiting Pluto Square Natal Midheaven
Progressed Midheaven Square Natal Pluto

LIGHT

Transiting Pluto square the natal Midheaven or a progressed Midheaven square natal (or progressed) Pluto can symbolize rebirth of a life purpose. A plan greater than oneself can stimulate actions. Conquering impatient attitudes builds depth. One may deal directly with conflict. A meaningful career can attract abundance. Individuals can feel like they are on a mission.

Providing for the needs of others may lift a selfish consciousness to new awareness. Taking control of shortsighted, reckless actions can stabilize one's life. Individuals can balance dependency needs. A passionate release of energy into career could be satisfying. Surviving a crisis or a key challenge promotes growth.

SHADOW
Transiting Pluto square a natal Midheaven or a progressed Midheaven square natal (or progressed) Pluto can express as compulsive power urges. War without compromise creates enemies. Life can become a series of worlds to conquer. A fear of emotional closeness leaves an empty feeling.

One may always be starting over. Broken careers and homes are a repeating melody. An individual may be her own worst enemy. A lack of consistency in dealing with responsibility can be a problem. All-consuming public lives may destroy intimacy. Lack of trust leads to using people. An outward show of power hides insecurity.

Quincunx: Transiting Pluto Quincunx Natal Midheaven
Progressed Midheaven Quincunx
Natal or Progressed Pluto

LIGHT
Transiting Pluto quincunx the natal Midheaven or progressed Midheaven quincunx natal (or progressed) Pluto is the "Yoga of empowering a life purpose." Individuals may utilize untapped resources.

Ambition can be dynamically reborn. Setbacks are turned into initiative. A "Yes, I can" attitude prevails.

SHADOW
Transiting Pluto quincunx a natal Midheaven or a progressed Midheaven quincunx natal (or progressed) Pluto can connote raw, coarse actions. A person might be destructive physically and mentally. A karmic pattern of self-destruction repeats.

Self-hatred can be devastating. Not forgiving those who have trespassed is limiting. A lack of trust may have roots in an unforgiving past. Angry moods may disrupt life. An individual could repress her initiative for growth. Personal power may be burned out. A lack of pride can be disorienting.

Opposition: Transiting Pluto Opposing Natal Midheaven
Progressed Midheaven Opposing
Natal or Progressed Pluto

LIGHT
Transiting Pluto opposing the natal Midheaven or a progressed Midheaven opposing natal (or progressed) Pluto can symbolize

the birth of a new, inner security. Unfinished emotional business is resolved.

Feelings can be expressed more openly. Personal power can come forth from one's soul. The death of old concepts gives birth to new enthusiasm. A controlling type may learn to let go. Not listening can become a willingness to understand. An individualist can find roots. One stops running away from ghosts in the closet. The ending of a key life chapter and letting go of the past may be important. A life of negativity can rise into a creative purpose.

Expressing personal creative power brings confidence and balance. Tapping into family ancestry can foster a clearer purpose. The game plan can fill with new energy. Roots may support growth. One may learn to appreciate loved ones. Home can become a place of inspiration and retreat. A new self-mastery may be displayed. Commitment to success in the outer and inner worlds can occur. Making changes to a home such as remodeling can be enjoyable.

SHADOW

Transiting Pluto opposing the natal Midheaven or the progressed Midheaven opposing natal (or progressed) Pluto can manifest as following the easy way out. A desire for immediate gratification aborts long-term plans. The game plan is hijacked by an insatiable attraction to danger.

An individual may be difficult to care about. A restless soul has no time for intimacy. Sexuality is in focus, but no permanent bonds or roots. Seemingly uncontrollable and obsessive urges may promote destruction. Lack of self-confidence can cause fear of risk taking. Excess dependency undermines self-motivation. This person could dominate on the home front. She could take out lack of success on loved ones.

The life may be void of imagination. A person may fear societal ridicule. Living a life for someone else is limiting. Emotions could seem uncontrollable. Compulsive, subconscious addictions could uproot the life. Insecurities may be denied.

Individuals may express smothering behaviors. A desire to be a parent of the world can offend others. A need to give and take space may be ignored. One may dump emotional problems onto convenient targets. Dealing with the loss of a loved one can be difficult. This is often a soul-searching time period. Introspection is commonly highlighted. Getting through painful experiences can be the strength that points the way to a brighter future.

SOFT ASPECTS
Sextile: Transiting Pluto Sextile Natal Midheaven
           Progressed Midheaven Sextile
               Natal or Progressed Pluto

Trine: Transiting Pluto Trine Natal Midheaven
Progressed Midheaven Trine
Natal or Progressed Pluto

LIGHT

Transiting Pluto sextile the natal Midheaven or a progressed Midheaven sextile natal (or progressed) Pluto can symbolize ease in expressing a life purpose. Searching can be rewarded.

Individuals can seek a meaningful life. New understanding could be brought to one's community. An individual can possess physical or psychological resources. A clearer focus of energy is possible. A high-energy person can become a better manager of time; a procrastinator can find self-motivating energy; a shy person can learn to value accomplishments; an ego-centered type may acknowledge the power of others.

Transiting Pluto trine the natal Midheaven or the progressed Midheaven trine natal (or progressed) Pluto can express as sharing resources. One can support movements (or cultural changes). One's vision can uplift others. A person can learn patience. Success may increase personal power. An intense life purpose can attract support. A career that expands growth is possible. A field of study may be mastered. New pride can open creative doors.

SHADOW

Both the Pluto/Midheaven sextile and trine can express as constant complaining. A compulsive need for approval may sabotage the life purpose. There can be hidden hatred or anger. A silent rage becomes explosive when overly frustrated. A desire to be number one could be all-consuming. Intensity can drown a clear game plan. Strategy needs to dry out in the land of reason.

DAWN

Pluto/Midheaven aspects can express as emotionally embracing one's life purpose. Personal power can bring one into new creative potential. Self-mastery can emanate into one's entire world. Deeper life experience can be shared with others.

CHAPTER TWELVE

PLANET/NODES OF THE MOON ASPECTS

Aspects formed by planets to the north and south nodes of the Moon reflect a special urge for soul growth. These are some of the deepest paths to fulfillment.

The north node symbolizes our challenge to build new spiritual, mental, and physical resources. The south node points to our past life tendencies. It is our recorded personal history. Many of our subconscious desires can be traced to south node symbolism.

Aspects formed by progressed or transiting planets to the Moon's nodes activate our passion to balance present and past. It is important to integrate our past behaviors with the evolving present. The promise of an awakened present can be found in embracing the north node. Progressed and transiting planets can bring the past and present into a symbolic crisis. Our choices can set us free.

PROGRESSED SUN/MOON'S NODES ASPECTS

Progressed Sun/Nodes of the Moon

Process:	Drawing Strength by Facing Past Life Themes
Ally:	A Creative Spirit
Illusion:	Over identification with Limitations

The progressed Sun/nodes of the Moon aspects can symbolize a dramatic time. Individuals may release the grip of a limiting past. They can draw from past-life strength in this incarnation. Subconscious impulses can be balanced with the needed direction for this lifetime.

Individuals can display creative courage. The entire life can go through great changes. This is a major overhaul of habits, creative energies, willpower, and shadows.

INTENSE ASPECTS
Conjunction: Progressed Sun Conjunct North Node of Moon
Progressed Sun Conjunct South Node of Moon

LIGHT
Progressed Sun conjunct the north node of the Moon can denote embracing one's vitality. A new surge of energy may come forward. One can awaken to enjoy this incarnation. One may fall in love with life. A new passion for relating and creativity emerges. Willpower can be stronger (and clearer).

Individuals may relax. They stop fighting a natural flow. One may attract positive forces. Love and appreciation can increase greatly. A late bloomer can find himself. A person may feel refreshed. Old ways of being are no longer satisfying. One may make up for lost time. Life can feel like a gift.

Progressed Sun conjunct the south node of the Moon can point to forcefully altering karmic habits. Irrational behaviors can be faced. One may willfully decide to go to the "light."

Individuals can make peace with the past. One may forgive himself or others. One's load is lightened. The past is no longer the key motivating force. A person may derive self-satisfaction by channeling compulsive drives into creative actions. Great self-realization can occur. Hidden allies and resources can be discovered. Past-life pain and escapism can be surrendered.

SHADOW
The **progressed Sun conjunct the north or south nodes of the Moon** can denote extremely willful behavior. One can become too pushy. Dictatorial attitudes can alienate others. A lack of flexibility can be problematic.

One can become too self-centered. A big ego can make a person insensitive to others. Intuition may be drowned out by a loud need for attention. Creative energies can freeze. One may feel pulled to compulsive behaviors. Individuals can chase one illusion after another. A desire for recognition can lead one to play false roles.

A loss of self-confidence is possible. One may listen to voices of the past echoing inadequacies. A need to move forward is thwarted. Pride keeps one from getting needed help. A person may surrender too much power to others. One may lose spontaneity. Self-doubt and worry are not very fulfilling.

Square: Progressed Sun Square North and South Nodes

Quincunx: Progressed Sun Quincunx North or South Nodes

LIGHT
The progressed Sun square the Moon's nodes can symbolize resolving internal conflicts. One may creatively solve challenges. A life of extremes can be balanced.

Individuals may break away from self-destructive past-life patterns. Constant crises can be transcended. A pattern of inconsistent behaviors can be resolved. A habit of forcing issues can be calmed by patience. Heartfelt creativity can manifest. Individuals can regain lost confidence. Shared love can be a catalyst for growth. A sad heart can find inner strength.

The progressed Sun quincunx either the north or south node of the Moon can point to getting the life back on course. This aspect is the **"Yoga of creatively answering karmic challenges."** A person can search for deeper meaning. One can find challenges that bring out willpower. An individual may control compulsive urges. One can understand motivations for actions.

Individuals can confidently step in a new direction. Past-life themes can be slowly integrated into the current life.

SHADOW
The progressed Sun square or quincunx the Moon's nodes can express as a lack of motivation. Individuals can wander aimlessly. A person can feel caught in limbo (between past and current lives). People can lack the willpower to overcome limiting behaviors. They can reenact karmic habits. New growth is thwarted by past-life pulls.

A person can feel separate from himself. Creative self-expression does not flow. One is playing roles without emotional intensity. Joy and happiness can be lacking. One may feel driven to achieve power and control. The simple things in life are taken for granted. Taking from life becomes the primary goal.

People can forget to reward themselves. "All work and no play" becomes a pattern. They can neglect love.

SOFT ASPECTS

Sextile:	Progressed Sun Sextile North or South Nodes
Trine:	Progressed Sun Trine North or South Nodes

LIGHT
The progressed Sun sextile or trine the Moon's nodes can denote happiness. One's life may be permeated with creative expression. One may confidently venture away from self-destructive actions. He may be surrounded by loving people. Past-life strengths may boost willpower. One may be stimulated by new challenges.

Intense individuals can go with the flow. Time is made for more pleasurable experiences. Individuals can release creative energies without as much environmental tension. One may feel in harmony with universal forces.

SHADOW

Progressed Sun sextile or trine the Moon's nodes can express as stagnation. People lack creative passion. They may not pursue creative growth. Self-motivation can be missing. One may stubbornly resist new challenges. Individuals may deny their compulsive behaviors. They go with the karmic flow. Escapist behaviors are ignored. Individuals may rationalize with the best. Power may be a subtle drive. One may deceive self and others. A lack of character and integrity add to negative traits.

DAWN

Sun/Moon's nodes aspects can express as beautiful self-realization. Past and current life themes can be sources of strength. One may display creative courage. Life can be filled with hard work and pleasurable experiences. The present may creatively express past-life tendencies.

PROGRESSED MOON/MOON'S NODES ASPECTS

Progressed Moon/Nodes of the Moon

Process:	Nurturing Soul Growth
Ally:	Hunger for New Transitions
Illusion:	Following Familiar Worn Out Behaviors

The progressed Moon/nodes of the Moon aspects can denote an emotional cleansing. People can feel the power of intuition. Individuals can tune into life processes, understanding the underlying order. People can feel secure with their lives. People may become aware of past-life themes. Self-defeating habits can be pulled up by their roots. One may recognize subconscious impulses. Emotional sharing and intimacy can blossom.

Conjunction: Progressed Moon Conjunct North Node
　　　　　　　　Progressed Moon Conjunct South Node

LIGHT

Progressed Moon conjunct the north node of the Moon can symbolize a refreshed emotional nature. One may embrace an important life transition. Emotional energy can be cleansed. A person may feel freed from guilt, helplessness, self-pity, and other emotional pitfalls. One may feel a new lease on life. Movement into new directions that build security can begin. More emotional strength may be available. One may feel she has paid her dues.

Close peers can be important allies. One may receive emotional support from others. A desire for home, family, and security may reflect a need for roots. The love nature can branch out into new directions. Deep, primal, spiritual impulses can awaken. A person can feel a bond with life forces. A reverence for life can surface. One can more intimately interact with life. Making peace with the past is possible. Past-life habits can be positively integrated into the present.

Progressed Moon conjunct the south node of the Moon can symbolize a forceful release of subconscious energies. One can become more conscious of emotional intensity. Irrational behaviors can be balanced. One's understanding of life can deepen greatly. Self-defeating behaviors can be converted into strengths. Facing a painful and escapist past can bring growth. Emotional disorientation can become intuitive clarity.

One may gain insight into past lives. Talents and gifts of past lives can be combined with new challenges. One may learn from the wisdom and lessons of past mistakes. Individuals can go beyond the traps that have ensnared the family. (The progressed Moon conjunct the north or south node can point to this.) A new path for the family ancestry can emerge through the individual. Reaching out for clarity and guidance can bring new horizons.

SHADOW

The **progressed Moon conjunct the north or south node of the Moon** can express as a disillusionment with one's life. Individuals may feel helpless and confused. Life can seem empty or meaningless. Compulsive subconscious energies can bring self-undoing. Refusing to face escapist tendencies can be problematic. One may willfully follow the dark side. Self-deception can dominate. One may be a stranger to himself, and a mystery to others. The same irrational behaviors that have aborted ancestral paths can occur again. Substance abuse, emotional imbalance, etc., can be embraced. One may not see the value of a new challenge. Adherence to the old and comfortable can keep a person in confining situations.

Individuals can lack a consistent path. They can be in constant confusion. A habit of pulling up and starting over again can be a form of escapism. Individuals may fear closeness. Self-examination creates tension.

Square: Progressed Moon Square North and South Nodes

Quincunx: Progressed Moon Quincunx North or South Nodes

LIGHT

The progressed Moon square the Moon's nodes can indicate acting on intuitive impulses. One may change karmic tendencies. Insecurity no longer holds one back. One may face hidden issues. Emotional blockages can be relieved. Deeper, soul-felt experiences call. Individuals can feel guided by invisible forces. One can make a new way in the world. Individuals may stop living in an illusion. A person may live a life more reflective of her own needs. Extreme dependency on others can be transcended.

The **progressed Moon quincunx either the north or south node of the Moon is the "Yoga of a deeper intuitive search for meaningful symbols."** An extremely action-oriented person may slow down to a more natural pace; a very serious and methodical nature can find a greater flow; a passive person discovers a new passion for life; a lonely heart can find love.

Individuals can stop expecting too much from others. One's own gifts and abilities can be found. A person can find her own center. Love need not be desperate. An individual can become comfortable with her own space.

SHADOW

The **progressed Moon square or quincunx the nodes of the Moon** can express as a lack of magic in life. Practicality and logic may block intuition. One may fear intuitive processes.

Individuals may be lost in idealism. Floating in dreams never touches reality. One can lose direction. Commitments can be shallow or meaningless. Worldly success can exclude a private life. One may lack the needed support systems to survive a personal crisis. Love can be taken for granted.

People might learn nothing from past experiences. A lack of emotional depth leads to a life of disappointments. Individuals may lack the emotional strength to survive adversity. Clinging to the past can be limiting. The same old karmic patterns ensnare the present. One may lose power due to a lack of emotional clarity.

SOFT ASPECTS

Sextile: Progressed Moon Sextile North and South Nodes

Trine: Progressed Moon Trine North or South Nodes

LIGHT

The **progressed Moon sextile or trine the Moon's nodes** can point to enjoying self-satisfaction. One may put energy passionately into relationships, family, and career. People may open new life chapters. A cosmic marriage with life takes place. Individuals can find peace within and without.

A rocky journey can mellow; inner conflict can find peace in a creative journey; love may flow more naturally and spontaneously; self-hate can turn to self-acceptance.

Stimulation comes from peers and loved ones. A falling in love with life can bring confidence and inspiration. Aesthetic impulses come forward naturally. One may feel energized. The fighting for one's life that can occur during the intense aspects is not as evident in the soft aspects. An individual can still express intuitive passion, but without the same burnout.

SHADOW
Progressed Moon sextile or trine the nodes of the Moon can express as a needy nature. One may too quickly seek protection in others, getting caught in their life paths. One's own way is blurred.

Individuals can get too protective of others. Too much nurturing pulls one away from her own path. Let others learn for themselves.

A lack of emotional depth makes one too vulnerable to upsets. Individuals can lack the emotional strength to survive a crisis. Individuals may resist a cooling-out period. Constant emotional stress drains the psyche. Signals to slow down are ignored. A failure to learn from the past can occur. One can continue on a self-defeating path. Karmic themes echo escapism.

DAWN
Moon/nodes of the Moon aspects can indicate new dynamic choices. Life can be filled with challenges. Individuals may possess great intuitive clarity. Solving problems from within bring light to outer circumstances. Karmic tendencies can be turned into allies. Old behaviors that distracted our growth now empower our choices.

PROGRESSED MERCURY/MOON'S NODES ASPECTS

Progressed Mercury/Nodes of the Moon

Process:	Integrating the Past and Present
Ally:	Clear Perception of Karma
Illusion:	Sweeping Self-Destructive Habits Under the Rug

Mercury/Moon's nodes aspects can reveal a growing awareness of the work individuals are here to do. A reflective nature can separate past karmic pulls from the present. An individual can find new order in life.

Mercury's perceptive qualities can combine with our instinctive tendencies to till new growth-promoting soil. A more conscious awareness of life's mysteries can begin.

INTENSE ASPECTS
Conjunction: Progressed Mercury Conjunct
North or South nodes

LIGHT
Progressed Mercury conjunct the north node of the Moon can point to mental decisiveness. One may perceive a new, fulfilling direc-

tion. Perceptions and intuition can flow together. Extremes can be balanced. Objectivity may help clarify emotional issues. Negative mental tapes can be replaced with a more positive framework. Scattered energy can be more concentrated. Nervous anxiety can be transcended.

Individuals may develop clearer perceptions of others. A disoriented mental or emotional nature may get grounded. People may stop projecting their own doubts and fears onto others.

A tendency to overanalyze life can be overcome. A worrier can learn to trust intuition. A skeptic can learn to "lighten up." Individuals who change directions constantly can learn to stay on course.

Progressed Mercury conjunct the south node of the Moon can symbolize turning around self-destructive tendencies. Individuals can gain a clearer perception of karmic themes. One may become less fixated on negative energy. Subconscious shadows can be brought to the conscious level. Inner conflicts can be faced. One may decide to deal with past limitations.

Individuals can gain insight into irrational behaviors. Understanding compulsive thoughts is liberating. A more flexible nature can develop. Rigid thinking can yield to new options. New inspiration can take place. A tired intellect can be moved by powerful emotional releases. Individuals may become more feeling. An intellectualizer can stop hiding behind a clever mind.

SHADOW
The **progressed Mercury conjunct the north or south node of the Moon** can symbolize a loss of perspective. Individuals may be disoriented by subconscious fears. Past-life themes can be confusing. People may not change negative habits. An extremely suspicious nature makes intimacy difficult. A rigid mental nature makes change difficult. One's concepts can be based on inaccurate perceptions.

A lack of faith could occur. Individuals can enslave themselves to limiting situations. A loss of clear mental perceptions can throw relationships out of balance. Not communicating clearly can occur. Emotions may be hidden. Individuals can fail to face emotional problems. They may hide from problems.

Square: Progressed Mercury Square North and South Nodes

Quincunx: Progressed Mercury Quincunx North or South Nodes

LIGHT
Progressed Mercury square the Moon's nodes can denote trust in one's perceptions. A person may resolve a conflict of intellect and emotions. A negative focus can seek the positive. Individuals can stop creating their own problems.

Writing and speaking skills can be accentuated. One may show communication talents. Thoughts may be deep and penetrating. People may go beneath the surface of situations. New meaningful symbols can stimulate new social contacts.

Progressed Mercury quincunx either the north or south node of the Moon is the "Yoga of finding new mental strength." Individuals may turn around self-doubt. A tendency to criticize self or others can be modified. An overly perfectionistic nature can learn to flow with life's natural rhythm. Individuals may stop projecting personal dislikes onto others. People can be more reflective.

SHADOW
The progressed Mercury square or quincunx the nodes of the Moon can manifest as nervous anxiety. Individuals can be driven toward a perfection that is not attainable. Expectations of self or others may be unreasonable. Individuals can lack depth. Perceptions might be too subject to the whims of life changes. People can lack a perceptive clarity that will carry them through hard times.

Individuals can become too concerned about their faults. Giving up on oneself blocks growth. Individuals can lack trust in feelings. Running to the intellect retards emotional growth. Intuition can be overruled by logic. One may pay too much attention to karmic themes. Concentrating on the negatives about oneself keeps new growth stagnant.

SOFT ASPECTS
Sextile: Progressed Mercury Sextile North or South Nodes
Trine: Progressed Mercury Trine North or South Nodes

LIGHT
Progressed Mercury sextile or trine the Moon's nodes can indicate tremendous mental stimulation. Many new seeds for this and future lifetimes being planted.

Intellect may be energized by self-acceptance. A new attitude regarding communication can come forward. A person can more adeptly communicate feelings. One's perceptions of life can be less in conflict. Life can have order. The environment no longer promotes stress.

The psyche can be filled with consciousness-raising experiences. New books, classes, and travel lift the spirits. A bored mental nature finds new enthusiasm.

SHADOW
The progressed Mercury sextile or trine the Moon's nodes can manifest as not separating fact from fiction. One may disrupt routines. Panic occurs easily.

Mental willpower can be lacking. Looking for easy answers leads to indulgence in old behaviors. Indecisiveness may leave one in limbo. Not thinking for oneself can lead to a confused existence. A lack of insight can occur. Individuals might be too easily pushed into situations they wanted to avoid.

DAWN

Mercury/nodes of the Moon aspects can symbolize new mental horizons. Perceptions can be elevated by new learning.

One may integrate the promise of the north node with past-life memories associated with the south node . The intellect can stop focusing on negatives. Life challenges can be faced with a decisive spirit.

PROGRESSED VENUS/MOON'S NODES ASPECTS

Progressed Venus/Nodes of the Moon

Process:	Deepening Value System
Ally:	Developing Inner Beauty
Illusion:	Chasing External Appearances

Progressed Venus/nodes of the Moon aspects can connote deep relationship impulses. Individuals can balance relationships. A need for peace and comfort could inspire personal changes. Excessive sensuality can be transcended. Deeper relationship values can be found. One may conquer compulsive relationship drives.

INTENSE ASPECTS
Conjunction: Progressed Venus Conjunct North Node
Progressed Venus Conjunct South Node

LIGHT

Progressed Venus conjunct the north node of the Moon can symbolize awakened social instincts. An inhibited person may go beyond a reserved nature. A need to share love can be born. Individuals may yearn for more balanced lives. Control can be gained over compulsive needs for a relationship. One may find inner beauty. New symbols can inspire growth. A person may find greater self-worth. Individuals can learn of life's natural abundance. A belief in poverty can be surrendered. People can reward themselves for hard work.

The self-indulgent can become less crazed with pleasing the senses. One can become intoxicated by passionate, creative energy. Self-love can lift one through obstacles. An aesthetic expression can bring material and emotional satisfaction.

Progressed Venus conjunct the south node of the Moon can point to making an ally of past-life energies. One may form a new relationship with irrational behaviors.

Relationships may strengthen one's determination to find a true balance. Intense emotional needs can be put to good use. One may do well in business or financial dealings that call for intuitive negotiations. One may attract peers and lovers working on similar karmic themes. Both people can help each other grow spiritually. An individual can learn to accept faults. Irrational blame of others can be surrendered.

SHADOW

The **progressed Venus conjunct the north or south nodes of the Moon** can express as a loss of self in sensual desires. Individuals can be emotionally unpredictable. Intimacy and caring become feared experiences. One can move too fast through life. Physical pleasure and social stimulation reach extreme proportions. Life can become an external show.

Individuals can lack the determination to sustain long-term relationships. A lack of emotional clarity can make for unusual relationship patterns. One may carelessly hurt others. Inauthentic relating causes one to move in and out of situations.

People can remain too long in unhealthy relationships. Too much dependence on others (for material or emotional needs) can be a problem. A lack of self-esteem can bring relationship or career confusion. One may be too sensitive concerning rejection. Forgiving oneself is still an ideal but not reality.

Square: Progressed Venus Square North and South Nodes

Quincunx: Progressed Venus Quincunx North or South Nodes

LIGHT

Progressed Venus square the Moon's nodes can denote resolving a lack of self-esteem. Individuals can find greater self-confidence. Past-life compulsive drives to lose oneself in relationships can be transcended. Power could be distributed more evenly between people. A desperate drive for fulfillment through relationships can be overcome. A greater understanding of emotional needs can calm extreme intensity. Relationships become based on mutual respect. Values can deepen. A tendency to live emotions through others may be modified.

Progressed Venus quincunx either the north or south nodes of the Moon is the "Yoga of finding a more valued life path." Individuals can find a refreshing, new lease on life. Wounded hearts can look into the motives for relationships. A lack of self-esteem can be turned around. A clear emotional nature can attract a more balanced life. One may stop living a life of extremes. The life is no longer a constant soap opera.

One may tap into past-life pitfalls. One does not repeat the same mistakes. One may stop expecting too much from others.

SHADOW

Progressed Venus square or quincunx the Moon's nodes can express as emotional disorientation. The life can be a series of emotional and financial disasters. Individuals may lack common sense. They can waste energy and resources foolishly. Too many ups and downs create instability.

A lack of depth in relating can be shown. Relationships can be based on surface appearances. A failure to learn from karmic excesses may be apparent. A lack of love can lead to food or substance abuse.

SOFT ASPECTS

Sextile: Progressed Venus Sextile North or South Nodes

Trine: Progressed Venus Trine North or South Nodes

LIGHT

Progressed Venus sextile or trine the nodes of the Moon can reflect a natural harmony with the environment. A very intense person can learn to move without burnout. A passive person can become stimulated by peers. A new eagerness to interact can bring growth.

A restlessness with old habits can bring a fresh start. Laziness or apathy can be conquered. One can awaken to the beauty of life. An angry individual can find peace. Self-worth can reach new highs. One may stop being too sensitive to criticism. A fear of rejection no longer inhibits social and creative impulses.

SHADOW

Progressed Venus sextile or trine the nodes of the Moon can manifest as gullibility. A desire for acceptance can be extreme. Individuals may sacrifice their own values. Self-esteem can be too influenced by opinions of others. The path of least resistance can be followed. An inner confusion attracts strange relationships. One may not follow intuition. An inner voice can be resisted. Life can lack meaning. Individuals may lack real purpose. Escapism related to past-life themes can occur.

DAWN

Venus/Moon's nodes aspects can point to a deepening value system. Individuals can overcome past-life habits of extremism. Relationship needs can be balanced. A compulsive desire for relationships can be sobered by a clearer self-esteem. One may be strengthened by tuning into emotional intensity.

PROGRESSED MARS/MOON'S NODE ASPECTS

Progressed Mars/Nodes of the Moon

Process: The Power of Decision Making

Ally: A Clear Identity

Illusion: Loss of Self

Progressed Mars/nodes of the Moon aspects can denote an intense time. Individuals can move ahead forcefully. The past may no longer be a convenient excuse. One can busily pursue new goals. The life can be put on course. An already smooth sailing existence can catch the wind of opportunity.

INTENSE ASPECTS
Conjunction: Progressed Mars Conjunct North Node
Progressed Mars Conjunct South Node

LIGHT
Progressed Mars conjunct the north node of the Moon can symbolize revitalizing energy. This can be a dramatic awakening. A procrastinator can slowly get going. A type "A" personality can find a greater purpose.

One may face karmic challenges more directly. One gets lost in the past less often. Individuals can embrace a strong identity. They may find a sudden motivation. People have more energy than usual. The life takes on more exciting challenges. A person may establish a personal turf.

Progressed Mars conjunct the south node of the Moon can be an about face, away from self-defeating behaviors. Self-hatred can be transcended. Self-confidence increases.

Impatience can be moderated. A selfish tendency can grow more sensitive to the needs of others. A territorial consciousness can open up its borders. Inconsistency can find follow-through. One may do more in a shorter time. An angry person can better direct feelings. One may cut away from limiting circumstances. A bold step into new territory lifts one above problems.

SHADOW
Progressed Mars conjunct the north or south node of the Moon can denote self-destruction. One may take anger and frustration out on himself. Good situations can be left too quickly. A hurried pace causes one to repeat the same mistakes. A reckless mentality leaves much unfinished business.

A selfish nature easily hurts others. A person may have a narrow, self-serving focus. Territorial consciousness results in well-protected borders. Individuals may hide emotional intensity behind a "macho-facho" display. A hard heart can keep others at a distance.

People may have a weak identity. Assertion instincts can hit an all-time low. A refusal to be motivated can leave one stalled.

Square: Progressed Mars Square North and South Nodes

Quincunx: Progressed Mars Quincunx North and South Nodes

LIGHT
Progressed Mars square the nodes of the Moon can indicate forcefully facing karma. Strength and determination can reach new heights.

Goals may seem within one's reach. An inner conflict can be resolved through action. Sitting on the fence is no longer a problem. One may participate more actively in life. A passion for the present can emerge. One may make peace with the past. A growing identity brings satisfaction.

Progressed Mars quincunx either the north or south node of the Moon can point to new self-satisfaction. One can gain more self-control. Raw energy finds a focus. This is the **"Yoga of tuning into raw intensity."**

One may outgrow childish temper tantrums. Angry outbursts are no longer needed to grab attention. Individuals fearing action can learn to take charge. Initiating qualities can be born. A hurt ego can recover. A tired psyche and body find strength. One may stop being his own worst enemy. Self-destruction is transcended. One may slow down and experience more depth. Patience becomes a virtue.

SHADOW
Progressed Mars square or quincunx the nodes of the Moon can express as a lack of self-insight. One may be too disturbed by outer events. An unclear sense of self leads to trouble.

One may enter situations too forcefully. A lack of control over raw energy can overwhelm others. Being in too much of a hurry to conquer karma can bring more trouble. A warrior may need some reflection about a course of action.

Individuals can lack assertion. Worry about consequences keeps one from initiating. Irrational drives can create extremes. A reckless nature can take crazy chances.

SOFT ASPECTS
  Sextile: Progressed Mars Sextile North or South Nodes
  Trine: Progressed Mars Trine North or South Nodes

LIGHT
Progressed Mars sextile or trine the nodes of the Moon can indicate a time of sowing. Individuals can move ahead without feeling environmental conflict. One may show great poise during difficult situations. A tolerance for discord gives one self-assurance. A decisive nature prevents inner conflict.

People can show sensitivity to others. Assertion and cooperation can be displayed. A hard-driven individual avoids creating senseless wars. Comfort with one's identity attracts cooperation from others. A person can be a catalyst for change. Past-life themes can be integrated into positive attitudes. One may turn anger into growth-promoting actions.

SHADOW
Progressed Mars sextile or trine the nodes of the Moon can express as angry moods. One may fail to cope with conflict. Sensitivity for self or others may be lacking. Individuals can lack the courage to initiate change. Hiding behind others can stifle growth. Identity can be flighty, based on soap opera or comic-book heroes. A hunger for new challenges is lost.

Individuals may expect something for nothing. Running away from challenges drains inner strength. People can lack patience. Jumping from one project to another leads nowhere. The life can lack direction. Insights are shallow.

DAWN
Mars/Moon's nodes aspects can sharpen identity. Assertion and present-life needs are mutually reinforcing. One can face a long-awaited challenge. One may stop running to the past and look into the mirror of present challenges.

JUPITER/MOON'S NODES ASPECTS

Transiting Jupiter/Nodes of the Moon

Process:	The Faith to Face the Present
Ally:	Eclectic Impulses
Illusion:	Inflated Self-Confidence

Transiting Jupiter/nodes of the Moon aspects can connote an illuminating faith. People can go forward with new hope. Past setbacks are no longer a thorn in the path. A "way" can be found. Individuals can adopt a broader vision. Stimulating knowledge permeates the life. People feel guided to new resources.

INTENSE ASPECTS
Conjunction: Transiting Jupiter Conjunct North Node
Transiting Jupiter Conjunct South Node

LIGHT
Transiting Jupiter conjunct the north node of the Moon can point to a new chartered path. A life in a rut can find new meaning. One may discover greater insights through travel, books, education, or spiritual searches. One can attract abundance at this time. One can bring good forces through a positive attitude. Not looking back can lead to new opportunity.

Eclectic interests can conquer problems. Teaching and communication skills can be talents. One may find a teacher who inspires greater learning. The life philosophy can broaden immensely. Self-understanding can expand.

Transiting Jupiter conjunct the south node of the Moon can mark transcending karmic pulls. One may find the faith to deal with the past. A lack of faith can be transcended. The negative is not so compelling. Lack of abundance no longer dominates.

Extreme overconfidence can be balanced. Narrow and judgmental attitudes can be surrendered. New understanding brings more tolerance for others. Foolish wandering can turn into a meaningful search. A too serious individual can find a lighter heart. Running to greener pastures can become believing in the present. A lack of reasoning power can be aided by new, eclectic growth.

SHADOW

Transiting Jupiter conjunct the north or south nodes of the Moon can express as extreme self-righteousness. One may be convinced that his way is the best. Others are missing out. A narrow perspective limits one. Arguing incessantly over principles can wear out relationships. A need to always be right is irritating.

Traveling in search of greener pastures can leave behind good situations. One may compulsively gamble on a new, hasty risk. Patience my be lacking. One may bite off more than he can chew.

A lazy attitude can block new learning. Complacency puts inspiration and faith to sleep. Negative beliefs thwart abundance.

Square: Transiting Jupiter Square North or South Nodes

Quincunx: Transiting Jupiter Quincunx North or South Nodes

LIGHT

Transiting Jupiter square the nodes of the Moon can symbolize finding the faith to resolve a life conflict. Individuals can attract guidance from universal forces. This can come through the power of one's beliefs. People may go to counselors and healers who offer insight into problems. People can stop running away. They find the strength to go through problems. Knowledge can balance emotional confusion. One can see beyond obstacles. Faith is born from a greater vision.

Transiting Jupiter quincunx the north or south node of the Moon is the "Yoga of finding new alternatives." Individuals can embrace new hope. Spiritual strength fosters growth. People can move courageously into new directions. A more reflective nature may combine with actions. One moves with a greater awareness. Negative attitudes can slowly become positive; the too confident can become more cautious; the wasteful can become more prudent; the fearful can discover faith.

SHADOW

Transiting Jupiter square or quincunx the nodes of the Moon can express as wasteful actions. A life of excess can result in exhaustion. A lack of focus and discipline yields little satisfaction. Individuals can lack the courage to live principles. A lack of faith can retard growth. A stubborn resistance to new knowledge inhibits flexibility.

Past-life themes related to extreme judgment of others can surface again. One may hastily throw away growth-promoting situations. Pompous behavior does not win admirers. Self-centered attitudes can bring a loss of perspective. Taking principles to the extreme loses reality. Individuals can think they are above universal or physical laws.

SOFT ASPECTS

Sextile: Transiting Jupiter Sextile North or South Nodes

Trine: Transiting Jupiter Trine North or South Nodes

LIGHT

Transiting Jupiter sextile or trine the nodes of the Moon can denote spontaneous faith. People may discover a more expansive life purpose. The future never looked brighter. One may enjoy an abundant present. One's principles are in synch with life.

People may tap into a greater enjoyment of life. Worries and tensions are released. New learning experiences fulfill a thirst for knowledge. Travel can be especially therapeutic. One may conquer past-life behaviors that have stunted growth. A more positive approach attracts abundance. A person can feel rewarded for hard work. An individual lacking initiative can be moved by the winds of inspiration.

SHADOW

Transiting Jupiter sextile or trine the nodes of the Moon can express as an exaggerated sense of self. Individuals can create situations like General Custer at Little Big Horn. One might foolishly defy the odds. Too much confidence (due to a "going with the flow") can result. A reckless abandonment of common sense brings difficulties. Wasteful actions reflect superficial knowledge. One may lack insight into situations. A passion for one's own opinions inhibits input from others. A "soft" faith can run away during a crisis. Individuals may lack conviction to morals and principles. They may not practice what they readily preach!

DAWN

Jupiter/Moon's nodes aspects can point to a strong belief in a life vision. Expanding one's horizons attracts new challenges. Self-discovery becomes a mission in life. This can feel like "no turning back." The time is today. The search for greater knowledge through travel (on the physical and mental planes) stimulates self-illumination.

SATURN/MOON'S NODES ASPECTS
Transiting Saturn/Nodes of Moon

Process:	Consolidating Past and Present
Ally:	Wisdom from the Past
Illusion:	Nothing Else to Learn

Transiting Saturn/nodes of the Moon aspects symbolize consciousness of karmic patterns. One seeks to balance new energies and recorded personal history. These aspects are important for soul growth.

INTENSE ASPECTS
Conjunction: Transiting Saturn Conjunct North Node
Transiting Saturn Conjunct South Node

LIGHT

FIRE/AIR
Transiting Saturn conjunct a north node in a fire sign (or house) and opposing a south node in an air sign (or house) may symbolize learning patience. An individual may take responsibility for actions (fire). One may become more perceptive (air).

A person who has lacked initiative (due to a fear of failure) may develop new confidence. An individual may mature and develop meaningful commitments. Past-life themes denote possible confused mental perceptions. The north node in fire is pointing to a need to solidify identity. The person may be learning to pay more attention to his own needs. The mental focus of south node in air can combine with action focus of north node in fire to become acting on perceptions.

Transiting Saturn conjunct a north node in an air sign (or house) and opposing a south node in a fire sign (or house) can symbolize new concentration. One may become more conscious of others. The opposite south node in fire points to past-life themes related to insensitivity and recklessness. One may be learning to think (air) before leaping (fire). A new alertness (air) may lead to a better timing of actions (fire). One can turn the raw energy of the south node in fire into productivity. One's mental horizons can recharge by forging these elements together.

Transiting Saturn conjunct a south node in a fire sign (or house) opposing a north node in an air sign (or house) can denote confrontation with a karmic pattern. This represents a deepening of soul growth. Someone can take control of self-destructive habits. A person may need to take responsibility for actions. Someone with a long streak of impatience may overcome this pattern. This can be a person who previously has been too self-centered. The opposite north node is pointing to more awareness of others.

If one has denied his own initiative and identity, he may take a bold first step to be himself. One's perceptions (air) may break through a fear of action (fire). The powerful, wild south node in fire can combine with the mentally cool north node in air to find new creative options. One may conquer fears, inhibitions, and lack of consciousness. Actions may have a deeper meaning.

Transiting Saturn conjunct a south node in an air sign (or house) opposing a north node in a fire sign (or house) can symbolize controlling mental energy. One may perceive his thoughts are too shallow. One may develop a new mental depth.

A person may desire to be taken more seriously. A new pride (fire) in self can come forward. One may show a new assertiveness. The mental dexterity of the south node in air can alchemize with the zest for life of the north node in fire. A new positive outlook can begin. One may search for new challenges. A person can conquer a fear of change and welcome life transitions.

EARTH/WATER

Transiting Saturn conjunct a north node in an earth sign (or house) and opposing a south node in a water sign (or house) can connote finding stability. An individual can redefine career goals. One may choose a career that is a more authentic self-expression.

A south node in water might indicate a consciousness filled with escapism. The divine discontent in the water element can make stability difficult. A person may stop evading responsibility. A life of extremes may be balanced by sensible earth.

The powerful intuitive and aesthetic drives of the south node in water can combine nicely with the grounding energy of the north node in earth. An individual can find peace and accept life as it happens. One's past-life memories and intuitive visions (water) can reinforce life ambitions (earth).

Transiting Saturn conjunct a north node in a water sign (or house) and opposing a south node in an earth sign (or house) can denote defining emotions. One may transcend a fear of commitment. A person may overcome a fear of intimacy. He may accept a painful past history or early childhood problems.

A person may balance dependency needs. A new confidence in expressing feelings may develop. One may overcome extreme negativity. The hardworking security consciousness of the south node in earth can combine with the perfectionistic and intuitive themes of the water element into realizing one's greatest dreams.

Transiting Saturn conjunct a south node in an earth sign (or house) and opposing a north node in a water sign (or house) can denote facing a life of denial. This can be a person who was austere and serious. One may find his feeling side.

A person could live out the other extreme. He might be too attached to physical appetites or solely interested in logical reasoning. Values can be heavily materialistic. One may tune into his north node in water. A new spiritual and intuitive consciousness may grow.

The physical and sensual south node in earth can combine with the sensitive north node in water into a new awareness. One may become a more giving person. An individual can find a new faith. One may transcend extreme pulls of the physical plane.

Transiting Saturn conjunct a south node in a water sign (or house) and opposing a north node in an earth sign (or house) can depict confronting escapism. The cosmic chiropractor is pointing to a need to balance idealism (water) and realism (earth).

Lack of faith may be a karmic pattern. Too much devotion to limiting causes can be turned around. One may balance a life of giving away too much to others. Extreme dependency on others (water) may be balanced with self-sufficiency (earth). An individual may boldly assume responsibility and make decisions.

One's karmic pattern may be not knowing how to set limits and follow-through on ambitions. Individuals can solidly plan and structure their lives. A new respect for the physical plane can develop. One can mature greatly.

The divine discontent of the south node in water can combine with the determination of the north node in earth to become satisfaction. Much can be accomplished materially.

SHADOW

FIRE/AIR

Transiting Saturn conjunct the north node in fire/opposing a south node in air or transiting Saturn conjunct a south node in fire/opposing a north node in air can express as an extreme lack of discipline. Perceptions (air) and actions (fire) can be in constant conflict. People can wildly disregard authority and constraints (Saturn). One may fail to mature.

Saturn can denote a rigid mind-set (air) and inflexible actions (fire). One may foolishly make the same mistakes due to a failure to change attitudes. He can judge others harshly. One may suffer burnout from a refusal to slow down. Type A personalities can become workaholics. They can become all business and forget the lightness of these elements.

People may fear spontaneous thoughts or actions. They sit on the fence of life (as a spectator). Individuals may adopt a cultural mind-set that keeps them apart from others. They may lack insight into those who differ in background. A narrow mind-set can be limiting. A person can get attached to being an authority figure. A fear of losing control keeps one from trusting others. A fear of honest communication can frustrate partners.

EARTH/WATER

Transiting Saturn conjunct a north node in earth/opposing a south node in water or transiting Saturn conjunct a south node in earth/opposing a north node in water can express as too much belief in observable reality. Intuition (water) is swallowed by physical plane experience (earth). People can get too controlling (fearing vulnerability). They can control their environment (earth) or feelings (water). A person can become a loner. Nobody is needed. Individuals can become dictatorial.

Some people give into depression. A person can have little self-respect. He may deny himself rewards. Dead-end jobs and relationships can result. One's domestic situation can be out of balance. Too much dedication to work (or family) could be stressful. A person may feel too responsible for others. People can feel like failures. Their time can be disorganized and undisciplined. A person may feel ruled by the demands of parents, bosses, children, or spouses.

An individual can get quite illogical in this node combination. An earthy (material) consciousness combined with a strong watery dependent nature can result in strange experiences. One can feel spaced-out and lose touch with reality. Ideals may slip away.

An individual can overidentify with karma. The water element symbolizes a release of karmic material. A person may tune into deep, unconscious layers. One may run away from himself. One's idealism may be crushed by reality. A person may not deal well with real life. An escape into fantasy or substance abuses makes for an abortive journey.

Square: Transiting Saturn Square North and South Nodes

LIGHT

FIRE/AIR

Transiting Saturn square fire/air nodes can indicate people move with more caution. Common sense and the wisdom learned through "past" experiences are used. A new steady direction is satisfying. A more sober attitude brings stability. Things of lasting value are appreciated. Commitment is no longer a forbidden word.

EARTH/WATER

Transiting Saturn square earth/water nodes can manifest as organizing one's life. People may stop fighting themselves. Responsibility and dependency needs can be solved. Escapism may be conquered. Ideals get grounded. Old problems can be solved. A new commitment to ambitions brings confidence. A guilty person can find new faith; an overly materialistic individual can find more emotional content; a lonely person can find love.

SHADOW

FIRE/AIR

Transiting Saturn square fire/air Moon's nodes can be an abortive journey. One may fail to learn from his past (of this life and previous lives). Individuals may not slow down. They can ignore body signals. They may repeat mistakes. An individual could suffer from a scattered consciousness.

One may be too stimulated by power drives. Self-importance can distort perceptions. Rigid concepts can create inflexible actions. A "play by my rules" philosophy alienates others. Excessive pride can lead to loneliness. Spontaneity may be blocked. A lack of pride can stifle future plans. One might be afraid to communicate. The liveliness of fire/air could be deadened by fear.

EARTH/WATER

Transiting Saturn square earth/water nodes can manifest as caution and more caution. One's life can move in reverse. People can give into a painful past. A fear of resolving early childhood (or past-life issues) can frustrate the present. Life could feel like a dead weight. Individuals can become too responsible for others. They may be parenting excessively. Holding onto the past might become a compulsive power motive. Clinging to an insecure existence can be a disaster.

People give up too easily. Irrational fears stifle creativity. A blocked emotional nature is frustrating. Running from commitments leads back to nowhere. A lack of roots is frightening and disorienting. Workaholism can be a problem. Individuals can grow overly serious and worried. Work may become an escape from problems.

Quincunx: Transiting Saturn Quincunx North Node
Transiting Saturn Quincunx South Node

The quincunx of transiting Saturn to the nodes of the Moon is the "Yoga of staying determined." A person can learn to control compulsive habits.

LIGHT

FIRE/AIR

Transiting Saturn quincunx fire/air nodes can manifest as gaining focus regarding actions and perceptions. **Transiting Saturn quincunx the nodes in fire** can indicate more centered actions. New self-control can be reached. The impulsive can slow down; the angry can clarify issues; the passive can begin realizing ambitions. A false ego (or extreme attention needs) can be confronted. People who give up too easily can learn determination; wasteful individuals can conserve energy and resources; irresponsible and impatient individuals find the patience to assume responsibility.

Transiting Saturn quincunx the air nodes can reflect more realistic perceptions. An individual's ideas may easily integrate into society. A fear of authority figures can be transcended. A scattered mentality can be organized. Changeability gives way to decisiveness.

EARTH/WATER

Transiting Saturn quincunx the Moon's nodes in earth can be a lesson in defining ambitions. Worn out paths may be cast aside. A renewed commitment to deepest ambitions is possible. Individuals may reach back for extra strength. Cultural myths can be conquered to realize one's own potential.

Transiting Saturn quincunx the Moon's nodes in water can overcome a guilty past. Missing pieces may be found. A disoriented person can find groundedness; an idealist some reality; someone with no ideals an imagination. Self-destructive, past-life habits finally are resolved. Escapism is no longer a false ally.

SHADOW

FIRE/AIR

Transiting Saturn quincunx the Moon's nodes in fire can connote rigid actions. A person may resist wise advice. Excessive pride can cloud judgment. Impatience could lead to disaster. Status-seeking can lead to shallow consciousness. One may repeat karmic mistakes associated with power. Striving for success can be ruthless. Being an authority figure seems the only goal.

Transiting Saturn quincunx the Moon's nodes in air might indicate a rigid sense of direction. Intellect can become stagnant. A desire for excessive stimulation could lead to restlessness and fickleness. The life may have no clear focus. One can be the pawn of authority figures. Karmic aloofness and intellectualism can become unruly. The present is still another enactment of a rigid past.

EARTH/WATER

Transiting Saturn quincunx the Moon's nodes in earth can manifest as work and more work! A life devoted to ambition can be out of balance. The emotions or private life are ignored. Practicality may kill intuitive insights. A life with no dreams can be dry. Commitments might be all status related. This person could deny himself success. A fear of failure could be the culprit. Some individuals try too hard. Spontaneity is dormant.

Transiting Saturn quincunx the Moon's nodes in water can manifest as excess dependency. People can rely too heavily on others for strength. A need to believe in oneself or in a greater power is denied. Life problems can be denied. Individuals can remain in nongrowth-promoting situations. Life can be disorganized. Karmic fear of responsibility can occur here. An emotional heaviness can thwart success. One may fear closeness. Loneliness and depression (due to emotional denial) are possible.

SOFT ASPECTS

Sextile: Transiting Saturn Sextile North or South Nodes

Trine: Transiting Saturn Trine North or South Nodes

The soft aspects formed by transiting Saturn to the Moon's nodes can be a time of appreciating one's life. An aware person who is really working to gain higher consciousness can use these soft aspects to enjoy greater understanding.

One may feel rewarded for working on karmic habits. One's environment can be satisfying and in synch with a life purpose. Ambitions can receive the support of family, community, and authority figures. One may be recognized for accomplishments.

LIGHT

FIRE/AIR

Transiting Saturn sextile/trine a fire/air node polarity can reflect a new excitement regarding ambitions. Individuals can find a creative spark. A stagnated existence can find new life. The **Saturn sextile** to fire nodes can denote looking into motives for actions. Air nodes organize ideas. The **Saturn trine** to fire nodes can indicate working for long-term ambitions. Air nodes take each day seriously.

An individual with a lot of intense aspects natally can find these aspects pleasurable. Type "A" personalities with the fire/air nodal polarity may learn to slow down. Deepening perception (air) and patience (fire) can occur. Working wiser (rather than only harder) can be refreshing. Hard work may bring deserved recognition.

EARTH/WATER

Transiting Saturn sextile/trine an earth/water node polarity can denote the realization of ideals. One may make good on potential. A new level of handling crises can result. One may feel more in control.

The **Saturn sextile** can bring earth to develop expertise; water to play an intuitive hunch. The **Saturn trine** can encourage earth to an even greater determination for success; water to risk a failure to fulfill a dream.

SHADOW

Transiting Saturn sextile/trine a fire/air node polarity can manifest as ignoring life's physical laws. One can feel indestructible. Type "A" personalities could become too aggressive. The **Saturn sextile** to fire nodes can symbolize "bossy" or dictatorial actions; air nodes can become too rigidly attached to ideas; the **Saturn trine** to fire nodes can connote a lack of limits. A person could block his own spontaneity. (The caution of Saturn symbolizes a fear of failure.) The **Saturn trine** to air nodes can indicate inflexibility. One could resist focus or discipline. The harmonious trine may indicate a lack of concentration.

EARTH/WATER

Transiting Saturn sextile/trine an earth/water node polarity can symbolize too much material focus. The **Saturn sextile** to earth nodes can become workaholism; water nodes can fear making dreams visible. Stagnation could occur. Saturn represents hitting the brakes. Earth and water lack the self-initiating quality of fire and air.

   Transiting Saturn trine earth nodes can become compulsive devotion to status. (This can dominate the entire life.) An individual could lack the stamina to reach his destination. He might expect things to come too easily. **Transiting Saturn trine water nodes** can represent a lack of ideals. One may be too hardened by life. This could be a person too dreamy to realize full potential.

DAWN

Transiting Saturn/Moon's nodes aspects can indicate bringing past and present into balance. One may gain control over too little or too much focus on certain life themes. Saturn is the sobering remedy to many karmic ailments. The cosmic chiropractor's transits to our Moon's nodes can indicate adjusting behavior. A person does not always like what he sees during these aspects. It can be a painful dose of reality. However, this is the time when one may truly walk from darkness into the light.

URANUS/MOON'S NODES ASPECTS

Transiting Uranus/Nodes of Moon

Process:	Living the Freedom of the Present
Ally:	Unique Visions
Illusion:	Fear of Unique Qualities

Transiting Uranus/nodes of the Moon aspects denote transcending karmic habits through dynamic awakening. One may accelerate soul growth. A careless individual can take one step forward and three steps back. Transiting Uranus aspecting the nodes of the Moon denotes one might alter karmic habits. These aspects can indicate one mentally imagines new habits (north nodes) and develops a new objectivity regarding irrational behaviors (south node).

INTENSE ASPECTS
Conjunction: Transiting Uranus Conjunct North Node
Transiting Uranus Conjunct South Node

LIGHT

FIRE/AIR

Transiting Uranus conjunct a north node in a fire sign (or house) and opposing a south node in an air sign (or house) can denote a more unique self. A new inspiring attitude can develop, clarifying irrational thought processes (south node in air). A pride in one's individuality may drive one into creative actions. Mental focus (airy south node) may reflect more respect for self and the needs of others. The individual may learn to act on impulses (fire) rather than only thinking (air).

Transiting Uranus conjunct a north node in an air sign (or house) and opposing a south node in a fire sign (or house) can discover new mental insights. Flashes of clarity — like never before — can come. One may relate to others flexibly. Goals appear more attainable. One could choose new peers. A new confidence in communication may occur. One may seek equality in relating (air) and drop an exaggerated sense of self (fire). Thoughts (air) interfaced with courage (fiery north node) can become an exhilarating search for truth and a clear identity.

Transiting Uranus conjunct a south node in a fire sign (or house) opposing a north node in an air sign (or house) can depict a sudden reversal of a karmic pattern. "Instant karma" can occur in Uranus conjunction aspects to the south node. A conscious person can adjust quite quickly. A person may learn to rest before burning out.

A mental perception may get the most out of high-energy periods. This is a high voltage aspect. Uranus can combine with the irrational fire of the south node to seek immediate gratification. One may perceive underlying drives for attention, competitiveness, and forceful opinions. The opposite north node calls for more reasoning ability. This is similar to Uranus transit conjunct the north node in fire but more potentially volatile. One might conquer an inflated ego with transiting Uranus conjunct the south node in fire.

A karmic pattern of losing self in others may be the focus. The individual may become justifiably more selfish in fulfilling goals (or needs). The opposite north node symbolizes keeping sight of the reasons for fiery actions. The attention span may be rather short. One may fulfill the north node in air by concentrating and clarifying thoughts. She may curb compulsive recklessness.

Transiting Uranus conjunct a south node in an air sign (or house) is opposing a north node in a fire sign (or house). One may deal with nervous energy. Finding a creative outlet may reveal hidden talent in a communication field. One may tap into a new goal. Individuals may be lifted into a cause greater than self. Ideas (air) may inspire others into action (fire). A person can make mental connections previously lacking. A new courage in communicating ideas can develop. A new confidence can be found in learning.

EARTH/WATER

Transiting Uranus conjunct a north node in an earth sign (or house) and opposing a south node in a water sign (or house) may be new skills. One may provide for his own welfare (north node in earth). A new sensitivity to the needs of others can occur (south node in water). A person may go beyond logic or practicality (earth) to trust intuition (water). One may learn discipline and responsibility (earth) to conquer escapism (water).

Transiting Uranus conjunct a north node in a water sign (or house) and opposing a south node in an earth sign (or house) can be more aware. One's intuition may sharpen greatly. The mental objectivity of Uranus can sharpen the clarity of the intuitive, watery north node. The stability of the opposite earth south node can ground this intuitive energy into lasting value.

An individual may learn to trust intuition. Too much belief in the logical (earth) could limit dreams (water). A person may reach new feeling depths. One may allow for more emotional content.

Transiting Uranus conjunct a south node in an earth sign (or house) and opposing a north node in a water sign (or house) may transcend physical consciousness. People may have difficulty rising above the physical plane. The opposite north node is pointing to intuition (water).

One may reach a higher consciousness. The north node in water can show more flexibility and compassion. A new sensitivity can develop. A person may find a higher faith (or greater connectedness with a higher power). Feeling less responsible for situations and trusting a higher power can relieve self-imposed pressure. Perhaps a person failed to take responsibility (or honor commitments) as a past-life pattern. One may follow through on responsibility. A new attitude of cooperation can occur.

Transiting Uranus conjunct a south node in a water sign (or house) and opposing a north node in an earth sign (or house) can be transcending self-destructive habits. One's emotional intensity stirs powerfully. One may gain more faith in self and in a higher power. Past-life aesthetic talents may become awakened.

The opposite north node in earth is pointing to finding order. An individual may use creature comforts to remedy a life of too much denial.

One may transcend perfectionistic tendencies. Humor and putting thoughts into order may release emotional pressures. A person can break away from dependency on others. A person can balance closeness (water) and distance (Uranus) in the life. The north node in earth can symbolize taking care of material needs.

SHADOW

FIRE/AIR

Transiting Uranus conjunct the north node in fire/opposing south node in air or transiting Uranus conjunct a south node in fire/opposing north node in air can be an excessive "me" focus. Behaviors might be selfish. The fire element can typify an angry individualist with little insight into the needs of others. The communication themes of air could become eccentric thinking.

People can get too expansive, and suffer from burnout. They may have little regard for physical limitations. An undisciplined nature (with an inability to focus on goals) can occur. Impatience with self and others may be the key problem.

One may exaggerate the truth. Perceptions can be inaccurate. One could blame others for problems. One can have a tremendous pride (fire) problem. An argumentative nature could result.

Both fire and air, when combined with Uranus, can symbolize a speedy nature. One may miss important details. A lack of attention to the needs of others can be a problem.

Transiting Uranus conjunct a north node in air/opposing the south node fire or transiting Uranus conjunct a south node in air/opposing a north node in fire can express as scattered energy. Ideas can be too electrically charged to focus.

Rigid thinking can make cooperation difficult. One may lack adaptability and resist change. Transitions could be upsetting. A resistance to new learning can dull one's consciousness.

An individual may become too fixated on thinking. An inability to express emotion or compassion can alienate others. One may think rather than act.

A tremendous drive to individuality can make stable relationships difficult to establish. People can be very changeable. The drive for stimulation can become a constant need. One may not want to be limited by commitments.

EARTH/WATER

Transiting Uranus conjunct a north node in earth/opposing south node in water or transiting Uranus conjunct a south node in earth/opposing north node in water can run away from commitments. One may lack sensitivity.

A person can become consumed by material goals. One may have trouble understanding the intangible. A lack of psychological depth can make for shallow life experiences.

The water element points to dependency issues. One may lean on others too much for support. A person could be uncomfortable with closeness. One may vacillate quickly from one extreme to the other.

Transiting Uranus conjunct a north node in water/opposing a south node in earth or transiting Uranus conjunct a south node in water/opposing north node in earth can express as aloofness. One may be difficult to perceive. Extreme emotional confusion may make relationships unstable. The entire life may be in constant flux. Extreme mood swings may dominate the consciousness. A person can fight her intuition. One may enter disastrous situations.

People may have little faith in intuition (or in a higher power). Substance abuses can be problematic. Individuals can be too devoted to others. An individual may live emotions and creativity through another person. A person may fear her own power. A denial of feelings, sensitivity, and emotional strength can occur.

Square: Transiting Uranus Square North and South Nodes

LIGHT

FIRE/AIR

Transiting Uranus square fire/air nodes can denote one's impulses and perceptions are working together. An individual may find a new confidence in planning future goals. Excitement concerning new self-awareness can occur. One may boldly display a new identity. People can awaken to new heights. There is no end to the imagination. The past can be something to conquer. The present and future beckon with hints of self-discovery.

EARTH/WATER

Transiting Uranus square earth/water nodes can symbolize transcending limited vision. One may rise above addictive habits (that have been karmic roadblocks). A greater awareness of others (and less selfishness) can occur. One may adopt a new humility. Dependent individuals may discover that self-indulgence is okay.

A surprise about-face from limiting karmic patterns can occur. The present becomes a new chapter of experimentation. The opinions of others are less important than before. This can be a refreshing time.

SHADOW

FIRE/AIR

Transiting Uranus square fire/air nodes can denote erratic, out-of-control behavior. One may lose purpose. Follow-through can be absent. Too much energy and no direction produces tremendous tension. An individual can be short-fused. Impatience and aloofness may alienate others. A lack of sensitivity and cooperation will not win admiration. Past habits can be repeated. The present and future might be a mixture of careless actions and off-key perceptions. Individuals may have little interest in commitment. A "digging up the seed" mentality may dominate.

EARTH/WATER

When **transiting Uranus squares earth/water nodes**, indecision may cause missed opportunities. An individual's ability to relax (earth) may clash with emotional tension (water). One can be trapped by not resolving past-life material. An individual can rationalize her way around issues. The present is a meaningless journey. Individuals may resist higher consciousness. They can settle for the boring and non-stimulating, running away from real growth. This can be an insecure time. One may feel caught between where she would like to be and the past.

   Quincunx: Transiting Uranus Quincunx North Node
                   Transiting Uranus Quincunx South Node

LIGHT

Transiting Uranus quincunx either the north or south node can denote finding a new direction. This quincunx is the **"Yoga of finding one's own way."** Thoughts and actions (air/fire nodes) or ideals and reality (water/earth nodes) may be brought to new clarity.

FIRE/AIR

Transiting Uranus quincunx fire/air nodes can manifest as new actions and perceptions. **Transiting Uranus quincunx fire nodes** can symbolize mental objectivity about actions. A person may perceive the outcome of situations before rushing into trouble. A new pride can stimulate growth.

   Transiting Uranus quincunx air nodes can show a new ability to prioritize needs. One may move boldly ahead with less distractions. Mental sharpness can replace self-doubt; sarcasm can be substituted by greater diplomacy; aloofness can give way to joint cooperation; experimentation can stimulate what was once a lack of curiosity.

EARTH/WATER

Transiting Uranus quincunx earth/water nodes can symbolize rising above changes. Physical (earth) or emotional (water) security can blast into new territory. **Transiting Uranus quincunx the nodes in earth** can indicate bold new enterprises. An unimaginative mind can suddenly spark creative thoughts. An already-centered individual can enjoy even more life options.

   Transiting Uranus quincunx the nodes in water can denote gaining emotional clarity. A dependent type can find the roots of freedom. A free spirit can include others in dreams. The future can bring new hope. A creative person may tap into genius.

SHADOW

FIRE/AIR

Transiting Uranus quincunx fire/air nodes can symbolize inconsistency. **Transiting Uranus quincunx fire nodes** can symbolize full steam ahead with no stability. Burnout due to a fast pace can result. Plans do not materialize. Lack of foresight delays actions. Impatience and arrogance can disrupt opportunities. Insecurity concerning identity is possible. Individuals may live their lives nervously. People lacking pride or self-confidence can live too much through others.

Transiting Uranus quincunx air nodes can denote mental jitters. Nervous anxiety can deplete energy. A refusal to feel or express emotions can alienate others. Relationships may be shallow and impersonal. Individuals may have trouble setting priorities. Unneeded details clutter the life. Many loose ends distract from the overall purpose.

EARTH/WATER

Transiting Uranus quincunx earth/water nodes can denote being lost. Transiting Uranus quincunx earth nodes can connote burning bridges too quickly. Individuals can fight creative impulses. New situations can be resisted. Looking for freedom in material security takes away from new insights. People may depend too much on others for material stability.

Transiting Uranus quincunx water nodes can symbolize emotional disorientation. Individuals can be too emotionally dependent on others. A fear of freedom could stunt growth. The future can be scary. Transitions might cause breakdowns. A loss of perspective can cause confusion. Devotion to limiting people and causes is enslaving.

SOFT ASPECTS

 Sextile: Transiting Uranus Sextile North or South Nodes

 Trine: Transiting Uranus Trine North or South Nodes

LIGHT

The soft aspects formed by transiting Uranus to the Moon's nodes can be stimulating and reassuring. In these sextile/trine aspects, people may feel that life circumstances are giving the green light. Confidence can exude. One may feel more at rest within herself.

FIRE/AIR

Transiting Uranus sextile/trine a fire/air node polarity can denote new mental dexterity. An upbeat era can usher in. A person can joyously welcome new challenges. She may cause fewer of her own troubles. A new direction can stimulate growth. The **Uranus sextile** can excite fire to initiate and air to think quickly; the **Uranus trine** can encourage fire to develop longer range in vision; air to embrace its ideas.

Uranus can lift the natural outgoingness of fire and air to high levels of spontaneous self-expression. New challenges are welcomed.

EARTH/WATER

Transiting Uranus sextile/trine an earth/water node polarity can express as breaking away from inertia. A security-oriented individual can experiment. The mud formed by earth and water can be dried by the detached Uranus. A new perspective regarding stability can occur. The **Uranus sextile** can push earth to act on new insight and entice water to untangle dependency needs. The **Uranus trine** can bring earth into a more universal understanding and water to value its freedom.

SHADOW

FIRE/AIR

Transiting Uranus sextile/trine a fire/air node polarity can manifest as not learning from the past. Selfish attitudes can blind perspectives. The **Uranus sextile to fire nodes** might be a match to gasoline. A person may overreact to situations (or need too much intensity). The **Uranus sextile to air nodes** can be too much mental electricity. Excessive stimulation seems required. The **Uranus trine to fire nodes** can be bombastic attitudes. A "grass is greener" philosophy can dominate. The **Uranus trine to air nodes** can be mental defensiveness. Indecision can be a problem.

EARTH/WATER

Transiting Uranus sextile/trine an earth/water node polarity can be too much attachment to the past. Status quo or peer pressures can dominate. Rebelliousness can be denied. Dependency needs are unclear.

   Transiting Uranus sextile earth nodes can be stubborn ideas. People can be too fixated on worn-out roles. **Transiting Uranus sextile water nodes** can deny individuality. Closeness and distance become a separating issue. **Transiting Uranus trine earth nodes** can wait for the future to happen. A lack of self-starting can be a problem. **Transiting Uranus trine water nodes** can denote disorienting attachment to others. Goals may be unclear. Surrender to past karmic escapism is painful.

DAWN

Transiting Uranus/Moon's nodes aspects can add vitality and self-confirmation. Breaking away from the habitual can be illuminating. Walking one's own path is exciting and refreshing.

   One must be careful to not move carelessly during the turbulence sometimes associated with these particular aspects. They are threshold aspects. We often are leaving old selves behind. A new direction and freedom awaits those who can tune into the highest frequency of these aspects.

NEPTUNE/MOON'S NODES ASPECTS

Transiting Neptune Nodes of the Moon

Process: Unifying Past and Present

Ally: Choosing Inspiring Symbols

Illusion: Escaping into Fantasy Worlds

Transiting Neptune aspecting the nodes of the Moon denotes finding unity between past and present lives . Incorporating faith in self and/or a higher power can be a major ally.

INTENSE ASPECTS

Conjunction: Transiting Neptune Conjunct North Node

Transiting Neptune Conjunct South Node

LIGHT

FIRE/AIR

Transiting Neptune conjunct a north node in a fire sign (or house) and opposing a south node in an air sign (or house) can denote raising actions (fire) to a more conscious level. Foggy perceptions (air) may become clearer. Self-centeredness can become more universal. A shortsighted individual can develop intuitive insight. Past-life themes (south node) indicate possible rigid ideas. The impersonal tendencies of both fire and air may lift to a more emotional nature. Individuals may become more vulnerable. Emotional closeness can be a new experience. Creative symbols can give new life to old concepts.

Transiting Neptune conjunct a north node in an air sign (or house) and opposing a south node in a fire sign (or house) can symbolize a more intuitive consciousness. The intellectual may learn to feel. A cold thinker can find compassion. The opposite south node in fire points to past-life themes related to insensitivity. An individual can develop more awareness of others. Others can be included in decisions and planning. Air and fire themes are unified.

Transiting Neptune conjunct a south node in a fire sign (or house) opposing a north node in an air sign (or house) can transcend egocentric tendencies. A forceful nature can become sensitized to needs of others. A "haste make waste" attitude may be overcome. Watching (Neptune) can help one understand motivations for actions (fire). Intuition (Neptune) can balance perceptions (air).

A lost identity can become whole again. Self-hatred can turn into love; a fear of oneself turns into self-exploration; a very finite grasp of life becomes more universal.

Transiting Neptune conjunct a south node in an air sign (or house) opposing a north node in a fire sign (or house) can symbolize new trust in intuition. A thinker may stop denying emotions; an aloof type can seek closeness; scattered people may find unity. Individuals may act on ideals. Excessive thinking is transcended. Mental shallowness can become deeper understanding. A socializer can find a greater purpose in relating to others. Rigid ideas can be changed by new inspiring symbols.

EARTH/WATER

Transiting Neptune conjunct a north node in an earth sign (or house) and opposing a south node in a water sign (or house) can tune into the mysteries of life. One's unconscious instincts may come forward. A life directed at material security may elevate to more intuitive expressions.

Past-life emotional intensity (south node in water) may be integrated into substantial commitments (north node in earth). An individual can turn a negative outlook into faith. Emotional confusion can be changed into divine inspiration.

A running away from reality (south node in water) can be transcended. A new responsibility (north node in earth) can bring confidence. Past-life escapism and emotional disorientation can turn into intuitive strength.

Transiting Neptune conjunct a north node in a water sign (or house) and opposing a south node in an earth sign or house can indicate a heightened understanding. Great creativity can drive individuals. Past lifetimes of limited insights can be raised to new intuitive visions. A fear of making ideals real can be overcome. Imagination can awaken a sleepy consciousness.

People may freely express dependency needs. Closeness is no longer threatening. A spiritual awakening can occur. Universal love can inspire inner potential. Universal or collective symbols could be embraced. Tuning into one's own subconscious world can be enlightening.

Transiting Neptune conjunct a south node in an earth sign (or house) opposing a north node in a water sign (or house) can find faith in a higher power. Too much belief in the tangible can be limiting. Complete self-reliance makes life a burden. One may reach out for greater self-understanding.

A denial of material things can be due to excessive austerity. A low opinion of the self can become new faith. Rigid beliefs are softened, allowing more people into the life and gaining a deeper purpose. Negativity and skepticism can become hopes and dreams; hardness can turn to intuition; material dependency into discovering a subconscious; denial of feeling into greater sensitivity.

Transiting Neptune conjunct a south node in a water sign (or house) opposing a north node in an earth sign (or house) can indicate falling in love with intuition. Higher consciousness can bring growth. One can tap into an emotional intensity (south node in water) that was troublesome in the past. Facing internal conflict can solidify commitments (north node in earth). A lack of common sense can blossom into intuitive wisdom; running from responsibility can become faith in facing life issues.

Watery Neptune has a powerful symbolism when conjunct a watery south node. This could denote turning around self-destructive habits. A major life passage, filled with emotional clarity and excitement, is possible. Becoming aware of behavior patterns can help focus the life.

SHADOW

FIRE/AIR

Transiting Neptune conjunct a north node in fire/opposing a south node in air or transiting Neptune conjunct a south node in fire and opposing a north node in air can denote the fire has gone out. A lack of initiative can be disorienting. The natural inclination of fire to move ahead despite the obstacles is absent. Too much reflection can dissipate intensity.

Individuals can have visions of grandeur. Big-headedness could block perceptions. A shallow sense of beauty might throw one off course. Satisfying shortsighted needs can abort goals. Looking for easy answers can bring a lack of depth. A zealous (fire) devotion to causes may waste time and energy.

Transiting Neptune conjunct a north node in air/opposing a south node in fire or transiting Neptune conjunct a south node in air/opposing a north node in fire can denote indecisiveness or procrastination. Emotions (Neptune) and thoughts (air) can derail actions (fire). A desire to please others might be extreme. Individuals may misrepresent the truth to mislead others. A lack of directness can delay needs being met.

A refusal to communicate openly can occur. Karmic habits of running away from the truth can be displayed. A fantasy world may color one's reality. The future can be trapped by a confused past. Too many loose ends fog clarity. Not believing one can find solutions could be problematic. A refusal to look for inner answers might be the source of troubles.

EARTH/WATER

Transiting Neptune conjunct a north node in earth/opposing a south node in water or transiting Neptune conjunct a south node in earth/opposing a north node in water can symbolize too much material consciousness. Individuals may never be satisfied with what they have. Divine discontent can make them hard to please. One may attach too much importance to displaying wealth. A lack of inner resources compulsively throws one into external overload. Money and status become one's gods.

Individuals may deny themselves success. They may feel not worthy to enjoy abundance. Their standards for themselves can be too high. A lack of faith in a higher power (or in life's mysteries) can be limiting. Career confusion is possible. People may too easily find something wrong with a choice. Not sticking to a decision can interfere with success.

Transiting Neptune conjunct a north node in water/opposing a south node in earth or transiting Neptune conjunct a south node in water/opposing a north node in earth can manifest as guilt city! People can overidentify with being the cause of others' problems. Trying to save the world can be disastrous. A lack of faith in self or a higher power can accentuate guilt.

Too much dependency and helplessness can be disorienting. Emotional needs may be excessive. This could be a karmic tendency to have to be saved. Giving too much of the self away to others is debilitating.

A devotional path could be all-consuming. Blind faith can be trouble. Addictive love takes away from balanced relating. One could lack an understanding of intuition (water). Running away from higher consciousness into the material world can occur. Self-destructive habits can be extremely compulsive. A lack of love for self can cause one to dive into sensual cravings.

Square: Transiting Neptune Square North and South Nodes

LIGHT

FIRE/AIR

Transiting Neptune square fire/air nodes can bring new faith in actions and perceptions. Delaying instant gratification for a more collective experience can be important.

Communication confusion could be transcended. Perceiving situations intuitively can lessen too much intensity. "Watching" can moderate impatience and hasty decisions.

Initiation can replace procrastination. A new faith in ideals can instill a refreshing purpose. One can rise above self-centeredness. More compassion and sensitivity help one transcend a crass nature.

EARTH/WATER

Transiting Neptune square earth/water nodes can unify objective (earth) and subjective (water) realities. A new outlook on material and inner needs can be accomplished. Status and possessions are no longer the driving forces in a person's life. Deeper symbols inspire individuals to rise above obstacles. Reality and ideals can be mutually strengthening. One may conquer escapism through higher understanding. Individuals may balance dependency needs. Expressing love can become easier.

SHADOW

FIRE/AIR

The transiting square of Neptune to fire/air nodes can express as not dealing with situations directly. The life direction can be chaotic. A sense of direction is in doubt. Individuals may be threatened by the present. Others may foolishly disregard obstacles. Ignoring limitations can be as disastrous as a fear of risk-taking. Perfectionism can be a nuisance. One waits for that perfect moment that does not arrive. That convenient excuse foils opportunities. Past mistakes can appear in the present.

EARTH/WATER

Transiting Neptune square earth/water nodes can show a lack of faith. People may deny higher ideals. Life's ups and downs can disappoint us. Individuals can rely too much on others for emotional support. Faith in self may be denied. Too much clinging to others can be self-destructive. Running away from reality (earth) can be emotionally disorienting (water).

People can become too attached to outer success. Compulsive material drives can destroy a private life. Life's illusions (whether it be fame, wealth, or status) can intoxicate one's consciousness. The search for a perfect life may side-step an internal understanding. A divine discontent with life's simplicity can complicate life.

Quincunx: Transiting Neptune Quincunx North Node
Transiting Neptune Quincunx South Node

The quincunx of transiting Neptune to the nodes of the Moon is the "Yoga of transcending life's illusion." Finding outlets for ideals and faith can be challenging. Intuitive strength can be an important ally.

FIRE/AIR

Transiting Neptune quincunx fire/air nodes can manifest as conquering actions and attitudes that destroy one's faith. Developing positive attitudes can be important.

Transiting Neptune quincunx the nodes in fire can stop letting others do the inspiring or motivating. Too much passivity can give way to action. A greater collective cause for energies can be born. One may tune into the inner emotional motivations for rash actions.

Transiting Neptune quincunx the nodes in air can inspire more creative thoughts. Individuals can deepen communication skills. One may listen as well as talk. Fixed concepts might find refreshing perspectives. A life with no ideals may fill this vacuum. The intellectualizers can learn to feel. Conscious mind burnout can be refreshed by right-brain intuition. Resolving a disorienting past brings peace to the present. Getting the mind in order brings contentment.

EARTH/WATER

Transiting Neptune quincunx earth/water nodes can rise above a disoriented life. One may find calmer waters. Emotional turbulence settles down.

Transiting Neptune quincunx the nodes in earth can find people gaining imaging power; those with overactive imaginations may get more focused (earth); boring lives can find new inspiration; overstimulated lives pay attention to inner voices.

Transiting Neptune quincunx the nodes in water can show the workaholic (earth) finding satisfaction in private life (water). Emotional needs can inspire a new reason to live. Imagination can reveal hidden creative talents. The higher self can beg for attention. Self-pity can turn into balancing dependency needs.

SHADOW

FIRE/AIR

Transiting Neptune quincunx the Moon's nodes in fire can manifest as confused identity. An inflated ego can demand attention. A deflated ego may have no purpose. Actions and conscience could be in conflict. One may serve too many masters. Natural fiery intensity may be held back. A desire for invisibility may make one hard to understand. Guilt can keep one from expressing the true self. A passive nature keeps individuals in limiting circumstances.

Transiting Neptune quincunx the Moon's nodes in air can manifest as not perceiving situations clearly. One may be suspicious of others. Too much perfectionism can be irritating. Individuals may lose objectivity. Emotional overreacting can occur. People may hide their true feelings. Idealism and fantasy may cause one to easily fall in love. One can lack the determination to work through conflict.

EARTH/WATER

Transiting Neptune quincunx the Moon's nodes in earth can manifest as an insatiable desire for perfection. Individuals can lose sight of reality. A divine discontent can make stability difficult. A desire for fame could become compulsive. People may try to prove over and over again that they are a success. Physical-plane addictions can cause an abortive life journey. A lack of introspection leads to an unstable existence.

Transiting Neptune quincunx the Moon's nodes in water can manifest as a "subjective haze." Individuals could walk around in circles. A denial of love and roots may lead to an empty life. Instead of intuition, people get confused. Unresolved past issues could flood one's consciousness with doubt. A lack of faith might be destructive. Self-criticism can be difficult. Dependency needs could keep individuals enslaved to limiting relationships. Not expressing ideals can be painful. Guilt can be one's downfall. Difficulty in separating oneself from the karma of others is problematic. One may try too hard to save others. Self-sacrifice may be extreme.

SOFT ASPECTS

Sextile: Transiting Neptune Sextile North and South Nodes

Trine: Transiting Neptune Trine North and South Nodes

The soft aspects formed by transiting Neptune to the Moon's nodes can be an inner atunement. A person can find inner tranquillity. In the soft aspects, individuals can develop new spiritual resources. A karmic past can be transformed by new attitudes. The cosmic dream weaver can bring the gift of intuitive clarity.

FIRE/AIR

Transiting Neptune sextile/trine a fire/air node polarity can denote more sensitivity. People who have had to fight to make dreams come true may find it easier now. They may relax and enjoy the beauty in life. The Neptune sextile can entice fire to stop fighting against itself; air to combine intuition with its mental capability. The Neptune trine can inspire fire to fall in love with its visionary spirit; air to reach with the heart as well as the mind.

In these soft aspects Neptune can still symbolize high creativity. Individuals with many intense aspects natally can find this a refreshing time period.

EARTH/WATER

Transiting Neptune sextile/trine an earth/water node polarity can connote a higher understanding of life's mysteries. The world of form may not be so unsettling at this time. The Neptune sextile can take earth beneath desire for the obvious; water to live highest ideals. The Neptune trine can teach earth to trust the intangible; water to believe in its subjective beauty.

Soft aspects formed by transiting Neptune to the earth/water node polarity can connote coming to grips with escapism. The cosmic dream weaver can symbolize individuals are ready to embrace higher ideals.

SHADOW

FIRE/AIR

Transiting Neptune sextile/trine a fire/air node polarity can manifest as too much idealism. Fire can be a dreamy romantic; air a spaced-out mentality. The Neptune sextile to fire nodes can express as chasing illusions; air nodes may get too emotionally attached to goals. The Neptune trine to fire nodes can be act now and reflect later; air nodes may stay on the dream level only.

EARTH/WATER
Transiting Neptune sextile/trine an earth/water node polarity can manifest as a loss of ideals. Earth can be stuck in a safe niche; water unsure of its state of well being. The Neptune sextile to earth nodes can express as a devotion to the tangible; water nodes may hold onto the past. The Neptune trine to earth nodes can doubt what one cannot see; water nodes may hide in their own world.

DAWN
Transiting Neptune/Moon's nodes aspects can denote vital hopes and dreams. People who have surrendered their inspiring symbols can find new ones.

The cosmic dream weaver can heal many an ailing heart. It has a deep and everlasting love potion. We need to be careful how this attractive energy is used. If used foolishly it can bring one illusion after another. Our appetites for sensual fulfillment can rule us. If this energy is used wisely, there is no end to inner and outer beauty. These aspects emanate from a deep, spiritual source.

PLUTO/MOON'S NODES ASPECTS
Transiting Pluto/Nodes of Moon

Process:	Personal Power through Transcending Karma
Ally:	Penetrating Concentration
Illusion:	Trying to Conquer the World

Transiting Pluto aspecting the nodes of the Moon denotes one is developing a penetrating awareness. A capacity to bond together the present and past is possible. An individual can rise above the ashes of karmic habits. Issues are often related to channeling power urges. Emotional and sexual intensity can be involved.

I agree with other astrologers who have said that Pluto can indicate layers of old identities. This is often a karmic period in a person's life. Releasing and assimilating the past are both important.

INTENSE ASPECTS
Conjunction: Transiting Pluto Conjunct North Node
Transiting Pluto Conjunct South Node

LIGHT

FIRE/AIR
Transiting Pluto conjunct a north node in a fire sign (or house) and opposing a south node in an air sign (or house) may denote focusing emotional intensity. Personal power urges (Pluto) can fill the north node fiery enthusiasm with more fortitude.

A shallow perception (air) can find more depth in Pluto. Life's mysteries can stimulate a desire to penetrate subconscious fears. A hurried existence (fire) can find new power in strengthening perceptions (air); a lack of identity (fire) can be mentally invigorated (air) by satisfying emotional needs. The past can be a friend of the present.

Transiting Pluto conjunct a north node in an air sign (or house) and opposing a south node in a fire sign (or house) can symbolize a heightened awareness. Individuals can feel pulled into new, growth-promoting enterprises.

A desire to express more emotional intensity can occur. Balancing needs for attention (south node in fire) is possible. People can become more comfortable with their direction. One's own ideas can be embraced. Honest self-expression replaces desire to impress others.

Transiting Pluto conjunct a south node in a fire sign (or house) opposing a north node in an air sign (or house) can depict transcending unconscious actions. Power motives (Pluto) can be made more conscious. A self-confident individual can convert impulsiveness (fire) into positive growth. Scattered perceptions (air) can focus deeply.

Karmic patterns of egocentricity or possessiveness can be overcome. Others can be allowed to be themselves. Individuals may tap into their own personal power. Overly dependent people become more decisive.

Transiting Pluto conjunct a south node in an air sign (or house) opposing a north node in a fire sign (or house) can denote transcending an aloof existence. One may encounter life more directly (fire). Pluto can symbolize taking air into more emotional expression.

A thinker (air) can find more depth. One who lacks self-confidence can find new self-mastery. The indecisive can time a decision more precisely.

Pluto can bring fire nodes to courageously deal with past issues. The present and future are seen with transformed eyes. The air nodes can look back at the past with a deeper understanding. The present and future offer confirmation of a bigger life purpose.

EARTH/WATER

Transiting Pluto conjunct a north node in an earth sign (or house) opposing a south node in a water sign (or house) can denote rising above limiting circumstances. Feeling stuck may be transcended. New mastery of skills (earth) can solidify ideals (water). Overcoming lack of imagination can lead one into higher consciousness. People may find a broader life purpose.

Dependency needs can be resolved. Pluto is personal power. Individuals may find a leveling point in terms of needs. The common sense and self-reliance of earth blends with the needy tendencies of water.

Transiting Pluto conjunct a north node in a water sign (or house) opposing a south node in an earth sign (or house) can symbolize intuitive intensity. Life's doors may miraculously open. A life of fighting oneself may be empowered by clearer ideals. The subjective dimensions of water soothe a life suffering from worry. Rising above guilt and excess perfectionism (water) can help transcend a feeling of failure (earth). The cosmic composter, Pluto, can turn lost ideals (water) into new hope. Attachment to material security (earth) becomes less compulsive.

Transiting Pluto conjunct a south node in an earth sign (or house) opposing a north node in a water sign (or house) denotes diving below, through, and above negativity. Rigid, worn-out behaviors can be buried. Material consciousness can become less compulsive. One stops running to the south node during emotional insecurity. The watery north node can become self-nurturing. Self-love can be a new experience; sharing love a great realization.

Transiting Pluto conjunct a south node in a water sign (or house) opposing a north node in an earth sign (or house) symbolizes solving irrational fears. New strength can be born. Escapism can be converted into responsible pursuits. Limiting paths can become personal satisfaction. Subjective life dimensions (water) can be great resources. Objective existence (earth) can find a new breath of life.

The longing for love and unity in past lives can be sobered by the reality of earth. The great alchemizer Pluto can help bridge the gap between our ideals (water) and daily life (earth).

The fusion power of the Pluto conjunction can bring earth nodes to pay more attention to how they got here. The present and future seem more of a miracle than a foregone conclusion. The water nodes can travel deeply into the subconscious. Fears and hidden symbols are lifted to new consciousness. Shadows of the past no longer interfere with the light of the present and future.

SHADOW

FIRE/AIR

Transiting Pluto conjunct a north node in fire/opposing a south node in air or transiting Pluto conjunct a south node in fire/ opposing a north node in air can express as a "might is right" attitude. Power drives can be extreme.

The fusion power of the Pluto conjunction can bring fire nodes to think in terms of the grandiose (and lose sight of little important things). Self-love and admiration reach extremes. Fire nodes can cloak themselves in the power of past-life habits. A refusal to change self-serving ways paves the road to trouble. Willfulness may not compromise. The objectivity of situations is lacking.

Air nodes can be ruthlessly impersonal. A lack of empathy or compassion surrounds a cold, calculating nature. The same sarcastic tendencies of past lives carry over into this lifetime. Individuals may have difficulty with decisions. Emotional instability can weaken mental clarity. The past may still be greatly unresolved.

Fire nodes can lack self-understanding. Power instincts may be out of balance. Individuals may fear their own power, or be too power hungry. Depending too heavily on others can stop fire energy in its tracks.

Air nodes can lose objectivity. A lack of trust can cause separation from others. Life can be intellectualized but not felt. Very emotional individuals could have a problem with clear thinking. They may lose power quickly in emotional situations. Negativity can be a source of trouble. Looking for the worst brings negative results. A lack of flexibility brings limited possibilities.

EARTH/WATER

Transiting Pluto conjunct a north node in an earth sign (or house)/opposing a south node in a water sign (or house) or transiting Pluto conjunct a south node in an earth sign (or house)/opposing a north node in a water sign (or house) can express as a collision of objective and intuitive worlds. People can hold onto the material world compulsively. Some fear reality. An inability to find oneself emotionally can be trouble.

Earth nodes can get lost in the material world. Individuals may never own or possess enough. Work can become an obsession. A stubborn resistance to transition periods can bring emotional upheavals. One may lose that to which she clings. This could be life's way of teaching that one must find a deeper sense of self.

Water nodes can become too intense. The penetrating emotional symbolism of Pluto can combine with water nodes in a refusal to face the past. Individuals may hide emotional vulnerability. A lack of continuity in the life can be unsettling. Extremes can be too appealing. The world may be felt as a threat. Irrational fears cause emotional outbursts.

Water nodes can become too dependent on outside forces. A lack of self-trust attracts a bizarre destiny. People keep stumbling into their past issues. Ghosts come out of the closet. The shadow forces dominate. People may fear closeness as a threat to losing power. Self-defeating, subconscious thoughts may be a source of problems.

Square: Transiting Pluto Square North and South Nodes

LIGHT

FIRE/AIR

Transiting Pluto square fire/air nodes can move beyond limiting circumstances. Fiery impatience and airy coolness can be combined. Individuals may pay more attention to hidden messages. Fast moving fire/air types can become more aware of life as a process. Communication and actions can deepen greatly.

Individuals could look to the past to resolve issues in the present. The future depends heavily on the building blocks of past and present. Self-centeredness might be composted into respecting the needs of others. Courage can become a plunge into unknown territory. Individuals may enjoy clear action and intellectual intensity.

EARTH/WATER

Transiting Pluto square earth/water nodes can seek a happy medium between physical and emotional worlds. Individuals can rise above compulsive desires. Old wounds can heal in the present. Individuals can draw strength from a powerful past by facing limitations. A new belonging can bring stability. Understanding inner motives frees emotional intensity. The present can fill with inner trust.

SHADOW

Transiting Pluto square fire/air nodes can point to a timidity in being oneself. A lack of pride could be problematic. Life circumstances can lack challenge. Some people go overboard with extremes. Everything is a crisis! A tendency to only see the positive could lead to trouble. A "must-win" attitude (with no compromise) can make relating difficult. Manipulation of others might be a motive.

Past mistakes can be repeated in the present. Self-delusion keeps one entrapped in the darkness. The present and future fill with uncertainty. Those lacking initiative trip over the same self-doubts. The foolhardy look for more karmic debts.

EARTH/WATER

Transiting Pluto square earth/water nodes can denote extreme dependency problems. Either too much clinginess or emotional isolation can result. A compulsive tendency to worry can be draining. Insecurity can nag at one. Individuals may be stuck in the past. They insatiably strive to change the past rather than accepting the present. Life's simplicity is ignored rather than enjoyed.

Quincunx: Transiting Pluto Quincunx North Node
Transiting Pluto Quincunx South Node

The quincunx of transiting Pluto to the nodes of the Moon is the "Yoga of finding true power." Karmic pulls can be especially powerful at this time. Avoiding past pitfalls is important.

LIGHT

FIRE/AIR

Transiting Pluto quincunx fire/air nodes can manifest as strength during emotional crises. Adversity lifts one to new personal power.

Transiting Pluto quincunx fire nodes can result in actions with a deeper purpose. Karmic habits of impatience can be transcended. Individuals can take pride in themselves. Fire can shed excess pride.

Inflated egos find they are very finite in a much larger world. Swiftness of action can become highly refined. Arrogance can turn into humility.

Transiting Pluto quincunx air nodes can denote transformed mental processes. One comes closer to life (rather than being aloof). Fixed ideas can mix with new intuitive insights. Subconscious irrational drives are surrendered.

EARTH/WATER

Transiting Pluto quincunx earth/water nodes can conquer addictive, self-defeating urges. Subconscious, shadow forces can be brought under control.

Transiting Pluto quincunx earth nodes can transcend physical appetites. Material security can be more moderate. Those people denying themselves material rewards may learn to relax more. Extreme diets and work habits can be balanced by rest and relaxation. Conquering lifetimes of karma in a few days is not likely. Individuals may learn to accept themselves and others.

Transiting Pluto quincunx water nodes can symbolize rising above emotional disorientation. Past-life traumas and dramas can be blended into more realistic expectations. Emotional intensity may become less draining. Channeling subconscious urges into creative pursuits is possible. Moods may be brought under control. Healing the past frees blocked psychic energy.

Earth nodes can rise above compulsive drives for order and security. The present can go beyond old routines. **Water nodes** can tap into the intuitive power hidden in the past. The subconscious can become an important ally of the present. The future can become a gift.

SHADOW

FIRE/AIR

Transiting Pluto quincunx fire nodes can manifest as being out of touch with feelings. People can be swept to and fro by life with little purpose. An impatience with self and others is bothersome. A lack of reflection can produce few insights. Head-on collisions with life may result. Individuals may hold back on assertion. Angry outbursts (due to repressed feelings) can occur. Individuals can become bitter (due to missed opportunities). People may depend too much on others for encouragement.

Transiting Pluto quincunx air nodes can manifest as a disorganized mental nature. Compulsive thoughts can be out of control. One may manipulate the ideas of others. Some individuals depend too much on the advice of others. One's own mental creativity is repressed.

EARTH/WATER

Transiting Pluto quincunx earth nodes can manifest as false power. Wealth and power can become too much the life purpose. Physical appetites can throw life out of balance. Individuals may give away too many of their resources. They can be taken advantage of financially, sexually, etc. Workaholism could be a problem. Individuals may work until they drop. The life may lack time for love or closeness (water).

Transiting Pluto quincunx water nodes can manifest as extreme dependency needs. Individuals can be too hungry for love and closeness. The other extreme is a lack of trust regarding intimacy. People may fall in love with individuals who take advantage of them emotionally. People may devote energy to powerful leaders. The spiritual impulse of water must be careful to devote itself to worthy causes. A lack of self-honesty can be problematic.

SOFT ASPECTS
Sextile: Transiting Pluto Sextile North and South Nodes

Trine: Transiting Pluto Trine North and South Nodes

The soft aspects formed by transiting Pluto to the Moon's nodes can accept the deeper meaning of life. An individual with a sincere desire to change difficult behavior patterns can find success. The soft aspects often have a greater flow than the "hard" ones. The environment can feel like wind behind our sail. Personal power can be positively channeled into relationships.

LIGHT

FIRE/AIR
Transiting Pluto sextile/trine a fire/air node polarity can express emotional intensity. A deepening awareness of motives for actions is possible. One's mental nature can feel less bombarded by outside forces. The Pluto sextile can bring fire nodes to look at the possible outcome of situations before leaping. Air nodes can learn to control anxiety. The Pluto trine can show fire acting on impulse for the common good; air nodes can easily handle crises.

EARTH/WATER
Transiting Pluto sextile/trine an earth/water node polarity can symbolize the coming together of hard-earned rewards. A birth chart with a lot of intense aspects may find this a delightful period. The Pluto sextile can stimulate earth to seek understanding beyond comfort and practicality; water can turn dreams into a passion for self-realization. The Pluto trine can elevate earth to go beyond self-preservation; water to go beyond irrational fears.

SHADOW

FIRE/AIR
Transiting Pluto sextile/trine a fire/air node polarity can show power to hide insecurity. Individuals may stay prisoners of their problems. The Pluto sextile to fire nodes can be a false show of confidence;

air nodes can become unreasonable and demanding. The Pluto trine to fire nodes can denote either too much confidence, or an extreme lack. Type "A" personalities could feel invincible. Dependent individuals can be unassertive. The Pluto trine to air nodes can become a journey into sarcasm. Negative thoughts can pollute the consciousness.

EARTH/WATER
Transiting Pluto sextile/trine an earth/water node polarity can be stuck in rigid or limiting behaviors. The Pluto sextile to earth nodes can indicate a fixation on limitation. A compulsive fear of lack creates insecurity. The Pluto sextile to water nodes can express as tension regarding dependency needs. A moody and restless nature may make closeness difficult. An individual may have trouble accepting simplicity. Emotional turmoil becomes a way of life.

Transiting Pluto trine earth nodes can be someone expecting success without trying. Individuals may be too eager to find a life purpose through status and wealth. Power can become too important. The Pluto trine to water nodes can manifest as a secretive nature. Individuals can manipulate others by appearing helpless. Addiction to more powerful individuals could occur even in this trine. Emotional nature may be in need of a tune-up.

DAWN
Transiting Pluto/Moon's nodes aspects can be vital in transforming outdated behaviors into productive action. Composting our self-defeating behaviors into winning attitudes is possible. These aspects can show people tapping into new personal power. We may inherit intuitive strength from our own past lives. The penetrating intensity of these aspects can awaken a deepening life purpose. The bonding process with our own destiny can reach new heights. The choices we make can free us from ignorance.

CONCLUSION

I hope the readers of this book have found the terrain enjoyable and fruitful. Astrology offers a great lens to more clearly view the processes at work in our lives for any time period. Each of us is in an endless process of self-discovery. I wish each of you great fulfillment and success in meeting the challenges before you. May your path to study astrology and life stay intriguing and exciting!

How to Order Progressed and Transit Charts

To use this book properly, you will need a chart that indicates the progressed or transiting locations of the planets in your horoscope.
The publisher offers a **Chart Service** whereby you can order a Progressed or Transit Chart.

We suggest our 4-color Student Chart for only $5 because you don't have to know how to read astrological glyphs or, our Basic Natal Chart for only $4, if the glyphs are important to you.

There is a $2 postage and handling charge per order.

Call Toll Free
1-800-888-9983

Monday - Friday, 9AM to 5PM Pacific Time
We accept MasterCard, VISA and AMEX

OR

Send your check or money order
with your place of birth (city & state), date of birth
and time of birth (hour & minute, AM/PM) and:
for progressed charts: the progressed date
for transit charts: the transit place (city & state),
date and time (hour & minute, AM/PM) to:

ACS Publications
PO Box 34487, Dept. RYF94
San Diego, CA 92163-4487

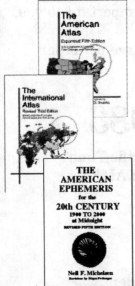

Titles from Steven Forrest

Also by ACS Publications

Survey

What were your two highest expectations
of *Roadmap to your Future*?

1. _____

Toni

254

547

2. _____

5364

How well did we fulfill those expectations?

_____

_____

_____

_____

_____

_____